Practical Plone 3

A Beginner's Guide to Building Powerful Websites

Alex Clark

Clayton Parker

Darci Hanning

David Convent

John DeStefano

Jon Stahl

Martin Aspeli

Matt Bowen

Ricardo Newbery

Sam Knox

Steve McMahon

Tom Conklin

Veda Williams

[PACKT] PUBLISHING

BIRMINGHAM - MUMBAI

Practical Plone 3

First published: February 2009

Production Reference: 1270109

Published by Packt Publishing Ltd.
32 Lincoln Road
Olton
Birmingham, B27 6PA, UK.

ISBN 978-1-847191-78-6

www.packtpub.com

Cover Image by Nick Powell (Nickcoolus@gmail.com)

Credits

Authors
Alex Clark
Clayton Parker
Darci Hanning
David Convent
John DeStefano
Jon Stahl
Martin Aspeli
Matt Bowen
Ricardo Newbery
Sam Knox
Steve McMahon
Tom Conklin
Veda Williams

Reviewers
Andrew Burkhalter
Calvin Hendryx-Parker
David Glick
Erik Rose
Jon Baldivieso
Jon Stahl
Martin Aspeli
Sam Knox
Veda Williams

Technical Editor
Aanchal Kumar

Copy Editor
Sumathi Sridhar

Acquisition Editor
Rashmi Phadnis

Development Editor
Ved Prakash Jha

Production Editorial Manager
Abhijeet Deobhakta

Editorial Team Leader
Akshara Aware

Project Team Leader
Lata Basantani

Project Coordinator
Lata Basantani

Indexer
Hemangini Bari

Proofreader
Dirk Manuel

Production Coordinator
Shantanu Zagade

Cover Work
Shantanu Zagade

About the Authors

Alex Clark is a Plone Consultant from Bethesda, MD, USA. He runs a thriving Plone consultancy along with his wife, Amy Clark. Together, they service a wide variety of government, corporate, and non-profit organizations in the greater Washington, D.C., area and worldwide. For more information, please see http://aclark.net. This is his first book and he hopes that people enjoy the result and are inspired to use Plone!

I'd like to thank my wife Amy for her tireless efforts in supporting my Plone career, and the Plone, Zope, and Python communities for being so amazingly supportive and inspiring.

Clayton Parker has been creating dynamic websites using Plone since 2004. He started out at Six Feet Up, Inc. as a Systems Administrator, which gives him an interesting take on Plone deployment. In 2007, Clayton started using zc.buildout to manage and deploy Six Feet Up's Plone sites. As a Senior Developer at Six Feet Up, he has created and contributed to buildout recipes in use by the Community.

Darci Hanning has a BSEE from Washington State University (Pullman) and received her MLIS from the University of Washington. She brings over 15 years of software and web application development experience to her position as Technology Development Consultant at the Oregon State Library. For the past three years she has been using Plone to create and deploy dynamic, easy-to-maintain websites for small libraries in Oregon. Since Spring 2006, she has been providing technical leadership for the Plinkit Collaborative, a multi-state cooperative, to deploy Plinkit in Colorado, Illinois, and Texas. She has presented on both Plone and Plinkit at national and international conferences, recently served as President of the Plone Foundation Board, and was selected as a "2008 Mover and Shaker" by Library Journal.

I would like to thank the Plone community at large for their ongoing support of Plinkit and the management team of the Oregon State Library for their enthusiastic support of my Plone-related endeavors. Without their support I would not have been able to participate in this community-driven project.

David Convent contributed several times to the Plone documentation effort with tutorials and how-tos covering the main themeing techniques. He developed DIYPloneStyle, a product and tool that helps theme developers to get started with basic generated code. The effort that was started with DIYPloneStyle is now merged in the themeing templates of ZopeSkel, which he maintains. David is currently employed at the Royal Belgian Institute of Natural Sciences. He's been working there for the MARS (Multimedia Archaeologichal Research System) project, a collaborative system based on Plone that is designed for Archaeologists and Anthropologists, and is now helping the web team at the institute.

I'd like to thank Veda Williams for her kind help. I doubt I could have finished the work without her support and contributions.

John DeStefano has accrued over 10 years' worth of experience in writing technical information and working with web-based technology. He has written documentation and technical training material for commercial and open-source products, including Adobe Dreamweaver and Flash, Microsoft Visual Studio and Windows Server; web programming languages, including ASP.NET, SQL, and XML; and technical certification, including Network+ and Oracle Database.

John has been rolling out, administering, and hacking (his own) Plone sites since 2006, and has contributed information and technical edits to the vast store of documentation on Plone's website.

John resides in Long Island, New York, with his wife, Jody, and their four children: Benjamin, Zachary, Sophia, and Jacob. He is currently a technical engineer in the Physics department at Brookhaven National Laboratory.

Jon Stahl is the Director of Web Solutions at ONE/Northwest, in Seattle, Washington, USA. He has over thirteen years of experience in technology consulting for nonprofit organizations, and leads a team of Plone consultants who have collectively launched several hundred Plone-powered sites for environmental organizations. Jon serves on the Plone Foundation board of directors, and is an active leader in the Plone community. His blog is at `http://blogs.onenw.org/jon`.

Martin Aspeli is an experienced Plone consultant and prolific Plone contributor. He served on the Framework Team for Plone 3.0, and is responsible for many new features, such as the improved portlets infrastructure, the "content rules" engine, and several R&D efforts relating to Plone 4.0. He is a former leader of the Plone Documentation Team, and has written a number of well-received tutorials that are available on plone.org. He is also the author of *Professional Plone Development*, and was recognized in 2008 by Packt Publishing as one of the "Most Valuable People" in open source content management systems.

Matt Bowen is a web developer for a Public Relations firm in Washington, D. C. Matt has a keen interest in helping non-technical people to share their knowledge over the web, and uses Plone to empower them to do so.

I'm extremely grateful to the Plone community, and especially the members of my local Plone user's group, ZPUGDC; without the community, I'd have never learned enough to contribute to this book, nor would any of us feel passionate enough to do so. From the larger community came our organizers (Martin and Veda) and our many reviewers, who made this practically possible. Finally, I relied on my family (mom, dad, and little brother) for their encouragement, and Laura Worthington for support and plenty of help in getting the wording right.

Ricardo Newbery is a web applications developer and consultant with over fifteen years of experience working with Internet technologies. A former physics researcher supporting the Research, Development, Test and Evaluation Division of the U.S. Naval Command, Control and Ocean Surveillance Center (NCOSC NRaD), Ricardo also taught Physics and Information Systems college courses for over ten years before chucking it all in recently, to move to beautiful Central Oregon and focus on developing his own consultancy (http://digitalmarbles.com) while mule deer and quail loiter outside his office window.

A member of the Plone community since 2004, much of Ricardo's current consulting work involves customizing Plone installations and optimizing high-performance web applications. Ricardo is the current release manager for CacheFu, a Plone add-on product used to help accelerate Plone web sites.

I want to thank Tammy Tatum for her advice and for proofreading my ramblings; and Miles Newbery for letting me read aloud my drafts instead of *Green Eggs and Ham* and making a good show of being impressed for a five year old.

I also want to thank Martin Aspeli for coming up with the idea for this book; John Stahl and Erik Rose for reviewing my drafts and coming up with some great suggestions; Alexander Limi and Alan Runyan for coming up with Plone in the first place; Geoff Davis for starting the CacheFu project; the Squid and Varnish proxy developers for helping me to work out how to simplify the presentation of complex cache behavior; and finally, the many contributors to CacheFu who have helped to make my job so much easier.

Sam Knox hails from Seattle, Washington where he works as the Support Manager for ONE/Northwest—a consulting group focused on helping environmental non-profits adopt and effectively use online technology. ONE/Northwest has served hundreds of organizations in the Pacific Northwest and beyond over the past 12 years. Sam regularly conducts Plone trainings and writes end-user documentation for a wide variety of audiences and skill levels. He also is primarily responsible for the highly successful online Plone documentation website, `LearnPlone.Org`.

I would like to thank my friends and colleagues at ONE/Northwest for their support, and the Plone community at large for creating the best Content Management System available today.

Steve McMahon lives in Davis, California, where he's a partner in Reid-McMahon, LLC, a web-development partnership specializing in developing Plone-based web sites for non-profit organizations.

Steve is currently the maintainer for the Plone Unified Installer and the OS X installer. He's the developer of the popular PloneFormGen add-on, and is the current release manager for the Plone Help Center. He was elected to the Plone Foundation Board of Directors in 2007 and 2008 and has served as Foundation secretary.

Tom Conklin is an Information Technology manager for a manufacturing company in the Syracuse. New York metro area. Tom has a keen interest in building business solutions in a way that makes IT transparent to the end users.

I want to thank my wife and kids for having the patience during the times when I latch on to a technology solution that I truly believe in. Over the past few years, Plone and Asterisk® (the Open Source IP PBX phone system) have captured my attention and imagination with regard to what is possible in solving everyday business problems. I also want to thank the Open Source community. The power of many dedicated people working towards superior solutions creates an environment of continual improvements, and no limits toward striving for a better way to solve a problem.

Veda Williams has worked in software development for 18 years, and as a Plone skinner for 3 of those years. She currently works for ONE/Northwest in Seattle, Washington. Veda is an editor for the documentation section of plone.org, and in addition to this book, she is writing a book on theming for Plone, due out in Spring 2009.

I would like to thank my colleagues, David Glick and Andrew Burkhalter, for filling in my knowledge gaps and providing generous assistance in reviewing my chapters; David Convent for his attention to detail; Rob Miller, for allowing me to borrow some of his material on GenericSetup; and our reviewers and authors who stepped in at the last minute to make this book happen.

About the Reviewers

Andrew Burkhalter comes from beautiful Seattle, Washington. He co-founded the Seattle Plone user group, assisted in the running of the 2006 Plone conference in Seattle, was a reviewer for Martin Aspeli's *Professional Plone Development*, and maintains several add-on products for Plone, many of which allow Plone to work in seamless and powerful ways with Salesforce.com. Over the years, he's touched in some way 100+ small-to-medium Plone-powered sites.

Six Feet Up's, Inc. co-founder **Calvin Hendryx-Parker** has 11 years of experience in fields as diverse as systems engineering, data modeling and information architecture. As Systems Engineer for Epylon, an enterprise-class company providing integration services to public sector entities, Calvin implemented ERP systems, deployed marketplace application servers and spearheaded network trouble-shooting.

As co-founder and Director of Engineering for Six Feet Up, Inc., Calvin oversees open source content management systems implemented in Plone, CMF and Zope. He is a proponent of web standards to ensure inter-operability with other platforms, and serves as the company's System Architect to promote project scalability and extendibility.

David Glick has helped to build and deploy over 25 Plone websites for environmental organizations in the Pacific Northwest, as a web developer at ONE/Northwest. He is an active contributor to the Plone collective and Plone core, and is passionate about making Plone easier to use for developers and non-developers alike.

Erik Rose is a consultant, developer, writer, and all-around nice guy at WebLion, the internal Plone consultancy at Penn State University. He has written several popular Plone products — including FacultyStaffDirectory, WebServerAuth, and CustomNav — and has spoken at world and regional Plone conferences about security, software architecture, and documentation. His attention to Plone's speed stems from his recent WebLion Hosting project, which provides a reliable and unattended way to set up and update the heterogeneous mob of departmental Plone servers at the university.

Jon Baldivieso works for ONE/Northwest in Portland, OR (US). He has been building sites using Plone since 2003.

Table of Contents

Part 3 – Now that I've got the basics, I'd like to learn how to...

Preface

Plone makes it easy to build and maintain powerful, user-friendly websites with cutting-edge collaboration and content management features. Thousands of companies, nonprofits, educational institutions, government agencies, and individuals around the world use Plone to power their websites.

Plone's out-of-the-box features, along with hundreds of free, open-source add-on Products, make it easy to build feature-rich, high performance public websites, intranets, extranets and custom web applications. Plone's wide-ranging feature set includes:

- An intuitive graphical HTML editor
- Automatic resizing of images
- A flexible permission and workflow system
- Human-readable, search-engine friendly URLs
- Full-text indexing of all content, including Word and PDF files
- Accessibility support for visually impaired users, including compliance with WAI-AA and US Section 508 standards

Plone is developed and supported by a worldwide community of thousands of individuals and hundreds of companies. The Plone Foundation, a nonprofit organization comprised of Plone community members, administers its intellectual property and trademarks.

Plone is written in Python, the popular, powerful, and easy-to-use programming language used by Google and thousands of other companies around the world. Plone uses the Zope web application server, and runs equally well on Windows, Mac OS X, and Linux/Unix.

This book will help you to get a Plone-powered website up and running. It covers everything from downloading and installing Plone, to using Plone to create and manage web content, to customization of Plone's functionality and visual appearance, and finally, to deploying your site "in the wild". Like Plone itself, this book is a community effort, with various Plone community members contributing chapters.

What this book covers

The book is divided into four parts:

Part 1 – Background

Chapter 1 Introducing Plone—Jon Stahl
What is a CMS? What is Plone, and where did it come from?

Chapter 2 Installing Plone—Steve McMahon
Learn how to get Plone up and running on Windows, Mac OS X, and Linux.

Chapter 3 A Brief Tour of Plone—Tom Conklin
Get an overview of Plone's user interface and key features.

Part 2 – I want to...

Chapter 4 Create Web Pages—Sam Knox
Learn how to create and publish web pages with Plone's built-in visual editor.

Chapter 5 Add News Items, Events, Links, and Files—Tom Conklin
Learn about the other standard content types, such as news items, events, and files.

Chapter 6 Structure the Content in My Site—Tom Conklin
Learn how to use folders and Collections to structure your content.

Chapter 7 Safely Manage Different Versions of Content—Darci Hanning
Understand Plone's built-in versioning features.

Chapter 8 Delegate Content Management to Other People—Tom Conklin
Learn how to create users and groups and give them permissions over various parts of your site.

Chapter 9 Manage Approvals and Other Workflow for My Content—Matt Bowen
Customize your security model by creating a workflow.

Chapter 10 Show Additional Information to Users and Visitors—Jon Stahl
Learn about Plone's Portlet features.

Chapter 11 Automate Tasks with Content Rules—Alex Clark
Build intelligence into your content management through the use of Content Rules.

Chapter 12 Control My Site's Configuration—Alex Clark
Detailed explanations of the various Plone control panels.

Part 3 – Now that I've got the basics, I'd like to learn how to...

Chapter 13 Set Up a Repeatable Environment using Buildout—Clayton Parker
Set up a development environment with various debugging tools.

Chapter 14 Find and Install Add-ons That Expand Plone's
Functionality—Steve McMahon
Learn how to find and install add-on components that are freely available online.

Chapter 15 Build Forms—Jon Stahl (with Steve McMahon)
Create web forms quickly and easily.

Chapter 16 Create New Content Types—Matt Bowen
Create custom content types to capture and manage specific information.

Chapter 17 Customize Plone—Veda Williams
Learn how to customize Plone's various UI components.

Chapter 18 Change the Look and Feel—David Convent, Veda Williams
Create a custom theme for your site.

Part 4 – My boss wants me to...

Chapter 19 Take My Site Live—Steve McMahon
Learn how to configure a live Plone server.

Chapter 20 Make It Go Faster—Ricardo Newbery
Configure a web cache to make Plone faster.

Chapter 21 Connect to Your LDAP/Active Directory Repository—John DeStefano
Let your users log in with their existing usernames and passwords by connecting to
an existing LDAP/Active Directory server.

What you need for this book

Plone runs under Windows, Mac OS X, and virtually all flavors of Linux/Unix, which means that you will be able to work through virtually the entire book on your desktop or laptop computer. Plone comes with "batteries included", which means that you don't need anything particular installed on your machine in order to get started. Plone's point-and-click installer will download and install a complete Plone web hosting environment, consisting of Python, Zope and Plone.

Who is this book For

If you want to get a Plone site up and running quickly and don't want to get involved in programming, this book is for you. This book is aimed at beginners who want to configure and customize Plone to meet their content management needs.

The book doesn't expect programming skills, although some knowledge of fundamental web concepts such as HTML and HTTP may be helpful. Some basic programming skills will be beneficial for the advanced topics.

Conventions

In this book, you will find a number of styles of text that distinguish between different kinds of information. Here are some examples of these styles, and an explanation of their meaning.

Code words in text are shown as follows: "Your Zope/Plone instance will be created in your Products or Applications directory in a folder named Plone, depending on your operating system."

A block of code will be set as follows:

```
[buildout]
...
eggs =
    ...
    plonetheme.mytheme
develop =
    src/plonetheme.mytheme
zcml =
    plonetheme.mytheme
```

When we wish to draw your attention to a particular part of a code block, the relevant lines or items will be shown in bold:

```
<genericsetup:registerProfile
  name="default"
  title="Andreas09 Theme"
  provides=""Products.GenericSetup.interfaces.EXTENSION""
  />
```

Any command-line input or output is written as follows:

```
Selected and implied templates:

 ZopeSkel#basic_namespace  A project with a namespace package
```

New terms and **important words** are introduced in bold. Words that you see on the screen, in menus or dialog boxes for example, appear in our text like this:

Then select the **Debug / development mode** checkbox and click on the **Save** button.

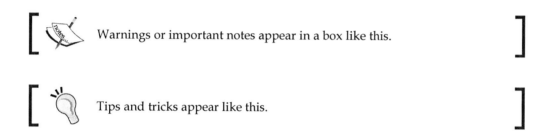

Warnings or important notes appear in a box like this.

Tips and tricks appear like this.

Reader feedback

Feedback from our readers is always welcome. Let us know what you think about this book—what you liked or may have disliked. Reader feedback is important for us to develop titles that you really get the most out of.

To send us general feedback, simply send an email to feedback@packtpub.com, making sure that you mention the book title in the subject of your message.

If there is a book that you need and would like to see us publish, please send us a note via the **SUGGEST A TITLE** form on www.packtpub.com, or send an email to suggest@packtpub.com.

If there is a topic that you have expertise in and you are interested in either writing or contributing to a book on, see our author guide on www.packtpub.com/authors.

Customer support

Now that you are the proud owner of a Packt book, we have a number of things to help you to get the most from your purchase.

Downloading the example code for the book

Visit `http://www.packtpub.com/files/code/1786_Code.zip` to directly download the example code.

The downloadable files contain instructions on how to use them.

Errata

Although we have taken every care to ensure the accuracy of our contents, mistakes do happen. If you find a mistake in one of our books—maybe a mistake in text or code—we would be grateful if you would report this to us. By doing so you can save other readers from frustration, and help us to improve subsequent versions of this book. If you find any errata, report them by visiting `http://www.packtpub.com/support`, selecting your book, clicking on the **let us know** link, and entering the details of your errata. Once your errata are verified, your submission will be accepted and the errata added to any list of existing errata. Any existing errata can be viewed by selecting your title from `http://www.packtpub.com/support`.

Piracy

Piracy of copyright material on the Internet is an ongoing problem across all media. At Packt, we take the protection of our copyright and licenses very seriously. If you come across any illegal copies of our works in any form on the Internet, please provide the location address or website name immediately so we can pursue a remedy.

Please contact us at `copyright@packtpub.com` with a link to the suspected pirated material.

We appreciate your help in protecting our authors, and our ability to bring you valuable content.

Questions

You can contact us at `questions@packtpub.com` if you are having a problem with any aspect of the book, and we will do our best to address your issue.

Part 1

Background

Introducing Plone

Installing Plone

A brief tour of Plone

1
Introducing Plone

Hi there!

Welcome to Plone!

The chances are that you're reading this book because you're thinking about using Plone to manage your web site content, or because you are a part of an organization that is already using Plone, and you need to figure out how to use it... on the double! Take a deep breath and relax. You're at the right place.

This book, *Practical Plone*, will help you get started with using Plone, the world's most powerful and easy-to-use open source content management system. You're in good company: hundreds of thousands of people around the world use Plone to build and maintain web sites. Plone is used by Fortune 100 corporations, small nonprofits organizations, universities, governments, scientific research organizations, and 'just plain folks'. Plone's flexibility, ease of use, power, and extensibility make it suitable for almost any project that revolves around publishing content online and managing it over time.

 See `http://plone.net/sites` for a selective list of Plone sites around the world.

In this introductory chapter, **Jon Stahl** will introduce you to the general concept of content management systems and Plone in particular. We'll offer a brief overview of the worldwide community of people who use, create, maintain, and support Plone—a community you now stand on the threshold of joining! We'll briefly explain open source software and the freedom that Plone's license grants you. We'll conclude this chapter with a brief overview of the topics to consider as you plan a web site.

What is a content management system?

In the early days of the Web, most people wrote web pages by hand, in raw HTML. That worked well — for a while. Then, as the Web expanded, people wanted to publish increasingly-complex web sites and maintain them over time. Raw HTML wasn't enough, and it turned out that the first-generation of graphical HTML editors, such as Dreamweaver and FrontPage, weren't enough either. More sophisticated systems for creating and managing thousands (or millions!) of pages were needed, and from this need, modern CMSes were born.

A content management system is a software application that allows you to create, edit, and publish information on the Web in a consistent, structured way.

Content management systems provide a wide range of features that support the process of creating and editing the content, including:

- **Separation of content from presentation**: By keeping the presentation (formatting) separate from the content (text, images, and so on), content management systems help to ensure that the web site content is formatted in a consistent way. Non-technical users don't need to be concerned with the details of how things should look.

- **Security**: Gone are they days when a single person published all of the content on a web site. With different people contributing content to a web site, it's important to ensure that people are only doing the things they're supposed to be doing. Content management systems provide security and workflow mechanisms that let you define and enforce appropriate permissions for your site.

- **Site structure**: Content management systems understand how different pieces of content relate to each other, and can automatically construct appropriate site navigation elements.

- **Searching**: Content management systems typically include powerful search tools that help users find the content on the site that they're looking for.

- **User interactivity**: Modern web sites invite user participation through commenting, rating, bookmarking, and the creation of new content. Content management systems let site users participate and help turn web sites into lively places for building communities.

In short, content management systems are the beating heart of most modern web sites. By automating routine tasks, they allow web site authors to focus on writing compelling content, and by opening up new horizons of interactivity, content management systems turn web sites into living, breathing communities.

What is Plone?

Plone is one of the world's most popular and powerful content management systems. People love Plone for its wide range of features and its exceptional ease-of-use. System administrators love it for its security and stability. Programmers love its modular, component-based design, and the ease with which it can be customized and extended. But Plone is much more than *just* a content management system. It is a flexible, extensible framework for building custom web site applications. Moreover, Plone is also a vibrant global community of users, consultants, and developers.

In short, Plone is both a powerful piece of software for building and managing web sites, and the global community of people who support it.

Plone: the product

Plone is one of the world's most popular, powerful, and easy-to-use content management systems. Plone makes it easy for people to build and manage web sites without any knowledge of HTML, web servers, or computer programming.

Plone has too many built-in features to be listed here, but a few highlights are:

- An intuitive, graphical HTML editor
- Automatic resizing of images
- Granular, role-based permissions, and an advanced workflow engine
- Versioning, staging, and locking of content
- Human-readable and search-engine friendly URLs
- Full-text indexing of all content, including Word and PDF files
- Accessibility support for visually-impaired users, including compliance with WAI-AA and US Section 508 standards

 A complete list of the features of Plone 3 can be found at:
`http://plone.org/products/plone/features/3.0`

Plone: the framework

Plone can also be customized and extended to meet almost any content management or web site development need. There are hundreds of free add-on products for Plone, and you can easily build your own to handle more specialized needs.

Plone is written in the programming language Python, and is built on top of the Zope web application server and its **Content Management Framework (CMF)**. These systems provide Plone with a powerful underlying framework and make it easy to add new features to Plone. Plone's use of Python and Zope also allow us to leverage a wide range of Python software not written specifically for Plone.

Plone runs equally well on Mac OS X, Windows, and *nix. A commercially-supported distribution of Plone for Windows and **Internet Information Service (IIS)**, called **Enfold Server**, is also available.

Plone: the community

Plone isn't the product of a company. As an open source project, it's the product of a community. Plone started in 2001 as a collaboration between Alexander Limi and Alan Runyan. It quickly blossomed into a worldwide community of thousands of users, integrators, and developers. It is this community that builds, improves, documents, supports, and implements Plone.

In many ways, Plone is this community. Plone-the-software continues to change (in some cases quite radically), but Plone-the-community, with its core values of openness, accessibility, democracy, and friendliness, is the bedrock upon which Plone's ongoing success is built.

By picking up this book, you stand upon the doorstep of this warm, open, and friendly community. We invite you to come on in and stay awhile.

You can connect with us both online and in the real world.

Online

The main online channels for the Plone community are its email lists and the **#plone IRC (Internet Relay Chat)** channel. You can find these at `http://plone.org/support`, and these are the best ways to get help with Plone.

In the real world

Plone has a strong culture of face-to-face gatherings. Local Plone user groups meet regularly in cities around the world. The Plone community has an annual global conference, as well as a number of smaller regional 'symposia'. Various Plone consultants offer regular training classes. In addition, much Plone development takes places through 'sprints'—small groups of people getting together for intensive, pair-programming development and mentoring sessions.

You can find an up-to-date list of Plone user groups at
`http://plone.org/support/local-user-groups`.

> **What does the name 'Plone' mean, anyway?**
>
> It doesn't mean anything. Plone is the name of a defunct electronic music band from England. When Alan and Alex first started discussing the project-that-would-become-Plone, they soon discovered their mutual admiration for the band Plone, and decided to name their software after it. It could be observed that the name 'Plone' continues a long open source tradition of giving incredible products obscure names that belie their true quality and power.

What does it mean that Plone is open source?

Plone is open source software. This means that you enjoy four fundamental freedoms with Plone:

1. The freedom to run Plone for any purpose.
2. The freedom to study and modify Plone.
3. The freedom to copy Plone.
4. The freedom to improve Plone, and release your improvements to the public, so that the whole community benefits.

The underlying source code of Plone is freely-available for anyone to look at, modify, and distribute. Plone is licensed under the **GNU Public License (GPL)**, which guarantees this freedom, and requires that anyone who distributes modified versions of Plone do so under an equivalently free license.

The Plone codebase is owned by the Plone Foundation, a US-based 501(c)(3) nonprofit corporation. The Plone Foundation, which was created with help from the Software Freedom Law Center, is modeled on the highly successful 'software conservancy' model of the Apache and Mozilla Foundations. The Plone Foundation provides legal protection for Plone, enforces its licensing terms, and promotes Plone and the Plone community. The Plone Foundation does *not* direct the development of Plone—the Plone community does that.

People who make substantial contributions to the Plone community can apply for membership in the Plone Foundation. The Plone Foundation is governed by a board of directors that is elected by the membership of the Foundation.

For more information about Plone's licensing terms, see `http://plone.org/about/copyright`. For more information about the Plone Foundation, see `http://plone.org/foundation`.

Planning your web site

Before you dive into installing and exploring Plone, it may be helpful to think a bit about the purpose, structure, and strategy of the web site that you're trying to build. Some questions to consider include:

Audience

Who will the users of your site be? Will they only be readers, or will they also be contributors? Will your site be public-facing, or internal to an organization?

Outcomes

What will your users want to do when they visit your site? What information, interaction, or services are they seeking? What are your objectives, as the site owner, for your users? How will you measure whether your site is succeeding?

Content and site features

Once you know your audience and your outcomes, you can start identifying the content and site features that will help your web site users accomplish their goals (and yours!).

Does your site require highly-structured content items such as a browsable catalog of products? Do you want your site visitors to be able to interact with your content by leaving comments or ratings, or through other interactivity? Do you need a blog, a discussion forum, or forms to gather data from your site visitors? Do you have a large library of existing content that you want to migrate into Plone?

Business rules

Many web sites implement 'business rules' which vary from the simple to the complex. A simple business rule can be 'pages need to be approved by a manager before going live'. A more complex set of business rules can be all the logic associated with an online store.

What business rules will govern the content and features on your site? Will certain sections of your site be restricted to certain users? Will the content need to be approved before publishing? Are your business rules very generic, or highly particular to your organization?

Graphic design, branding, look, and feel

Plone provides a spares, modern, out-of-the-box look, but most web site projects require some level of customized graphic design. Plone can be made to look like almost anything, if you are willing to spend the time on the design and implementation.

How ambitious are your design requirements? Is there an existing brand identity or other graphic design elements that you need to incorporate? Who will be responsible for the creative design work?

Integration with external systems

Many organizations have existing IT systems that they want Plone to interact with, such as a centralized directory server for user logins, or an existing relational database system. Plone 'plays nice' with many types of existing IT systems, but it's always wise to identify any integration requirements up front, because such integration often involves custom configuration and coding.

Hosting/deployment

Once you've built your site, where will you deploy it? How much traffic do you expect? How will you back up your site? Who will manage the server that hosts your site?

Who will maintain and edit the site?

Web sites are living things, and require ongoing care and feeding in order to remain healthy.

Who will provide the ongoing content creation, editing, and maintenance that your site requires? Do they have the resources that they will need to get the job done? Will they need training on using Plone?

Need more information on web site planning?

The **Web Style Guide** is a great high-level guide to the process of planning a web site. You can find it at http://webstyleguide.com/

Summary

In this chapter we've learned:

- What a content management system is
- About the Plone open-source content management system
- About Plone's key features
- About the Plone community
- About planning a web site

In the next chapters, we'll dive into the process of actually building and launching a web site with Plone!

2

Installing Plone

Plone is the CMS behind some of the web's largest, most complex sites. However, you can install and run it on your workstation or laptop quickly and easily.

In this chapter, **Steve McMahon** will show you how to install Plone for learning, testing, or development purposes on Windows, Mac OS X, or Linux platforms, using installation kits provided by the Plone community. We'll also look at the steps required to install Plone from source code.

Background

Plone runs atop the Zope web-application server, which is written in, and requires, the Python programming language. A working installation of Plone thus requires Plone, Zope, and Python. Each of these is a substantial package, and they have to be set up correctly in order to work together.

Fortunately, the Plone community has developed installers that gather together all of the required components and set them up in an immediately-useful configuration. Installers are available for all of the major operating system platforms: Windows, Mac OS X, and the Linux/BSD/Unix operating system family. We'll go over the use of each of these installers in detail.

If you want more control over the installation process than is offered by the installers, or if you wish to install Plone on a new platform, you may wish to install the individual components yourself from source code. This should be possible on any POSIX-compliant platform, and we'll also go over the basics of this type of installation.

Downloading Plone installers

To find the current release of Plone and its installers, visit `http://plone.org/products/plone`. You'll be offered several downloads, including:

- **Plone for all platforms**: This is an archive of Plone itself, ready for use if you've already installed the appropriate versions of Python and Zope.

- **Plone for Windows**: This is the installer for Windows 2000/XP/2003/Vista.

- **Plone for Linux**: This is the so-called "Unified Installer" not only for Linux, but also for all varieties of BSD, Solaris, and Unix. It also works with Mac OS X, but most Mac users will find one of the Mac-specific installers more convenient.

- **Plone for Mac OS X**: This will generally be available in versions for Intel and Power PC processors. Users of recent-vintage Macs should choose the Intel version.

You may also find packages for some specific Linux versions. In general, it's preferable to use the Unified Installer than to use a platform-specific package. Platform-specific packages should be used only by those with a very strong commitment to the packages-only school of system administration. The Plone community will usually struggle to support installations based on platform-specific packages, such as RPMs or DEBs.

Download the installer for your operating system platform, and proceed to the following Windows, Mac, Linux, or source-code install sections. We'll be up and running in no time.

Installing on Windows

The Windows installer is an executable program that will install Python, Zope, and Plone. It sets up Plone to run as a service (meaning that it runs in the background) and includes a controller program to start and stop the service and perform major configuration.

Running the Windows installer

The Plone Windows installer you've downloaded should have a filename like `Plone-3.2.0.exe`. The filename will be specific to the Plone version, and may also include a build number for the installer version. Open this file to run the installer.

This should bring up a welcome screen. The Windows installer follows the standard Windows installer wizard format. You should click on **Next** to continue. The second page of the wizard will ask you to accept that Plone is licensed under the GNU Public License. Assuming you agree, click on the **I accept the agreement** option button and then click on **Next**. This will bring you to the following dialog box that allows you to specify the installation target directory:

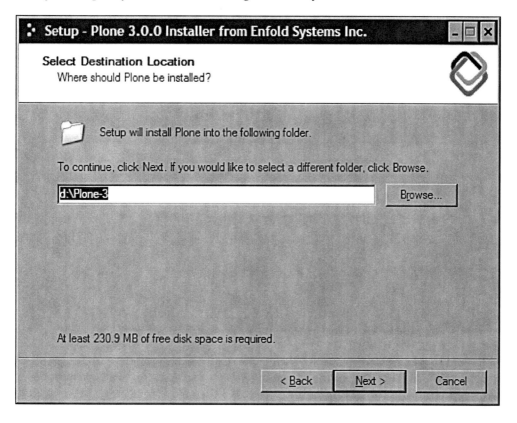

If you're setting up a production server, there may be many considerations, such as drive speed and backup strategy, that go into selecting an installation target. For a test or development installation, though, the primary consideration is that there will be ample disk space to include both the installed components and your developing web sites. Click on **Next** once you've specified a target install directory, and you'll move into the administrative account setup dialog box.

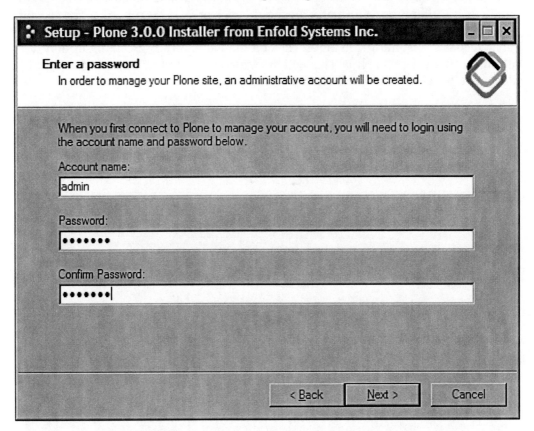

You'll need to use the account name and password you specify here to do initial administration of your site, so make a note of them and click on **Next** to move to the options confirmation dialog box.

If your destination is correct, go ahead and click on the **Install** button to proceed. Expect the installation to take a substantial amount of time. Unlike some binary installers, the Plone Windows installer is not just extracting files into the target directory. Much of the install time will be spent using the newly-installed Python to compile Plone's libraries and Zope's libraries into efficient byte code. The installer also creates a Plone site object inside a new Zope database.

Go ahead and click on the **Finish** button once the installer finishes all that work.

Running Plone

Take a look, now, at your Windows **Start | All Programs** menu. There should be a new **Plone** item, containing several options.

The **Plone** shortcut, with Plone's three-dot logo, is the Plone controller, which you'll use to start, stop, and configure the Plone service. The **Python** item will open an interactive Python interpreter that you can use to explore Python. **Links** is a set of web links to convenient online resources.

The **Development** sub-menu has two very useful options:

- **Plone Debug**: This runs Plone in a foreground console window in debug mode. Debug mode gives you advanced diagnostics, and can be particularly useful in tracking down why a particular add-on module won't load.

- **Setup Environment**: This opens a Windows command-line console with environment variables set to point to your Zope/Plone install and its Python libraries. This helps you run Python scripts in an environment similar to the one used by Zope and Plone.

For starting and stopping Plone, you'll want to use the Plone controller application. Run it and you'll see the status of the Plone service, and a button that will allow you to start Plone (if it is not running already).

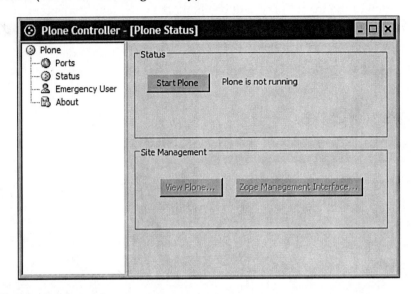

Setting ports

If you're running any other Internet services on the installation computer — such as Microsoft's **Internet Information Server (IIS)**, then before starting Plone, take a moment to check the port assignments. Click on the **Ports** item in the left pane. The right pane will then display the ports assigned to the Plone service.

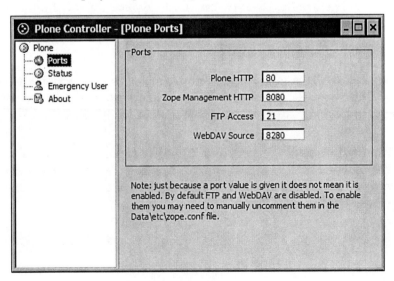

As it is freshly installed, the Plone service will be set up to use port **80** for a Plone web site, port **8080** for the through-the-web **Zope Management Interface**, **21** for **File Transfer Protocol,** and **8280** for **WebDAV**. (FTP and **WebDAV** make it easy to move files in bulk into your Plone site; they are disabled by default, and you may ignore them unless you need them.)

Port 80 is the standard port for **HTTP**. If you already have a web server (such as IIS) running on the target computer, there is a very good chance that it's already using port 80. If so, you will need to choose an alternate port for the Plone web interface. Port 81 or 8081 might be a good choice.

 Running IIS and Plone on the same ports is one of the most common installation mistakes on Windows.

Starting and stopping the Plone service

After considering your port choices, click on **Status** in the left pane to return to the Status view. You may now start Plone by clicking the **Start Plone** button. This will take a moment, particularly the first time, but you will soon see the status indicator change to say **Plone is running**.

You may now use the Site Management buttons—**View Plone...** or **Zope Management Interface...**—to open web browser views of Plone or the ZMI. We'll talk about what to expect in the *Testing Your Installation* section following the platform-specific installer sections.

To stop Plone, click the **Stop Plone** button on the status pane.

Customizing startup

When you use the controller application to start and stop Plone, you are starting and stopping a **service**—a program that runs as a background process with no window of its own. The controller starts, stops, and shows the status of the service, but it's otherwise not connected to it. After using the controller to start Plone, you may close the controller, and Zope/Plone will continue to run on your computer. This is typical for applications such as web servers that provide the Internet services.

The Plone Windows installer configures the Plone service to start automatically when you start your computer. This is reasonable for a server configuration, but may not be what you want if you're wanting to use your new Plone installation for testing or development.

To change the startup behavior of the Plone service, run the Windows **Services** administration tool (**Start | All Programs | Administrative Tools | Services**).

Look for **Zope instance at ...** at the end of the services list and double-click on it.

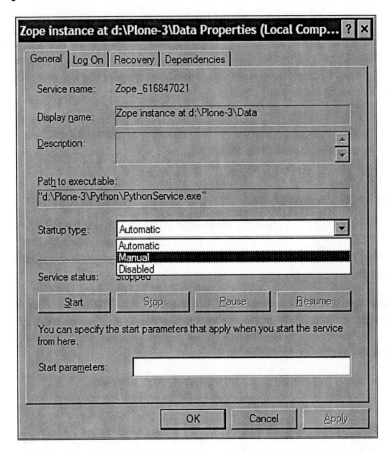

Startup type Automatic will cause the service to start automatically with the computer. Change it to **Manual** if you want to avoid this; you may then use the Plone controller to start and stop Plone.

The installation layout

When you installed Plone, the installer put both the programs and objects database into the target directory. Much of this is Python and Zope, and will not change as you update your site. The **data** subdirectory is where Plone itself, the add-on products, and the object database are installed. This is what the Plone documentation will often refer to as your **Zope Instance**.

Uninstalling

You can uninstall Plone by using the Windows Control Panel's **Add or Remove Programs** applet. Uninstalling Plone will leave your target directory in place, with the object database and custom products, untouched. Delete the directory manually if you no longer need these.

Installing on Mac OS X

The Plone installer for Mac OS X is available in two versions: one for each of the two processor families in use with OS X—specifically, PPC, and Intel. Both may be downloaded from http://plone.org/products/plone. For recent vintage Macs, choose the Intel processor version. The installation procedure is identical for both.

The OS X installer makes great use of the Unix foundations of the operating system. It provides an easy-to-use graphical installer, but gives you all of the power of a Unix installation of Plone.

Running the installer

Download the OS X installer and you'll see that, like many OS X applications, it is distributed as a disk-image file. Double-click on the image file and OS X will effectively open a virtual disk drive.

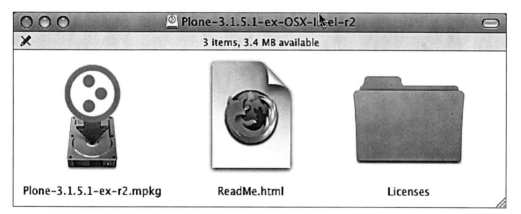

The .mpkg file is the package installer; its name will vary with different versions of Plone. Double-click on it to start the actual install process.

In the first couple of installation steps, the installer will allow you to read the ReadMe.html file and ask you to confirm your agreement that Plone is distributed under the GPL. You'll then be offered a chance to choose an installation target drive.

Custom install options

The next step in the installation process gives you a choice of a standalone or ZEO cluster installation. The standalone installation is the simplest, and the best one to use for development purposes. The ZEO cluster installation offers opportunities for load balancing, and is better suited for production installs. Choose **Production Mode** to perform the installation as administrative user (you'll be asked for a password when the installation process runs). This will set up Zope to run under a special user identity with a security profile more appropriate for a production server.

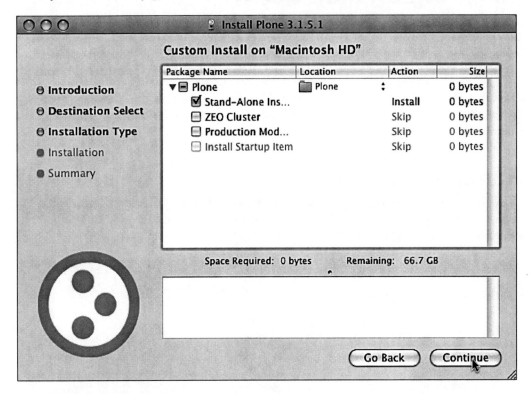

Adding a startup item will up set your computer to start Plone whenever the computer starts.

Finishing up

You should be able to click through the rest of the installation process. At some point, you'll be required to enter a password for the Zope admin users.

When the install process finishes, open up a finder window and navigate to your Applications directory. You will discover a Plone folder.

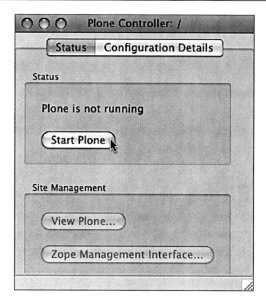

This folder will include the components of Python and Zope, plus a `zinstance` (for standalone) or `zeocluster` (for ZEO cluster) folder that will contain the configuration files, the object database, and Plone itself.

Starting and stopping Plone

When you start or stop Plone, you'll actually be starting or stopping the Zope web applications server. To start Zope in a standalone installation, use the Plone Controller application to start, monitor, and stop Zope and Plone. For more complex installations, or if you just like to use the command line, open a terminal window with the **Terminal** application. Look for it via the finder in the `Utilities` folder, which is inside `Applications`. Then, issue the start command you found in the `readme.txt` file. Typically, it will look like this:

```
your-computer:~ stevemcmahon$ /Applications/Plone-3.1/zinstance/bin/
plonectl start
Password:
. daemon process started, pid=15464
```

This starts Zope running as a service, independent of your terminal session, and you can then safely close the terminal application. Zope will keep running until you explicitly stop it, or until the computer is shut down. To stop Zope, use the terminal application again to issue the command line:

```
your-computer:~ stevemcmahon$ /Applications/Plone-3.1/zinstance/bin/
plonectl stop
```

The command will vary with your Plone version. The `adminPassword.txt` file you found earlier is your guide to the exact command.

Also, it's handy to be able to start Zope in the foreground/debug mode:

```
your-computer:~ stevemcmahon$ /Applications/Plone-3.1/zinstance/bin/
plonectl fg
```

If it is started in this way, Zope will stay connected to your terminal session and will print diagnostic messages to the terminal.

Uninstalling Plone

Removing a Plone install from OS X is easy. First, make sure that Zope isn't running; stop it if necessary. Then, use the Finder to delete the `Plone-3.1##` (the name will vary with your version) folder from the Applications folder.

Installing on Linux

Although it is offered under the title **Get Plone for Linux/BSD/Unix**, the **Unified Installer** is meant to install Plone on any Unix work-alike operating system. It's been tested on all of the common varieties of Linux, FreeBSD and OpenBSD, Mac OS X, and Solaris 10.

The Unified Installer is actually a source installation kit. It bundles together the source code for Plone and all of Plone's major dependencies, along with a shell script that builds and configures the components. Using it to install Plone is often as simple as downloading the kit, unpacking it, and issuing a single command. You will need to be comfortable with opening a terminal (or shell) session and issuing shell commands.

Installation options

The Unified Installer is versatile, and may be used to prepare Plone for use in configurations ranging from a production-ready, load-balanced cluster to a testing and development installation in a user home directory. As the latter requires no special privileges, and is easiest to understand, we'll cover it in this chapter. However, you should know that you can also use the installer for more advanced installations. The installer's `README.txt` documents the advanced options.

Preparing your system

A few common development tools are required to use the Unified Installer. These may already be installed on your system, but if you've never built packages from source before, you may need to do some preparatory tool installation. In particular, you will need the GNU tools: **GCC (GNU Compiler Collection)**, **G++ (GNU C++)**, and **make**.

The simplest and quickest way to see if you already have these tools installed is to open a terminal window (or use **SSH** to open a remote shell, if it's not your workstation), and just try to run the commands gcc, g++, and make:

```
steve@ubuntu:~$ gcc
gcc: no input files
steve@ubuntu:~$ g++
g++: no input files
steve@ubuntu:~$ make
make: *** No targets specified and no makefile found.  Stop.
```

If you receive a **command not found** response to any of these commands, use your platform's package manager to install the appropriate package. If you don't have root access on the install target, you'll need to contact your system administrator and ask them to install these common tools.

Extra packages

There are a few optional system library packages that you may want to install to add features. These include **readline, libssl, libxml2, wv**, and **xPDF**. These are mainly desirable for production servers. See the README.txt document file included with the Unified Installer for details of the roles played by these packages.

Downloading and unpacking the Unified Installer

Open a web browser and visit http://plone.org/products/plone. Copy the link location for **Get Plone for Linux/BSD/Unix**. Open a shell session on the installation target computer and download the Unified Installer to your home directory. wget is a handy tool for this.

```
steve@ubuntu:~$ wget http://plone.googlecode.com/files/Plone-3.1.0-
UnifiedInstaller.tar.gz
...
09:57:51 (294.24 KB/s) - Plone-3.1.0-UnifiedInstaller.tar.gz' saved
[25236282/25236282]
```

Note the `tar.gz` filename extension of the file that you just downloaded. This is sometimes written `.tgz` and indicates a **gzip** compressed tar archive, sometimes called a **tarball**.

Now, unpack the archive by using the `tar` utility:

```
steve@ubuntu:~$ tar zxf Plone-3.1.6-UnifiedInstaller.tar.gz
```

Substitute the name of the installer that you have downloaded. Filenames will vary with Plone and installer versions.

This will create a `Plone-3.1.6-UnifiedInstaller` directory (the name will vary with the Plone version). In it, you should find a `README.txt` document, along with an `install.sh` script and package, and script subdirectories. It's always a good idea to take a moment to review the `README.txt` file.

Running the Unified Installer

Change your current directory to the newly-created installer directory:

```
steve@ubuntu:~$ cd Plone-3.1.6-UnifiedInstaller/
```

You're now ready to run the Unified Installer's `install.sh` script. Use the `standalone` command-line option to indicate that you want to create a simple Zope/Plone install:

```
steve@ubuntu:~/Plone-3.1.6-UnifiedInstaller$ ./install.sh standalone
Stand-Alone Zope Instance selected
Rootless install method chosen. Will install for use by system user steve
...
Installing Plone 3.1.6 at /home/steve/Plone-3.1
...
```

Now, sit back and watch the console messages stream by. The install script does a lot of work. In sequence, it will perform source installations of the following:

- Python
- PIL (the Python Imaging Library)
- ElementTree (a Python XML library)
- Python SetupTools
- Zope
- Plone

The install script may also install local copies of **zlib** (compression) and **libjpeg** (photographic image manipulation) libraries if you don't have development versions of these on the computer already. It will also initialize a Zope object database and create a Plone web site inside it.

Don't worry about the messages flying by. If any part of the install fails, the install script will stop and display an error message. When the process is complete, you can expect to see a concluding message containing an administrative password, start and stop instructions, and the success message:

```
...
Plone successfully installed at /home/steve/Plone-3.1
See /home/steve/Plone-3.1/zinstance/README.txt
for startup instructions
```

Make note of the administrative user name and password, then read the README.txt file in the zinstance directory for start and stop instructions. If you need to check your password again, you'll find it recorded in the adminPassword.txt file in the zinstance directory.

Starting and stopping Plone

You can now start Zope and Plone with the command line:

```
$HOME/Plone-3.1/zinstance/bin/plonectl start
```

Substitute the directory created by your installation for Plone-3.1; this will vary with Plone versions. $HOME is just shorthand for your home directory. A successful start will display a message like this:

```
. daemon process started, pid=15054
```

Where pid is the identifier for the process.

This starts Zope and Plone running in the background, detached from your shell session. You may close the Window or switch to some other work. Plone should keep running until you take action to stop it, or shut your computer down.

To check if Plone is running, use the command:

```
$HOME/Plone-3.1/zinstance/bin/plonectl status
```

And, to stop it, use the command:

```
$HOME/Plone-3.1/zinstance/bin/plonectl stop
```

In all of these cases, what you're actually starting and stopping is the Zope web application server. Plone is an application installed to run on Zope.

You may also find it very useful to be able to start Zope/Plone in **foreground** mode. In this mode, Zope will run in debug mode and will print diagnostic messages to the terminal window. You will not be able to run other programs in this shell session until you stop Zope, and if you close the terminal window, you will shut down Zope.

```
$HOME/Plone-3.1/zinstance/bin/instance fg
```

The installation layout

The installation process created a directory with a name such as `Plone-3.1` in your home directory. This directory contains the Python and Zope builds and a `zinstance` directory that contains the configuration files, the object database, and a few utilities. `zinstance` is often referred to as your Plone **instance** directory.

Installation options

We briefly mentioned previously that the Unified Installer may be used to create different types of Plone installations. In particular:

- If you run the installer while logged in as root (or using the `sudo` command), Plone will be installed in your system's `/usr` directory, and will be set up to run under the `plone` user ID
- If you use the command-line option `zeo` rather than `standalone`, the installer will set up a **Zope Enterprise Objects (ZEO)** cluster configuration, which provides excellent load-balancing and control options

Both of these options are a good idea if your goal is a secure, robust install for a production server. Both add unnecessary complications, though, if you're only after a test or development installation.

Installation from source

The installers do a great job of installing and configuring Plone and the required components for you. So, why would you want to, or need to, install from source? Some reasons may be:

- There's no installer for your platform, and no simple adaptation of the Unified Installer will work
- You may need to use an already-installed version of Python
- You may want to put the parts together yourself so that you can see how they really fit
- You may want to do some serious development work with Plone or may want to track cutting-edge development.

Let me emphasize, however, that installation from source is more work and will require a much better understanding of your platform's development tools and the Plone components.

We will not cover a source installation in depth here; consider this to be just an orientation. More details will be provided in Chapter 13.

The software stack: Python, Zope, and Plone

Plone is built on the Zope web application server, which is largely written in Python, with some C language components. Plone is very picky about the versions of Zope that it runs on, and each Zope version, for its part, is very specific about its required Python version.

Plone 3.1.6, for example, requires Zope version 2.10.6. Later versions of Zope in the 2.10.x series are most likely to be acceptable. Zope 2.10.x runs under Python 2.4.5; later versions in the 2.4.x series are also likely to work.

The general strategy for a source installation is:

1. Install (or ensure that you have already installed) an acceptable version of Python.
2. Install the Python Imaging Library to work with the proper copy of Python.
3. Add the Python `ElementTree` library.
4. Install Zope with configuration instructions to use the proper copy of Python.
5. Create a working instance of Zope.
6. Install the Plone components into the working Zope instance.

Traditional source install

Traditionally, all of these steps are completed by visiting web sites, downloading the compressed archives (tarballs), unpacking, building, and testing, and then installing them. You may be able to take one big shortcut: download the Unified Installer for Linux, and use the contained packages for your builds. The `install.sh` script that the Unified Installer uses to build components is also a great source of practical hints for building components.

The most common mistake in traditional source installs is using the wrong copy of Python to build the components. Your system may have several versions of Python; you need to use only one of them, and that one must be compatible with the Zope version.

A better build with buildout

The Python, Zope, and Plone developer communities have been working on a better way of taking care of most of the steps for building Plone: using the zc.buildout Python library. You'll still need to build an appropriate Python installation yourself, but this is a particularly a good build method if your goal is to track Plone or advanced Plone product development, or to contribute to that development yourself.

Using buildout for a Zope and Plone installation is covered in more detail in Chapter 13, where we look at creating a development environment for customizing Plone.

Testing your installation

After you've installed and started Plone, you'll want to make sure it's working properly.

First, let's check the Zope web application server. Start up a web browser and navigate to http://localhost:8080/manage. If you've installed Plone on a remote server, replace localhost with the name or IP address of this server, for example, http://192.168.1.100:8080/manage.

You will be asked to authenticate. Use the administrative login ID (usually admin) and the password created during the installation. Then, you should see the **Zope Management Interface (ZMI)**.

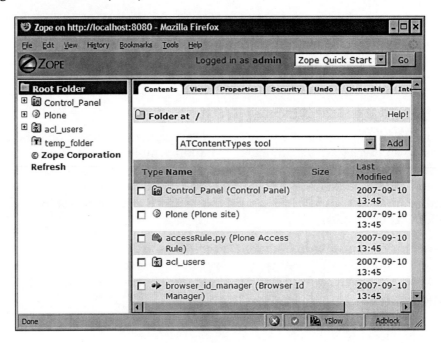

If your browser doesn't connect at all, first check to make sure that Zope is indeed running. If you've changed the port configuration for Zope, make sure that you've substituted your new port number for 8080. If Zope is running and the URL is correct, it is likely that a firewall (hardware or software) is blocking access to the Zope service. Check your firewall settings, or ask your firewall administrator to check them.

If the browser connects, but you can't authenticate, recheck your administrative login ID and password.

If you've successfully found the ZMI, look in the left pane for a `Plone` object. The Windows, Linux, and OS X installers should have created one for you. If you're installing from source, though, you'll need to add your own Plone site object. Look for the drop-down selection next to the **Add** button and select **Plone Site** from the list. Click on the **Add** button and fill out the form to add a working site. `Plone` is probably a good choice for an initial identifier, if only to maintain some compatibility with the way the installers set it up.

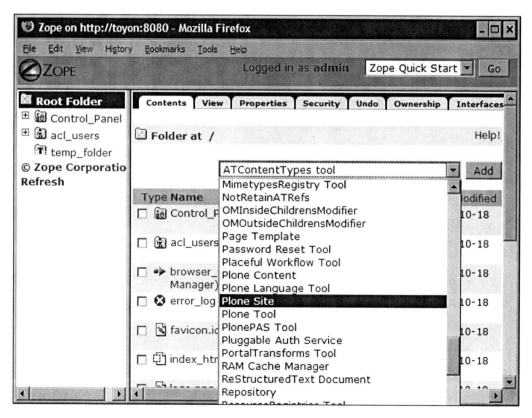

After testing the ZMI, confirm that Plone is available by visiting `http://localhost:8080/Plone` (again, adjust for your host and port configuration). Expect to see an empty Plone site.

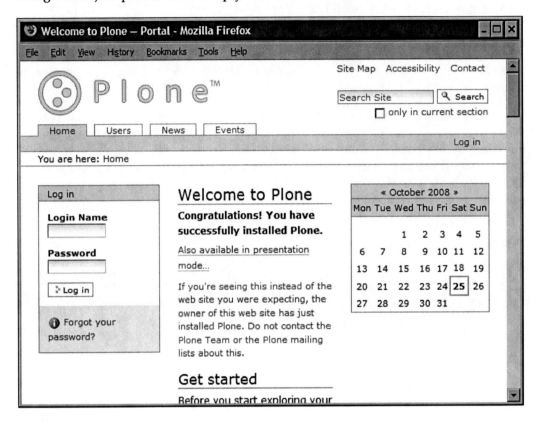

Summary

In this chapter, we have learned:

- How to find an appropriate Plone installer
- How to install Plone on popular platforms
- How to start and stop Plone on each platform
- How to quickly test the Plone installation

You should now be ready to begin configuring and administering your new Plone installation.

3
A Brief Tour Of Plone

Plone is a web browser based CMS where users of the system can focus on adding content to the site in a collaborative environment. Navigation and page layout is handled as a layer that web designers and developers can build or extend upon. The default install of a fresh Plone site has an excellent structure already created. So, unless specific customization is desired, you can mainly focus on adding content. To get comfortable with logging on and navigating within a Plone site, the examples in this chapter will be using the default Plone structure. We will focus on elements that are typical of many Plone-based sites. From time to time, you will see 'covered later', or 'advanced topic'. This is due to the depth of functionality that Plone offers. This chapter is about getting your feet wet.

In this chapter, **Tom Conklin** explains how to log into a Plone-based site, and explains the basics of navigating around a site, by going over common web page elements and terminology.

Logging into a Plone based site

When you first get your Plone site, you are presented with a section where you can log in. Depending on how the site is configured, you could have had an account set up by the site administrator, or you may be able to create a user account yourself by clicking on the **New User** link, as shown in the following screenshot:

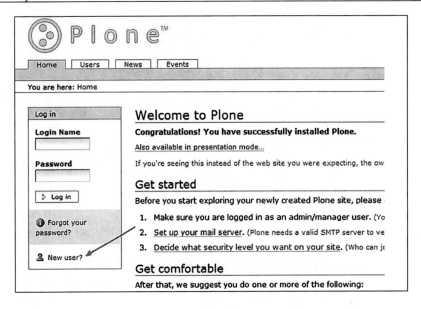

After clicking on the **New user?** link, you are presented with the following page:

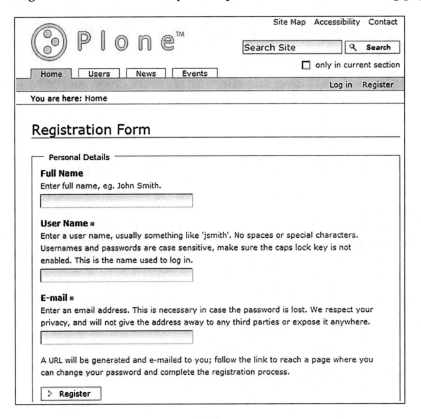

After filling out the form with your **Full Name, User Name**, and **E-mail**, the site will autogenerate an email message and send it to the address specified (assuming that a mailhost has been specified), along with a hyperlink, so that you can complete the registration process.

If you then check your email account, you should see something similar to what is shown in the following screenshot. The subject line is based on the title of the Plone site. In this case, the site that sent this email is called **Plone Dev Site**. For your system, it will use the name that the administrator created specifically for your site. If you can't find the email, check to see if your mail system has treated it as unsolicited email (spam).

 The system-generated message indicates that the user is set to expire if registration is not completed 168 hours. This is helpful in case the email went to an unintended user.

Clicking on the hyperlink brings you to a page where you can set up your password:

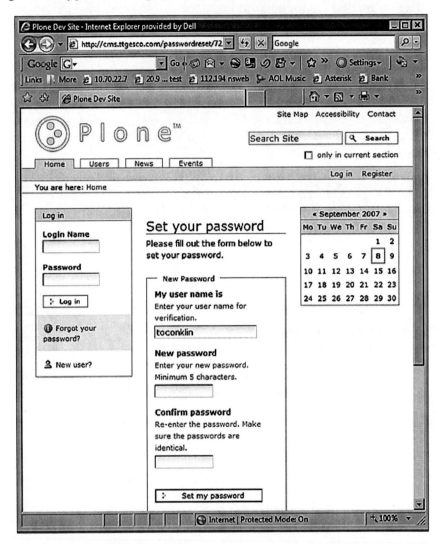

Once you have set up your password, you can log into the site.

Cookies must be enabled in order to log into Plone.

Once you are logged on to the site, you are presented with a layout that stays fairly consistent no matter where you are in the site.

Portlets

Before we navigate through the home page, we'll cover the topic of **portlets**. The name portlet gets its name from the term **portal**. A portal can be defined as an entry point or front door to a web site. When viewing a new Plone site, you have the following features built into your site:

- Navigation
- News items
- Events-calendar
- Recently-changed items

All of the above items are dynamic in nature, and Plone handles the navigation to these items via portlets, which are small entry points to those topics. The following is a screenshot of the navigation portlet:

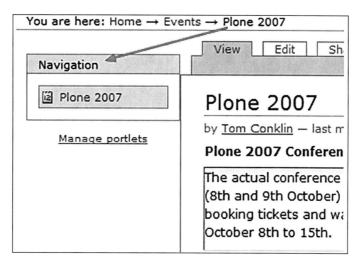

As your site grows in depth, the portlet functionality will be a great asset to your visitors as they navigate through the site. Here we see additional portlets—specifically the news, events, and calendar portlets.

Navigating the home page

We will now go over the various elements on the main page to get you familiar with navigating through a Plone site. We'll travel around the **Home** page, as seen in the following screenshot, going clockwise though the page starting with the default Plone logo, and going through all of the linked elements.

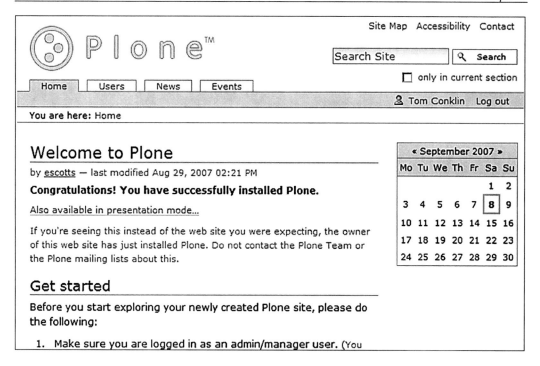

Logo

The **logo** on a Plone site is consistent on all pages, and always links back to the home page if you click on it. The chapter on theming explains how you can change the Plone logo to your own logo, if desired. What's important to point out is that even with your own logo, a user clicking on it will still be taken to the top level of the home page, no matter where they are within the structure of the site.

Site Map

The **Site map** link takes you to a page that lists all of the pages that you have permission to view.

Accessibility

The **Accessibility** link takes you to a page that describes how to navigate though Plone using only the keyboard.

Contact

The **Contact** link takes you to a page that lets you provide feedback to the site administrator.

Search

The **Search** function gives you the ability to search either the entire site, or just within the section that you are in. The amazingly-quick **LiveSearch** dynamically displays results as you are typing your search term. The more specific you are, the more precise your results will be:

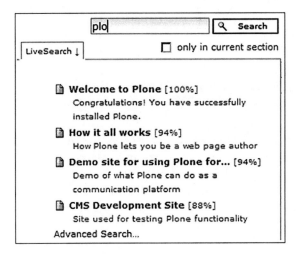

User link

The **User** (logged-in user) link takes you to a page that lets you configure your own personal dashboard. Within this area, you can configure your own portlets, which contain hyperlinks to areas within the Plone site, as well as links to external sites that offer **RSS (Really Simple Syndication)** feeds.

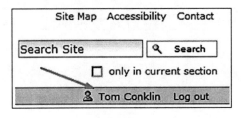

The next section will focus on how you can make changes to your dashboard after clicking on your name.

Personal dashboard

The following screenshot shows the **Dashboard** view. This view is your own personal page that you can configure to contain items of interest. For example, if you have a **Manager** or **Reviewer** role, you will be able to see links to all of the items on the site that are waiting for you to review and/or publish via a configured portlet. The Manager and Reviewer roles will be covered in Chapter 8.

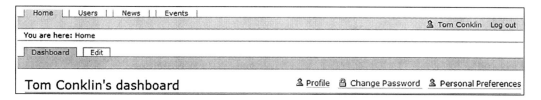

When you are in the **Dashboard** view, you have several additional links: **Profile**, **Change Password**, and **Personal Preferences**. We will cover each of these in the following sections.

Profile

The **Profile** link has placeholders for your **Location, Portrait, Biography,** and a link to a **personal page** (covered later), as well as a section that lists all of the content that you have created or edited recently.

While in the **Profile** section, you can select the **Edit** tab and then make various changes to:

- Your name
- Email
- Location (Optional)
- Language (Optional—Defaults to site default)
- Biography (Optional)
- Home page (Link to an external web site if desired)
- Content Editor when making web pages (Advanced topic covered later)
- Enable external editing (Advanced topic covered later)
- 'Listed in searches' checkbox
- Allow editing of Short Names (Advanced topic covered later)
- Portrait (Optional—you can upload an image here)

The **Edit** tab within the **Profile** section is a link to your **Personal Preferences** page, and the **View** tab within **Personal Preferences** is a link to your **Profile** view page.

Change password

The **Change Password** section lets you change your password. You must enter your current password, a new password, and the new password again to confirm the characters typed the first time, and then click on the **Change Password** button to effect the changes.

Dashboard edits

Going back to your **Dashboard** page, you can click on **Edit**, and change the portlets that will be displayed when you view this page. By default, Plone is set up to show up to four columns. Initially, you have **News**, **Events**, **Recent Items**, and **Review List** set up. You can define and arrange the portlets that are important to you using the drop-down lists above each column, as shown in the following screenshot:

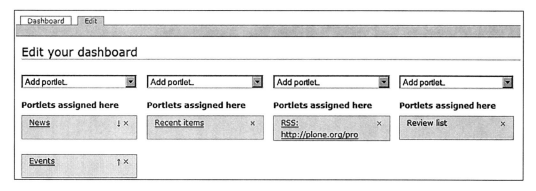

As displayed above, you can even define your own RSS portlet from an external site. In the third column from the left in the preceding screenshot, a **RSS Feed** from Plone has been assigned to a portlet via the drop-down selection:

The following portlets are enabled for the profile:

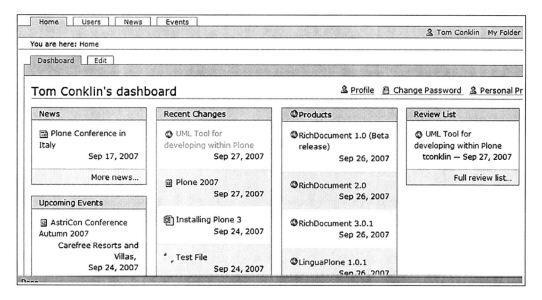

Tabs on the Home page

Let's return now to the home page of our site. We need to go over a few other navigational items on our Plone site.

By default, a Plone site shows the following **tabs**:

- **Home**
- **Users**
- **News**
- **Events**

Home tab

The **Home** page shows the initial page that everyone sees, and it's the same default **Home** page that you would see when clicking on the logo, as described previously.

As additional sections of the site are created, the administrator can enable additional top level folders to be displayed as a **tab**. The tabs can also be controlled more explicitly, as explained later in Chapter 6.

Users tab

The **Users** tab allows you to search for other users on the Plone site, based on various criteria such as login **Name**, **E-mail**, **Full Name**, **Group**, and **Role(s)** as shown in the following screenshot:

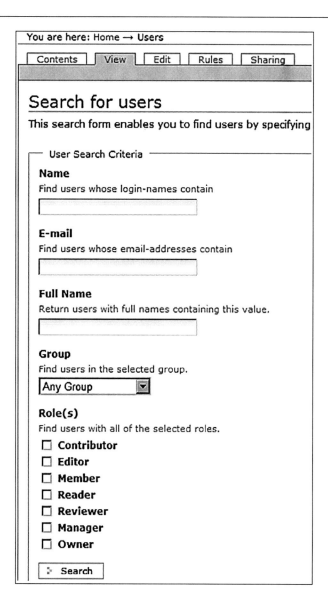

News

Items that have been created as News Items in the site will be displayed when you click the **News** tab.

Events

All **Events**, which includes future as well as past entries that have been created in the site, will show up on this page. **News** and **Events** will be covered in depth in Chapter 5.

Breadcrumbs

Breadcrumbs is the term that is used to describe the links shown above the content as you navigate though the site. Getting back to a previous page higher in the navigation, even if you are many pages deep within a site, can by accomplished by clicking the desired hyperlink.

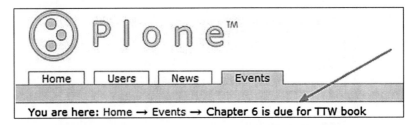

My folder

Depending on how your site is configured, you may have an additional link called **My Folder.** By default, this feature is not enabled.

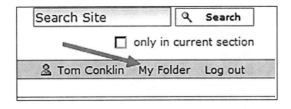

This folder is created when the user account is created, and is typically only used in an Intranet environment. It is not advisable to enable this on external sites where users can register themselves, as the risk of spambots increases.

The **My Folder** section is well-suited for allowing new users to practice making web pages, uploading files, and so on, in order for them to get comfortable with the system. Content created in these sections can easily be moved to another section using Plone's cut and paste functionality, which can be found on the **Contents** tab.

Colophon

The section that appears at the bottom of all the pages is called a **colophon**.

> The Plone® CMS — Open Source Content Management System is © 2000-2007 by the Plone Foundation et al.
> Plone® and the Plone logo are registered trademarks of the Plone Foundation. Distributed under the GNU GPL license.
>
> Powered by Plone   Valid XHTML   Valid CSS   Section 508   WCAG

In a web site, a colophon is a description of the tools, systems and resources used to create the web site and keep it operational. The colophon serves to acknowledge and give credit to all of the resources that are combined to produce the site. In Plone, the colophon usually appears at the bottom of the page, under the footer (which usually contains contact information), and typically has the 'Powered by Plone' button, the accessibility button, web standards, and other buttons.

Summary

As mentioned at the beginning of this chapter, the navigation and layout of a Plone site remains consistent throughout the site. As you will discover in later chapters, this is typically true even for custom Plone sites. From a usability standpoint, site users and visitors can rely on your Plone site to be very predictable, no matter how deep the content gets.

In this chapter, we have learned:

* How to log into to a Plone based site
* How to retrieve your password
* How to change your password
* How to personalize your personal preferences
* What a portlet is
* About main page elements and navigation on a typical Plone site
* Some basic Plone terminology

Part 2

I want to...

...create web pages

...add news items, events, links, and files

...structure the content in my site

...safely manage different versions of content

...delegate content management to other people

...manage approvals and other workflow for my content

...show additional information to users and visitors

...automate tasks with content rules

...control my site's configuration

4
Create Web Pages

Creating web pages is one of the most essential tasks in managing a web site. Up to this point you've familiarized yourself with the various elements of a fresh install of Plone, so you are now ready to learn the basics of page creation, editing pages, creating hyperlinks, and managing images. We'll also introduce you to the text formatting tools included with Plone.

In this chapter, **Sam Knox** will take you through the essentials of creating web pages in Plone.

Viewing site contents

Now that you've learned how to log in and find your way around a Plone web site, you're ready to start creating web pages. A **Page** in Plone is one of the most fundamental content types. Think of a page as a blank canvas to which you can add text, images, links, and other media. There are other, more specialized content types to choose from, but pages often comprise the bulk of the content of a Plone web site.

If you've just logged in to your site, click on the **Contents** tab to take a look at the site contents. You should get comfortable with using the **Contents** tab to find things until you've learned how to build the navigation structure of your site. You should see a screen that looks something like the following screenshot:

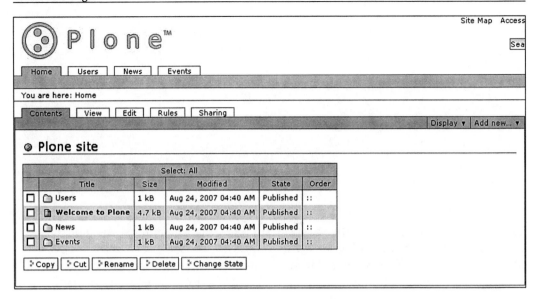

This view shows you some basic information about the contents of your web site. As you are working with a fresh copy of Plone, you will see a few content objects that were automatically created when you installed Plone. There are a few folders here, and one page, called **Welcome to Plone,** which is the page you see after logging in. Let's look at how to create a new page of your own.

Adding a new page

Note the **Add new...** menu on the far right of the green taskbar. Click on it, and choose **Page** from the drop-down menu.

Now you are on the **Add Page** screen. There are three main elements to consider when creating a new page:

1. **Title**: Appears at the top of the page as the main heading.

2. **Description**: Appears as bold text, just below the title.

3. **Body Text**: The contents of the page.

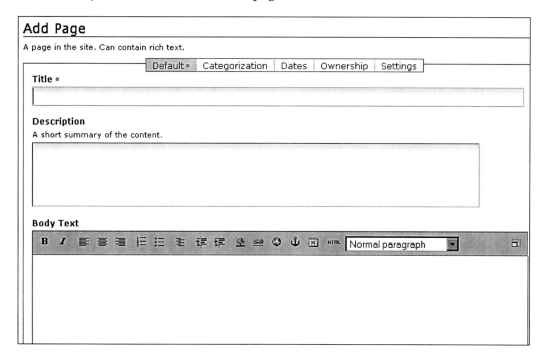

The **Default, Categorization, Dates, Ownership, and Settings** tabs that appear above the **Title** field are used to provide additional metadata about the content item, and to change settings such as whether to allow or disallow comments. These functions will be covered in subsequent chapters of this book. For now, you can ignore these tabs.

Title

A page's **Title** field fills two important roles. Firstly, the title acts as the heading for the page, appearing both at the top of the page as well as in your web browser's title bar. Secondly, the title is used to generate the URL, or web address, for that particular page. For example, if the page title happens to be "The Cascade Mountains", the web address that would be generated would be `http://www.mysite.com/the-cascade-mountains`.

Keep in mind that the **Title** is a required piece of information. You cannot create a page without it. If you try to navigate away from the **Add Page** screen without providing a title, Plone will prompt you to create one.

Description

The **Description** field also serves several different functions. Firstly, the description appears in bold text, immediately below the **Title**, and above the **Body Text**, when the page is viewed. Secondly, when using the search tool included with Plone, the search results will be displayed with the **Title** first, and with the **Description** immediately after the title. The **Description** is also used in other listing views that Plone generates.

Finally, Internet search engines such as **Google** will generally pay a lot of attention to the text you put in the **Description**. So writing a succinct and accurate description of your content will help greatly with **SEO (Search Engine Optimization)**. The description is not a required field, but it is quite useful and you should get into the habit of using it.

Body Text

The **Body Text** field is where you'll put the main content for your page. This is where you will add hyperlinks, images, headings, tables, and other content. Note that there is a toolbar with several icons at the top of the **Body Text** section.

You probably recognize many of these icons from using popular word processing programs. You can hover your mouse pointer over an icon, and the name of the icon will appear. These icons represent the formatting tools available to you in Plone. Some of the functions you'll find in the toolbar include:

- Creating headings and subheadings
- Creating numbered lists and bulleted lists
- Formatting text
- Creating hyperlinks
- Inserting images
- Inserting tables

Go ahead and start typing some text into the **Body Text** field. Once you have entered a few lines of text, try some of the formatting tools. Highlight some text and click on the style drop-down menu (which defaults to **Normal paragraph**) and select **Subheading**.

You've now created a subsection for the page. The following screenshot is an example of what this might look like:

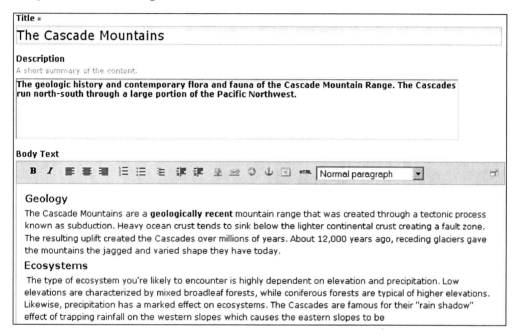

Using the formatting tools

There are several tools included in Plone that allow you to format paragraphs and characters of text. You can find these controls in the toolbar of the **Body Text** field. To format some selected text, simply highlight it by holding down your left mouse button and dragging the highlighted area over the text that you want to format, and then clicking the icon or selecting the menu item of your choice. In this section, you'll learn how to use the various formatting icons and the style drop-down menu.

Bold and Italics

The bold and italics buttons (shown in the following figure) allow you to do very simple text formatting. Both are used to highlight important text, but on the web, bold is used far more than italics. Italics are often used to communicate a note or suggestion to the reader, whereas bold is typically used for emphasis, and to assist the reader in scanning the page.

To use the bold formatting, highlight some text and click the **B** icon. You can also remove the bold formatting by highlighting some bold text and clicking the **B** icon.

To use the italics formatting, highlight some text and click the **I** icon.

Left, center, and right align

By default, any text entered in to the **Body Text** field is left aligned. Center align will center the text in the middle of the page, and right align will shift text over to the right. The alignment icons can also be used to set the alignment of images and tables. The left, center, and right alignment icons are shown in the following figure:

Numbered and bulleted lists

Use the list icons (shown in the following figure) to create ordered and unordered lists on a page. Start by separating each list entry with a simple line break (press *Enter* once). Then highlight the entire list and click on either the numbered or the bulleted list icon, depending on the type of list that you want. If you want to add more entries to your list after it's been created, simply position your cursor to the right of one of the list lines and press *Enter* once. This will create a blank list line in which you can type additional content.

Note that when you choose to use a numbered list, a new drop-down menu appears to the right of the style drop-down menu, so that you can choose the style of numbering, as shown in the following screenshot:

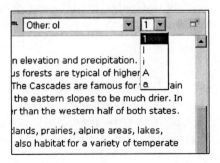

This drop-down menu allows you to choose Arabic numbers, uppercase Roman numerals, lowercase Roman numerals, or uppercase or lowercase letters for your numbered list.

Definition list

Sometimes, you may find that you want to define several terms on your web page by creating a glossary listing or a simple dictionary. Plone provides you with the **definition list** icon (shown in the following figure) to help you accomplish this:

Start by typing the first term in your definition list. Then highlight it and click on the definition list icon to activate definition list formatting. Next, press *Enter* once and the next line getting automatically indented. Use this line to provide a definition for the term. Press *Enter* again to move to the next term. When you are done with your definition list, press *Enter* twice to end the definition list formatting.

Lowland
> Low elevation ecosystems usually characterized by broadleaf trees and mild temperatures. The elevation profile of these areas are quite flat allowing for spreading river valleys and plains. Many of Earth's cities are in this zone.

Upland
> Higher elevation than lowlands, uplands are characterized by higher angle slopes and increasing precipitation. Conifers and broadleaf trees can both occupy this zone.

Montane
> In the Cascades, the montane region is usually where the broadleaf forests start to thin out and the conifers begin to dominate. Montane refers to the zone up to, but not exceeding tree line. Precipitation increases and average high temperates decline in this zone.

Alpine
> Usually refers to the areas at or above tree line. Alpine vegetation grows close to the ground in the form of hardy, woody perennials such as heather and low bush huckleberry. Some *Krumholtz* (twisted and stunted) trees can survive in this region, but they grow very slowly and are usually fir or spruce.

Indent text

In Plone, indentation (also called **quote level**) implies more than simple paragraph indentation. Use it for quotations, for excerpted text, or for an easy way to call attention to important text such as a tip or a hint. Simply highlight the text that you want to indent and click on the indent icon (the one with the right-facing arrow, shown on the right in the following figure). Each quote level will place a blue vertical bar to the left of the text to separate it from normal paragraph text. There is also an icon for reversing the indent formatting (the icon with the left-facing arrow).

The indent tool also allows you to create several levels of indent to create an interesting visual hierarchy. Each time that you click on the indent icon you are adding another quote level. Take a look at the following example:

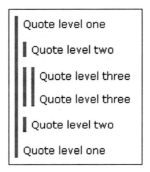

The styling of the indented text can be modified using CSS, which we will discuss in Chapter 17.

Using the style menu

The style menu is the drop-down menu located just to the right of the **HTML** icon, and is a very useful formatting tool in Plone. The **Normal Paragraph** style (shown in the following figure) is the default style when you start typing text into the **Body Text** field of a page, but you also have several other choices.

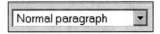

As with all other formatting, simply highlight the text that you want to format and select the desired style from the drop-down list menu. Here's a quick summary of Plone's default styles:

- **Normal Paragraph**: If you want to revert some formatted text back to the default paragraph style, choose this option.

- **Heading**: This creates a heading of the same size as the heading generated from the **Title** field of the page. However, when you apply this style, you also get a blue horizontal line just under the heading. Use this to start a major new section on the page.

- **Subheading**: This creates a subheading, which is smaller in size than the **Heading** style. Use this to create subsections on your page.

- **Literal**: This style is useful if you want to display mathematical formulas or lines of computer code. It's a good way to offset content that must be read "literally" from other content that may have stylistic components.

- **Discreet**: This will render the text with a grey color, and slightly smaller than **Normal Paragraph**. It's useful for notes to your site's visitors that should sit lower in the visual hierarchy than other styles.

- **Pull-quote**: This style will right-align the text, color it orange, and also apply the same vertical blue bar that you saw in the indent or **Quote level** style. **Pull-quote** is useful for leaving notes to your site's visitors, such as a "see also" note, or for giving useful tips.

- **Call-out**: This is similar to **Pull-quote**, but is not right-aligned, but is slightly indented. This can be used for emphasis or for leaving notes to your site's visitors.

- **Page Break**: Not a text style as such, **Page Break** is used if you want to control where page breaks should be, for the purpose of printing. You don't need to select any text to apply this style to; simply use it between the lines of text where you want the page break to be. This is useful if the page you are creating is to be printed, and you want to make sure that the sections are split across pages.

- **Clear Floats**: This calls a CSS style that removes floats of the selected element. This is useful for removing text wrapping around an image, for example.

- **(remove style)**: Use this if you want to remove a formatting style. Note that when you use this feature, the text will revert to `<no style>`, and not back to **Normal Paragraph**.

All of the above-mentioned styles are considered **paragraph styles**, which means that the style will affect the entire paragraph, and not just the text that you've highlighted. For example, if you have a paragraph of text and you highlight only the first few words and choose the **Subheading** style, all of the text in the paragraph will become a subheading.

- **Highlight**: This puts a yellow background color behind the text. **Highlight** is a **character style**, which means that it can be applied to any length of text, and not just to whole paragraphs. This style is the only default character style that comes with Plone, but eventually you'll learn how to create your own custom styles.

Examples of each style

The following is an example of each of the styles, and how they appear on a page:

This is Normal Paragraph text. Notice the amount of space between this line, and the line beneath it.

This is a Heading

This is a Subheading

This is the Literal text style.

This is Discreet text style

This is a Call-out
This is a Pull-quote

This is text with (remove style) applied. Notice that there is less space between lines, than there is with the Normal Paragraph style.

Character styles can be applied to any amount of text, like this Highlight style.

Saving your work

It's a good idea to save your work from time to time, especially when you've been working on a page for a while. At the bottom of the **Add Page** screen, you'll see two buttons: one is **Save** and the other is **Cancel**. **Save** will complete the page creation process, while **Cancel** will abandon it and the current work will be lost.

Once you've saved your work, you should see a confirmation message just above the title, to let you know that the page was successfully saved, as shown in the following screenshot:

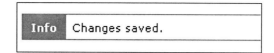

Also note that your page title now appears in the navigation tabs along the top of the screen, below the Plone logo, assuming that you have not modified how the tabs at the top are rendered.

Editing a page

Now that you've created your first web page and saved the contents on your Plone site, you may want to go back and edit your page. There are two ways of editing page content. In both cases you must first be viewing the page that you want to edit.

Edit all parts of a page

Click the **Edit** tab in the green toolbar to enter the **Edit Page** mode. In this mode, you will be able to change the content of all of the three fields for a page (**Title, Description**, and **Body Text**) just like you could when you first created the page. Remember to click on **Save** at the bottom when you are done editing, or **Cancel** if you don't want to keep your changes.

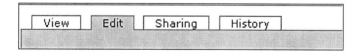

Edit a single part of a page

Let's say you just want to make a quick change to one of the page fields, such as correcting a spelling error in the **Description**. Plone provides a way for you to make the change without having to enter the full **Edit Page** mode.

When viewing the page that you want to edit, simply hover your mouse pointer over the page field that you wish to edit and notice the border that appears. Simply press the left mouse button once to edit only that part of the page. Both the **Save** and **Cancel** buttons appear for your use.

Editing the HTML of a page

If you are familiar with HTML, you can edit the raw underlying HTML of the **Body Text** field. Click on the HTML button, and you'll be able to view and edit the HTML of your page body. Simply click on the same button again to switch back to the normal graphical editing mode.

Using full screen mode

The full screen mode expands the editor window to take up the full width of your computer monitor. Some people prefer to edit in this mode because they find it easier to concentrate on just the text they are editing, instead of looking at the body text in the context of the rest of the elements on the page. Keep in mind that the layout you see in full screen mode will change when the page is saved. Switching to full screen mode does not change the actual width of the body text.

Creating hyperlinks

Hyperlinks are essential for creating a usable web site. They're also one of the things that make the Internet so unique. Instead of a book that has a clear beginning, middle, and end, a web page is a single point in a vast network linking many of the world's computers together. Following the links from page to page and from site to site is what gave rise to the idea of "surfing" the Internet. Links are a great way of pulling a site visitor deeper into your web site, or for pointing them to useful resources elsewhere on the web.

In Plone, there are two main types of links: **Internal Links** and **External Links**. An Internal Link is a hyperlink to a page on the same web site. An External Link is a hyperlink to a page on a different web site.

Internal Links

If you haven't done so already, go ahead and create at least two web pages of your own. Navigate to one of the pages and click on the **Edit** tab on the green toolbar.

Now you should be looking at the **Body Text** of your web page. Highlight some text that you want to create a link for and click on the Internal Link icon shown in the previous figure.

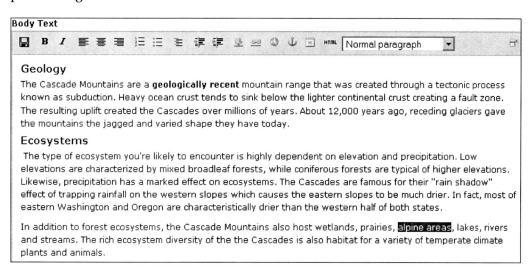

The following **Insert Link** window will appear now:

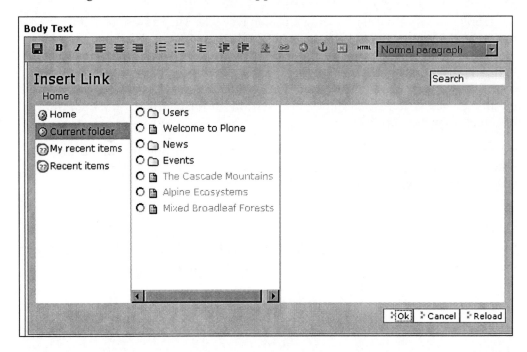

Note that you can navigate around in this window to find the page that you want to link to. If you don't see any pages at first, try clicking on **Home** in the leftmost column. This should bring up a listing of the contents for your web site, as shown in the preceding screenshot. You can also use the **Search** box in the upper right corner of the **Insert Link** window to locate the page that you want to link to.

Then, select the page to create a link to. In the following screenshot, we've chosen to create a link to the **Alpine Ecosystems** page:

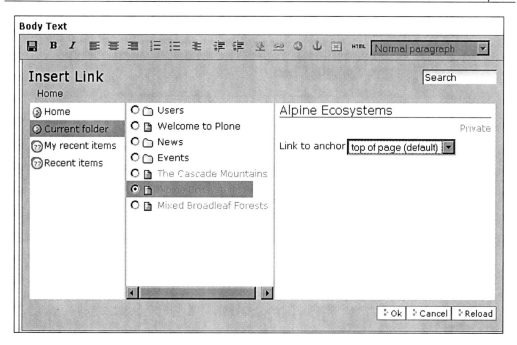

For the time being, ignore the **Link to anchor** menu and just proceed with the default selection. Click on the **Ok** button in the lower-right corner of the **Insert Link** window to finish creating your Internal Link.

You're all done! Save the page that you are working on to try out the link. Your linked text should appear slightly blue and underlined, to differentiate it from normal unlinked text.

External Links

As stated above, External Links are for linking to a web site other than the one you are working on. The process for creating an External Link is similar to that of creating an Internal Link.

Start by editing a page and highlight some text that you want to create an External Link from. Click on the following External Link icon:

Now you need to type in the complete web address of the target page. Plone provides the first part of the link, the **http://** (which must be included) to make things easier. Thus if you want to link to the Plone web site, you would type www.plone.org just after the **http://** part.

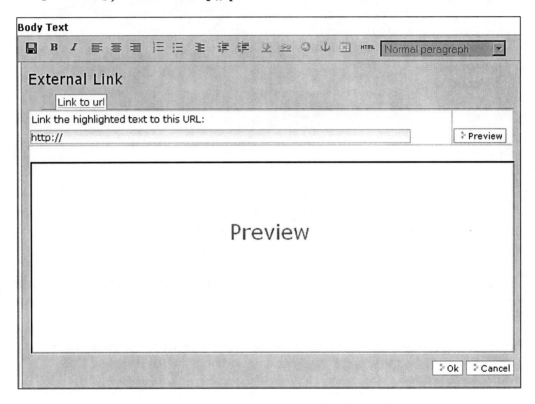

Alternatively, you can copy and paste web addresses from your browser into the link field. This makes things easier if the link you want to use is long and difficult to remember.

Use the **Preview** button on the rightmost side of the dialog box to make sure that the web site address that you've provided is valid, and that the correct page exists at that address.

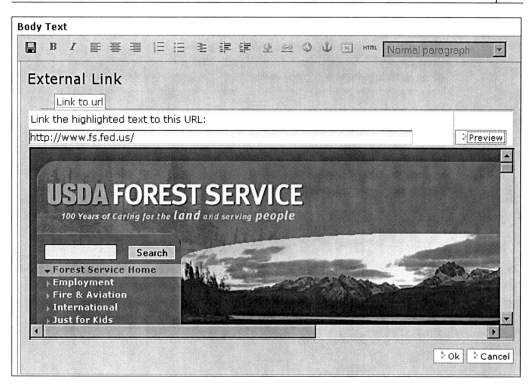

Click **Ok** in the lower-right corner of the **External Link** window to finish creating the link. Now save the page you were working on, to complete the operation.

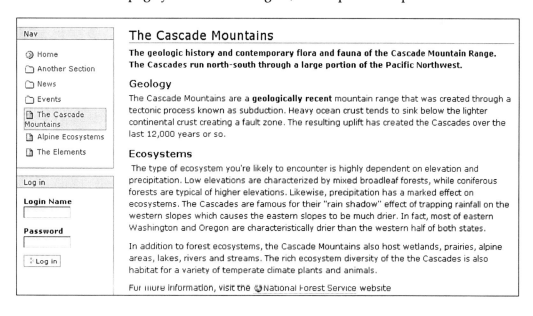

Notice that the text of the External Link has a small icon next to it, as shown in the following figure:

> For more information, visit the National Forest Service website

 If you want to create a link that sends an email, just follow the directions for creating an External Link, but instead of typing in a web address, remove the **http://** text and replace it with `mailto:emailaddress@isp.com`. Then click on **Ok** to finish creating the Email Link.

Linking to a specific part of a page: anchors

Anchors are a way of linking directly to a *specified part* of a page. For example, if you have a rather long page with many sections, you may want to create an anchor for each section and a link to that anchor so that your site visitor doesn't have to scroll up and down the page manually looking for the correct section. The anchor icon is shown in the following figure:

 Anchors are sometimes referred to as *bookmarks* or *internal targets*.

Consider the following page—a list of many chemical elements:

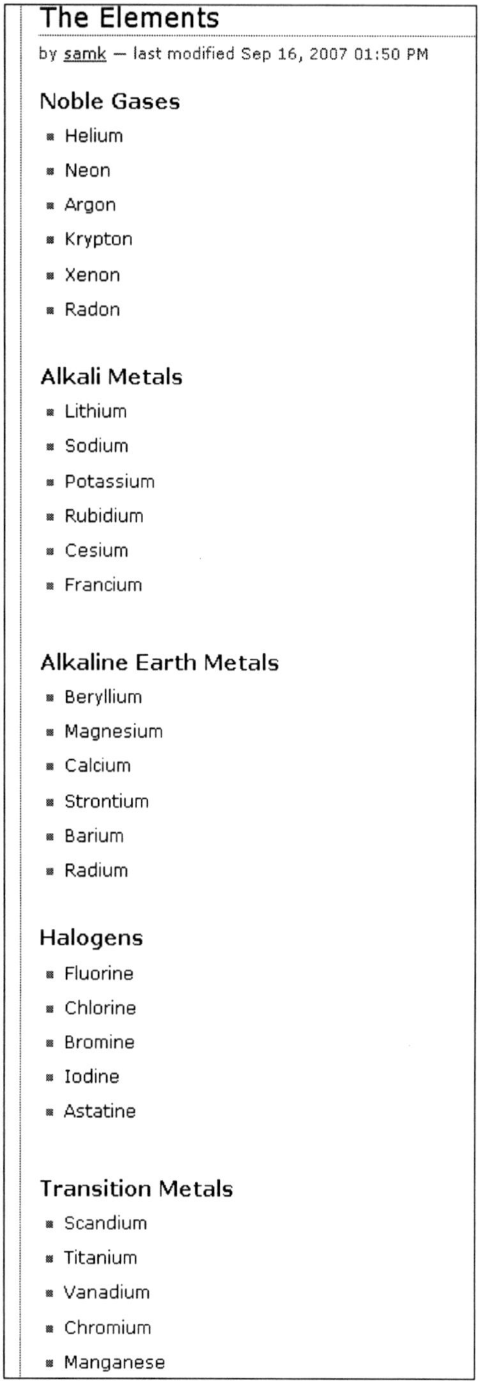

The Elements

by samk — last modified Sep 16, 2007 01:50 PM

Noble Gases

- Helium
- Neon
- Argon
- Krypton
- Xenon
- Radon

Alkali Metals

- Lithium
- Sodium
- Potassium
- Rubidium
- Cesium
- Francium

Alkaline Earth Metals

- Beryllium
- Magnesium
- Calcium
- Strontium
- Barium
- Radium

Halogens

- Fluorine
- Chlorine
- Bromine
- Iodine
- Astatine

Transition Metals

- Scandium
- Titanium
- Vanadium
- Chromium
- Manganese

Because this list is broken up into subsections (**Noble gases, Alkali Metals,** and so on) it is possible to create a link that goes directly to each section, by creating an anchor.

Defining the anchors

We'll start by defining where the anchor is going to be. The best thing to do in this case is to create one anchor for each **Subheading** on the page.

To begin, click on the **Anchor** icon. In the **Anchors** window, note the two tabs: **Link to anchor** and **Manage Anchors**. Click on **Manage Anchors** to define the anchors for this page.

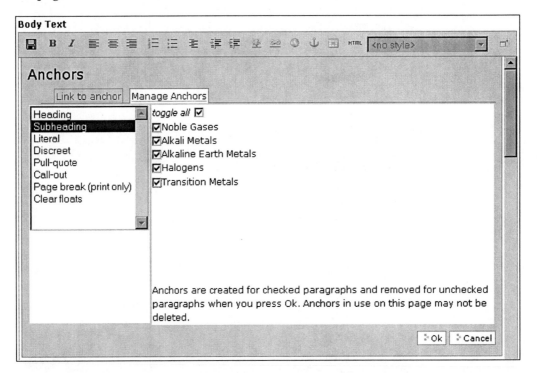

Note the list of paragraph styles on the left (**Heading, Subheading,** and so on). You must select a paragraph style to display a list of the items that you can create anchors for. Because in the example page there is only the **Subheading** style in use, you won't see anything appear in the list on the right until you click on **Subheading**. But when you do, you will see all of the text elements on the page that have the **Subheading** styling applied to them.

Starting with **Noble Gases**, we'll select each checkbox for all of the subheadings in the list and click on **Ok** to finish. You've now created an anchor for each of the subheadings on your page. Should you want to delete an anchor, simply return to the **Anchors** window and *deselect* the checkbox next to the anchor that you wish to remove.

This is only the first step in creating some working anchors. You won't see much change at this point.

Linking to an anchor from a different page

Now that the list of anchors is defined, we can create an Internal Link that points directly to one of these anchors. Let's go ahead and create a link from another page to the **The Elements** page.

We'll start by creating an Internal Link. Highlight the text that you want to create the link for and then click on the Internal Link icon.

Next, navigate to the page that you want to link to (in this case, **The Elements**). Click on the **Link to anchor** drop-down menu on the right to get the list of anchors that you've defined already.

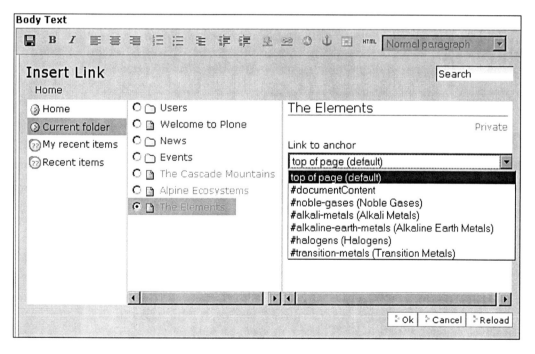

From here, choose the appropriate anchor. In keeping with our example, we'll choose **Halogens**.

The link has now been created. When the page is saved, you can follow the link you've just made and it should take you not only to the correct page, but also to the exact position you identified as the anchor.

Linking to an anchor on the same page

Let's say you want to link to an anchor that is on the same page as the link is. Using the Anchor icon, you can easily create such a link. Let's consider the **Elements** page from the above examples. Here's some sample text that makes a reference to the list of transition metals. The words **Transition Metals** are highlighted because we want to link to the anchor of the same name.

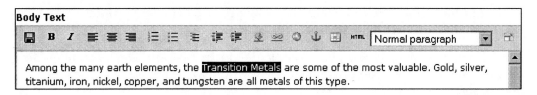

Next, click on the Anchor icon. You should see the **Anchors** window. Leave the **Link to anchor** tab selected and click on the appropriate style from the menu on the left (remember, we've been working with subheadings). This will bring up a list of defined anchors that you can link to, as shown in the following screenshot:

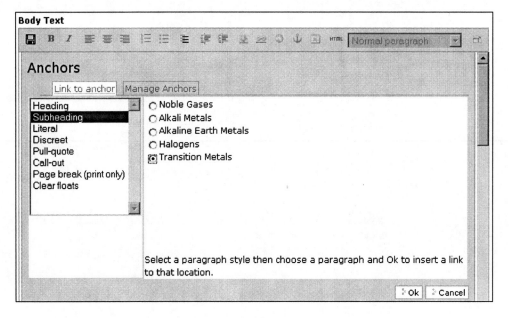

Select the anchor that you wish to link to (**Transition Metals** in this case) and click on **Ok**.

Working with images

Up to this point, you've been working only with text and hyperlinks. Now we'll learn how to work with images in Plone.

Uploading an image

Before you can place an image into a page, you must **upload** the images to your web site. In essence, this means that a copy of the image must be transferred from your computer to your Plone web site. A common practice is to create an `images` folder in which to store all of your images. You don't have to do things this way, but it may help you to keep your content organized on your site.

Navigate to the location to which you wish to upload your image, then click on the **Add new...** menu item and select **Image** from the drop-down list:

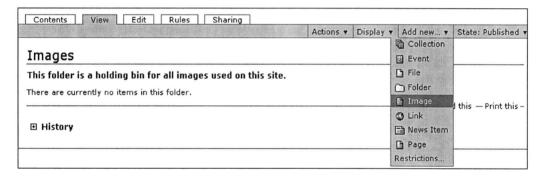

You should now see the **Add Image** screen. Just like pages, images need a **Title** and, optionally, a **Description**.

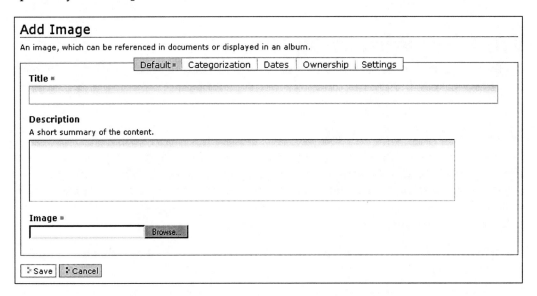

Complete these fields and then click on the **Browse...** button and navigate to the image on your computer's hard drive. Once you have located the image, click on it to select it, and then click the **Save** button on the **Add Image** screen. Now the image file is a part of your web site. The next thing to learn is how to insert the image on a page.

Inserting an image on a Page

Navigate to the page you wish to insert the image on. Edit the page, and choose the location for the image by positioning the cursor on the page where you want the image to appear. Click on the **Insert Image** icon to display the Insert Image screen. An example of this screen is shown below:

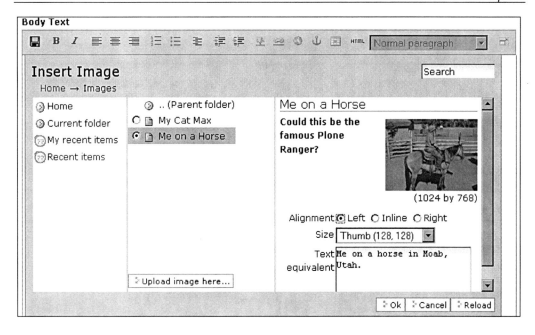

The **Insert Image** screen is divided into three sections. On the left are some navigation links to help you find the image file. Often, it helps to click on **Home** to see the full contents of your site. You can then select your **Images** folder, or whatever folder the image is located in. The middle section shows you what images are in the folder you have chosen. Click on an image file in the list, and the image details will appear in the rightmost section.

Notice that the image details section displays the **Title (Me on a Horse)** and the **Description** below that. You can also see a preview of the image, and the image dimensions.

Next, select an **Alignment, Size,** and if you wish, change the **Text equivalent**. These values are used as follows:

- **Alignment:** This controls how text will wrap around the image and on what side of the screen the image will be aligned.
- **Size:** You have several resizing options on this menu, covering a wide range of sizes.
- **Text equivalent:** Have you ever hovered your mouse over an image and seen a little description pop up? What you're seeing is the **Text equivalent** (also known as alt-text, or tooltip text). The text equivalent automatically uses the **Title** of the image, but you can change this if you want to.

When you have finished making your selections, click on **Ok** to insert the image. The page should then appear as follows:

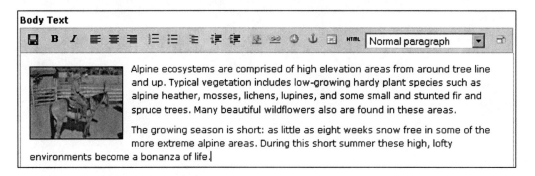

The **Thumb** size and the **Left** alignment are chosen for this example. You can see how the text wraps to the right of the image.

If you want to remove the image, simply click on it and press the *Delete* key.

> To create an image a link, simply click on the image and use the link buttons in the same way as you would for text (see above).

When you have finished inserting images on the page, make sure that you save the page before moving on to something else.

Preparing images for the web

When choosing the images you want to use on your site, you need to be aware of some basic best practices. Not everyone who uses the Internet has a fast, broadband connection, nor does everyone have a nice high-resolution monitor. In addition, there are certain web standards with regard to the type of image file that you are using. In designing a web site, your goal should be to reach as wide an audience as possible. As such, you must prepare your images with the following ideas in mind:

- **File format**: GIF and JPEG are the most widely-supported formats. Modern web browsers also support PNG format, but older browsers may have trouble with PNG images.

- **File size**: The larger the file size, the slower the display time for your web pages, especially for users on a slow Internet connection. Try to keep your images to under 50kb in size.

- **Image dimensions**: The physical size of the image is usually expressed in pixels. Use images that have a width that is less than the width of the **Body Text** field of your pages. Typically that means less than 500 pixels wide. If you want to display a larger image, insert a small version on the page and then link to the large version by using an internal link.

 Modern digital cameras are capable of taking very high resolution pictures. although you can upload large image files into Plone, you may find that they quickly consume your disk space and slow down your site. It is a wise idea to crop, scale down, and compress large images before uploading them to your web site. Plone itself cannot do this for you without using plugins, but there are many excellent software packages that can. Popular open source programs for image editing include the **GIMP** and **Paint.NET**. Commercial options include **Microsoft Photoshop Elements, Jasc Paint Shop Pro, and Adobe Photoshop**.

Controlling the layout of a page: tables

Let's say you have a long list of items that you want to display on a single web page, such as all the elements in the periodic chart. You could simply list them all out in a single vertical column, but that would make your page rather long, and force your site visitors to scroll down the page a great deal to see all of the content. This is where **tables** come in.

Tables create a grid of rows and columns into which you can place content and display text or images side-by-side. There are a few basic table styles, which control the appearance of the table, to choose from. Start by editing a page, and click on the following **Insert table** icon:

 A word of caution: You cannot superimpose a table over pre-existing content. If you insert the table on top of text, you'll lose all the content! You must start by creating the table first, and *then* add content into the table cells.

A window will pop up, to let you choose the **Table Class**. There are several to choose from, some of which look only slightly different from some of the others. Select the number of rows and columns, indicate whether you want to use headers for the table columns, and then click on **Add Table**.

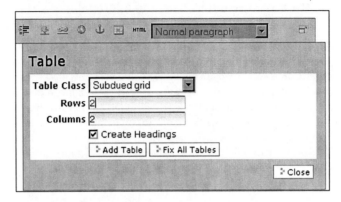

At first you'll just see a tiny grid, but the table will re-size itself as you type text into the cells. Here are examples of what each **Table Class** looks like in practice. All of these have two rows, two columns, and the headings turned on:

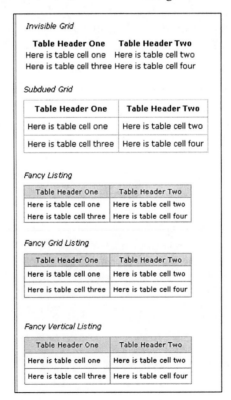

As you can see, the differences are subtle in some cases, but you should be able to find a style that works for the layout that you are envisioning. It will take you some time to get used to working with Tables, so be patient. Experiment often, and don't forget to save your work!

 If you wish to add additional rows or columns to an existing table, simply click inside a table cell. Small **x** and some little arrows will appear. Up and down arrows add rows above or below the current row, and left and right arrows add columns to the left or right of the current column. The **x** is there in case you want to remove a row or a column from the table. Use *Ctrl+z* to undo your work if you make a mistake.

Publishing your work

In this chapter, you've been working on your Plone site as a logged in user. The pages that you've created will appear in the top navigation tabs. However, try logging out and then finding the pages you've created — the navigation tabs for your pages aren't there anymore! Before the outside world can see your pages, you must **publish** them.

You may have noticed that when you view your pages (when logged-in), they are labeled **Private**. By default, when you create new pages, they are considered private. This allows you to work on a page "behind-the-scenes." Then, when you are ready to display the page publicly, you need to publish it.

Publishing a page

To publish a page, you should first, navigate to the page that you wish to publish. Note the **State** menu item on the rightmost side of the green toolbar. Click on this menu item and select **Publish** from the drop-down list.

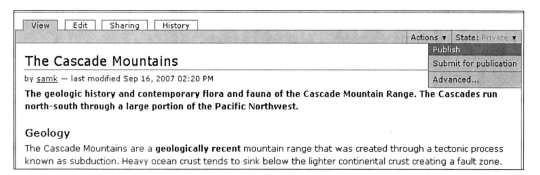

For now, you can ignore the **Submit for publication** and **Advanced** options in the **State** drop-down menu. These functions will be covered in subsequent chapters of this book. If you do not see the **Publish** option, it is probably because you are not logged in as an administrator. The default workflow assumes that non-administrators have to get their work reviewed by a reviewer before it can be published. You will learn more about workflow and the **State** tab in subsequent chapters.

That's all there is to it. Now if you log out of your site, you should see the page you've just published, available as a navigation tab.

Publishing multiple pages

In the previous section, you learned how to publish a single page. You can also publish multiple items in a directory at once, rather than one at a time. This can be done through the **Contents** tab for the folder.

First, navigate to the folder in which there are pages that you wish to publish. Then click on the **Contents** tab on the green toolbar. Note that the publishing state is indicated by color—Red is private content, and blue is published content. Select the checkboxes next to the content that you want to publish and then click on the **Change State** button below the folder contents list.

You are then taken to the **Publishing process** page. There are several things that you can do here, but for now, look at the bottom of the page. Select the **Publish** option, and click on **Save** to continue.

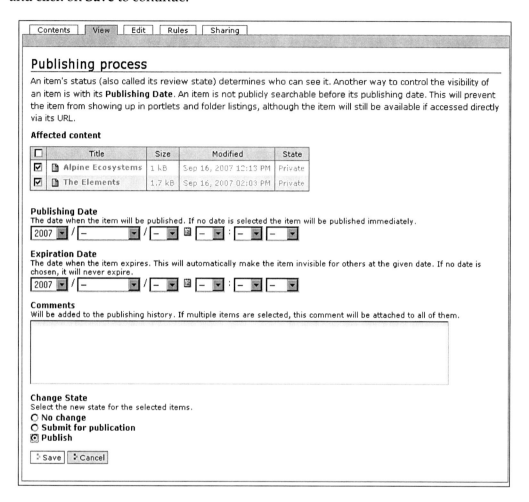

Publishing a folder

Let's say you want to publish a folder that contains other content items. Plone gives you the choice of publishing only the main folder, or all of the contents of the folder as well. Here is an example of this latter scenario:

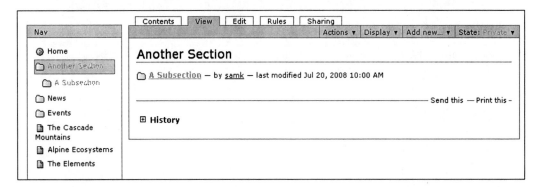

Here we have a folder called **Another Section**, and a second folder within it called **A Subsection**. We wish to publish both **Another Section** and the folder contained within it.

First, navigate to one level above the folder that you want to publish. In this case it's the home page or the root level of the site. Then click on **Contents** in the toolbar to see a listing of all of the content items. Note that the text of **Another Section** is colored red, to indicate that is in a **private** state.

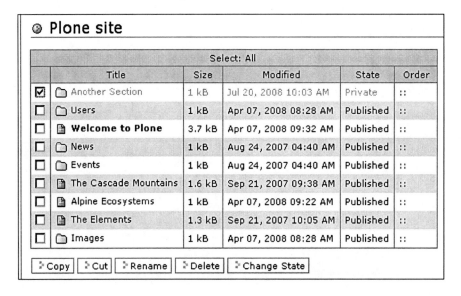

Select the checkbox next to **Another Section** and then click on **Change State** button. You should now see the **Publishing process** page, as shown in the following screenshot.

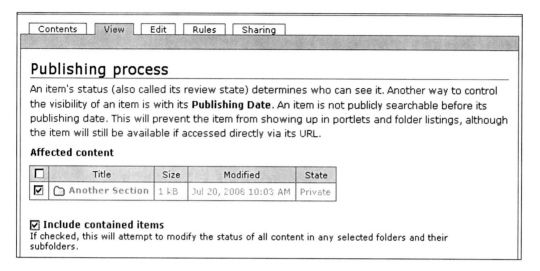

Note the checkbox labeled **Include contained items**. By selecting this checkbox, you can choose to have all of the contained content items published along with the main folder you are publishing. To finish, choose **Publish** at the bottom of the page and click on **Save**.

You can check the results by clicking on the folder you have just published. The folder and all of its contained items should now be displayed as published items, in the familiar blue text color, as shown in the following screenshot:

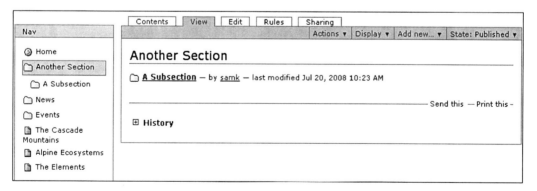

Summary

There's a lot of information in this chapter that you will use when working on a Plone web site. All of the basics of creating pages, formatting text, inserting images, and creating hyperlinks are covered here. In addition, we have introduced the idea of publishing content and of user roles. These are foundational skills that you'll need to learn in order to successfully manage a Plone web site. The information in this chapter is particularly important if you are responsible for publishing content to a Plone web site.

5

Add News Items, Events, Links, and Files

Now that you have learned how to create pages, you are ready to move on to creating other types of content items to populate your web site.

In this chapter by Tom Couklin, we will focus on:

- Creating news items
- Creating events
- Creating hyperlinks to internal and external web sites
- Uploading files to your Plone site

By using these types of content items, you are making your site dynamic, with various topics that could be relevant to your audience. Having news items and events gives visitors the impression that the site is current and should be checked on a regular basis. Creating hyperlinks and making electronic files available in a user-friendly way helps to give your site a polished look and feel.

News items

As you have seen, Plone sites have built-in sections called portlets, which display short listings of additional content. The news items that we will create will take advantage of this concept. Once your news item has been created and published, it will be available to the users of your site, directly from the portlet. By clicking on the item listed in the portlet, the user is taken to the full news item.

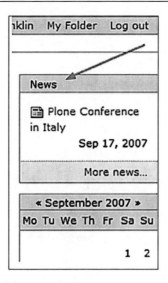

Creating a news item

You can create news items from anywhere that the site administrator has enabled this capability. You can find out if this is the case by clicking on the **Add new...** link and seeing if the option **News Item** is available in the drop-down list, as shown in the following screenshot:

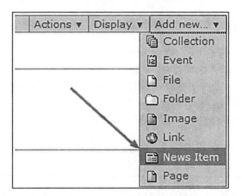

After you choose the **News Item** option, you are taken to the following page, to create the item:

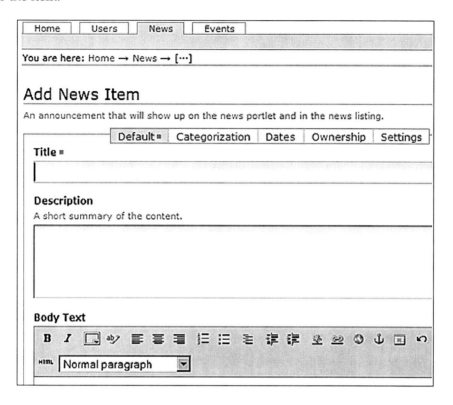

This will look the same as you saw in the chapter on creating pages. Just as with pages, you must provide a **Title**, and you should also add a **Description** for your news item. The **Description** field will be helpful to your site visitors, because once your news item is available, moving the mouse over the news headline in the portlet will show the description text, as shown in the following screenshot:

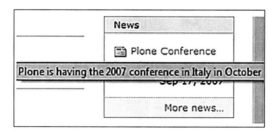

The body text can be created using the graphical HTML editor, and the HTML editing functionality that you learned in Chapter 4 is available to you. Formatting and linking your **News Item** is exactly the same as for page creation.

Unlike pages, news items also include fields for a related image and a caption:

Image
Will be shown in the news listing, and in the news item itself. Image will be scaled to a sensible size.

[　　　　　　　　　　] [Browse...]

Image Caption

[　　　　　　　　　　　　　　]

Change note
Enter a comment that describes the changes you made.

[　　　　　　　　　　　　　　]

[Save]　[Cancel]

When a user clicks on the main **News** navigation tab, they will see a listing of all of the news items. Clicking on (for example) **Plone Conference in Italy** takes the user directly to this page within the site. The following screenshot is an example of what a news item looks like when displayed within the news section. By default, Plone also makes this content available via a RSS feed, or you can send a news item to someone via an email message.

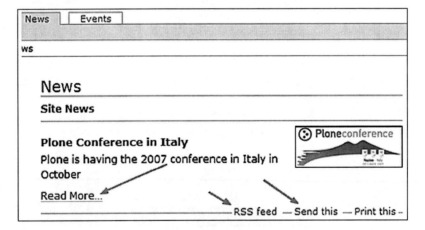

When the user clicks on the **Read More...** link he or she will be taken to the full article:

As you can see, the item itself is very similar to a regular page, with the exception that an image that is included. The image itself can actually be larger in size than the size shown on the page. The user can click on the image to view the image actual size. Plone dynamically resizes the image to better fit it within the context of the article. However it is always a good idea to resize your images before uploading them to your site.

If you have editing (or more powerful) rights to the news item, you can revisit and edit the news page, as well as look at any revisions that have been made it it (by yourself or by other users). If necessary, you can revert the news item to a previous version from the history section.

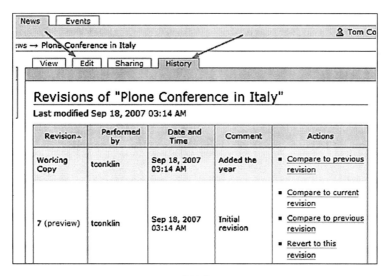

The **History** section shown in the preceding screenshot is available for all content items created by you or by others. This functionality is covered in more detail in Chapter 7. This functionality is especially helpful when more than one person is collaborating on a piece of content.

The news folder

In the default setup of Plone, one of the navigation tabs is **News**. The News folder contains a default **Collection** item, which automatically generates a listing of news items located anywhere on your site.

Collections will be covered in more detail in Chapter 6.

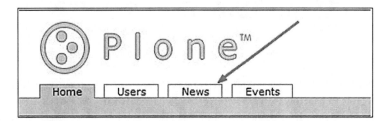

While you are in the **News** section, if you look at the **Add new...** drop-down option, you will see that the default is to have only **News Item** available for posting in this section.

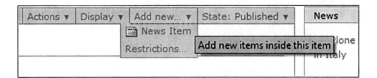

The **RSS feed** link is an available option for allowing visitors to subscribe to the **News** section of your site. Without any coding on your part, News content is RSS enabled! Users of your site can stay up-to-date as and when new content is added.

The following screenshot shows what it looks like when you subscribe to the news section in Firefox 2.x:

Events

Events are another basic content type in Plone, and share many of the same basic fields as news items and pages.

The events folder

A default Plone site has an **Events** folder. Similar to the **News** folder discussed above, this contains a collection that lists all of the events created within the site.

Creating events

To add an event within the **Events** section, click on **Add new...** and choose **Event** from the drop-down list.

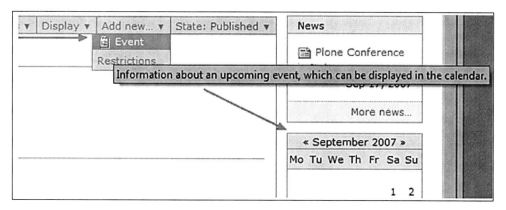

As noted in the tool tip, Event items are linked to the **Calendar Portlet**.

The following is a list of fields within the Event content type that are different from what we have seen so far for pages and news items:

- **Event Location**: Adding content in this section can assist your search engine, and give more context to your event.
- **Event Starts (Mandatory)**: Events are meant to have a beginning and ending time and date.
- **Event Ends (Mandatory)**: See Event Starts (Mandatory), above.
- **Attendees**: This can be helpful for showing who is participating. The search engine can also pick up on names entered here.

- **Event Types**
    - **Existing Categories**: This gives you the ability to add keywords that can be used for site collection criteria
    - **New Categories**: Use this if you need to include the existing categories
- **Event URL**: Link to additional information.
- **Contact name**
- **Contact E-Mail**
- **Contact Phone**

The following screenshot shows how the fields are presented within Plone:

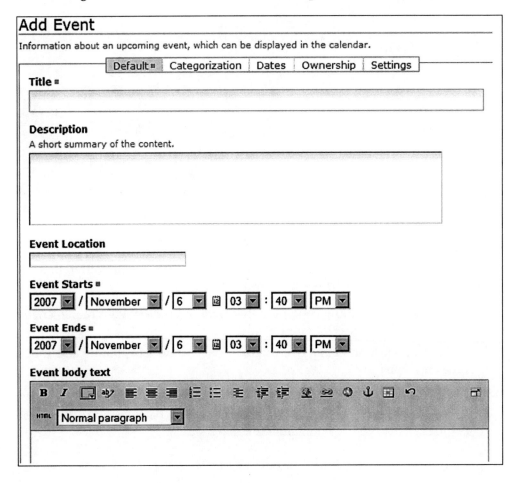

After the section for the event body text, you will see the following fields:

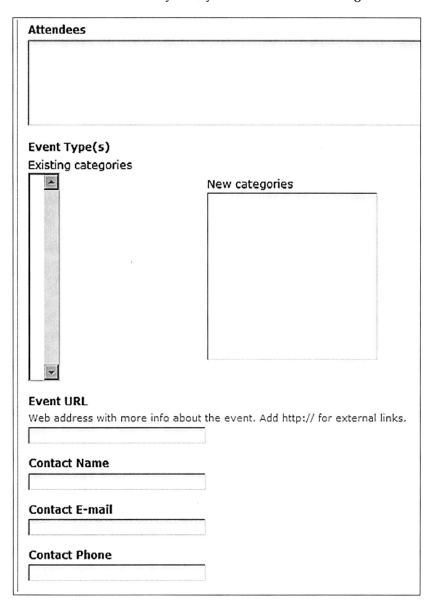

As noted above, apart from the **Title**, only the start and end dates of the event are mandatory. Plone lets the editor decide if any of the other items that are typically associated with an event should be filled out.

The following is an example of an event that has been filled out with all options complete:

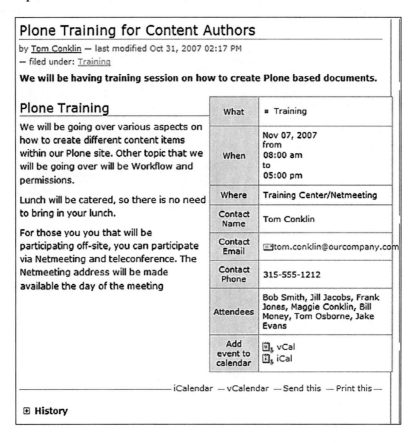

Most of what is shown in the preceding screenshot is self-explanatory, with the exception of the **What** option, which can be specified via the **Categories** tab.

Handy, out of the box features include the ability to import a calendar item into either an Apple iCal calendar or Microsoft Outlook. You can also send a link to this page to someone via email, or print the event details:

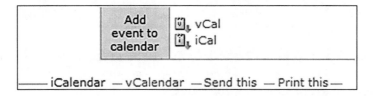

Using the vCal and iCal links

When you click on the **vCal** icon or link, you get the following pop up (in Firefox):

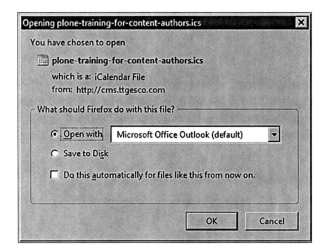

You can choose to either open this file, or save it to disk. On choosing **Open**, or on double-clicking after downloading, the file opens in an Outlook form. You can make additional edits to the event details, or just save it to your calendar.

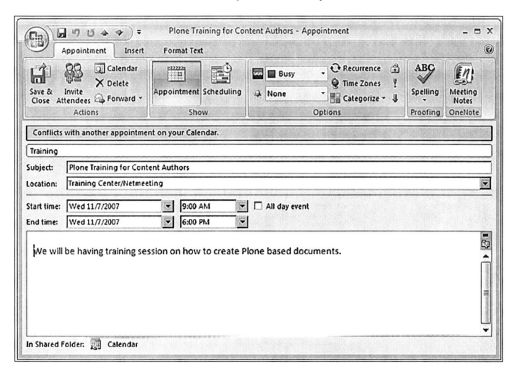

After saving the event, it is added to your Outlook calendar.

The same type of functionality is available to users of Apple-based computers who use the Apple Calendar, when the **iCal** option is selected.

Links

In Chapter 4, you learned how to create internal and external hyperlinks within pages by using the graphical HTML editor. Plone also offers the ability to create links as standalone content objects, rather than as part of the body text of a page. Link objects can be very useful as you build your site structure. Let's explore how to put them to use!

To begin, click on **Add new…** and then choose **Link**:

Once you are in the create/edit mode, you will need to enter a **Title** (mandatory), then a **Description**, and the **URL** (mandatory) of the destination. Unlike the **Kupu** editor, the **Link** edit screen does not have a live preview, so you should try to play it safe by copying and pasting the URL from the actual site, rather than trying to retype the URL by hand.

Creating this link page does not offer too much to the users just yet. We'll now take a look at expanding what the link functionality can do. A nice feature within Plone is the ability to allow users to provide comments on web pages. This can be enabled by going to the **Settings** tab (while in edit mode) and selecting the **Allow comments** checkbox:

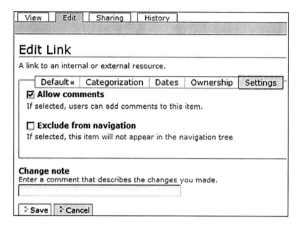

Now, when a registered user visits the page, he or she can add comments related to the link:

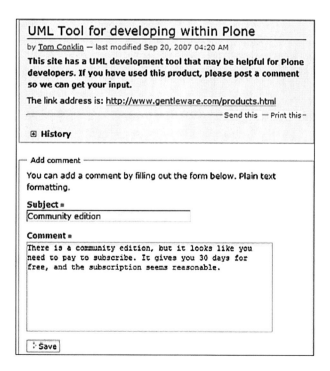

Unregistered users will be able to see the page, including the comments, as shown here:

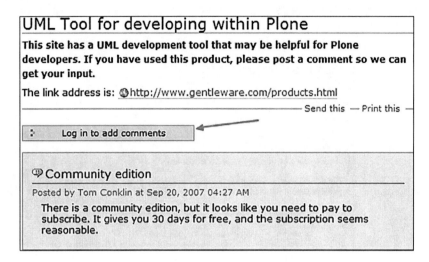

If you are a registered user and have not logged in yet, you can follow the **Log in** link to add your comments.

An additional purpose for using the link object is for organizing your content based on specific criteria. Taking the example above further, we could add more link pages that are related to additional UML tools. All of these link pages can then be made part of a **Collection**. Your site could then contain an additional navigation structure that allows visitors and members to navigate through this collection.

The most common use case, however, is to add a link object to your navigation. If you want your users to be able to access external sites while they are on your site, this is an easy way to provide this capability. Note that the links in your navigation will only take you to the desired location if you are logged out of your site. Logged-in users (managers) will be taken to a page that displays the link and gives them an opportunity to edit the link.

Files

Many web sites need to include non-HTML content such as PDFs, Microsoft Office and/or OpenOffice documents, CAD files, MP3s, ZIP archives, and so on. Plone's **File** content type lets you upload and manage any kind of file type on your site. Assuming that the appropriate supporting programs are installed on your server, Plone can automatically index and search the text in Word, PDF, and other document formats.

Adding a file

From the menu, select **Add new...** and then select **File**.

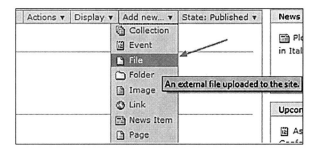

The **Title** field must be specified on the page that is displayed next, and optionally, a **Description**. It's again important to note that the better the title and the description, the better the visitor's experience is. Meaningful titles and descriptions will ensure that the visitor is getting the file he or she needs.

A file placed on a site may be there for a long time, and it's important to know if you're looking at 'newsletter-may-2008' or 'newsletter'. Be specific!

After clicking on the **Browse...** button, you are able to search your local drive (or network drives) to select the desired file. Once it's selected, click on **Save**.

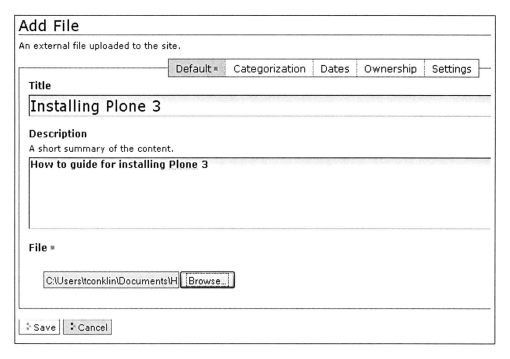

After uploading the file to the site by clicking on **Save**, the file becomes available to the users of your site. There's no need to publish the file, as files do not use the standard publishing workflow.

Performing a LiveSearch on the word 'guide', for example, shows the dynamic results, and the document with the attached file that was just created.

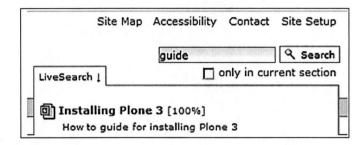

Some important information that is displayed on the page pointing to the uploaded file is:

- Who put the file there
- The date on which it was uploaded
- The file type

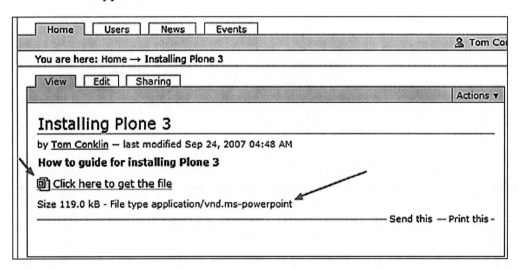

Also note that the link states **Click here to get the file**. You may also just see a link to the file. Clicking on this link will download the file to your local machine.

Summary

In this chapter, we have learned:

- How to create a news item
- How to create an event item
- How to create a link to an external website
- How to upload a file

Using what you have learned in this chapter, you should now have a good understanding of how to make News, Events, Links, and Files available to your site's visitors and members.

6

Structure Your Content

If you have been following this book chapter-by-chapter, you have learned how to create pages, news items, events, links, images, and files. This has given you some good background on creating content in Plone. Now, **Tom Conklin** will show us how to structure and organize your content so that your site is poised to grow.

Just like building a house, you need to have a strong foundation and framework to support a site that is built to last, without needing any major rebuilding in the future. Proper planning from the beginning will go a long way toward having a site that is easy to maintain.

Real world information architecture tips

Based on what your users need and/or want to see, you need to structure your content within topics, or **high-level containers** that are typically content-specific sections. As an example, we will take a look at `http://Plone.org`.

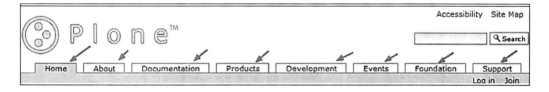

When visitors enter a Plone site, no matter how deep they go, the navigation tends to stay the same. The following screenshot shows that a visitor is in the **Documentation** section of the site, with the opportunity to drill down within this section for additional documentation topics:

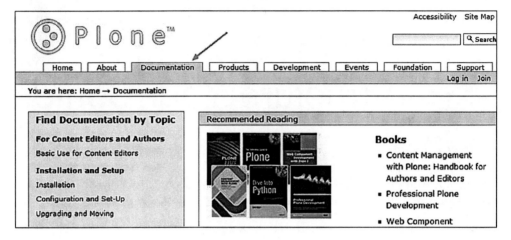

By default, Plone has a portlet that shows the navigation aids on the left-hand side of the browser, which helps the visitors navigate within the subject matter. In this example, there are several subsections below **Development**.

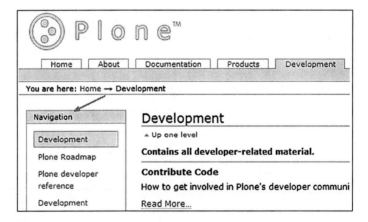

Structuring your content

When planning your site, you must first decide how you want to structure your content. The structuring can be worked out through brainstorming sessions with other people involved with your site, in order to come up with a structure suits your business objectives. Investigating other sites that share your organization's model could be a good starting point towards developing your final solution.

To really understand how Plone can be an effective solution for your content delivery needs, we will take a look at how to implement Plone for a High School web site. In this type of structure, you will see how some content is targeted at all users, while other content is tailored to specific users.

We will use the following high-level topics for demonstration purposes:

- Home
- News
- Events
- Academics
- Sports
- Clubs
- PTO (Parent-Teacher Organization)
- Alumni

In order to create these sections, we will first create folders for the above sections, into which you will add content. Each of the above sections will be visible in your top-level navigation. Within each top-level folder, we will also create subfolders to help you to structure your content.

To create a folder, go to your homepage, select **Add new...** and choose the **Folder** option from the drop-down list, as shown in the following screenshot:

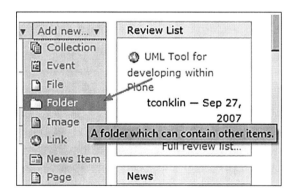

Specify the **Title** and the optional **Description**. In this case, we will create a folder for the **Academics** section:

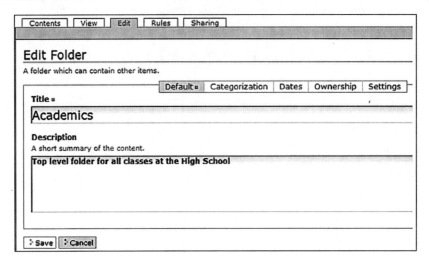

We're going to just keep the defaults here; we will cover the **Settings** tab shortly.

Click on **Save**, and then make sure that your folder has been published:

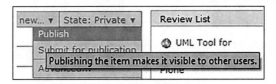

Now take a look at the overall navigation structure:

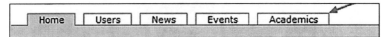

There is now a new tab in your navigation bar, which represents a container for holding all of the content that will be part of the academics section of the site. You will follow the same process to create the rest of the top-level tabs.

First, we will need to make a change to the default tab behavior in Plone. Specifically, we want to remove **Users** as a top-level navigation item. Removing it from the tab navigation does not mean that it no longer exists; we're just making sure that items that are more important to this specific site are shown to the visitors and users.

To remove **Users** from the navigation bar, click on the **Users** tab, and then select **Edit**. Once you are in **Edit** mode, there is the section where you can select **Settings**. You can then select the **Exclude from navigation** checkbox.

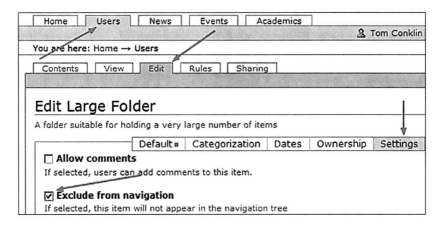

After saving your changes, you can see that the tab **Users** is no longer part of your navigation:

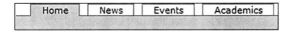

Using the same process for adding new folders, we'll add **Sports**, **Clubs** and **PTO**. We end up with the following:

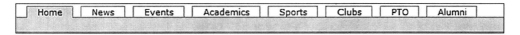

Now that we have the top-level structure in place, we can focus on what will need to go within each topic. The process is similar, with the difference being that you need to be within the given topic before creating the next level of folders.

When you create folders in the **Home** section, you have the ability to create top-level tabs. Creating folders within the other top-level folders you create allows you to be more specific for the given topic. We will use the example of the **Sports** top-level tab for creating an additional folder/site structure. We will need to create the following sub-folders:

- Football
- Basketball
- Soccer
- Track and Field
- Lacrosse
- Baseball
- Softball

To do so, we must drill down into the **Sports** folder and add new folders within it. Once you have added these folders under the **Sports** section, the **Navigation** to the new folders is available in the leftmost side of your browser window:

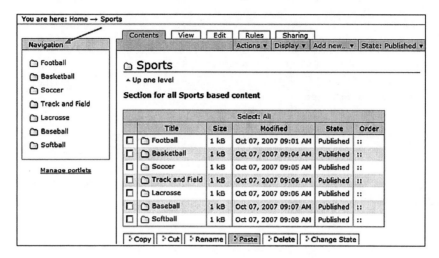

Note that the navigation shows only the contents of the current folder. This can be adjusted via the **Manage portlets** link, which is available on the home page, below the left and right columns. This link is also accessible via http://www.mysite. com/@@manage-portlets, where www.mysite.com is the name of your Plone site. Simply set the **Start Level** to **0** and save your changes.

Now that the structure for the **Sports** folder is in place, let's take a look at how you can change the order of display of the folders. If the football season is over, it may make sense to move this category to the bottom of the navigation. To change the order of the **Football** folder, go to the **Contents** view under **Sports**, then click in the **Order** column for the **Football** row. The row will turn yellow, and the cursor will change to a four-headed arrow, which indicate that the content object can be moved. Drag the row up or down in the list, to the desired location.

	Title	Size	Modified	State	Order
☐	🗁 Basketball	1 kB	Oct 07, 2007 09:04 AM	Published	::
☐	🗁 Soccer	1 kB	Oct 07, 2007 09:05 AM	Published	::
☐	🗁 Track and Field	1 kB	Oct 07, 2007 09:06 AM	Published	::
☐	🗁 Lacrosse	1 kB	Oct 07, 2007 09:06 AM	Published	::
☐	🗁 Baseball	1 kB	Oct 07, 2007 09:07 AM	Published	::
☐	🗁 Softball	1 kB	Oct 07, 2007 09:08 AM	Published	::
☐	🗁 Football	1 kB	Oct 07, 2007 09:01 AM	Published	:: ✛

Select: All

⟩ Copy | ⟩ Cut | ⟩ Rename | ⟩ Paste | ⟩ Delete | ⟩ Change State

Now, when you click on the top level of **Sports**, the navigation listing appears in the new location that you have just defined:

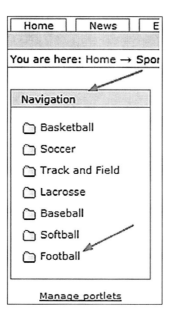

Now, let's take the new folder structure created under the **Sports** section, and create some more folders that are specific to each sub topic.

Select a folder, and then go to the **Contents** tabbed page. In this example, we will create the following folders under the **Soccer** folder, which is under the **Sports** folder:

- Varsity
- Boys
- Girls
- Junior Varsity
- Boys
- Girls
- Boosters

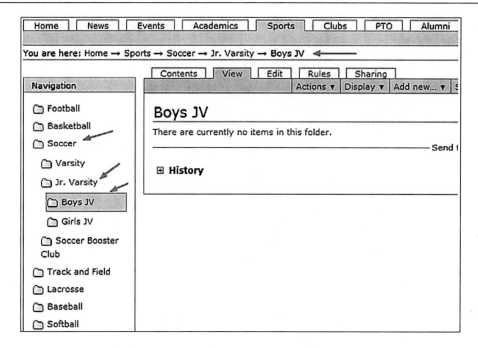

As identified in the preceding screenshot, the breadcrumbs navigation shows the progression through the site. You can also see how the navigation within the **Sports** section can grow to fit specific content.

> You will see in Chapter 8 how you can add specific roles, such as contributors within the **Sports** section, and add additional contributors even deeper. An example of this would be a Girl's JV soccer coach being able to add content to the **Girl's JV soccer** section, but nowhere else.

By understanding these concepts that apply creating folders for your navigation structure, you will be well on your way to having consistent navigation throughout your site.

Adding Collections to your site

As your site is expanding, you may find that one section is too narrow in scope, and needs to be placed into multiple sections on your site. The example we will use is for the Booster Club to be in the **Home** section of the site, the **Sports** section, as well as the **Club** section, but not as a top-level tab. Additionally, the content that is created in each of the sections will be available in the **Home** section of the site, but the authors will have only the permission to add content from within their own folders. We will accomplish this by using what is called **Collections**.

Collections look like Folders, and in the previous versions of Plone, they were called **Smart Folders** and **Topics**. Their name has now been changed to Collections due to the fact that they are not truly folders; they are actually queries of items that follow specific criteria.

To create a new collection, go to the section where you want it to be created (in this example, we will go to the **Home** section). Click **Add new...** and choose **Collection** from the drop-down list:

You are then presented with the following form, where you specify the mandatory **Title**, the optional **Description**, and the **Body Text**:

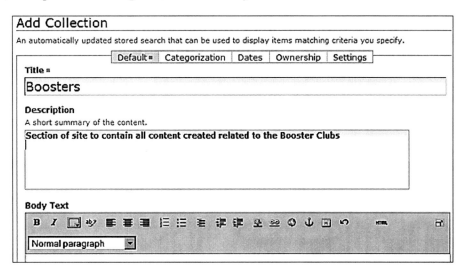

Click on **Settings**, and then select **Exclude from navigation.** We will leave everything else with the default values for now, so clicking on **Save** will hold the current state of the object even though it will not have any functionality just yet.

You will be able to return to this object by navigating to **Home,** and going to the **Contents** tabbed page, where you can see your new collection. Also notice that the icon for this object is a 'multiple pages' icon (and not a folder or single page icon).

Clicking on the **Boosters** link will take you to the following page:

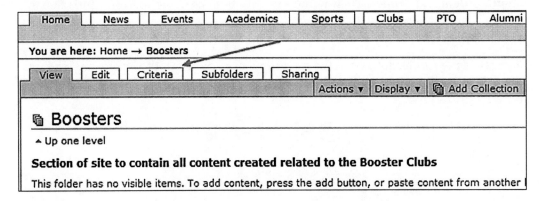

Note that we now have a new tab to work with, called **Criteria**. We will get back to this section shortly. We first need to tag items within our site so that this new object can be included in the collection criteria that we are looking for.

Let's now go back to the **Boosters** section folder under **Soccer**, select the **Edit** tab, then select **Categorization**, and finally enter **BoosterInfo** in the **New Categories** text box, and then click **Save**:

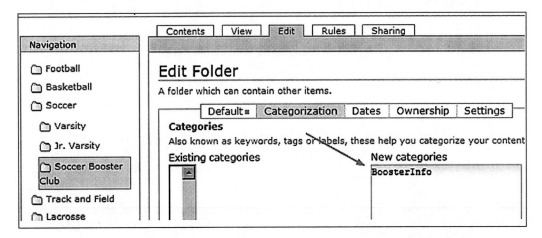

Now, when you refresh your view on this folder, the **BoosterInfo** is in an existing category, and is available for selection from other content types, so the following is displayed:

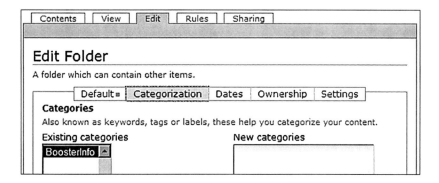

Now, let's go back to the **Booster** collection that we had created previously. Select **Criteria**, then under **Field name**, select **Categories**, and under **Criteria type**, choose **Select values from list**.

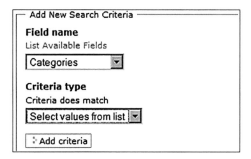

Finally, click on the **Add criteria** button.

You are now presented with a form that you can use to complete the process. Select **BoosterInfo** in the **Values** list (right now it just shows the one item).

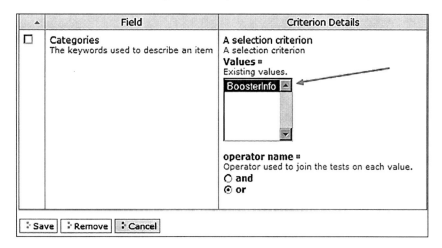

Now, when we go back to the **Boosters** Collection view, we can see the results of what we have just set up:

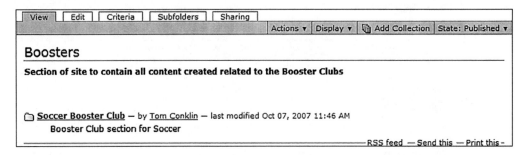

We see a folder for the **Soccer Booster Club**, and clicking on that link takes us to the actual **Soccer Booster Club** folder, which is present elsewhere on the site:

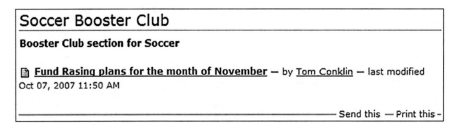

This is not a big deal yet. The visitor could have simply gone to that section via the standard navigation. As the topic is about Boosters, let's go to another section that has Booster information—**Clubs**. Then we will add a folder called **Academic Booster Clubs**. Go to **Categorization**, select **BoosterInfo**, and then click **Save**:

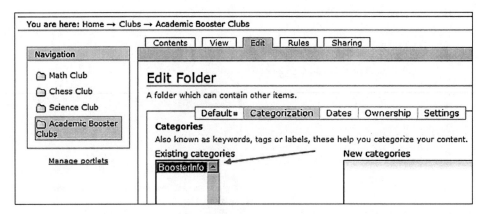

This folder is now set up and ready for content to be added to it. All content that is added to this folder will be available via the collection created in the **Home** section.

After creating a new page within this new section, we can carry out a tests to check that our collection is working correctly, by viewing it. Here is the result:

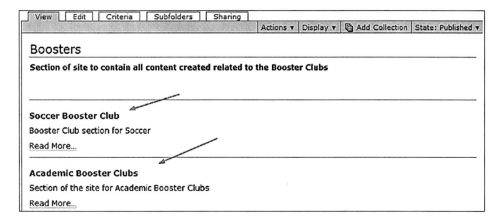

You may be thinking: "so what, what's the big deal"?. By itself, it still isn't all that useful. But we have an additional tool to use in order to complete this exercise. When you create a Collection, you are also creating an object that is RSS-enabled by default. Now, visitors who are interested in any of the booster clubs can subscribe to the Booster Collection, and receive a notification when content is added:

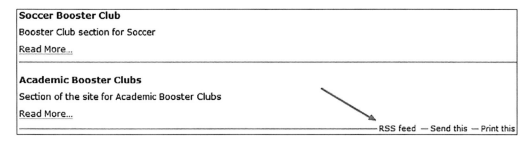

The following is the result after adding the RSS feed within FireFox:

We have only scratched the surface of using the Collections functionality within Plone. As you get more comfortable using Collections, you will find that you can configure them with many different criteria such as item type, date, creator, and so on that will ensure that specific results are returned.

For example, you may wish to set up a criteria along the lines of "Show me all of the items in folder X, where there is a keyword of a OR b, AND the state is published." Collections are very powerful for aggregating content that may be scattered across your site.

Additional Collections

The **News** and **Events** sections also take advantage of the Collections functionality. We can use this built-in functionality by creating **News** and **Events** items within each topic area, and have the results displayed within **News** and **Events** portlets for all of the site visitors to see.

We must first ensure that the contributors to each specific area have the ability to create these types of items within the section that they are responsible for. By posting News and Events within their own area, Plone automatically populates the news and events portlets in those sections. By changing the criteria to recognize only the **News** and **Events** items listed in a given folder, we can prevent other unrelated news and events items from appearing.

In addition, as the **News** and **Events** sections are actually Collections, site visitors can subscribe to the RSS feeds for this type of content.

Restricting types of content

As you grow your site and delegate the creation of content within specific folders to certain contributors, you may also want to prevent these contributors from creating other types of objects, such as collections. We can disable this functionality by removing the objects from the **Add new...** menu and clicking on the **Restrictions** option.

Let's re-visit the **Sports** section. By default, contributors have the ability to add the following types of content:

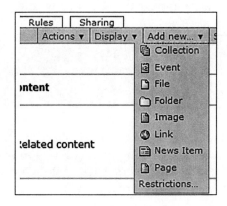

We only want to allow the contributors to create the following content types:

- Events
- News Items
- Pages

After clicking on **Restrictions...** we can disable the items that we don't want to be available for use by deselecting the appropriate checkboxes:

Restrict what types of content can be added

Type restrictions
Select the restriction policy in this location.
○ **Allow the standard types to be added**
◉ **Specify types manually**

Allowed types
Controls what types are addable in this location.
☐ **Collection**   ☐ **File**   ☐ **Link**
☑ **Event**   ☐ **Folder**   ☑ **News Item**
☐ **Favorite**   ☐ **Image**   ☑ **Page**

Secondary types
Select which types should be available in the 'More...' submenu *instead* of in the main pulldown. This is useful to indicate that these are not the preferred types in this location, but are allowed if you really need them.
▣ **Collection**   ▣ **File**   ▣ **Link**
☐ **Event**   ▣ **Folder**   ☐ **News Item**
▣ **Favorite**   ▣ **Image**   ☐ **Page**

⁝ Save   ⁝ Cancel

The result of this action is the following functionality, for someone with Contributor rights:

Assuming that people have been assigned rights to create these items, they will have content published in their specific sections (Sports, Boosters, and so on).

This content will be available within the collection's results. For example, the specific sections will include the **News** and **Events** flagged as **BoosterInfo**, and the default **News** and **Events** sections and portlets on the **Home** level will also include these items, as the default criteria for these sections are more general.

Moving content

Now that you know how to create folders and understand all the content items that ship by default with Plone, you may be asking yourself: "What if I created content in one section, but it really needs to be in a different section?". This kind of change is inevitable in any site, and Plone has an easy way of moving content to where it is needed.

Let's start off by creating some content in the **Sports** Section, and then move this into the **Clubs** section.

We will first go to the location where the content that needs to be moved currently exists. In this example, the content is in the **Football** section. Let's go to the **Contents** tabbed page for this section:

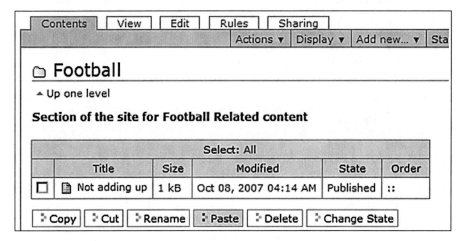

Select the checkbox to the left of the **Not adding up** item, and then click on the **Cut** button. Now go to the folder where the content belongs. Make sure that you are on the **Contents** tabbed page:

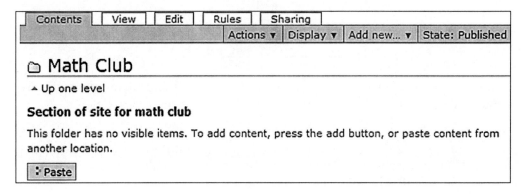

Click the **Paste** button, and now the item will be in the correct location:

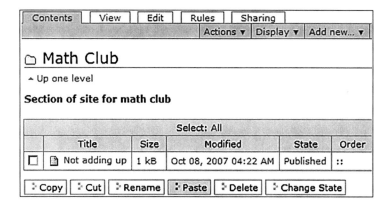

This same functionality is available for moving and/or copying entire folders. An example of doing this is when you are first building your site, and you want to have identical folders within each subsection. Previously, we created **Varsity**, **Jr. Varsity**, and **Soccer Booster Club** under the **Soccer** section. We can copy these three folders and place them into the **Football** folder:

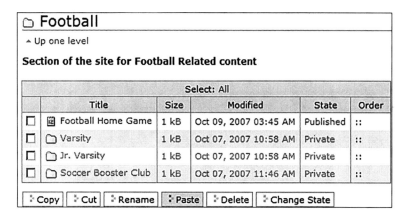

Now we just need to click the **Change State** button to publish them. You may also need to make other minor changes, such as changing **Soccer Booster Club** to **Football Booster Club**. Because this object was copied, the categorization keyword we created for the booster folder (**BoosterInfo**) is also set up within the copied folder.

If you have content items within the copied folder, you will also need to publish the individual items, even after publishing the folders. You can also delete objects at this point, if they are not relevant to your new section.

Changing the order of pages

You may have a scenario where you want the visitor to be able to 'page through' the content that you have created. An example would be a manual, or a long document that you need to break up into sections.

In the following example, we will create a series of pages within a folder called **School Handbook** in the **Academic** section with **page navigation,** and then move around some of the pages so that the page flow in the correct order.

Go to the correct folder, select the **Edit** tab, then select **Settings,** and select the **Enable next previous navigation** checkbox.

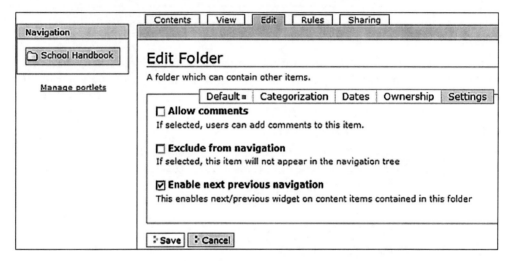

Now we can go and add some pages to this folder. When we add pages, they are listed in the order of their creation, so we will make an obvious mistake:

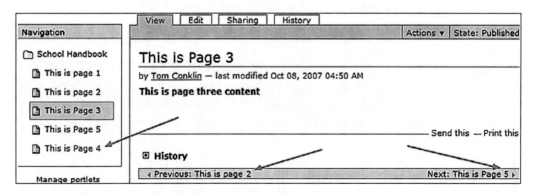

We have the navigation working, but we need to correct the error of the pages being out of order. We do this by going to the **Contents** tabbed page of the **School Handbook** folder, and then selecting **Page 4**:

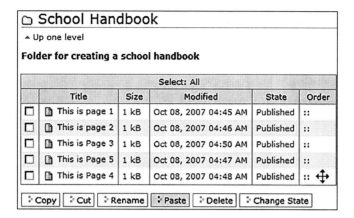

We then drag it to above **Page 5**:

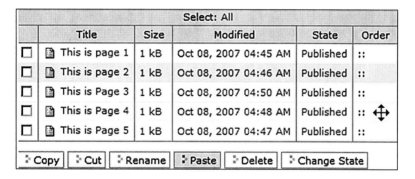

When you view your handbook again, you will see that the order has now been changed:

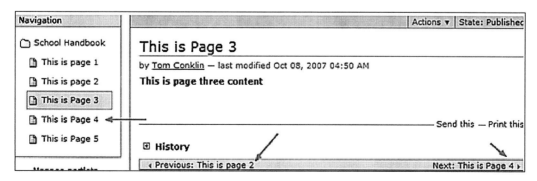

Summary

In this chapter, we have learned how to:

- Organize your content
- Create folders
- Organize folders based on topics and groups
- Create Collections
- Move files from one folder to another
- Copy folders
- Create page navigation
- Move the order in which pages are displayed in the navigation

We've dug in a bit deeper into Plone's end user architecture. You should now have the confidence to start adding content to your site in an organized and effective manner.

7
Safely Manage Different Versions Of Content

Essential capabilities of content management are the abilities to view the 'change history' of a content item, to compare various versions with one another, and optionally, to revert to a previous version of a content item.

In this chapter, **Darci Hanning** discusses how to use versioning in Plone to examine the history of changes made to a content item, to preview and compare versions, and to revert to a previous version of a content item.

Introducing versioning

Now that you have learned how to add various types of content, from pages to events to news items, we're ready to introduce a feature of Plone called **versioning**, which is an important part of content management. The content items you work with in your Plone site may go through many changes over time. Plone provides versioning information to help you manage your content from the time it was initially created through to the current version.

By default, Plone provides versioning for the following content types:

- Pages
- News Items
- Events
- Links

Other content types can be configured to provide versioning through the Plone Control Panel under **Types**. You can read more about this in Chapter 12.

 Although you may enable the **File** type to use versioning, the only changes that are tracked are those items actually describing the **File** (for example, **Title**, **Description**, and so on). The changes to the contents of the **File** are not tracked.

Creating a new version

Versions are created each time you save your content. Note that there is a **Change note** field at the bottom of the **Edit** page for content items with versioning enabled:

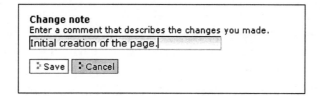

The information entered in the **Change note** field will be stored along with other versioning information, which you are able to view through the **History** tab.

Viewing the version history

You can view the list of all of the versions of a content item by clicking on the **History** tab for that content item. In the **History** view that you can see in the following screenshot, the most recent version is listed first. Clicking on any of the column headers will re-sort the listing based on that column heading.

| View | Edit | Sharing | History |

Revisions of "Cascade Range in Oregon"

Last modified Sep 26, 2007 04:29 PM

Revision▲	Performed by	Date and Time	Comment	Actions
Working Copy	admin	Sep 26, 2007 04:29 PM	Updated formatting.	■ Compare to previous revision
2 (preview)	admin	Sep 26, 2007 04:29 PM	Initial revision	■ Compare to current revision ■ Compare to previous revision ■ Revert to this revision
1 (preview)	admin	Sep 26, 2007 04:25 PM	Added more content to the page.	■ Compare to current revision ■ Compare to previous revision ■ Revert to this revision
0 (preview)	admin	Sep 26, 2007 04:16 PM	Initial creation of the page.	■ Compare to current revision ■ Revert to this revision

The most current version is always labeled **Working Copy** in the **History** view.

Previewing previous versions

To preview a specific version, simply click the **preview** link of the desired revision. In the following example, revision 3 has been identified, and will be displayed if this link is clicked:

Revision▲	Performed by	Date and Time	Comment	Actions
4 (preview)	admin	Sep 26, 2007 05:46 PM	Updated content; final version before publishing.	■ Compare to current revision ■ Compare to previous revision ■ Revert to this revision
3 (preview)	admin	Sep 26, 2007 04:29 PM	Updated formatting.	■ Compare to current revision ■ Compare to previous revision ■ Revert to this revision
2 (preview)	admin	Sep 26, 2007 04:29 PM	Initial revision	■ Compare to current revision ■ Compare to previous revision ■ Revert to this revision

On the subsequent page, you may either click on the **jump down** link to the point of the content preview:

Revision▲	Performed by	Date and Time	Comment	Actions
4 (preview)	admin	Sep 26, 2007 05:46 PM	Updated content; final version before publishing.	■ Compare to current revision ■ Compare to previous revision ■ Revert to this revision
3 (jump down)	admin	Sep 26, 2007 04:29 PM	Updated formatting.	■ Compare to current revision ■ Compare to previous revision ■ Revert to this revision

or you may scroll down the page in order to see the actual preview:

Preview of Revision 3

New Page

A sample page in Plone

Plone is powerful and flexible. It is ideal as an intranet and extranet server, as a document publishing system, a portal server and as a groupware tool for worldwide collaboration.

Plone is easy to use. The Plone Team includes usability experts who have made Plone easy and attractive for content managers to add, update, and maintain content.

Plone is standard. Plone carefully follows standards for usability and accessibility. Plone pages are compliant with US Section 508, and the W3C's AA rating for accessibility, in addition to using best-practice web standards like XHTML and CSS.

Plone is easy to install. You can install Plone with a click-and-run installer, and have a content management system running on your computer in just a few minutes.

Plone is international. The Plone interface has been translated into over 40 languages, and tools exist for managing multilingual content.

Comparing versions

From the **History** view, you can compare any version with the previous version by using the **Compare to the previous revision** link in the **Actions** column. You can also compare any previous version with the current version by using the **Compare to current revision** link.

In the following example, the previous version of the page (**revision 7**) is being compared to the current version of the page (**revision 8**):

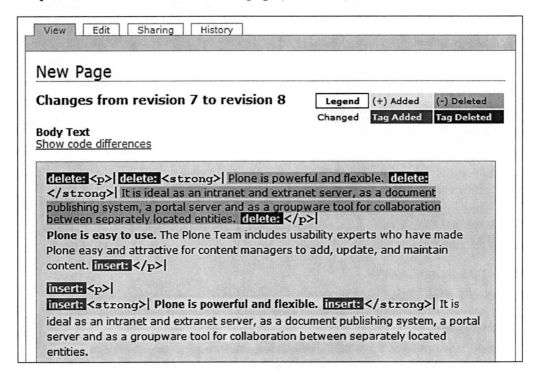

This comparison view will color-code the following types of changes between versions:

- Content added
- Content deleted
- HTML tags added
- HTML tags deleted
- Content changes

In the above example, the first paragraph (highlighted in the left column) was actually moved farther down the page (highlighted in the right column). Note how changes to HTML tags are indicated by the colored labels **delete** and **insert**.

If you are familiar with HTML, the **Show code differences** link provides an alternative view of the changes. The following is a screenshot of the code (or HTML) differences view, comparing the two revisions after clicking on the **Show code differences** link:

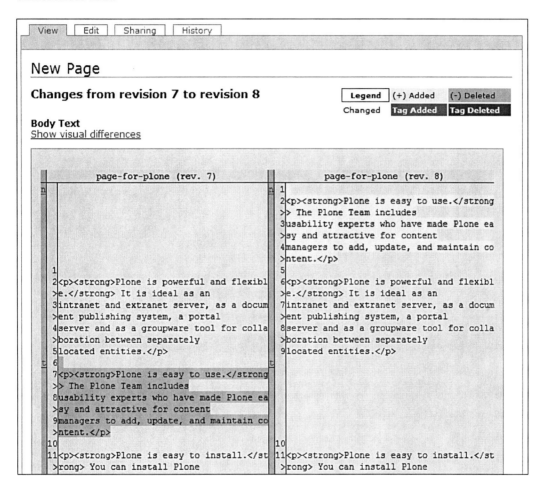

Note how the position of the text in this view reflects the actual location of where the text was in **revision 7** (left column), and where the text is currently located in **revision 8** (right column).

Reverting to a previous version

One of the most useful aspects of versioning is the ability to revert to a previous version. After using the preview links to verify that you have found the version you want to make the new current version, simply click on that version's **Revert to this revision** link:

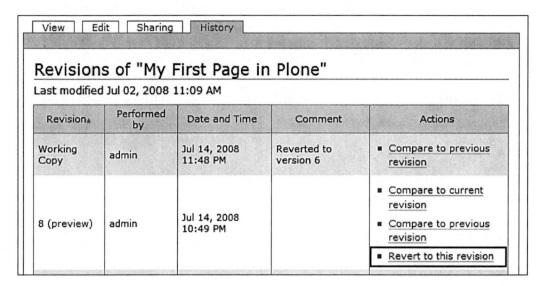

Clicking on the **Revert to this revision** link for **Revision 8** will create a *new version* of the content item. This new version will be identical to **Revision 8**:

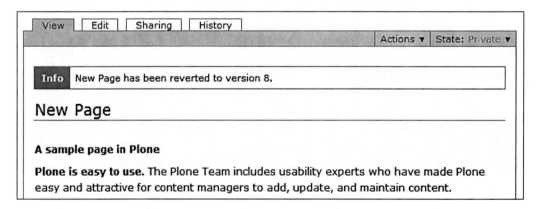

You will also notice that there is now a new revision in the **History**:

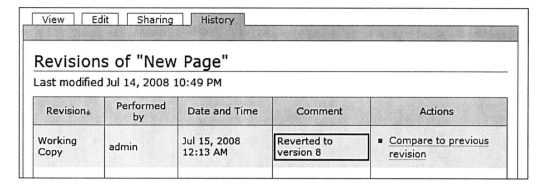

 The **Comment** column is automatically updated to indicate that the most recent version was created from reverting to **Revision 8**.

Summary

In this chapter, we have seen what a powerful tool versioning is, for managing each saved version of a content item. In particular, we learned:

- Which types of content item have versioning enabled by default
- How to view all of the prior versions of a particular content item
- How to preview a specific revision or version of a content item
- How to compare two versions of a content item
- How to revert to a previous version of a content item

8

Delegate Content Management to Other People

You have now learned how to create and organize your own content. Now, it's time for you to allow other people to create and edit content on your site.

In this chapter, **Tom Conklin** will show you how to create Users and Groups, and how to give them specific permissions to add, edit, and view the content on your site.

 This chapter requires that you log in with the Manager role.

Creating users and groups

Before you can delegate permissions to other users, you need to have some other users on your site. To create **Users** and **Groups**, you need to begin by entering the **Site Setup** section:

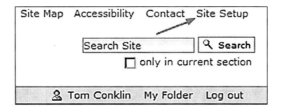

At this point, you will need to decide if you want to create users yourself, or let users add themselves without interaction on your part. We will first go over the basics of how to create a user account, and then move on to the various other ways in which Plone allows users to be created.

Creating a user

Start by navigating to **Site Setup**, then to the **Users and Groups** section from the control panel, and then select **Add New User**.

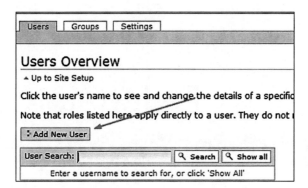

You are then presented with the following form to be filled out:

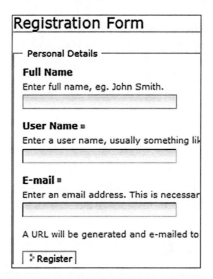

After you click the **Register** button, an email is sent to the email address provided, assuming that a mailhost has been configured for your site. The email will contain a link that will bring the user back to the site to complete the registration process.

 Plone will delete the account if it isn't accessed within 168 hours from time of initial creation.

Allowing users to register themselves

If you want to let users add themselves to your site, you need to select the **Security** link, and then select the **Enable self-registration** checkbox, as shown below:

Security settings

▲ Up to Site Setup

Security settings for this site.

─ Security settings ──────────────────────────────

☑ **Enable self-registration**

Allows users to register themselves on the site. If not selected, only site managers can add new users.

☐ **Let users select their own passwords**

If not selected, passwords will be autogenerated and mailed to users, which verifies that they have entered a valid email address.

☐ **Enable User Folders**

If selected, home folders where users can create content will be created when they log in.

☐ **Allow anyone to view 'about' information**

If not selected only logged-in users will be able to view information about who created an item and when it was modified.

[⁙ Save] [⁙ Cancel]

After saving the security settings, you can visit your home page, and you'll see the following portlet where an anonymous user can register themselves:

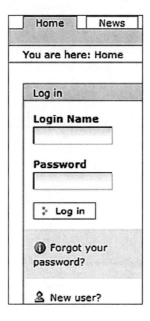

On clicking the **New user?** link, users will be brought to a page where they can fill out their details as described previously, with the only difference being that they are filling out the registration form, and not you.

Once they have registered, users are assigned to the Member role by default. Details of the various roles and their permissions are described in the *Roles and Permissions* section of this chapter.

If you are going to allow self registration, it's recommended that you do not enable the **Enable User Folders** option, as the user may truly be anonymous. You also shouldn't enable the **Let users select their own passwords** option, as that would let anyone create an account without verifying themselves as valid users via the email mechanism.

Creating users with initial passwords

If you want to control the creation of users, you will need to first ensure that the **Enable self registration** option in the **security section** is disabled.

If you have to assign an initial password for any new user, you should deselect the **Let users select their own password** checkbox.

Security settings

▲ Up to Site Setup

Security settings for this site.

┌ Security settings ─────────────────────

☐ **Enable self-registration**
Allows users to register themselves on the site. If not

☑ **Let users select their own passwords**
If not selected, passwords will be autogenerated and

☐ **Enable User Folders**
If selected, home folders where users can create cont

☐ **Allow anyone to view 'about' information**
If not selected only logged-in users will be able to vie

⁙ Save   ⁙ Cancel

Specifying these options will enable you, as the administrator, to create users and assign initial passwords to them. This can be useful in situations when you are setting up many accounts and want to bypass the email confirmation process, or in scenarios where users may not have email accounts.

 After a user has been authenticated for your site, they can go into the **personal profile** as described in a previous chapter and change their password.

Roles and permissions

Plone's security and permissions model is based on the idea of roles. A **role** is a bundle of permissions. For example, the **Reader** role may only have the permission to view content, while the **Contributor** role can view content and also add new content. Plone ships with a number of pre-defined roles, which cover most common situations. You can also define new roles, but that is beyond the scope of this introductory chapter.

Roles					
Contributor	Editor	Member	Reader	Reviewer	Manager
☐	☐	☑	☐	☐	☐

Plone's built-in roles are as follows:

Contributor

The **Contributor** role grants users the ability to add content to the site. Contributors can edit the content they have created, but cannot edit others' content. Contributors can copy and paste content objects into folders for which they have the **Contributor** permission.

Editor

The **Editor** role is more limited then the **Contributor** role in that editors can edit others' content but are not able to create their own content. The editor role also has the ability to **Submit for Publication**. The **Editor** role is useful when content needs to be proofread or edited before (or after) being published.

Reader

The **Reader** role has view permissions for the content items created that are in the private state. With this role, the user only can view content. No other action is available, as demonstrated by the following screenshot:

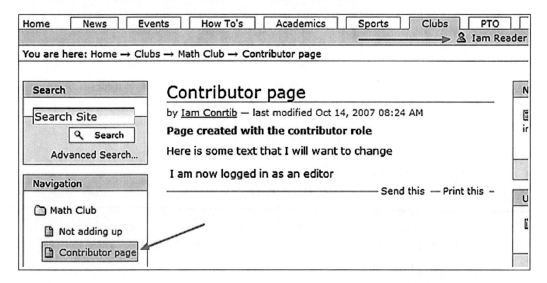

Reviewer

The **Reviewer** role has permission to publish items that are in the **Submit for Publication** state. They can't see items that are in the private state.

The reviewer can see items in the **Publish** queue via a portlet. By default, the **Review List** portlet is set up in the personal dashboard for the user, as well as on the right-side columns of the site:

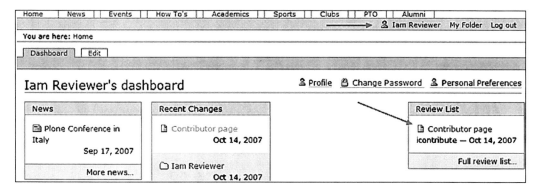

The reviewer also has the option to publish the page, send it back to the contributor, or go to the **Advanced...** options:

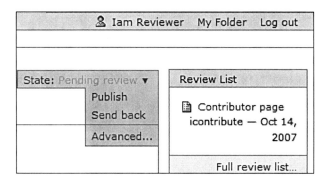

Within the **Advanced...** section, the reviewer can publish, send back to the contributor, or submit for publication on a specific date, as well as have the content expire (make unavailable to site visitors) on a certain date.

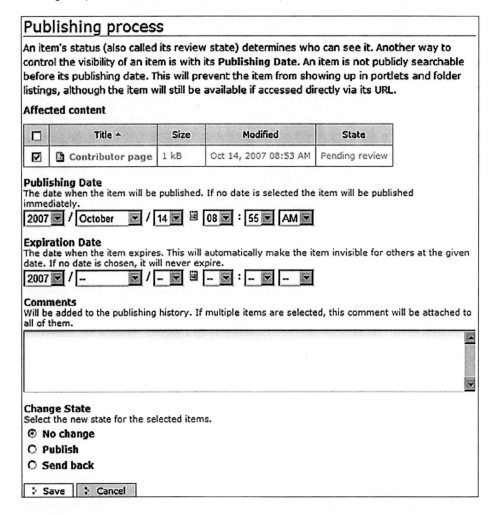

Manager

The **Manager** role is the **Site Administrator** role. It's also known as a **super user account**. This role has all possible permissions within the site, including access to the **Site Setup** section, where Users and Groups can be created. Typically, this role is reserved for a limited number of people. When applying permissions at the folder level within the site, a sharing tab is available to the **Manager** role so that specific permissions can be granted for that top-level folder, which then propagates down to all of the subfolders, either existing, or yet to be created.

As new subfolders are created, the **Manager** role can create new folder permissions within those subfolders, if necessary.

The tab **Sharing** shows our progress so far, as we have applied permissions to the **Clubs** folder structure:

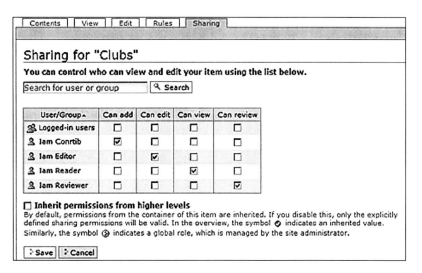

As can be seen in the preceding screenshot, we have only one role selected for each user account. As mentioned earlier, the **Reviewer** role currently can't see the private items. We could also assign the **Reader** role, which would enable access to the private content. We could even give more control to the Reviewer by selecting the **Can add** and **Can edit** permissions. Doing this would give the **Reviewer** role maximum control over the content where the permission is applied. This makes a lot of sense for smaller sites.

Using groups to control security

If you expect your site to grow beyond a handful of content contributors, you should consider assigning Roles to **Groups**, instead of to individual users, whenever possible. This will greatly ease the administrative burden as you add and remove users from your site.

For example, imagine that you have four specific sections of your site for which 10 different users have the Contributor role. As time goes by, one of the members of that group may no longer be involved. If you assigned the Contributor role to each user in each section individually, you would need to take that specific user out of each section.

If, on the other hand, you created a group and gave that group Contributor permission on the appropriate sections of your site, all you would need to do is remove one user from the group. By doing so, the permissions set up for the group takes care of all of the four sections, with this one change.

Creating groups

To create a new group, go to **Site Setup**, and then click on **Users and Groups**. Once you are in the **Users and Groups** section, click on the **Groups** tab.

In this section, you can define groups that will contain users. As you apply permissions throughout your site's folder structure, you can apply group permissions in addition to or in lieu of users. Plone's default groups are:

- **Administrators**

- **Reviewers**

- **Authenticated Users**

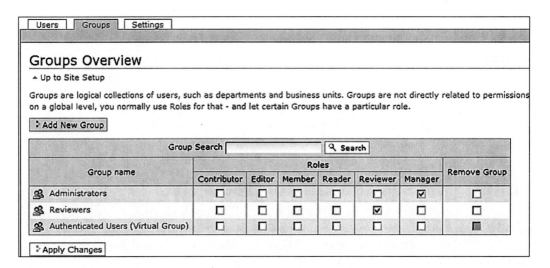

Assigning a user to the **Administrators** group gives that user the **Manager** role for the whole site. Assigning a user to the **Reviewers** group grants the **Reviewer** role to the user for all sections of the site. The **Authenticated Users** group is a **Virtual Group** that includes all of the logged-in users for your site. There are no assigned users in this group.

We will now create some groups that will make sense for the High School demo site used in Chapter 6.

We'll create a structure where parents can contribute pages for the High School's sports program. The coaches will have the Editor role, and the Athletics Director will have the Reviewer role. The Groups we will create are as follows:

- **Sports Contributors** (Assign registered parents to this group)
- **Sports Editors** (Assign coaches to this group)
- **Sports Reviewers** (Assign the Athletics Director to this group)

To create the new Groups, navigate to the **Groups** section, click on **Add new Group**, and then specify a name for the new group:

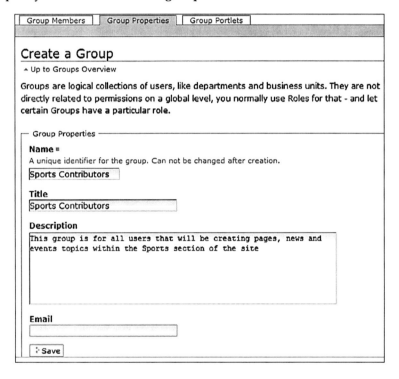

After we have created all of the groups, we can assign users to the groups, and then assign the groups to the **Sports** section.

 Don't assign any roles to the groups in the **Site Setup** section unless you want that group to have these permissions across your entire site. You can assign roles specific to users, and groups roles, within specific sections of your site. This will limit their roles to only what you explicitly define.

Adding users to groups

To add users to a group, you need to go to **Users and Groups**, and then click on the **Groups** tab. Click on the group name to which you want to add users. This will bring up a page where you can search for users. Once you have found the users to be added, select the checkbox next to their names:

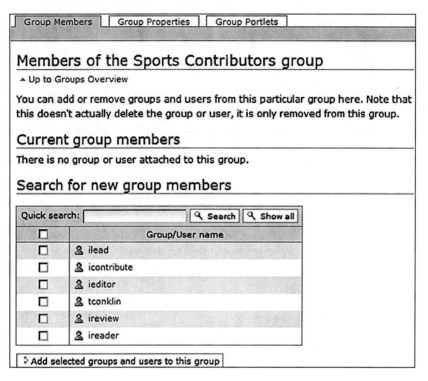

 You can also add a group as a member of another group.

Assigning roles to specific places in your site

We can now go to the **Sports** section, and apply the group permissions to it. Navigate to the **Sharing tab**, and then deselect the **Inherit Permissions from Higher Levels** option, as we want to have specific permissions within this section. We can display all of the users and groups that we want to add, but to limit the results, we can filter by typing in **sports**, as shown below:

Sharing for "Sports"

You can control who can view and edit your item using the list below.

| | sports | 🔍 Search |

User/Group	Can add	Can edit	Can view	Can review
👥 Logged-in users	☐	☐	☐	☐
👥 Sports Contributors	☑	☐	☐	☐
👥 Sports Editors	☐	☑	☐	☐
👥 Sports Reviewers	☐	☐	☐	☑

☐ **Inherit permissions from higher levels**
By default, permissions from the container of this item are inherited. If you disable this, only the explicitly defined sharing permissions will be valid. In the overview, the symbol ⊘ indicates an inherited value. Similarly, the symbol ⊗ indicates a global role, which is managed by the site administrator.

[Save] [Cancel]

By selecting the appropriate roles, the members of these specific groups will have the roles they need for their specific content areas.

This methodology provides a great solution for large sites as you can scale towards many different subject matter experts or authors.

Summary

In this chapter, we have learned how to:

- Enable self-registration
- Create user accounts with initial passwords
- Create user accounts with email verification
- Set up roles and permissions for users to be able to work in Plone
- Create groups
- Add members to a group
- Apply permissions via users and/or groups to folders

Using what you have learned in this chapter, you should be ready to add users and groups to your site. This, in turn, will enable your site members to start adding content to your site in a more controlled fashion.

9

Manage Approvals and Other Workflow for my Content

One of Plone's greatest strengths is its advanced workflow system. Workflows control access to and operations on content objects in Plone. You can use workflows to control who can see a page, who can modify an image, who can create an event, and who can see the contents of a given folder.

You can also define review processes for your content objects, giving various groups of users different levels of access to your content objects, depending on where the object is in the review process. For example, using one of Plone's stock workflows, you can require that after a user creates a page, the page is reviewed before it is available to the public.

In this chapter, **Matt Bowen** will teach you the fundamental concepts of Plone's workflows. He'll show you how to change the stock workflows, govern the content types on your site, and also how to modify these workflows to better suit your site's needs.

Background

Let's start with a definition, so that terms used later in the chapter are clear:

A workflow defines **states** (which are bundles of **permissions** for each **role**) for objects of a given content type, and **transitions** between these states (usually **guarded** in terms of permissions a user must have to execute those transitions).

Within that definition are several other terms that are important to understand. We'll start with permissions and build from there. Permissions are a low-level concept in Zope that determine whether a user can perform some action (such as View (an object), Modify (attributes of that object), or Add (some piece of content). To get an idea of the permissions available in Plone, head to your site's **Site Setup**, and then click on **Zope Management Interface** (known as the **ZMI**).

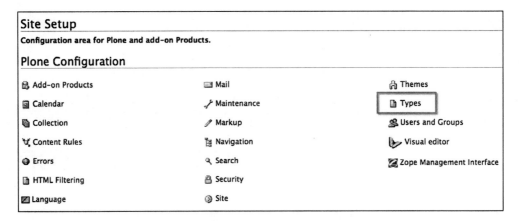

Once there, click on the **Security** tab near the top of the screen to see the lengthy list of permissions.

As you can see in the following screenshot, across the top of the columns, you'll see names such as **Manager**, **Reviewer**, and **Member**. These are the various roles a user might have for a given folder.

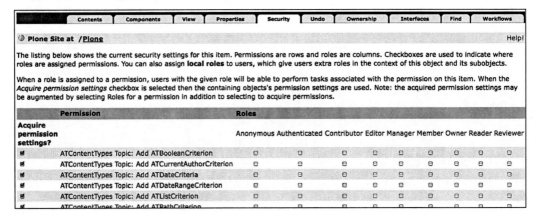

Roles

As the security tab implies, a role is a bundle of permissions for a group of users (any user who has that role) in a given context. Out of the box, Plone includes the following roles: **Anonymous, Authenticated, Owner, Contributor, Editor, Manager, Member, Reader**, and **Reviewer**. Anonymous, Authenticated, and Owner are slightly unusual, because Plone assigns them automatically; as you might expect, unauthenticated users have the Anonymous role, and logged-in users have the Authenticated role. Note that any permission that anonymous users have, all the other users have as well, even when they're logged-in. Also, a user will have the Owner role for any object that he or she creates.

So, for example, a logged-in user might have the Contributor role on your site, and this gives the user permission to **Add events** to your site. But that same user might not have the permission to delete any published content in the site.

Why are so few boxes checked explicitly? And what's up with "acquire?"

Zope (and consequently Plone) uses the concept of **Acquisition**, which can be complicated while programming, but makes security much simpler. With acquisition, a given container or object doesn't need to explicitly define all of the possible permissions for itself. Instead, it only needs to explicitly declare (or have set) the permissions that are important to its own security. Everything else is acquired from the container's context.

So, for example, your folders may not set a specific permission for **Modify portal content**, but instead can acquire which roles have that permission from the portal's root (your Plone site). This will be useful to keep in mind for later use; a permission you don't explicitly set in your workflow (and some that you do, if you want) will acquire permissions from its context and parents. So if. for some reason, users can cut and paste when you don't think they should, you might want to see which roles have the permission at your portal root, and then control it explicitly in your workflow.

The sheer number of permissions and checkboxes under the security tab can be somewhat overwhelming, and you're right if you feel a little nervous about changing anything here. In fact, changing security settings on the security tabbed page is usually a bad idea; workflow changes will override anything you modify from the security tabbed page, and workflow is a more systematic way to manage security.

In general, the only place where it's an acceptable idea to change security settings is the root of your site. Thankfully, with workflows, you don't have to fool around with the security tabbed page for any individual object—instead, you get to define how the security changes for entire classes of objects in a given state.

States

A state is a set of permissions for each role (on your portal) for a given object. For example, a page in the **private** state can only be viewed by its owner. The same page, when in the **published** state, can be viewed by anyone, but can only be edited by a manager. Typical states might include a draft stage, a review stage, a copy editing stage, and a publication stage. In each state, different groups of users might have the right to view, edit, or even delete an object. For example, a group of editors may be the only users who are allowed to edit a page in the copy editing stage, lest some other user introduces errors during that phase. During the draft stage though, all registered users might have access to modify a page, to ease collaboration.

Transitions

States, on their own, are not very useful, though—a page in the draft state needs some way to make it to the published state. Otherwise, the intended audience might never see it. This is where transitions come in. A transition is exactly what you would expect– a way to change the state of an object. Transitions are defined between two states (and yes, loops are possible). Naked transitions could be dangerous though. In our preceding example workflow, it wouldn't exactly be useful if a writer could transition a page out of copy editing. That's really the prerogative of the copy editor.

Thankfully, the authors of Plone's workflow engine realized this and now allow you to set guard roles that specify the roles required to execute a given transition. You are also allowed as many transitions as you want between states, so you could set up a workflow where authors have to send their pages for review, but managers (and only managers) can skip all the in-between states and push a page directly from private to published.

If you're poking around on the workflow tabbed page, you will actually notice several different kinds of transitions and guard options. Plone's workflow engine is incredibly flexible and powerful, and allows for automated transitions guarded by the Python code, which can evaluate complex rules. However, covering these extra features is beyond the scope of this chapter. If you're interested, I encourage you to read further in the documentation section of `plone.org` at `http://plone.org/documentation/tutorial/understanding-permissions`.

Changing your site's workflow

Different types of sites require different types of workflow and access, and Plone makes changing the workflows that govern your content easy. For example, you may have a site that will be used as an Intranet/Extranet. Plone provides a pair of workflows for this case (**Intranet/Extranet workflow** and **Intranet workflow for folders**). Thankfully, changing from **Simple Publication Workflow** to the **Intranet Workflow** is painless. You can find the workflows (and a bunch of other useful settings) for your site under **Site Setup** under the **Types** option, as shown in the following screenshot:

The **Type Settings** section lists all of your content types, and then the **(Default)** option. Within Zope/Plone, you can specify a workflow for each content type, or say that the type follows the default. By default, all of your types will use the **(Default)** setting. You can see this in the ZMI, if you click **portal_workflow** for your Plone site:

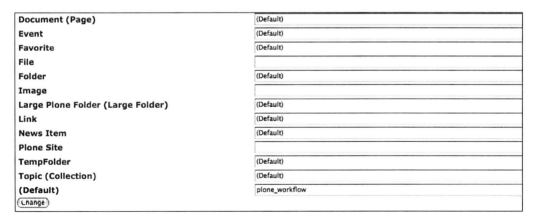

Out of the box, the default workflow is the **simple_publication_workflow**, which applies to of all the included content types, except **File** and **Image**. As files and images don't have workflows, they acquire all of their permissions from their containers, that is, if the user can access the folder containing an image or a file, the user can also access the image or the file.

To effect our change, we first have to change the **(Default)** from simple_publications_workflow to Intranet/Extranet workflow. Do this by selecting **Intranet/Extranet Workflow** from the **New workflow** drop-down.

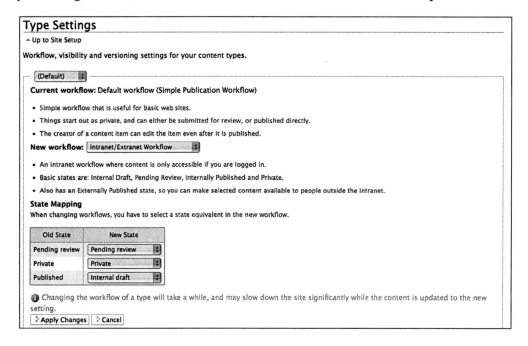

This will change the workflow for Pages, Events, Favorites, Folders, Links, News Items, and Collections to the **Intranet/Extranet Workflow**. Further, notice the **State Mapping** box—this lets you tell Plone which states in your current workflow correspond to the states in the new workflow. You'll want to make sure that **Pending review** maps to **Pending review**, **Private** to **Private**, and **Published** to either **Internally published** or **Externally published** (depending on how you think of your existing published content). This will ensure that any content that you have already created on your site ends up in an appropriate state when you change the workflow.

Once you've set up your state mapping, click on **Apply Changes**. Take a look at the note about the speed of this action and its effect on performance. If you have an administrative (non-public) instance of your site, it would be a good idea to use that version for this sort of thing. If you have a site with lots of existing content, changing the workflow on all of these objects is a long process.

This should take care of most of our objects. However, for this workflow, Folders have their own special workflow that is simple and efficient. So, after you've set a new default, select **Folder** from the type field's drop-down list at the top of the page. Then, under **New workflow**, select **Intranet Workflow for Folders**. The state mapping here is pretty simple, as the Intranet workflow for Folders has only two states—just be sure to map **published** to **Internal draft**. How you handle folders that are currently pending review will depend on your specific situation. Once you've made your selections, apply this workflow, and then take a little break while Plone modifies all the folders in your portal.

 It's always advisable to back up your site's data.fs file before making a large change of this nature.

Understanding Plone's supplied workflows

Plone ships with a variety of useful "stock" workflows that you can use for your portal, and these workflows even come with useful documentation that explains what they do. To better understand and investigate the descriptions that ship with the workflows, we'll use the ZMI and investigate the **Simple Publications Workflow** in detail.

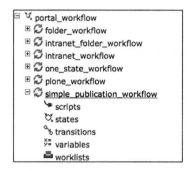

To explore the **Simple Publication Workflow**, we'll need to spend some quality time in the ZMI. You will find the workflows by expanding the [+] sign next to **portal_workflows** in the left-hand index frame of the ZMI. While you're at it, go ahead and expand the [+] next to **simple_publication_workflow** too.

In the **Types** configuration, Plone explains that the simple publications workflow "Things start out as private, and can either be submitted for review or published directly." So, clicking the states link in the ZMI, we should expect to see three states, and indeed, we do:

Workflow States at /Plone/portal_workflow/simple_publication_workflow/states

☐ **pending   Pending review**

       publish (Reviewer publishes content)

       reject (Reviewer send content back for re-drafting)

       retract (Member retracts submission)

☐ *** private   Private**

       publish (Reviewer publishes content)

       submit (Member submits content for publication)

☐ **published   Published**

       retract (Member retracts submission)

       reject (Reviewer send content back for re-drafting)

Note: Renaming a state will not affect any items in that state. You will need to fix them manually.

(Rename) (Delete) (Set Initial State)

Note that the **private** state has an asterisk (*) next to it, which indicates that this is the initial state for this workflow. When a user creates a new object that's governed by this workflow, it will start off in the private state. To learn more, let's click on ***private**, which brings us to the following screen, which offers a user-friendly description of the state and the possible transitions from the **private** state (which we'll talk more about later). From this screen, click on **permissions**, which will show you exactly what **private** means in terms of permissions by role:

Workflow State at /Plone/portal_workflow/simple_publication_workflow/states/private

When objects are in this state they will take on the role to permission mappings defined below. Only the permissions managed by this workflow are shown.

Acquire permission settings?	Permission	Anonymous	Authenticated	Contributor	Editor	Manager	Member	Owner	Reader	Reviewer
☐	Access contents information	☐	☐	☑	☑	☑	☐	☑	☑	☐
☐	Change portal events	☐	☐	☐	☑	☑	☐	☑	☐	☐
☐	List folder contents	☐	☐	☑	☑	☑	☐	☑	☑	☐
☐	Modify portal content	☐	☐	☐	☑	☑	☐	☑	☐	☐
☐	View	☐	☐	☑	☑	☑	☐	☑	☑	☐

Save Changes

From the preceding screenshot, we can see exactly what the users of a given role can do with an object in this state. For a **private** object, the object's owner, site managers, and editors can access information about the object (related to viewing the actual object through the web), change the date/time and location information of objects with those attributes (Plone Events in most cases), see the object in folder listings, modify (or edit) the object, and view the object itself.

Contributors and readers can see objects in the private state, but can't edit them (they lack **Change portal events** and **Modify portal content**). Remember that any other permission not listed by the workflow is acquired from the object's parent, so that permission for, say, viewing the history for an object governed by this workflow will be governed by the portal's default (only managers have this permission out of the box).

To see what happens when an object changes state, go back to the states overview, then select **published** and click on its **permissions** tab:

Workflow State at /Plone/portal_workflow/simple_publication_workflow/states/published

When objects are in this state they will take on the role to permission mappings defined below. Only the permissions managed by this workflow are shown.

Acquire permission settings?	Permission	Anonymous	Authenticated	Contributor	Editor	Manager	Member	Owner	Reader	Reviewer
☐	Access contents information	☑	☐	☐	☐	☐	☐	☐	☐	☐
☐	Change portal events	☐	☐	☐	☑	☑	☐	☑	☐	☐
☐	List folder contents	☑	☐	☐	☐	☐	☐	☐	☐	☐
☐	Modify portal content	☐	☐	☐	☑	☑	☐	☑	☐	☐
☐	View	☑	☐	☐	☐	☐	☐	☐	☐	☐

Save Changes

This time, anonymous (and thus everyone else), has significantly more access to the object. Because anonymous has **Access contents information**, **List folder contents**, and **View** permissions, any portal user can see this object in folder listings and visit the object through the web. Note that the object's owner, as well as site editors and managers, can still edit the published content. As an exercise, look at the pending state's permissions and see if you can tell what differs there from the permissions of the private and published states.

Now that we understand the states, we need to understand how an object moves between them. Astute readers will remember that transitions change an object's state, and sure enough, there's a **transitions** link for this workflow. Clicking on this link brings us to a list of the transitions, as well as which states they move an object between:

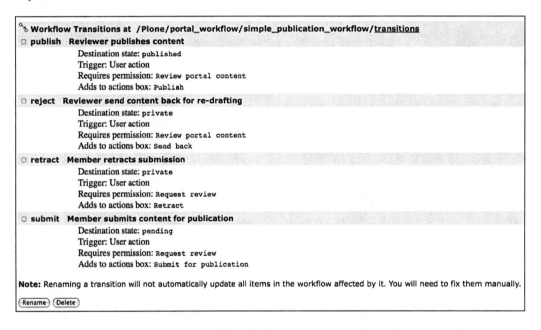

From the preceding screenshot, you can see most of the options that a user has available to them in order to change the state of a given object. Unfortunately, you cannot see the source-state for a given transition from this screenshot; that is listed on the **states** screenshot. Using our great memories (or multiple tabs in Firefox), we can figure out the paths, though.

From **private**, a user with the **Request review** permission (contributors on an out-of-the-box Plone site) can **submit** an object to **pending**. From there, a user with the **Review portal content** permission can either publish an object (putting it in the **published** state) or reject it (putting it back in the **private** state). Users with the **Review portal content** permission can skip the pending state and directly publish from **private**. This is useful and convenient for managers who may need to rapidly create and release content objects.

Now that you have understood these ZMI pages, you can fully evaluate Plone's other workflows and understand exactly what they change with each state. The **Type Settings** page provides useful descriptions of each workflow to save you time and trouble. However, as security in Plone is controlled through workflow, it would be useful to be able to evaluate exactly what a given workflow permits in some level of detail.

Making our own collaboration workflow

Using your understanding of Plone's workflows, it's time to create a new one. Imagine that your site requires a great deal of collaborative authoring by staff (a new role) that needs to be reviewed before it's published. Moreover, after something is published, the regular staff should not be allowed to edit it. Finally, we need a copy editor role and a copy editing state as these pages are written by multiple authors and take some solid editing to make them flow well.

This workflow sounds close to the **simple_publication_workflow**, but it's slightly different. Let's start by making a copy of the **simple_publication_workflow** in the ZMI. Visit **portal_workflow** again, and then select the **contents** tab.

Type	Name	Size	Last Modified
	folder_workflow (Community Workflow for Folders)		2008-10-25 11:50
	intranet_folder_workflow (Intranet Workflow for Folders)		2008-10-25 11:50
	intranet_workflow (Intranet/Extranet Workflow)		2008-10-25 11:50
	one_state_workflow (Single State Workflow)		2008-10-25 11:50
	plone_workflow (Community Workflow)		2008-10-25 11:50
	simple_publication_workflow (Simple Publication Workflow)		2008-10-25 11:50

Plone Workflow Tool at /Plone/portal_workflow — Help! — Add Workflow — Rename | Cut | Copy | Paste | Delete | Import/Export | Select All

Select the checkbox next to **simple_publication_workflow** and then click on **Copy**. After the page refreshes, click on **Paste**. You will now have **copy_of_simple_publication_workflow (Simple Publication Workflow)**, which will be listed at the top of the screen. Select the checkbox next to this, click **Rename**, and replace the name with **practical_collaboration_workflow**. After the page refreshes, click on **practical_collaboration_workflow**, and give it a good title (for example, "Practical Collaboration Workflow") and a short description (such as "Provides a way for contributors to create and collaborate on pages, along with review and copy editing states"). Save your changes. Now let's dig into the roles, states, and transitions.

First, we'll need to add two new roles: **Staff** and **Copy Editor**. To add a role, we work in the ZMI. First, go to the root of your site (at the top of the leftmost sidebar, called **Plone** if you used the unified installer). Then, click on the **Security** tab. Scroll to the bottom of the page, and enter **Staff** in the **User defined roles** box, and then click on **Add Role**. Do the same for **Copy Editor**.

Next, the new roles will need permissions. We'll model the **Copy Editor** along the lines of Plone's built-in **Editor** type, and **Staff** on the **Contributor** type. So, for **Copy Editor**, ensure that the same checkboxes are selected as for **Editor** (for example, **Access contents information**, **Manage properties,** and so on) and then make sure **Staff** matches **Contributor** (for example, **ATContentTypes: Add Document, Access contents information**, and so on).

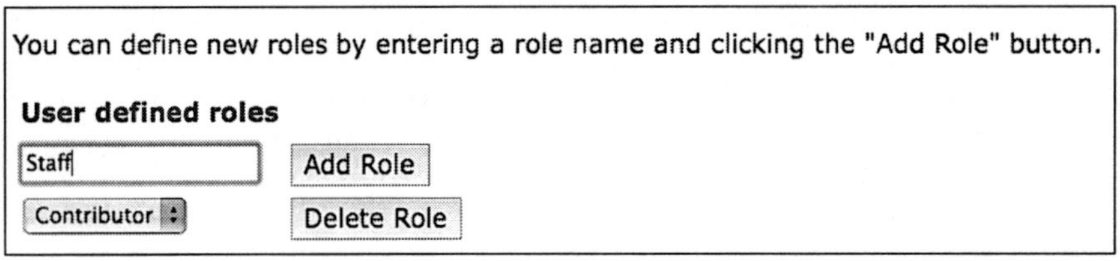

You can define new roles by entering a role name and clicking the "Add Role" button.

User defined roles

| Staff | | Add Role |
| Contributor ⬍ | | Delete Role |

Now that we have adequate roles, we can allow any staff to modify a **private** object. This way, our staff can collaborate on pages without showing them to the public. So, click the **States** tab, and then the link to the **private** state. These pages are still **private**—the public can't see them—so the title is probably ok, although you may need to change the description.

After you've written something useful and pithy, go to **permissions**. Here, we'll want to give **Staff** the rights to **Change portal events** and **Modify portal content**, as well as the other permissions that allow them to actually see the content. We may want to give **Copy Editors** the right to view content at this stage too, as staff may have questions for them. So select **Access contents information, List folder contents,** and **View**, as shown in the following screenshot. Save your changes, and bask for a moment—you've just modified a workflow:

⌂ **Workflow State at** /Plone/portal_workflow/practical_collaboration_workflow/states/<u>private</u>

When objects are in this state they will take on the role to permission mappings defined below. Only the permissions managed by this workflow are shown.

Acquire permission settings?	Permission	Anonymous	Authenticated	Contributor	Copy Editor	Editor	Manager	Member	Owner	Reader	Reviewer	Staff
☐	Access contents information	☐	☐	☑	☐	☑	☑	☐	☑	☑	☐	☑
☐	Change portal events	☐	☐	☐	☐	☑	☑	☐	☑	☐	☐	☑
☐	List folder contents	☐	☐	☑	☐	☑	☑	☐	☑	☑	☐	☑
☐	Modify portal content	☐	☐	☐	☐	☑	☑	☐	☑	☐	☐	☑
☐	View	☐	☐	☑	☐	☑	☑	☐	☑	☑	☐	☑

Save Changes

Moving on, let's do something similar in the **Published** state—this time though, we need to remove some permissions. Go back to the **States**, select **published**, and then select the **permissions** tab. Deselect the checkboxes for **Change portal events** and **Modify portal content** for the **Owner** role, as shown in the following screenshot and then save your changes:

⌂ **Workflow State at** /Plone/portal_workflow/practical_collaboration_workflow/states/<u>published</u>

When objects are in this state they will take on the role to permission mappings defined below. Only the permissions managed by this workflow are shown.

Acquire permission settings?	Permission	Anonymous	Authenticated	Contributor	Copy Editor	Editor	Manager	Member	Owner	Reader	Reviewer	Staff
☐	Access contents information	☑	☐	☐	☐	☐	☐	☐	☐	☐	☐	☐
☐	Change portal events	☐	☐	☐	☐	☑	☑	☐	☐	☐	☐	☐
☐	List folder contents	☑	☐	☐	☐	☐	☐	☐	☐	☐	☐	☐
☐	Modify portal content	☐	☐	☐	☐	☑	☑	☐	☐	☐	☐	☐
☐	View	☑	☐	☐	☐	☐	☐	☐	☐	☐	☐	☐

Save Changes

Now, we just need to add the **editorial review** state and change some transitions around. We need reviewed pages to go to editorial review, instead of directly to **published**. Back at the **States** tabbed page, add a state with the ID **editorial_review**, which will be added to the list of states.

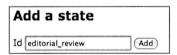

Add a state

Id `editorial_review`   (Add)

Now, let's make a transition into the editorial review. Head over to the **Transitions** screen, and add a transition called **submit_to_editor**. Select it from the list, and give it a title of "Submit to editor," and a description of "Submits an object for copy editing". For the destination state, select **editorial_review**, and under **Guard** we'll try something new—we will require the **Reviewer; Manager** role. We want reviewers to submit objects for editorial review, as there's no **Request editorial review** permission supplied with Plone. We add a semicolon and **Manager** after reviewer, because managers should be able to make any transition. In **Name (formatted)** add **Submit to editor**, and in **URL (formatted)** add `%(content_url)s/content_status_modify?workflow_action=submit_to_editor`.

It is the URL that gets called to change the workflow state. The URL uses a simple substitution (the `%(content_url)`) to get the URL of the current content. Then it appends **content_status_modify** to it, and then passes the argument of `workflow_action=submit_to_editor`, which tells Zope to perform the **Submit to editor** transition.

We also need to make one small modification to an existing transition. Publishing will now require different guards. So, from the transitions list, select the **publish** transition. Then, in the Guard boxes, remove the **Permission(s)** and add the **Role(s)** of **Manager; Copy Editor**. This will allow managers and copy editors, but not the reviewers, to publish content as we don't want any unedited content going up on the site.

Now that we have our transitions set, we can return to the **States** tabbed page and set up the states. From the states list, first select **pending** and deselect **publish** as a possible transition; replace it with **submit_to_editor**, as shown in this screenshot:

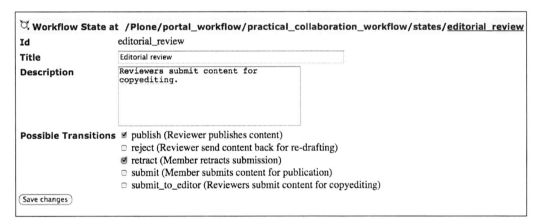

Save your changes, and then head over to **editorial_review**. On this screen, give the state a title (**Editorial review**) and a description (**Reviewers submit content for copyediting.**). Then, select the **retract** and **publish** transitions.

Once you've saved these changes, click on the **Permissions** tab, and set up some reasonable permissions. First, deselect **Acquire permission settings?** We want to explicitly set these permissions for the state. Now, give **Copy Editor, Editor,** and **Manager** all five permissions. Copy editors and managers should be able to view and modify the content, while the editor is a local role that should be allowed to edit content. For **Owner, Staff, Contributor,** and **Reader,** select **Access contents information, List folder contents,** and **View,** so that these users can still look at objects in the editorial review without disturbing the editor's work. When you're done, the permissions should appear as follows:

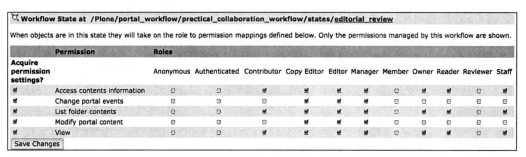

Workflow State at /Plone/portal_workflow/practical_collaboration_workflow/states/editorial_review

When objects are in this state they will take on the role to permission mappings defined below. Only the permissions managed by this workflow are shown.

Acquire permission settings?	Permission	Anonymous	Authenticated	Contributor	Copy Editor	Editor	Manager	Member	Owner	Reader	Reviewer	Staff
☑	Access contents information	☐	☐	☑	☑	☑	☑	☐	☑	☑	☐	☑
☑	Change portal events	☐	☐	☐	☑	☑	☑	☐	☐	☐	☐	☐
☑	List folder contents	☐	☐	☑	☑	☑	☑	☐	☑	☑	☐	☑
☑	Modify portal content	☐	☐	☐	☑	☑	☑	☐	☐	☐	☐	☐
☑	View	☐	☐	☑	☑	☑	☑	☐	☑	☑	☐	☑

Save Changes

With this last change, you're ready to set this workflow as your portal's default. So, back in Plone, in the **Type Settings**, select **(Default)** and set the **New Workflow** to **Practical Collaboration workflow**. As most of our states have the same names, it's easy to verify that the mappings are correct. So all that's left to do is to apply the change and wait. And with that, you have a new collaboration workflow:

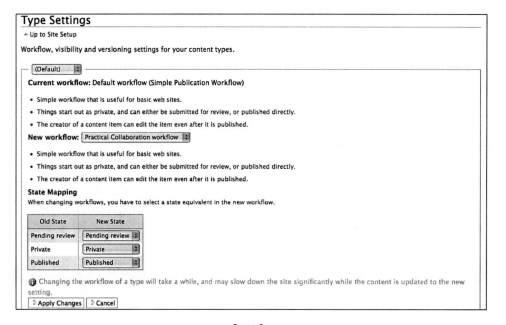

Type Settings

▲ Up to Site Setup

Workflow, visibility and versioning settings for your content types.

(Default) ▼

Current workflow: Default workflow (Simple Publication Workflow)

- Simple workflow that is useful for basic web sites.
- Things start out as private, and can either be submitted for review, or published directly.
- The creator of a content item can edit the item even after it is published.

New workflow: Practical Collaboration workflow ▼

- Simple workflow that is useful for basic web sites.
- Things start out as private, and can either be submitted for review, or published directly.
- The creator of a content item can edit the item even after it is published.

State Mapping

When changing workflows, you have to select a state equivalent in the new workflow.

Old State	New State
Pending review	Pending review ▼
Private	Private ▼
Published	Published ▼

ⓘ Changing the workflow of a type will take a while, and may slow down the site significantly while the content is updated to the new setting.

⟳ Apply Changes   ⟳ Cancel

Summary

In this chapter, we've learned:

- What workflows control, and when to use them
- How to change the workflows that govern our content
- How to modify an existing workflow to make it meet our needs
- How to create a new workflow to implement collaborative editing

Plone's workflow engine is extremely powerful and complex, and so there is a great deal to learn if you want to truly master workflows. If you find yourself making a lot of new workflows, you may find ArchGenXML to be of great help (visit `http://plone.org/documentation/manual/archgenxml2`).This is covered in Chapter 16, with respect to new content types but not workflows. It allows you to map out your workflows in **Unified Modeling Language** (**UML**) and then generate them as installable Plone products.

You will also probably want to brush up on your TALES expressions (visit `http://plone.org/documentation/tutorial/zpt`) so that you can write more interesting guard conditions. And, if you're particularly ambitious, you can write Python scripts that execute on workflow transitions, allowing for incredible flexibility in your workflows.

10

Show Additional Information to Users and Visitors

Web sites are not built with content alone. Most sites need additional chunks of contextually-relevant information such as navigation boxes, listings of recent items, and other bits of "sidebar" content. In Plone, these small chunks of content are generally known as **portlets**.

Plone's portlet system makes it easy to place chunks of additional information on your site. Plone ships with a variety of built-in portlets, and you can easily create custom portlets that meet your particular needs. You can associate portlets with different sections of your site, with different content types, and with different groups of users.

In this chapter, **Jon Stahl** shows how to manage the portlets on your web site. You'll learn how to create portlets, to control where they appear on your site, and to customize them.

What's a portlet, anyway?

A **portlet** is a chunk of information that can be shown outside of the main content area of a page. In the following screenshot of Plone's default home page, the **Log in** box and the calendar are portlets.

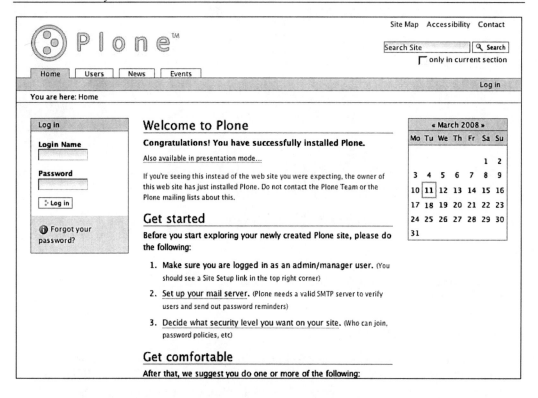

Plone's default theme has two **portlet managers** that control the assignment of portlets on the right and left sidebars of the page. You can place portlets into these slots on the page. It's also possible to add portlet manager slots to a custom theme so that you can display portlets in other areas of the page, but that's beyond the scope of this book. For more information, refer to: `http://plone.org/documentation/ how-to/adding-portlet-managers`.

There are two things that we need to know about portlets before we dive into adding them:

1. Portlets can only be added to portlet managers. They can't be added into the body content of your pages.
2. Portlets can be assigned to folders, content types, or user groups, and will cascade down through the site hierarchy unless you explicitly block inheritance.

Plone's built-in portlets

Plone ships with a generous assortment of basic portlets. Here's a quick list of Plone's default portlet offerings:

- **Login**: Shows Plone's login box to anonymous users; is hidden if a user is already logged in

- **Collection portlet**: Shows the results of a **Collection**

- **Review list**: Visible only to the users with the **Reviewer** role; this portlet shows a list of items that users have submitted for review before publishing

- **RSS feed**: Shows a list of items in an RSS feed

- **Classic portlet**: A wrapper for Zope 2 style portlets, which may have been developed prior to the advent of Plone 3 and its new portlet system

- **Calendar portlet**: Shows a simple calendar that highlights the dates of upcoming events for your site

- **Search**: Shows Plone's search box useful if you have chosen to disable the standard search box, and want to show it in a sidebar instead

- **Recent items**: Shows the most recently-published content items on your site

- **News**: Shows the most recently-published **News Items** on your site

- **Static text portlet**: Shows a chunk of static, editable HTML content; this is one of Plone's most versatile and useful portlets

- **Navigation**: Shows the navigation tree

- **Events**: Shows upcoming published events on your site

 You're only likely to use Classic portlets if you are using an add-on product that hasn't fully embraced the new style of building portlets, or if you are building your own custom portlets.

Add-on portlets

Many add-on products for Plone will supply one or more relevant portlets when the product is installed.

There are also additional standalone portlets available as separate add-on products. Among the most useful standalone add-on portlets are:

- **TAL Portlet**: A portlet that allows you to write your own simple portlets in Plone's templating language, TAL. Optionally, you could just write a Classic portlet.

- **Feedmixer**: A portlet that allows you to aggregate multiple RSS feeds into a single portlet.

These products can be found in the **Products** section of Plone.org.

Adding portlets

There are three ways to add portlets to your site:

1. Add portlets to specific locations on your site.

2. Add portlets that are associated with specific content types—for example, a portlet that shows on all News Items.

3. Add portlets that are shown only to specific groups of users in your site.

Adding portlets to specific sections of your site

We'll start with adding portlets to a specific section of your site, as this is the most common and the simplest thing to do.

Log in to your site (via the **Log in** portlet) and look at the bottom of the rightmost sidebar for the **Manage portlets** link.

This will take you to the **Manage portlets** screen.

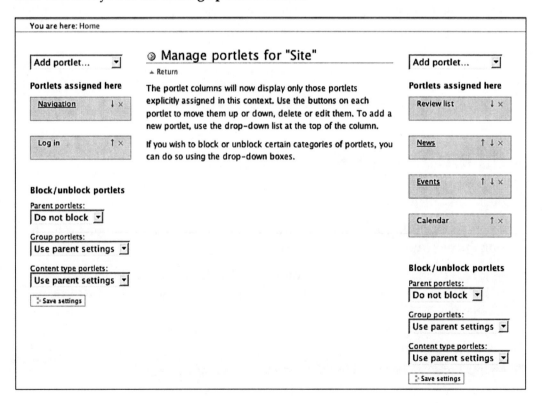

Managing Portlets Peacefully
Because you were on the front page of your site, when you clicked the **Manage portlets** link, you are now managing the portlets for your entire site. If you only want to manage portlets for a single section of your site, first navigate to that section, and then click the **Manage portlets** link. The header of the **Manage Portlets** screen will tell you which section of the site you are in.

The **Manage Portlets** screen tells you that certain portlets are already assigned to all of the pages of your site. In the example above, the left sidebar portlet manager has the **Navigation** portlet and the **Log in** portlet. The right sidebar portlet manager has the **Review List, News, Events** and **Calendar** portlets.

Moving and Removing Portlets
You can move existing portlets around within a portlet manager by clicking on the up and down arrows within the portlet. You can remove a portlet from the portlet manager by clicking on the red **X**.

To add a portlet to your site, select the **Add portlet...** drop-down menu at the top of either the right or left sidebar, and choose a portlet type to be added. For practice, let's try adding a static content portlet to the right sidebar.

This screen contains the familiar Kupu-powered rich text editing widget, along with:

- A **Portlet header** (title) field.
- A **Portlet footer** field.
- A optional hyperlink field, which will be clickable from the portlet header and footer.
- An **Omit portlet border** checkbox. If selected, this hides the portlet header, footer, and border. This is very useful if you only want to place an image or some floating text in your sidebar.

Enter some text into your new portlet, click on the **Save** button at the bottom of the screen, and then click on the **Home** tab to return to your site's homepage. You should now see your new static text portlet. If you click around the site, you'll continue to see the portlet on all of the pages of your site.

Adding portlets to specific content types

You can also assign portlets to specific content types on your web site. These portlets will be shown any time you are viewing that type of object.

Content type portlets are assigned via the **Types** control panel. You can access this by navigating to **Site Setup** and then choosing the **Types** option. Choose a content type (we'll use **News Item** in this example) from the drop-down list to see the configuration options for the content type, as shown in the following screenshot:

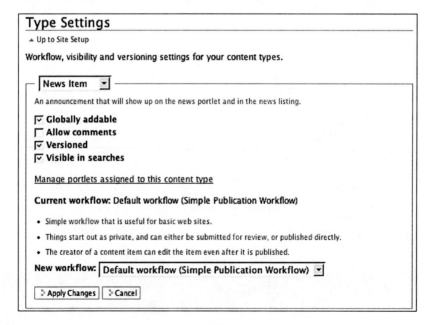

Then, click on **Manage portlets assigned to this content type**. You'll be taken to the following **Manage portlets** screen:

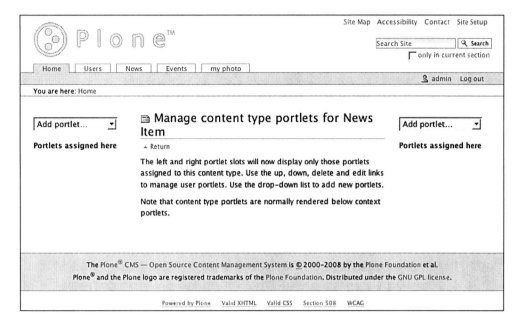

You can use the drop-down lists in the right and left sidebars to assign portlets to either column, as you've done previously.

A good test is to create a **Static text** portlet and assign it to **News Items**, and view a **News Item** to see if the portlet does indeed display.

Adding portlets to specific groups of users

The third and final way of assigning portlets in Plone is to assign them to specific groups of users. For example, you may wish to show some information only to site administrators.

Group-specific portlets are managed via the **Users and Groups** control panel. You can access this by navigating to **Site Setup** and then choosing the **Users and Groups** option.

Click on the **Groups** tab, then on the name of a group (we'll use **Administrators** in this example), and then on the **Group Portlets** tab, as shown in the following screenshot:

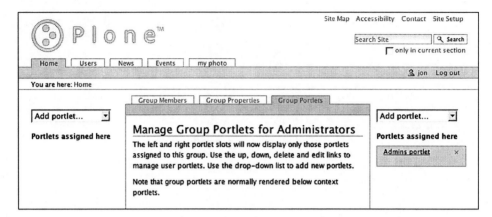

How does Plone know in what order to show different kinds of portlets?

If you are viewing a page, then Plone will display sets of portlets in the following order:

- Location-specific portlets
- Content type portlets
- Group portlets

If you want to change this ordering, you will have to write some custom code in an add-on product. That's beyond the scope of this chapter, but you can look at the README.txt file in the Plone's plone.app.portlets component for code samples.

Hiding portlets for specific content objects

Thanks to the magic of Zope **acquisition**, portlets that you assign at the top levels of your site will cascade down the site hierarchy and will appear on all of the objects at lower levels. In other words, if you assign a portlet to a folder, it will appear for all of the objects and subfolders inside that folder—unless you explicitly hide them by using Plone's portlet blocking system.

The key idea of portlet blocking is that, at any given location in your site, you can hide the portlets that would otherwise be inherited from parent locations, user groups, or content types. This provides you with great flexibility in how and where portlets should appear on your site.

Portlets are blocked from the **Manage portlets** screen for an object. We'll now walk through a simple scenario in which we block portlets from being inherited by a specific News Item.

If you've worked through the preceding examples for adding portlets, you will have assigned portlets to the root level of your site, to **News Items**, and to the **Administrators** group. Now let's try using portlet blocking to hide all of these portlets for one specific News Item.

Before you start, make sure that you:

- Have at least one **News Item** on your site
- Have assigned portlets to the root of your site, to the **News Item** content type, and to the Administrators group (we'll use simple static text portlets in this example)
- Are logged in as a user who is a member of the **Administrators** group

As we start, the view of your news item should look like this:

Click the **Manage portlets** link in either column. You'll be taken to the familiar **Manage portlets** screen:

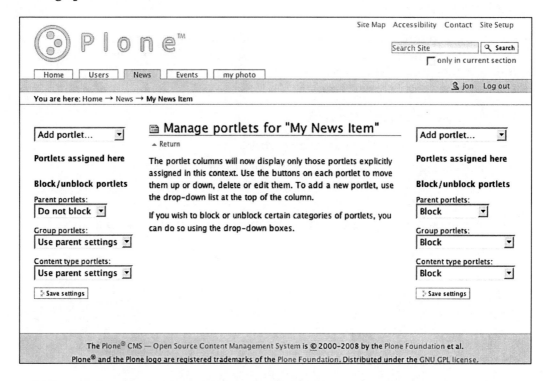

Note the **Block/unblock portlets** drop-down fields. These allow us to choose whether or not we want to block portlets from being acquired by this object. By default, an object will:

- Show the portlets assigned to its parent objects
- Inherit its parent object's settings for content type portlets
- Inherit its parent object's settings for group portlets

To block all of the portlets in the right-hand sidebar from being acquired by this particular **News Item**, set the **Parent portlets**, **Group portlets**, and **Content type portlets** drop-downs in the right-hand sidebar to **Block**.

Click on **Save settings**, and then click on **Return** to return to the view of your **News Item**, which should now look like this:

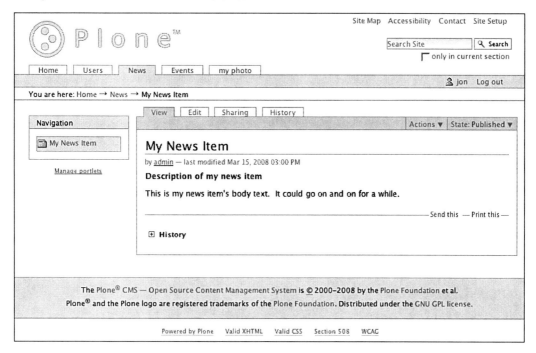

As you can see, you've blocked all of the right sidebar portlets that your **News Item** was acquiring by virtue of being underneath the root of your site, by being **News Item**, and by you being a member of the **Administrators** group.

Unblocking portlets that have been blocked

If you've blocked the content type or group portlets in a folder, you can unblock those portlets for individual objects inside that folder by selecting Do not block from the **Group portlets** and/or **Content type portlets** drop-down menus.

Can I unblock location-based portlets?

You can't unblock location based portlets; but you can re-add portlets to individual objects.

The combination of location, user group, and content type portlets, plus portlet blocking and unblocking is very powerful, but can't cover very complex rules for portlet inheritance. You will have to do some custom portlet programming in order to implement more complex schemes.

Creating new types of portlets

Plone makes it easy to create new types of portlets that include custom programming logic for your site. There are several ways to create custom portlets, but the simplest way to get started is to use the add-on product `collective.portlet.tal` which provides a new type of portlet, called a `TAL Portlet`. This portlet allows you to write simple bits of code using Zope's TAL templating language.

Let's walk through a quick example of building a custom TAL portlet, which will show a randomly-selected news item from your site.

Installing collective.portlet.tal

Before you can add a TAL portlet, you must download the product from `Plone.org/products` and install the add-on product `collective.portlet.tal` on your site. The best way to do this is to modify your `buildout.cfg` file.

Add `collective.portlet.tal` to the `eggs` and `zcml` sections of your `buildout`. Here's a code snippet with the changes made to it:

```
[buildout]
  ...
  eggs =
    ...
    collective.portlet.tal
[instance]
recipe = plone.recipe.zope2instance
...
zcml =
  collective.portlet.tal
```

Once you've made these changes, re-run `buildout` by issuing the following command:

```
$ ./bin/buildout
```

Refer to Chapter 14 for more information on installing add-on products.

Once you've added the product to your `buildout`, visit **Site Setup** and choose **Add/Remove Products**, to install `collective.portlet.tal` in your site.

Finally, add a few news items to your site so that we have something for our new TAL portlet to find.

Adding a simple TAL portlet

With the `collective.portlet.tal` produc in place, the following can happen:

1. Navigate to your Plone site.

2. Choose **Manage Portlets** in the right column.

3. From the **Add portlet...** drop-down list, choose **TAL Portlet**.

4. You'll see an empty text box in which you can enter a title. We will specify **Featured News Item** as our title. We'll soon see the code needed to feature a random one of our site's published news items.

5. In addition to the **Title** text box, you'll also see an HTML text area titled **TAL code**. Conveniently, this comes pre-populated with some boilerplate HTML and TAL code. Skim this, so that you get a feel for how this looks and what the common HTML structure is like, for a portlet in Plone.

As an immediate experiment, we will find the following snippet of code:

```
<dd class="portletItem odd">
  Body text
</dd>
```

We will modify this, slightly, to:

```
<dd class="portletItem odd">
  Is this thing on?
</dd>
```

Click **Save** and navigate through the site, and you should see your first TAL portlet in action. Of course, there's nothing in this example that couldn't be accomplished with a static text portlet. So let's navigate back to the **Featured News Item** portlet and make it a bit more interesting and dynamic.

Update the code in your TAL Portlet to include the following:

```
<dl class="portlet portlet${portlet_type_name}"
  tal:define="newsitems python:context.portal_catalog
              (portal_type='News Item', review_state='published');"
  tal:condition="newsitems">
  <dt class="portletHeader">
    <span class="portletTopLeft"></span>
    <span>
      Featured News Item
    </span>
    <span class="portletTopRight"></span>
  </dt>
  <dd class="portletItem odd"
    tal:define="random_newsitem python:random.choice(newsitems)">
    <a tal:content="random_newsitem/Title"
          href="[replaced by random news item link]"
          title="[replaced by random news item title]"
          tal:attributes="href random_newsitem/getURL;
            title random_newsitem/Title">[replaced by random news
                                          item title]</a>
  </dd>
  <dd class="portletFooter">
    <span class="portletBottomLeft"></span>
    <span>
      <a href="http://example.com/news">More news...</a>
    </span>
    <span class="portletBottomRight"></span>
  </dd>
</dl>
```

Now, let's go into more detail on a few of these sections, so that you understand what's happening. If at any point you need more context, try reading the excellent ZPT reference manual at `http://plone.org/documentation/tutorial/zpt`.

Variable declaration

TAL provides a mechanism for declaring variables. This is designated by the `tal:define` attribute, which can be added to an HTML tag. Within any given `tal:define` statement, any number of variables can be defined. The variable name is separated by a space from the code statement that will be executed to determine what value is assigned to the variable. Each variable line is terminated with a semicolon to signify that a new variable is to be defined in the next line.

Below, we add a new variable, `newsitems`, which consists of a search of the Plone site for all published pieces of content of type `News Item`.

```
<dl class="portlet portlet${portlet_type_name}"
   tal:define="newsitems python:context.portal_catalog
              (portal_type='News Item', review_state='published');"
```

The `python:` bit signifies that the ensuing statement should be interpreted as Python code, rather than basic TAL. This is required, so that we can pass several requirements (called "parameters") to Plone's catalog, which will determine the types of items that will be assigned to the `newsitems` variable. In our case, we request only the items of type **News Item** that are in the **published** state. We can now use the value of `newsitems` within the `<dl />` tag and within any HTML tag that is nested below the `<dl />` tag in the ensuing HTML (that is, child tags). This is referred to as the scope of this variable.

Conditionals

Another attribute, `tal:condition`, can be used to determine if everything below the given tag should be displayed. The following is used to make sure that we have found a `newsitem` before we move on with the rest of the code:

```
tal:condition="newsitems"
```

This is an attribute of the same `<dl />` tag.

Choosing a random item

As explained above, we'll want to declare another variable that can be used to represent our randomly-chosen item. We will give this the appropriate name of `random_newsitem`, and the Python code is really quite simple. Python has a helper library called `random`, and if we pass a list of items to the `choice` function of Python's `random` library, we're assured of one randomly-selected result in return.

```
<dd class="portletItem odd"
   tal:define="random_newsitem python:random.choice(newsitems)">
```

Now, anywhere within our `<dd />` tag, we can refer to the `random_newsitem` variable.

Filling in the value of an HTML tag

The `tal:content` attribute on an HTML tag has the effect of filling in the HTML tag with a given value. The catalog query from our initial `newsitems` variable returns what Zope calls "catalog brains". The details aren't important, but remember the fact that it's a high-level overview of the full piece of content, and various items are "indexed" for quick retrieval. One of these items is the `Title`, and our following statement asks us to fill the `<a />` tag with the title of our randomly-chosen news item.

```
<a tal:content="random_newsitem/Title"
```

Attributes on an HTML tag

If you're comfortable with HTML, you'll know that many tags have attributes. For example, the `<a />` tag has an attribute `href`, which is used for listing the destination of a hyperlink when the link is clicked on in a web browser. An `<img />` tag has a `src` attribute that specifies the location of the image to be displayed. In TAL, these attributes can be dynamically filled by using the `tal:attributes` attribute. Inside the quotes, the syntax looks similar to a `tal:define` attribute, but rather than setting up several variables for use, we're determining which attributes of a given tag will be valued with what. In our case, we fill the `title` attribute with the same value that will appear within the body of our `<a />` tag, and we fill the `href` attribute with another item that our catalog brain returns which is the absolute url of the randomly-chosen news item. This can be studied within the following snippet:

```
<a href="[replaced by random news item link]"
  title="[replaced by random news item title]"
  tal:attributes="href random_newsitem/getURL;
         title random_newsitem/Title">[replaced by random news
              item title]</a>
```

 The author prefers to include square brackets and a comment about what will happen within the various HTML elements as a reminder of how the code works, so that it looks more familiar to people who know HTML, but do not yet know TAL. However, these comments could be omitted entirely.

When this all is put together, the actual HTML will look something like this:

```
<a href="http://127.0.0.1:8080/talportlet/news/practical-plone-
         released"
  title="Practical Plone Released!">Practical Plone Released!</a>
```

If at any point during this process you notice a message similar to the following:

```
<!-- Page Template Diagnostics
Compilation failed
zope.tal.taldefs.TALError: *something went wrong*, at line 1, column 1
-->
```

it simply means that your HTML has a typo, and that you'll need to find the line in question and fix any issues. Common problems can include:

- Missing HTML tags (for example, a forgotten `</a>` closing tag)
- A mistyped TAL attribute (the author's favorite typo is `tal:defines`, rather than `tal:define`)
- A missing semicolon needed to separate a new variable or HTML attribute declarations

You can now click **Save** and navigate through the site. If you have more than one published news item within your site, clicking through the site should display all of your news items, eventually.

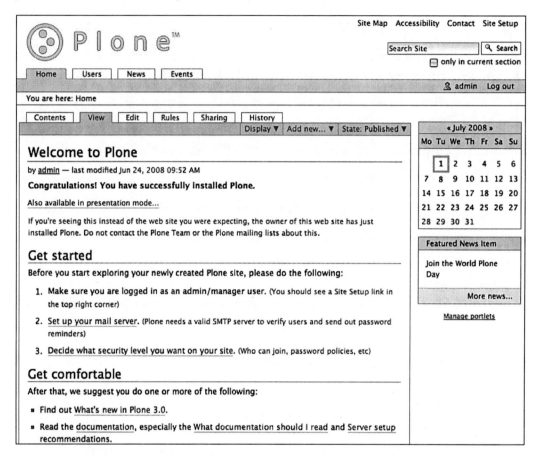

More information

A TAL portlet is a very simple way of creating custom portlets. More complex portlets can be created using filesystem-based development practices, but that's beyond the scope of this book.

There is considerable in-depth information on creating new portlets in the documentation section of Plone.org and in Martin Aspeli's book, *Professional Plone Development*.

Summary

In this chapter, we have learned:

- How to assign portlets to objects, content types, and groups of users
- How to re-order and remove portlets
- How to block portlets from being inherited
- How to create custom portlets

11

Automate Tasks with Content Rules

Now that you've learned how to add, structure, and manage content on your site, it's time to let your site to do something for you. Perhaps you'd like to receive an email when someone adds a page to your site, or automatically move published news items to a top-level news folder, or notify site users of a successfully-completed action.

In this chapter, **Alex Clark** introduces you to **Content Rules**, which enable you to do all of this, and more.

Understanding content rules

For many years, people wondered how to automate tasks in Plone. During this time, the installation of add-on products to perform specific tasks was usually required (for example, CMFNotification). With Plone 3, this is no longer necessary. Content rules allow you to define **Triggering events** and associate them with **Conditions** and **Actions** to automate many site tasks that you would otherwise have to perform by hand. The basic steps are:

1. Create a rule.
2. Select a Triggering Event.
3. Select an Action.
4. Assign the rule to a content object.

Content rules are created in the Plone Control Panel, and then activated via the **Rules** tab of a content object. You can also define content rules for the top-level site object.

Plone Control Panel
You can read more about the Plone Control Panel in Chapter 12.

Getting into action

Let's dive right in with a few practical examples of how to set up content rules.

Receiving an email when someone adds a page

If you would like to keep a close watch on your site's growth and progress, you may want to receive an email every time someone adds a new page to your site. You can achieve this by using a content rule with the "mail" action.

1. Create the rule:

    *   Click on **Site Setup**.

    *   Click on **Content Rules**.

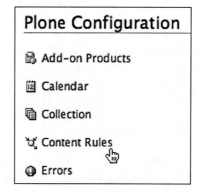

- Click on **Add content rule**.

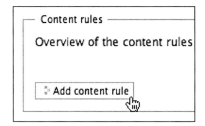

- Specify a **Title**.

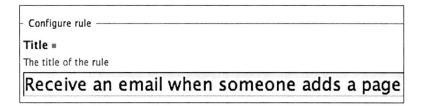

- Select the **Triggering event**.

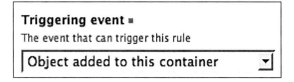

- Make sure that the **Enabled** checkbox is selected.

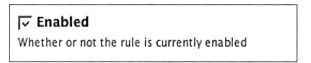

- Make sure that the **Stop executing rules** checkbox is left unselected (unless you want the rule to execute only once)

- Click on **Save**.

2. Add an action to the rule:

- Navigate to the **Edit content rule** form by clicking on the new rule.

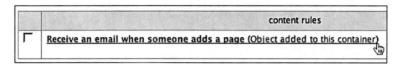

- Select **Mail action** from the **Add action** drop-down field, and then click **Add**.

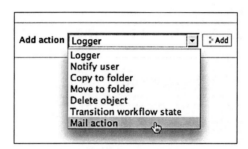

- Specify a **Subject**.

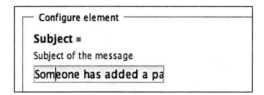

- Specify the **Email recipients**.

- Enter a **Message** of **Someone added '${title}' at ${url}**, and then click on **Save**.

3. Add a condition to the rule:
    - Navigate to the **Edit content rule** form by clicking on the new rule.
    - Select **Content type** from the **Add condition** drop-down list and click on **Add**.

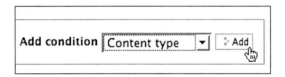

    - Select **Page**, and then click on **Save**.

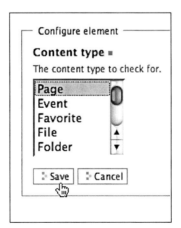

- The **Edit content rule** form should now look like this:

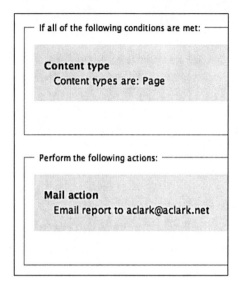

4. Activate the rule:

   - Navigate to the top level of your site by clicking on either the site logo or the **Home** tab.

   - Select the **Rules** tab in the content area.

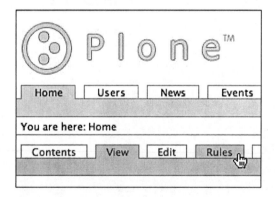

   - Select the new rule, and then click on **Add**.

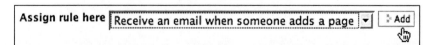

- Select the checkbox next to the new rule, and then click on **Apply to subfolders**.

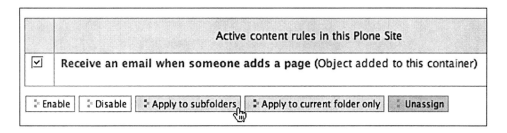

That's it! You can now test this rule by adding a page, then checking the email account that you configured in **Email recipients**. If you receive an email to this account, it means the rule was successful.

Mail settings

Make sure that you have correctly configured an SMTP server, SMTP port, Site 'From' name, and Site 'From' address in the **Mail** section of the Plone Control Panel, or this example will not work. You can read more about mail settings in Chapter 12.

Before we begin the next example, let's look at the content rules control panel in more detail. Again, you can get to it by navigating to the **Content Rules** control panel by clicking on **Site Setup,** and then click on **Content Rules**.

Note that the **Enable globally** checkbox is checked. You can deselect it, and then click on **Save**, to disable all of the rules at the same time:

The **Content Rules** section lists all of the rules for your site. If you completed the first example, it should now look like this:

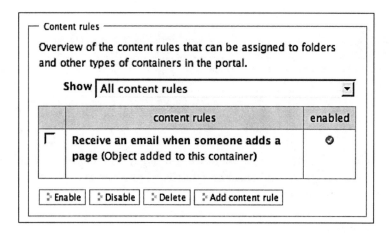

 You can use the **Show** drop-down list to filter by either trigger or current state—that is, whether the rule is enabled or disabled. By default, all content rules are shown.

Moving published news items to a top-level news folder

Now that you understand how to create and activate content rules, let's move on to a scenario where your rule actually modifies your site. In this example, let's imagine that you let users contribute news items in various places, but you want to collate all published news items into a single top-level folder.

You can do this on your site by following these steps:

1. Click on **Site Setup**.
2. Click on **Content Rules**.
3. Click on **Add content rule**.
4. Specify in the **Title: Move news items to /news-items**.
5. Select the **Triggering event: Workflow state changed**.

Your **Content Rules** control panel should now look like this:

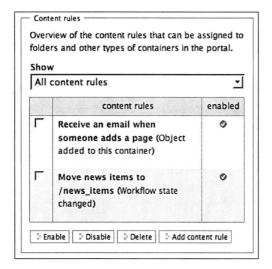

This rule should apply only to news items that have been published. So let's add conditions to check for the content type and the workflow state:

1. Select **Content type** from the **Add condition** drop-down list and then click on **Add**.
2. Select **News item**, and then click on **Save**.
3. Select **Workflow state** from the **Add condition** drop-down list and then click on **Add**.
4. Select **Published**, and then click on **Save**.

Your **Content Rules** control panel should now look like this:

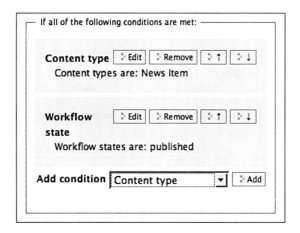

Next, we'll create an action to move published news items to a top-level news items folder. But first, using the skills we acquired in Chapter 6, let's create a top-level news items folder:

1. Navigate to the top level of your site by clicking on the either site logo or the **Home** tab.

2. Select **Folder** from the **Add new...** drop-down list.

3. Specify a **Title of News Items**.

4. Click on **Save**.

Your site should now look like this, with a new **News Items** tab in the global navigation area.

Now, return to the **Content Rules** control panel and add an action:

1. Navigate to the **Content Rules** control panel by clicking on **Site Setup**, and then on **Content Rules**.

2. Navigate to the **Edit content rule** form by clicking on the new rule.

3. Select **Move to folder** from the **Add action** drop-down list, and then click on **Add**.

4. Enter **/news-items** in the **Target folder** search box, and then click on **Search**.

5. Select the news-items option button from **Search results**, and then click on **Update Selection**.

6. Click on **Save**.

The **Content Rules** control panel should now look like this:

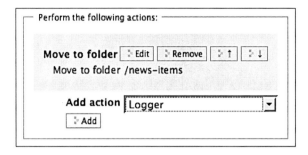

We're almost finished. The rule has been created; now we must activate it. You may recall the following steps from the first example:

1. Navigate to the top level of your site by clicking on either the site logo or the **Home** tab.

2. Select the **Rules** tab in the content area.

3. Select the new rule and click on the **Add** button.

4. Select the checkbox next to the new rule, and then click on **Apply to subfolders**.

The **Rules** tab should now look like this:

We have finished creating the rule, but another important step remains: testing. To test this rule, using the skills you acquired in Chapter 5, simply create a news item somewhere other than in the **News Items** folder and publish it:

1. Navigate to the top level of your site by clicking on either the site logo or the **Home** tab.

2. Select **News item** from the **Add new...** drop-down list.

3. Enter a **Title** of Test.

4. Click on **Save**.

5. Select **Publish** from the **State** drop-down list.

The published news item should now be located in the top-level news items folder. You can confirm this by doing the following:

1. Navigate to the top level of your site by clicking on either the site logo or the **Home** tab.

2. Click on the **Test** news item in the News Portlet:

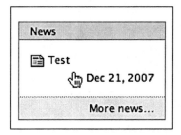

3. Notice that the breadcrumbs indicate that **Test** is inside **News Items**.

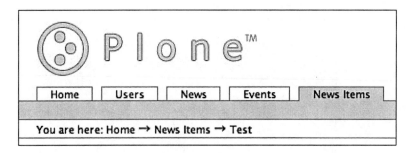

We have one more example to go, but first let's review some core concepts. Here is some terminology that by now you should be familiar with:

- **Content Rule**: Allows you to automate a task
- **Triggering Event**: Causes a rule to be executed
- **Condition**: Additional requirements for rule execution
- **Action**: The task to be performed

It is also important to be familiar with the triggering events, conditions, and actions that Plone ships with. We'll have a look at these in the following sections.

Triggering events

- **Object added to this container**: Triggered when new content items are created
- **Object modified**: Triggered when content items are edited
- **Object removed from this container**: Triggered when content items are deleted
- **Workflow state changed**: Triggered when content items, for example, when a news item is submitted for publication

Conditions

- **Content type**: Restricts rule execution by content type; for example, copies news items to the news items folder
- **File Extension**: Restricts rule execution by file extension; for example, copies files that end in `.zip` to the downloads folder
- **Workflow state**: Restricts rule execution by workflow state; for example, copies only published news items to the news items folder
- **User's group**: Restricts rule execution by user group; for example, notifies Reviewers of content edited by Contributors
- **User's role**: Restricts rule execution by user role

Actions

- **Logger**: Sends a message to your site's event log
- **Notify user**: Sends a message through the web, similar to Plone's system messages
- **Copy to folder**: Copies a content item
- **Move to folder**: Moves a content item
- **Delete object**: Deletes a content item

- **Transition workflow state**: Changes the state of a content item
- **Mail action**: Sends an email to someone

Keep these definitions in mind as you work through the last example and through your future content rules.

Notify site users of a successfully-completed action

You may want to notify the user in the previous example that his or her news item has been moved to the top-level news folder. Because a rule for this exists already, all we need to do is add another action. You can do this by following these steps:

1. Click on **Site Setup**.
2. Click on **Content Rules**.
3. Select the existing rule **Move published news items to a top-level news folder**. (Workflow state changed)
4. Select **Add Action: Notify User**, and then click on **Add**.

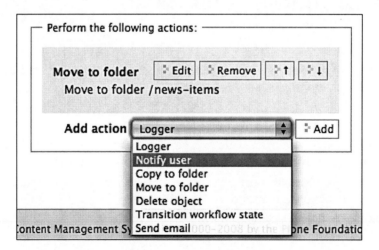

5. In the **Message** filed, enter **Your news item has been moved to /news-items!**

Your **Content Rules** control panel should now look like this:

As this rule is already active, all that is left is to test it:

1. Navigate to the top-level of your site, and create a news item.
2. Publish this new news item.
3. Confirm that you receive a notification, and an on-screen message, stating that the news item has been moved.

Summary

The content rules functionality is very powerful and can support a variety of use cases. In this chapter, you learned how to:

- Receive an email when someone adds a page to your site
- Automatically move published news items to a top-level news folder
- Notify site users of a successfully-completed action

It is also possible to register new triggering events, and provide new types of conditions and actions to build rules with. This is beyond the scope of this book, and requires some Python knowledge. But if you are interested, take a look at `http://plone.org` for relevant documentation. In particular, `http://plone.org/documentation/tutorial/creating-content-rule-conditions-and-actions` covers the topic of creating new conditions and actions.

12
Control My Site's Configuration

Throughout this book, you have used the Plone control panel to configure various settings, from controlling how the visual editor behaves, to customizing workflow for users and groups, to creating and assigning content rules.

In this chapter, **Alex Clark** describes the Plone control panel in detail. You will learn the following:

- Using the control panel effectively
- Configuring RSS syndication
- Configuring navigation actions
- Configuring the navigation portlet

The Plone control panel

You can access the Plone control panel by clicking on **Site Setup** in the site actions area in the upper-right corner of the screen:

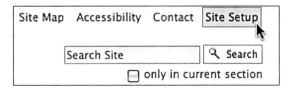

The control panel is shown in the following screenshot:

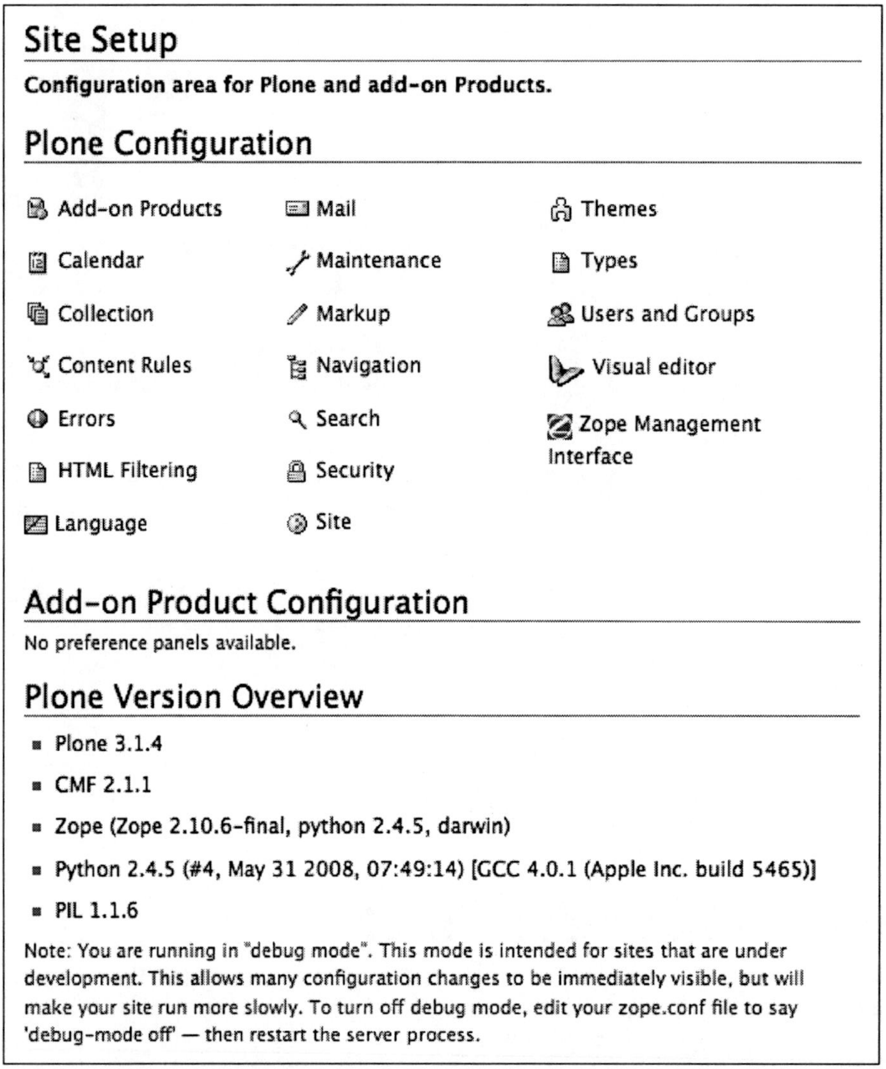

Site Setup

Configuration area for Plone and add-on Products.

Plone Configuration

🗃 Add-on Products	✉ Mail	🏠 Themes
📅 Calendar	🔧 Maintenance	📄 Types
🗐 Collection	✏ Markup	👥 Users and Groups
⚙ Content Rules	🗒 Navigation	▷ Visual editor
⊙ Errors	🔍 Search	🗔 Zope Management Interface
📄 HTML Filtering	🔒 Security	
🖼 Language	⊚ Site	

Add-on Product Configuration

No preference panels available.

Plone Version Overview

- Plone 3.1.4

- CMF 2.1.1

- Zope (Zope 2.10.6-final, python 2.4.5, darwin)

- Python 2.4.5 (#4, May 31 2008, 07:49:14) [GCC 4.0.1 (Apple Inc. build 5465)]

- PIL 1.1.6

Note: You are running in "debug mode". This mode is intended for sites that are under development. This allows many configuration changes to be immediately visible, but will make your site run more slowly. To turn off debug mode, edit your zope.conf file to say 'debug-mode off' — then restart the server process.

The Plone control panel contains three main sections:

1. **Plone Configuration**.
2. **Add-on Product Configuration**.
3. **Plone Version Overview**.

Although we will focus mostly on the preference panels in the **Plone Configuration** section, you should be aware of the other two sections. The **Add-On Product Configuration** section contains preference panels for add-on products. Not all add-on products have a preference panel, but those that do, place them here. The **Plone Version Overview** is a very useful section that contains information about the software stack used to run your Plone site. Here you will find the Plone version, CMF version, Zope version, Python version, and PIL version. The Plone version is obvious, but the other parts of the software stack that run your Plone site may require an explanation:

- **CMF**: The **Content Management Framework** is an add-on to Zope 2 that makes it easier to build content management applications. Plone uses it extensively.

- **Zope**: The **Zope 2 Application Server** is the application that runs when you start your Plone site. The CMF and Plone are installed "on top of" Zope 2.

- **Python**: The **Python Programming Language** is the programming language used (along with small amounts of 'C') to create Zope, the CMF, Plone, PIL, and just about any add-on that you may install on your Plone site.

- **PIL**: The **Python Imaging Library** is a Python library that makes it easier for programmers to manipulate images in their programs. Plone uses it extensively.

Walk-through of each preference panel

Now that we've discussed the Plone control panel in general, let's move on to the individual preference panels.

Add/Remove Products

The **Add/Remove Products** section is, appropriately, listed first, because it is arguably the most used. This is the first place that you go after installing an add-on product in the file system and restarting your Plone. It typically looks something like the example shown in the following screenshot:

Add/Remove Products

▲ Up to Site Setup

This is the Add-on Products install section, you can add and remove products in the lists below.

To make new products show up here, add them to your buildout configuration, run buildout, and restart the server process. For detailed instructions see **Installing a third party product**.

┌─ Products available for install ─────────────────────────────┐

☐ 🗟 **Marshall 1.0.0**
　　📄 Product Description

☐ 🗟 **NuPlone trunk**
　　Extension profile for NuPlone Product.

☐ 🗟 **OpenID Authentication Support 1.1**
　　Adds support for authenticating with OpenID credentials in a Plone site
　　📄 Product Description

☐ 🗟 **Workflow Policy Support (CMFPlacefulWorkflow) 1.3.1**
　　Add in Plone the capability to change workflow chains for types in every object.
　　📄 Product Description

☐ 🗟 **Working Copy Support (Iterate) 1.1.5**
　　Adds working copy support (aka. in-place staging) to Plone.
　　📄 Product Description

[⚙ Install]

└──┘

The products listed here ship with Plone, and you can safely ignore them unless you have a specific need.

To demonstrate the installation of an add-on product, let's suppose you have just installed the **RichDocument** (http://plone.org/products/richdocument) add-on product in the file system and restarted Plone.

Add-on product installation

Installing add-on products is typically done with buildout, and is covered in detail in Chapter 14.

Next, the **Products available for install** section will appear as shown in the following screenshot:

Add/Remove Products

⌃ Up to Site Setup

This is the Add-on Products install section, you can add and remove products in the lists below.

To make new products show up here, add them to your buildout configuration, run buildout, and restart the server process. For detailed instructions see Installing a third party product.

Products available for install

☐ 📖 **Attachment support 3.0.1**
    Simple attachment content types and widget
    📄 Product Description

☐ 📖 **Marshall 1.0.0**
    📄 Product Description

☐ 📖 **NuPlone trunk**
    Extension profile for NuPlone Product.

☐ 📖 **OpenID Authentication Support 1.1**
    Adds support for authenticating with OpenID credentials in a Plone site
    📄 Product Description

☐ 📖 **RichDocument 3.0.2**
    An extension of the default Page type to include image and file attachments

☐ 📖 **Workflow Policy Support (CMFPlacefulWorkflow) 1.3.1**
    Add in Plone the capability to change workflow chains for types in every object.
    📄 Product Description

☐ 📖 **Working Copy Support (Iterate) 1.1.0**
    Adds working copy support (aka. in-place staging) to Plone.
    📄 Product Description

⸭ Install

Select the checkbox next to **RichDocument 3.0.2** and click the **Install** button. Your **Installed Products** section should now look like this:

```
┌─ Installed products ──────────────────────────────────────────┐
│                                                               │
│  ☐ 🖼 Attachment support 3.0.1                                 │
│           Simple attachment content types and widget          │
│           📄 Product Description  📄 Install log              │
│                                                               │
│  ☐ 🖼 RichDocument 3.0.2                                       │
│           An extension of the default Page type to include image and file attachments │
│           📄 Install log                                      │
│   ┌──────────┐                                                │
│   │ Uninstall│                                                │
│   └──────────┘                                                │
└───────────────────────────────────────────────────────────────┘
```

Note that another product, **Attachment support 3.0.1**, has been installed automatically as a dependency of **RichDocument 3.0.2**. You can uninstall **RichDocument** in a similar way—by selecting the checkbox next to **RichDocument 3.0.2** and clicking the **Uninstall** button.

Typically, you will only visit the **Add/Remove Products** control panel when adding or removing add-on products, or seeing what is installed. When removing a product, you should uninstall the product first, stop Plone, remove the product directory from the file system, and then restart Plone.

Calendar

Next, in an alphabetical order, but not in an order of importance, is the **Calendar** preference panel, which is used to configure how the calendar portlet is displayed. As the calendar portlet is very resource-intensive (most people tend to remove it for that reason), this preference panel is not used very often. Plus, with the advent of the portlet infrastructure in Plone 3, this preference panel arguably belongs there instead. But as it currently resides in the Plone control panel, we will cover it here. This panel contains two sections:

- **First day of week in the calendar**
- **Workflow states to show in the calendar**

Normally, the first day of the week is Sunday. If you'd like to make it Saturday instead, follow these steps:

1. Select **Saturday** from the drop-down menu, as shown in the following screenshot:

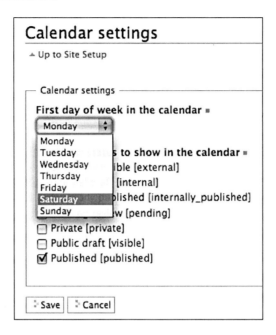

2. Click on the **Save** button.

Your calendar portlet should now look something like this:

Similarly, by default, only events that have been published are displayed. If you'd like to display the events that are in the private state as well, follow these steps:

1. Select the **Private [private]** checkbox, as shown in the following screenshot:

2. Click on the **Save** button to save your settings.

Now, using the skills you learned in Chapter 5, create a test event and confirm that it is displayed in the calendar portlet, as shown in the following screenshot:

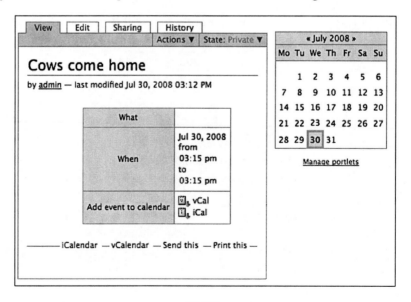

As you can see, the calendar portlet demonstrates how workflow states can affect your site's behavior.

Collection

The **Collection** control panel may appear daunting at first glance, and most beginners will not need to use it, but it can be very useful in some cases. The configuration panel contains two sections:

1. **Collection Indexes**.
2. **Collection Metadata**.

The panel appears as shown in the follows:

These tabs don't mean much to most people at first glance, so let's take a step back and explain what a Collection is, and why we care. A Collection is a folder-like object on your site that contains the results of a search query that you define. For example, if you have hundreds of user folders on your site, each containing hundreds of images, you can create a Collection to display all of the images in one place.

More about Collections
Collections are covered in detail in Chapter 6.

This is possible because Plone has a content type called **Image**, and Collections allow you to search for all objects of a certain type, in this case, the Image type. Collections use the Plone Catalog Tool, which contains a list of indexes that are best defined by the tool itself:

- Plone Catalog Tool Indexes: This list defines which indexes the Catalog will contain. When objects are cataloged, the values of any attributes that match an index in this list will be indexed.

In other words, all of the content objects on your site have attributes (such as content type, description, and category), and these attributes are searchable once the objects are defined in the catalog. Plone ships with many indexes out-of-the-box, and the **Collection Indexes** section of the Collection control panel allows you to control them.

Similarly, an excerpt from the Plone Catalog Tool best defines the **Collection Metadata** section.

- Plone Catalog Tool Metadata: This list defines what per-object metadata the Catalog will store. When objects get cataloged, the values of any attributes they may have that match a name in this list will be stored in a table in the Catalog. The Catalog then uses this information to create result objects that are returned whenever the catalog is searched. It is important to understand that when the Catalog is searched, it returns a list of result objects, not the cataloged objects themselves. So if you want to use the value of an object's attribute in a search, that attribute must be in this list.

By adjusting the settings in **Collection Indexes** and **Collection Metadata**, you can create more sophisticated queries when specifying the criteria for Collections. We will not address this in detail, as it is a fairly advanced topic, and this configuration panel is rarely used by beginners.

Content Rules

Content Rules are covered in Chapter 11, so we won't cover them again in detail here. However, it is worth mentioning that this is where you enable or disable your content rules site-wide, if and when you have the need to do that. For example, if several content rules are broken, rather than disable each of them individually, you can turn them all off at once. The control panel for content rules appears as shown here:

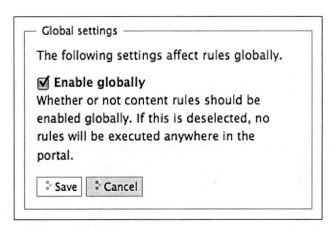

Deselect the **Enable globally** checkbox to disable all content rules.

Errors

As its name implies, the **Errors** control panel displays a log of errors (called exceptions) that have occurred on your site. By default, common errors are ignored, but to demonstrate its functionality, we can choose to display a common error, such as the one caused by a request for a page that does not exist. Follow these steps to create and view an error:

1. Click **Site Setup**.
2. Click on **Errors**.
3. Remove the text **NotFound** from the **Ignored exception types** text box, as shown in the following screenshot:

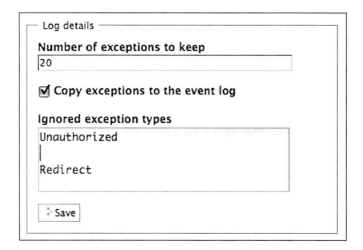

4. Click on **Save**.

Now, try to navigate to a page that you know does not exist, such as `http://localhost:8080/Plone/this-page-does-not-exist`. Reload the **Errors** control panel and you should see something like this:

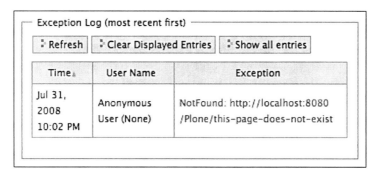

This means that a **NotFound** exception occurred. If you click on the **Exception** title, you can view the **Exception Details**, which will appear as shown in the following screenshot:

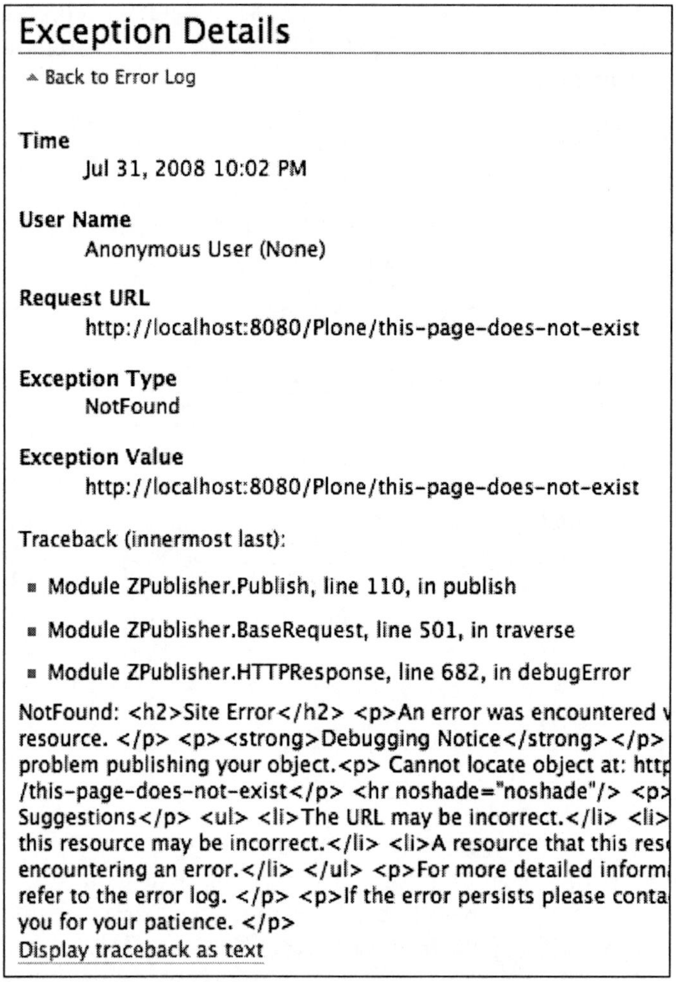

Exception Details

▲ Back to Error Log

Time
    Jul 31, 2008 10:02 PM

User Name
    Anonymous User (None)

Request URL
    http://localhost:8080/Plone/this-page-does-not-exist

Exception Type
    NotFound

Exception Value
    http://localhost:8080/Plone/this-page-does-not-exist

Traceback (innermost last):

- Module ZPublisher.Publish, line 110, in publish

- Module ZPublisher.BaseRequest, line 501, in traverse

- Module ZPublisher.HTTPResponse, line 682, in debugError

NotFound: <h2>Site Error</h2> <p>An error was encountered v
resource. </p> <p><strong>Debugging Notice</strong></p>
problem publishing your object.<p> Cannot locate object at: http
/this-page-does-not-exist</p> <hr noshade="noshade"/> <p>
Suggestions</p> <ul> <li>The URL may be incorrect.</li> <li>
this resource may be incorrect.</li> <li>A resource that this res
encountering an error.</li> </ul> <p>For more detailed inform
refer to the error log. </p> <p>If the error persists please conta
you for your patience. </p>
Display traceback as text

This kind of information can be very useful for troubleshooting when unexpected errors occur. If you click on the **Display traceback as text** link, you will see a page full of text that you can paste to a site such as http//paste.plone.org. Once you do so, you can then refer to that URL in an online chat (in #plone), or use Plone's email support lists to solicit help for the error.

HTML filtering

Here, you can add or remove restrictions that Plone places on HTML tags, attributes, and styles in your content. Before you change these restrictions, consider the following reasons not to do so:

- **Security**: Some tags, such as applet, embed, object, and script, are considered security risks because they allow your site to execute arbitrary code. Make sure you know exactly what you are doing before allowing such tags.

- **Uniformity**: Plone makes good use of CSS to make it relatively easy for you to style your content in a sane and manageable way. If you decide to include additional tags, attributes, or styles inline with your content, you may be sorry later when it comes to deploying a new look and feel, because you will have to hunt down and change these elements.

It isn't wrong to change the default behavior– just think carefully before doing so!

Enough of caution—it's time to modify some filters! Consider the use case of a picky boss who hates misaligned text with a fiery passion. With Plone's default settings, it is possible to change the alignment of text in your content by inserting an in-line text-align style. To demonstrate this, follow these steps:

1. From the front page of your default Plone site, click on the **Edit** tab.

2. Scroll down to the visual editor and click on the **HTML** button.

3. Modify the contents of the first **h2** tag to include the style **text-align: right**, as shown in the following screenshot:

Body Text

HTML

```
<p class="discreet">
If you're seeing this instead of the web site you were expecting, the owner
this web site has just installed Plone. Do not contact the Plone Team
or the Plone mailing lists about this.</p>
<!-- Fly in the face of the boss! -->
<h2 style="text-align: right">Get started</h2>
```

---

4. Click the **HTML** button again to return to the visual editor, and your page should now appear as shown in the following screenshot, with the text **Get started** aligned to the right:

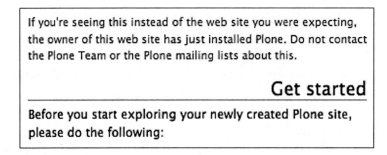

"Curses! Right-aligned text!" your boss will scream; but we can prevent this from happening again with a quick visit to the **HTML Filtering** control panel:

1. Click on **Site Setup**.
2. Click on **HTML Filtering**.
3. Click on **Styles**.

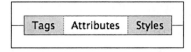

4. Select the **text-align** checkbox and click on **Remove selected items**.

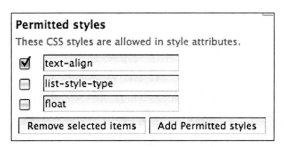

5. Click on **Save**.

Now, to prove to our boss that we have removed the offensive styles:

1. Revisit the front page.
2. Click on **Edit**.
3. Click on **Save**.

Your front page should have returned to normal (with all text aligned to the left). All your future attempts to align text to the right will now be squashed!

You can control tag filtering by adding or removing tags from the **Nasty, Stripped,** and **Custom** tag sections. **Nasty** tags are completely blocked, **Stripped** tags are removed but their contents remain, while the **Custom** tags section can hold tags that are needed, but are not a part of XHTML.

You can control tag attribute filtering by adding or removing tag attributes from the **Stripped attributes** and the **Stripped combinations** sections. **Stripped attributes** will be stripped from any tag when the content is saved, while the **Stripped combinations** option will strip the specified attributes from the specified tags only.

Language

One of the most powerful features of Plone is its multilingual support. If you are planning to deploy a multilingual site, or if you just want to play around with the feature, head to the **Language** control panel. Here you can configure the site language by carrying out the following steps:

1. Click on **Site Setup**.
2. Click on **Language**.
3. Select your **Site language** from the drop-down list.
4. Click on **Save**.

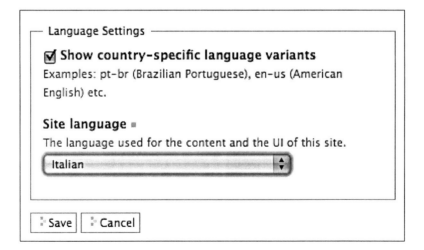

5. Click on **Save** again, and reload any page to display your site in the new language.

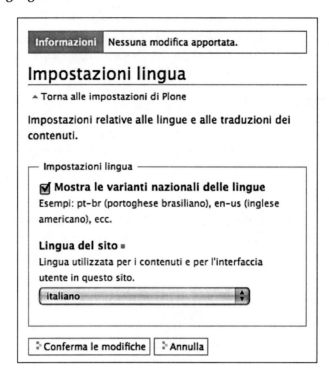

Additionally, you can choose to enable or disable country-specific language variants. In some cases, the language variant is very similar to the original language; in other cases, it's not.

Mail

The **Mail** control panel is one of the first places you will visit after installing Plone. In case you have any doubt, Plone reminds you to do this, with a not-so-subtle message, whenever you visit **Site Setup**:

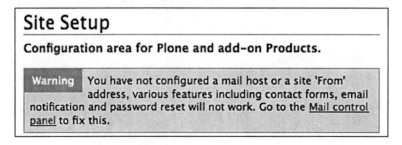

So let's do exactly that:

1. Click on **Site Setup**.
2. Click on **Mail**.
3. Enter **localhost** in the **SMTP server** field.

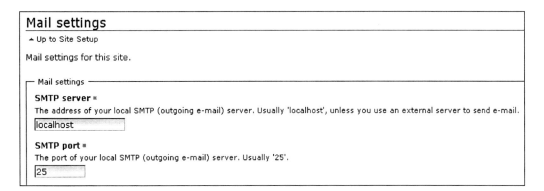

4. Enter your email address in the **Site 'From' address** field.
5. Click on **Save**.

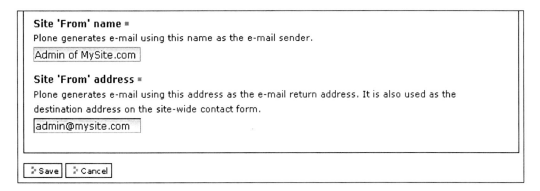

Once you fill in these fields, Plone will stop bothering you with warning messages each time you visit the **Mail** control panel.

You can configure the **Site 'From' name**, change the default **SMTP port** address (the default is **25**), and you can add an **ESMTP username** and **ESMTP password,** if your mail-hosting configuration requires this.

SMTP server

If you are running a mail server on your computer, then your SMTP server is typically **localhost**. You can run a mail server on most Linux, Mac, and Windows computers. For details, ask your system administrator.

Maintenance

Prior to version 3 of Plone, packing the database required a visit to the 'top level' of the Zope Management Interface (where your Plone site exists, alongside **Control_Panel**, **acl_users**, and **temp_folder**). The **Maintenance** control panel now saves you a trip. This panel can be accessed only by a user with a Manager role at the Zope root, a Manager role in Plone only will not suffice. To pack your database in Plone, log in with the same administrative account with which you created your Plone site, and then follow the steps below:

1. Click on **Site Setup**.
2. Click on **Maintenance**.
3. Notice the current size of your database before packing it.

4. Click on **Pack database now**.

5. Note that the size of your database has now shrunk significantly.

You can also view your **Zope Server uptime**, and start or shut down your server:

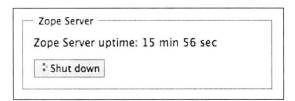

Markup

The **Markup** panel lets you control what text markup types are available when editing content. To demonstrate it, let's change the default format for content to text rather than HTML, using the following steps. By doing so, you will see how this type of configuration change can be useful.

1. Click on **Site Setup**.

2. Click on **Markup**.

3. Select **text/plain** as the **Default format**.

4. Deselect **text/html** and select **text/plain** in **Alternative formats**.

5. Click on **Save**.

Now, test your new configuration by adding a new page by carrying out the following steps:

1. Navigate to the top level of your site.

2. Add a **Page**.

3. Add some text to the page.

You'll notice the markup because it is still created by the visual editor. But we've chosen to display it as plain text. You may now want to return your site to the default configuration for the next example.

You can also enable **Wiki behavior** for your content in the **Markup** control panel. Let's do that now, by carrying out the following steps:

1. Click on **Site Setup**.
2. Click on **Markup**.
3. Click on **Wiki behavior**.

4. Select the **Page** checkbox and then click on **Save**.

Now, to test the new configuration, add some wiki syntax to a page, in the following manner:

1. Navigate to the top level of your site.
2. To edit the front page, click on its body.
3. Create a wiki link called **Plone Team**, and then click on **Save**. The syntax for wiki links is **((Plone Team))**.

Note that you are now prompted to click on **Plone Team** to create a new **Page**.

If you click on the link, you get a new page!

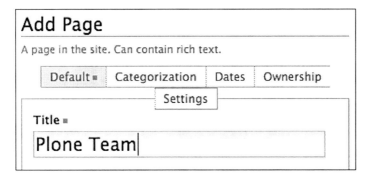

You can then add some text to describe how wonderful the Plone Team is! This is optional, of course.

Navigation

The **Navigation** control panel allows you to configure how both sections link (also known as **portal tabs**) and the sitemap is displayed. Navigation is covered later in this chapter, so we won't cover it here.

We've come a long way since the beginning of this chapter. For the next few relatively simple sections, we will not give detailed examples. Instead, you are encouraged to experiment on your own; change a setting or two, check the result, and repeat the steps.

Search

The **Search** control panel allows you to do two things:

- Enable or disable the **LiveSearch** feature, which returns results to the user instantly, as they type in the Search box.

- Configure which content types are returned in search results; by default, all 'Plone friendly' types are returned. (Many 'legacy' content types still exist, but are not used by Plone. You can safely ignore these.)

Security

The **Security** control panel allows you to configure the following four features, all of which are disabled by default:

1. Self-registration.
2. User-selected passwords.
3. User folders.
4. Display of 'about' information.

Site settings

The **Site settings** control panel allows you to configure some obvious features, such as the **Title** and **Description** of your site, along with several unrelated controls that ended up here because they didn't belong anywhere else.

The obvious settings are:

- **Site title**: Set the title of your site
- **Site description**: Set the description of your site

Both of these settings can affect how your site appears to the outside world via RSS feeds, and how search engines index it.

The less obvious settings are:

- **Show 'Short Name' on content**: Choose to display the 'short' name when editing content. If displayed, the short name can be edited, and will affect the URL. For example, if you create a page called 'Plone Team', it will be saved as 'plone-team', and the URL for the page on your site will be something like this: `http://localhost/Plone/plone-team`. Even if this option is disabled, the 'short' name can still be edited by selecting **Rename** from the **Actions** drop-down menu.

- **Enable inline editing**: This option is enabled by default, and allows you to turn the 'fancy' editing of forms on or off with KSS (Plone's AJAX framework). To put it in another way, it allows you to enable or disable the feature in Plone that allows you to edit HTML form data without submitting the form to the web server (via AJAX).

Plone's AJAX framework

You can read more about the KSS project at
`http://kssproject.org/`.

- **Enable link integrity checks**: This option is enabled by default, and simply warns the users when they are about to rename a content object that is linked from another content object.

- **Enable external editor**: This feature is disabled by default, and when it is enabled, it must also be enabled per user, in the user's preference panel. The external editor feature allows you to use a text editor of your choice, which is running on your local machine, rather than the **Visual Editor** known as **Kupu** that runs through the web interface. You can read more about configuring an external editor on Windows or Mac OS respectively at:

  - `http://plone.org/documentation/how-to/getting-externaleditor-zopeedit-working-on-windows`

  - `http://plone.org/documentation/how-to/getting-externaleditor-zopeeditmanager-working-in-firefox-on-mac-os-x`

External Editor on Linux

Unfortunately, at the time of writing, there is no tutorial for getting an external editor working on Linux, but the Windows and Mac OS concepts apply to Linux as well. In short, you have to install the external editor program, configure it to use your editor, and configure your browser to use the external editor when you click on an external edit link in Plone.

- **Expose sitemap.xml.gz**: This option is best explained by the control panel description, which says that it exposes your content as a file according to the `sitemaps.org` standard. You can submit this to compliant search engines such as Google, Yahoo, and Microsoft. It allows these search engines to crawl your site more intelligently.

- **Insert JavaScript inline for web statistics support**: This control panel option is also best explained by the control panel description, which says that it enables support for web statistics from external providers (for example, for Google Analytics). Paste the code snippets provided, and these will be included in the rendered HTML as entered near the end of the page.

Themes

The **Themes** control panel allows you to set the **Default theme**, but perhaps more interestingly, it allows you to configure three additional settings. Each is best explained by the description:

1. **Mark external links**: If enabled, all external links will be marked with link type specific icons. If disabled, the **External links open in new window** setting has no effect.

2. **External links open in new window**: If enabled, all external links in the content region open in a new window.

3. **Show content type icons**: If disabled, the content icons in folder listings and portlets won't be visible.

Additional Themes

You can install additional themes for Plone by searching for Plone products at `http://plone.org/products` and following the installation instructions provided with the theme. These instructions can also be found at `http://plone.org/documentation/how-to/how-to- install-a-3-x-theme-using-buildout`

We are nearing the end of the walkthrough. For the last few sections, due to the level of complexity involved, we will return to using fully-detailed examples.

Types

The **Types** control panel lets you control the workflow, visibility, and versioning settings for your content types. Note that selecting a content type from the drop-down menu automatically displays the settings for that type. Also notice the **(Default)** content type setting. All of your content types are configured to use this content type's workflow by default. If you change the workflow for **(Default)**, you are changing it for all of your content types. However, if you change it for any type other than **(Default)**, you will change it only for that type. This is not obvious when we use the control panel, but it is an important distinction to be aware of.

Let's start with a simple example, literally, by changing the **Simple Publication Workflow** to the **Single State Workflow** for **(Default)**:

1. Click on **Site Setup**.
2. Click on **Types**.
3. Select **Single State Workflow** from the drop-down menu, as shown in the following screenshot:

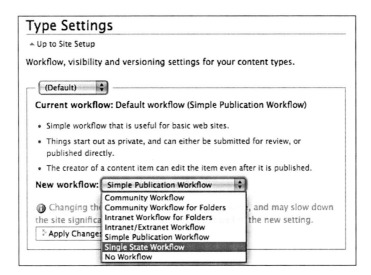

4. You will be presented with a section named **State Mapping**. In this case, there is only one state that we can map to, so there is no choice to be made. In other cases, you may have the opportunity to choose how your states are remapped.

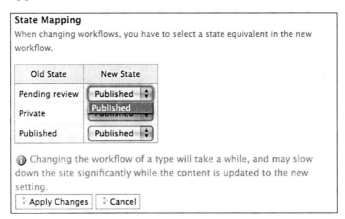

5. Click on **Apply Changes**.

Note that all content is now in the **Published** workflow state, and there is no option to change the states.

Other configurable options in the **Types** control panel, when working with rules for different content types, are as follows:

- **Globally addable**: If this option is selected, the selected content type will appear in the **Add new...** drop-down menu.

- **Allow comments**: If this option is selected, logged-in users will have the ability to add comments to the contents of the selected type.

- **Versioned**: If this option is selected, and if **Working Copy Support** is installed, content of this type will have a **Check out** option in its **Actions** drop-down menu, and a version of the object will be made available with each edit.

- **Visible in searches**: If this option is selected, content of this type will be returned in search results and in collections.

Working Copy Support and Workflow Changes

You can read more about Working Copy Support and Workflow Changes in Chapter 7 and Chapter 9, respectively.

Users and Groups

Here, you can add or remove users and groups to and from your site. In addition, Plone 3 features a new **Users and Groups settings** section, which allows you to alter your site's behavior if it contains a large number of either users or groups. This section is best explained by the text from the control panel itself:

- **Many users or groups**: This determines if your Plone site is optimized for a large numbers of users or groups. In environments with a lot of groups, it can be very slow, or even impossible, to build a list of all of the groups. This option tunes the user interface and behavior of Plone for this case by allowing you to search for users or groups, instead of listing all of them.

In other words, if selected, your site will display a search form, rather than a list of users or groups.

To get familiar with the **Users and Groups** control panel, let's walk through the creation of a new user. This will provide a good general understanding of how the control panel works, and hopefully facilitate future operation.

1. Click on **Site Setup**.

2. Click on **Users and Groups**.

3. Click on **Add new user**.

4. Fill in the form.

5. Click on **Register**.

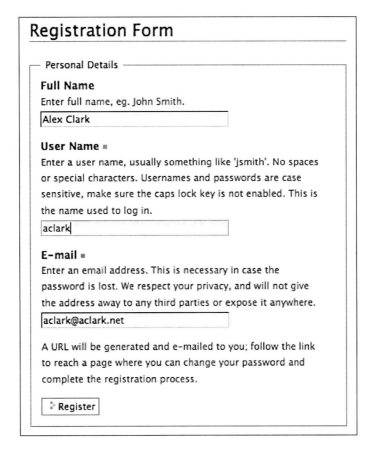

Personal Details

Full Name
Enter full name, eg. John Smith.

Alex Clark

User Name ▪
Enter a user name, usually something like 'jsmith'. No spaces or special characters. Usernames and passwords are case sensitive, make sure the caps lock key is not enabled. This is the name used to log in.

aclark

E-mail ▪
Enter an email address. This is necessary in case the password is lost. We respect your privacy, and will not give the address away to any third parties or expose it anywhere.

aclark@aclark.net

A URL will be generated and e-mailed to you; follow the link to reach a page where you can change your password and complete the registration process.

Register

Site registration options

By default, Plone will send the new user an email with instructions on how to set his or her initial password. You can change this behavior by exploring the options available in the **Security** control panel, which was described earlier in this chapter.

Once the new user has been registered, you can display and configure settings for them by clicking on the **Show all** button. You will see something similar to what is shown in the following screenshot:

| User name | E-mail Address | Roles | | | | | | Reset Password | Remove user |
		Contributor	Editor	Member	Reader	Reviewer	Manager		
aclark (Alex Clark)	aclark@aclark.net	☐	☐	☑	☐	☐	☐	☐	☐

User Search: [   ] 🔍 Search 🔍 Show all

⯈ Apply Changes

Here, you can add or remove users' roles, change users' email addresses, reset users' passwords, and remove users.

> **Groups and Roles**
> Chapter 8 contains more information on site roles, and on how to create groups to assign the roles to.

In the **Groups** section, you gain the ability to add, remove, and configure roles for your groups. From Chapter 8, you know that groups provide an easy way to assign a role to more than one user at a time. For example, if I expect to have a large number of people contributing book chapters to my site, I might create a group called **Writers**, assign to it the contributor role, and add the writers to that group. Let's try this now:

1. Click on **Site Setup**.
2. Click on **Users and Groups**.
3. Click on **Groups**.
4. Click on **Add New Group**.
5. Call it **Writers**.
6. Optionally, specify a **Title** and **Description**.

7. Optionally, you may choose to associate this group with an **Email** address, or, more likely, a list containing the email addresses of all of the people in the group.

We can now assign the **Contributor** role to our group, and then click on **Apply Changes**, as shown in the following screenshot:

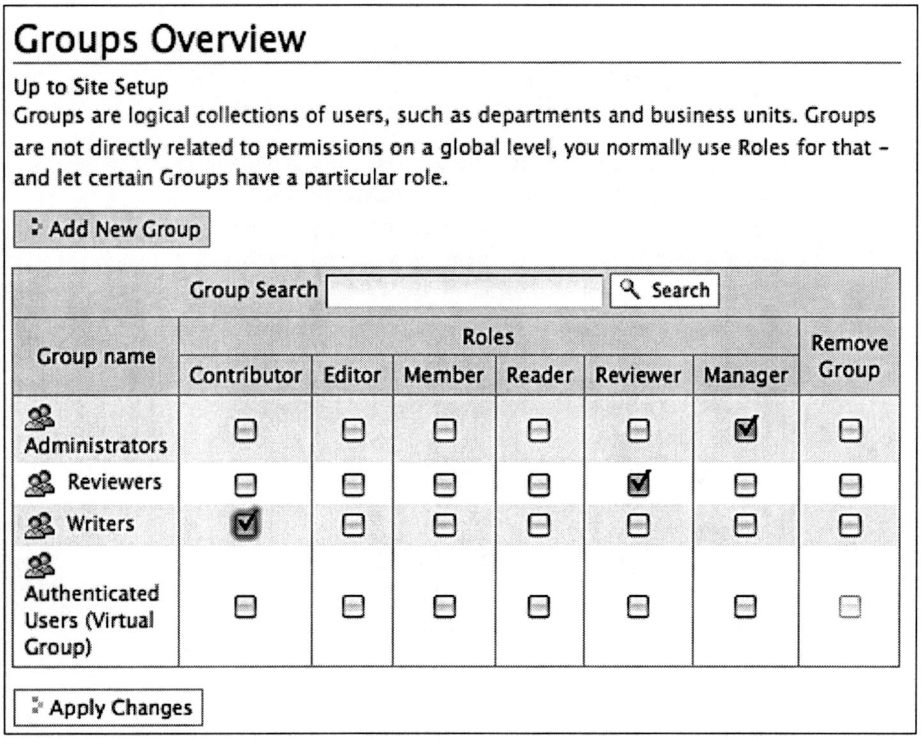

Groups Overview

Up to Site Setup
Groups are logical collections of users, such as departments and business units. Groups are not directly related to permissions on a global level, you normally use Roles for that – and let certain Groups have a particular role.

[**Add New Group**]

| Group Search | | | | | | | [Search] |

Group name	Roles						Remove Group
	Contributor	Editor	Member	Reader	Reviewer	Manager	
Administrators	☐	☐	☐	☐	☐	☑	☐
Reviewers	☐	☐	☐	☐	☑	☐	☐
Writers	☑	☐	☐	☐	☐	☐	☐
Authenticated Users (Virtual Group)	☐	☐	☐	☐	☐	☐	☐

[**Apply Changes**]

At this point, we can add members to our group, for example:

1. Click on **Site Setup**.
2. Click on **Users and Groups**.
3. Click **Groups**.
4. Click **Writers**.
5. Enter the name (not the user ID) of a user that you would like to add to this group and click on **Search**, or click on **Show all** to view a list of all of the users.
6. Select the user(s) and click on **Add selected users and groups to this group**.

Adding groups to groups

Groups can contain other groups. For example, a group of University employees may contain a group for Faculty and a group for Staff.

When you finish, the **Groups** section of your control panel should appear as shown in the following screenshot:

If you now utilize the **Contributor** role on your site, anyone in the new **Writers** group will be subject to that role. For example, you can create a top-level site folder called **Book Chapters** and share permissions with the **Contributor** group in the following manner:

1. Navigate to the top level of your site.
2. Create a folder called **Book chapters**.
3. Click on the **Sharing** tab.
4. Search for the **Writers** group.

You'll notice that Plone has already selected the **Can add** permission, and that this permission can't be disabled because, by default, the Contributor role assigns it. But you can choose to grant additional permissions here, such as **Can edit**, **Can view**, and **Can review**.

Sharing for "Book Chapters"

You can control who can view and edit your item using the list below.

Writers	🔍 Search

User/Group	Can add	Can edit	Can view	Can review
👥 Book writers	⊘	☐	☐	☐
👥 Logged-in users	☐	☐	☐	☐

☑ **Inherit permissions from higher levels**

By default, permissions from the container of this item are inherited. If you disable this, only the explicitly defined sharing permissions will be valid. In the overview, the symbol ⊘ indicates an inherited value. Similarly, the symbol ⊗ indicates a global role, which is managed by the site administrator.

Save	Cancel

Kupu visual editor

Also in the running for the most complicated control panel is the **Kupu visual editor** panel. This contains six tabbed configuration sections in all, and in case it is not obvious, Plone's default visual editor is called Kupu, as described in Chapter 4.

- **Config**: Basic Plone settings, including Link options, Captioning, Reference Browser, HTML View, Original Image Size, and Styles preferences.
- **Libraries**: Configure the contents of Kupu drawers.
- **Resource Types**: Configure the types of things that can go into a Kupu drawer, based on their content type.
- **Documentation**: Covers everything from installation, to usage, to migration from Epoz. If you are unsure about any of the other sections, you can read the documentation here.
- **Links**: This tab allows you to check and maintain links in Kupu-editable fields.
- **Toolbar**: Controls button visibility.

Most people can safely ignore these sections. Covering all of the sections would require a Kupu book by itself, but we will cover one setting—**Styles**.

Styles

There are two subsections in the **Styles** section of the **Config** tab of the **Kupu Configuration** panel: **Tables** and **Styles**. The **Styles** subsection allows you to add additional items to the styles drop-down menu. Users can then select these items, after selecting text, to wrap the text in the associated styles, rather than needing to enter the HTML code by hand. For example, perhaps you would like to make more headings available. By default, h2 and h3 are provided as Heading and Subheading, but Plone ships with unique styles for h1 through h6. We can provide h4, and call it **SubSubheading**, by carrying out the following steps:

1. Click on **Site Setup**.
2. Click on **Visual editor**.
3. Scroll down to the **Styles** section.
4. In the **Styles** field, add **SubSubheading | h4**.
5. Click on **Save**.

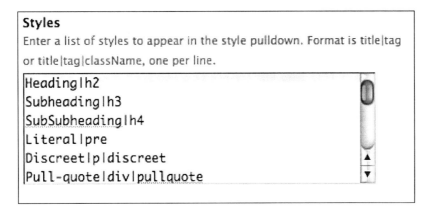

Now, edit some content, select some text, and apply the new style by carrying out the following steps:

1. Navigate to the top level of your site.
2. Edit the front page.
3. Select some text.
4. Select the **SubSubheading** style from the **Styles** drop-down menu.

Your page should end up looking something like this:

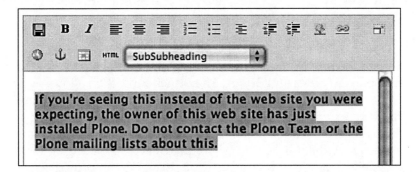

In the above example, the text automatically picks up the styling from the h4 text, which is already defined in Plone's default stylesheets. But you could easily create a new style and define it in the `ploneCustom.css` file. For example, we could add Big Blue Heading | bigblueheading to the styles list, where `bigblueheading` is defined in your `ploneCustom.css` file as:

```
bigblueheading {
    color:blue;
    font-size:1.2em;
    font-weight:bold;
}
```

Then, when editing a Plone page, this style would be available for selection.

Zope Management Interface

The **Zope Management Interface (ZMI)** is covered in various places throughout this book, and can be used to accomplish tasks that cannot be accomplished elsewhere through the web. As such, we will not cover it in any detail here, other than to provide some general advice. If something can be done through the Plone interface, it should probably be done there, and not via the ZMI. For example, don't cut and paste Plone content through the ZMI, because there may be additional methods called on Plone content objects that do not get called when the action is performed through the ZMI.

We've reached the end of the control panel walkthrough, and that was a lot to digest. Before we move on to the next section, here is a list of the 19 preference panels we have covered, for review:

- **Add/Remove Products**: Add or remove add-on products that have been installed on the file system.

- **Calendar**: Configure the calendar portlet's behavior, such as the first day of the week, and the workflow states to be displayed.

- **Collection**: Configure the Plone Catalog Tool indexes and metadata for your Collections.

- **Content Rules**: Define, change, or remove content rules, and also enable or disable them globally across the site.

- **Errors**: Contains error messages generated by your site, and allows you to configure how and when these messages are generated and displayed.

- **HTML Filtering**: Control the filtering of HTML tags, attributes, and styles in your content.

- **Language**: Configure the language of your site.

- **Mail**: Configure the SMTP server and port.

- **Maintenance**: Pack the database, view its uptime, and shut down or start up your Plone site.

- **Markup**: Control what markup is available when editing content.

- **Navigation**: Control the behavior of the site sections and the sitemap. Choose which content types are displayed, and what workflow state they must be in to be displayed. Decide if portal tabs are to be automatically generated, and if so, for which content types.

- **Search**: Enable or disable live search, and configure which content types are shown in the search results.

- **Security**: Enable or disable self-registration. Let users select their own passwords, enable or disable user folders, and allow or disallow anyone from viewing the 'about' information.

- **Site**: Configure the site title and description. Decide whether or not to display the 'short name' for content, enable or disable link integrity checks, enable or disable the external editor feature, expose `sitemap.xml.gz` in the portal root, and add JavaScript for web statistics support.

- **Themes**: Settings that affect the site's look and feel.

- **Types**: Workflow, visibility, and versioning settings for your content types.

- **Users and Groups**: Add or remove users and groups, assign roles, and optimize your site for use with many users and groups.

- **Kupu Visual editor**: Complex configuration options for the Kupu editor.

- **Zope Management Interface**: Advanced configuration options for non-beginners and, in some cases, beginners following specific instructions.

Syndicating content with RSS

Syndication of objects other than Collections can be configured, on a per-folder basis, via an "object action" that is disabled by default.

What is an action?

Actions are configurable objects that typically contain links. For example, **Site Setup** is an action that contains a link to the **Plone Control Panel**.

To enable this action, follow these steps:

1. Click on **Site Setup**.
2. Click on **Zope Management Interface**.
3. Scroll down and click on **portal_actions**.
4. Click on **object**.
5. Click on **syndication**.
6. Check **Visible**, and then click on **Save Changes**.

You will see something similar to the example shown in the following screenshot:

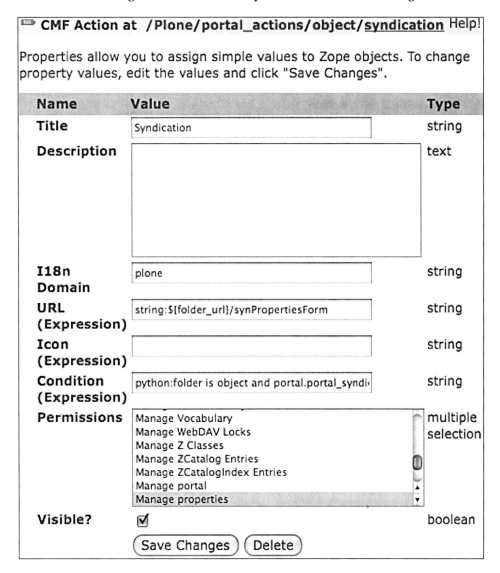

This will enable the **Syndication** tab on folder objects.

Now, let's syndicate the content in the top level folder of our site, by carrying out the following steps:

1. Navigate to the top level of your site.
2. Click on the **Contents** tab.
3. Click on the **Syndication** tab.
4. Click on **Enable Syndication**.

Once syndicated, your browser may tell you that a feed is available, as demonstrated by the blue RSS feed icon in the URL field in the following screenshot:

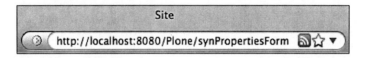

If the RSS icon is not displayed, you may need to visit the feed directly at `http://localhost:8080/Plone/RSS`, or by adding the suffix `/RSS` to the root URL for your site. Your browser may respond by asking you what you want to do with this feed, as shown in the following screenshot:

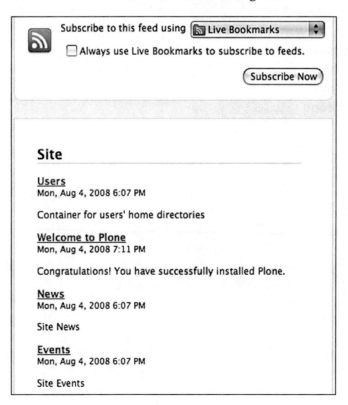

This brings us to our last section, which is about navigation. We covered navigation in the control panel, but there is much more to the story.

Navigation options

There are two additional ways in which we can configure our navigation: either through **Global Sections**, or through **Navigation portlet**.

Global sections

One of the most distinctive and popular features of Plone is the global sections (also known as **portal tabs**). These appear as shown in the following screenshot:

By default, you will get a new global section every time you add a new content object to the root of your Plone site. To demonstrate this, let's add a new top-level folder to our site.

1. Navigate to the top level of your site.
2. Select **Folder** from the **Add new...** drop-down menu.
3. Give it a name of **New Section**.
4. Click on **Save**.

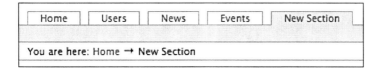

You will see a new global section called **New Section**.

In the preceding example, the new site section is displayed as required. However, sometimes, you don't want a new section to be added to the global navigation. Fortunately, it is easy to work around this:

1. Navigate to the top level of your site.
2. Select **Page** from the **Add new** drop-down menu.
3. Give it a name of **New Page**.
4. Click on the **Settings** tab.

5. Select the **Exclude from navigation** box and click on **Save**.

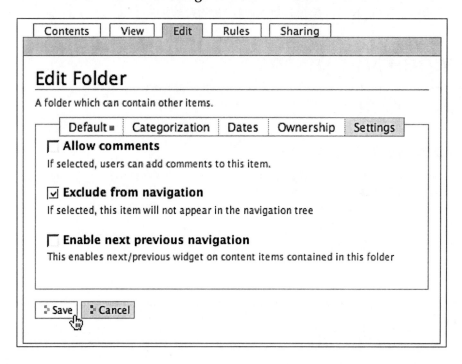

After selecting this option, Plone will not create a new global section called **New Page**. You can make additional configuration changes to the global navigation through the **Site Setup | Navigation** panel, disabling **Automatically generate tabs** and adding more tightly-controlled navigation items through the **portal_actions** option found in the ZMI. For more information, refer to the tutorial at: http://plone.org/documentation/how-to/changing-tabs.

Navigation portlet

Finally, we will cover configuration options for one of Plone's very noteworthy features — the Navigation portlet. This appears as shown in the following screenshot:

By default, you won't see the Navigation portlet in the root of your site, unless you specifically enable it by carrying out the following steps:

1. Navigate to the top level of your site.
2. Click on **Manage portlets** at the bottom of the rightmost column.
3. Click on the **Navigation** portlet assignment in the leftmost column.
4. Scroll down to **Start level**, and change its value from **1** to **0**.

The top level of your site will now look something like the following screenshot:

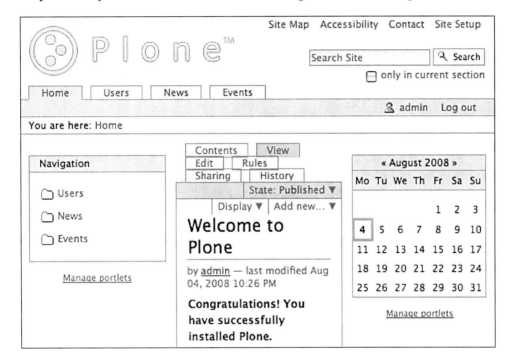

Let's click on **Manage portlets**, and then on the **Navigation** portlet assignment, to return to the **Edit Navigation Portlet** preference panel. There are several configurable options, explained as follows:

- **Title:** If you'd like to change the title displayed in the navigation portlet header, you can do that here. Enter **Site Navigation** in the **Title** field, and your navigation portlet will appear as shown here:

- **Root node:** If you'd like your navigation portlet to display the contents of a folder and not the top level folder, you can do that here. To demonstrate this, we can create a folder called **Navigation** that contains three more folders, and then set the root node to the **Navigation** folder.

  1. Navigate to the top level of your site.
  2. Create a new folder called **Navigation**.
  3. Create three subfolders called **Folder A**, **Folder B**, and **Folder C**.
  4. Navigate to the top level of your site.
  5. Click on **Manage portlets**, and then on the **Navigation** portlet assignment, to return to the **Edit Navigation Portlet** preference panel.
  6. Select the **Navigation** folder in the **Root node** section, and then click on **Update selection**.
  7. Scroll to the bottom of the form and click on **Save**.
  8. Navigate to the top level of your site. The navigation portlet will now look like this:

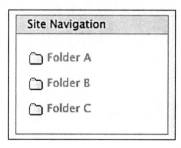

- **Search results**: This is a new feature in the latest 3.x Plone versions, which includes top-level object titles and URLs, option buttons for each object, and **Parent** and **Browse** buttons as well. The search option allows you to choose a folder that should serve as the root of your site. By default, it shows **Users**, **News**, and **Events**, but any folder could be selected, by using this widget.

- **Include top node**: Sometimes, this option is useful for providing an additional navigation link to the root of your site. If you enable this option and your **Start level** is **0**, your navigation portlet will appear as shown in the following screenshot:

- **Only show the contents of the current folder**: Using an example similar to the one mentioned previously, we can demonstrate this feature by carrying out the following steps:

    1. Navigate to the top level of your site.
    2. Create a new folder called **Navigation**.
    3. Create three subfolders called **Folder A**, **Folder B**, and **Folder C**.
    4. Navigate to the top level of your site.
    5. Click on **Manage portlets**, and then click on the **Navigation** portlet assignment, to return to the **Edit Navigation Portlet** preference panel.
    6. Select the checkbox **Only show the contents of the current folder**, and then click on **Save**.

7. Before making this change, from inside the navigation folder the navigation portlet looks like the following screenshot:

8. Afterwards, it will look like the following screenshot:

- **Start level**: Covered in the preceding example.
- **Navigation tree depth**: Last but not the least, the navigation tree depth setting allows you to configure the level at which the navigation portlet will stop displaying content. To demonstrate this using the previous current folder example, select the **Navigation tree depth** checkbox and then click on **Save**. Your navigation portlet should now appear as shown in the following screenshot, showing only one level of contents within the currently-selected folder.

This concludes the section on navigation, and the chapter on controlling your site's configuration in detail.

Summary

In this chapter you have learned:

- How to use the control panel effectively
- How to syndicate the contents of any folder
- How to configure navigation using options such as **Exclude from navigation**, and the navigation portlet settings

Part 3

Now that I've got the basics, I'd like to learn how to...

...set up a repeatable environment using buildout

...find and install add-ons that expand Plone functionality

...build forms

...create new content types

...customize Plone

...change the look and feel

13

Set up a Repeatable Environment using Buildout

Plone is a very powerful content management system. A part of the power comes from its extensibility in using third-party products and packages. You can set up a Plone instance, add a few products, and have a working site in no time. But what do you do if you want to release your new Plone site to production, or develop some new features with your colleagues?

In this chapter, **Clayton Parker** explains how to use `zc.buildout` to set up a repeatable Plone environment. This will enable you to spend more time working on your project rather than just setting it up.

Terms

In order to get the most out of buildout, there are some terms that we will need to understand. Here are explanations of the most common terms you will hear:

- A **Python Package** is a collection of Python modules set up in nested directories (sometimes referred to as a dotted namespace). An example is the `plone.app` package.

- A **Python Egg** is a way of packaging a Python package so that it can be distributed easily. It is what allows us to get of all the Python packages needed in our buildouts.

- The **Python Package Index** (`http://pypi.python.org`), also known as **PyPI** or **The Cheese Shop** (inspired by *Monty Python*) is a central repository of eggs that you can easily install using the `easy_install` command of `setuptools`.

- A **Zope Product** is a special Zope package that lives in the `Products` namespace. Zope products that are not 'eggified' are put into the `Products` folder inside the Zope instance. Plone products prior to version 3.0 that use the `Products` namespace are referred to as "old-style" Zope products.

- **ZCML** is the language that Zope 3 uses to configure components. Zope 3 does not load packages that are in a certain location automatically because Zope 3 no longer has special locations like the Products package has. Instead, you have to explicitly tell Zope 3 to load your package, by using a ZCML statement. This ZCML statement is sometimes called a **ZCML slug**. ZCML slugs are required for packages that do not live in the Products namespace, so that Zope will load the configuration files.

- A **Zope Installation** is what you get when you compile Zope.

- After you compile Zope, you create a **Zope Instance**. Prior to the invention of buildout, this is where all of the products and packages were manually installed.

- The **ZopeSkel** package is a set of **Paster** templates that allows you to create your own packages and buildouts by answering a set of questions. Paster is a pluggable command-line frontend that has commands to set up package file layouts. The templates provided by Paster are maintained by the community, to keep up with the latest best practices.

Why zc.buildout?

You need a way to organize and deploy your application. The aim of `zc.buildout`, called buildout for short, is to allow you to assemble an environment quickly. Buildout lets you describe your application by using an easy-to-use configuration language. Plus, there are a growing number of recipes that extend buildout to offer even more functionality.

Default settings

When developing Plone sites, you will want to set up a central cache for eggs, downloads, and Zope installations, by using buildout. This will avoid having multiple copies of all of these files for each buildout you install.

In order to set this up, you need to add a `.buildout` directory to your home folder. Inside the `$HOME/.buildout` folder, you can add a file named `default.cfg` with your default settings. Consider the following example:

```
[buildout]
eggs-directory = /path/to/home/.buildout/eggs
download-cache = /path/to/home/.buildout/downloads
zope-directory = /path/to/home/.buildout/zope

[instance]
event-log-level = debug
```

We are telling buildout to put all eggs, downloads, and Zope installations into the `.buildout` folder. This will save us a lot of time if we are working on multiple projects with similar dependencies. In order to use the cache directories, you will need to create them by hand. Here, we create them via the command line:

```
$ cd ~/.buildout
$ mkdir eggs downloads zope
```

> The defaults that you define in the `default.cfg` file only provide values for options that have not been set in your buildout. These settings will not override the settings you make in your `buildout.cfg`.

Buildout quick start

There are a couple of quick ways to get started with a buildout for your Plone project.

The easiest way is to go to the Plone web site (`http://plone.org/products/plone`) and download a buildout-based installer. As of Plone 3.2, all of the installers are buildout-based. When the installation is complete, you will have a buildout that contains everything that you need to run your Plone application.

The second way to get started quickly with a buildout-based project is to use **ZopeSkel**. To use ZopeSkel, you must have `easy_install`. If you do not already have `easy_install` on your system, please read and follow the installation instructions for `easy_install` at `http://peak.telecommunity.com/DevCenter/EasyInstall#installing-easy-install`. Make sure that you are installing `easy_install` into the copy of Python that is powering your Zope instance. Depending on your server configuration, this may or may not be your system-wide Python. Once `easy_install` is set up, run the following command:

```
$ easy_install -U ZopeSkel
```

Once you have installed ZopeSkel, you can see a list of the available templates by using the `paster create` command.

```
$ paster create --list-templates
Available templates:
...
plone3_buildout:  A buildout for Plone 3 projects
```

Using the same command, we can create a buildout from a template. The command will ask us a series of questions and then create the buildout.

```
$ paster create -t plone3_buildout myproject
...
Creating template plone3_buildout
```

Once your buildout has been created, you need to bootstrap it to generate the buildout command:

```
$ cd myproject
$ ls
README.txt  bootstrap.py buildout.cfg products/    src/     var/
$ python2.4 bootstrap.py
Generated script 'bin/buildout'.
```

To see all of the available options and commands for `buildout`, you can run the following command:

```
$ bin/buildout -h
```

You are now ready to build your application by running buildout.

```
$ bin/buildout
Generated script 'bin/instance'.
Generated script 'bin/repozo'.
...
```

When the buildout finishes grabbing all of the pieces of the application, you'll be able to start up your Plone instance. The script will have the same name as your instance part—in our case, `instance`.

```
$ bin/instance fg
```

Cooking with buildout

Buildout gives us the ability to define our application via configuration files. The building blocks of a buildout are **Parts** and **Recipes**.

Parts are the individual pieces that make up the complete application. A part is installed using a recipe. A recipe is a Python egg that knows how to parse the part's options and create the given piece.

There are a many useful buildout recipes available from the Python Package Index that provide a wide range of uses. The recipes can build your application from start to finish.

Buildout configuration

A buildout is configured using a `.ini` like syntax that is based on Python's `ConfigParser` module. The syntax is straightforward, and easy to use.

The configuration is split into sections using **headers**. A header consists of a word surrounded by square brackets. The `[buildout]` section contains the options for the buildout.

Options are defined using the syntax `option-name = value`. You can define multiple values for an option by separating each item with a space. You can also put each value on a separate indented line, as demonstrated in the following `develop-eggs` option:

```
[buildout]
parts = zope2 instance
develop-eggs =
  src/my.package
  src/my.other.package
```

 Indentation is important in buildout configuration files. Options and section names should always start at the beginning of the line. Multiple values need to be consistently indented so that buildout can properly read them.

In the preceding example, we have two options in the `[buildout]` section. The `parts` option has two values, and the `develop-eggs` option has two values. Comments must start at the beginning of the line, as shown in the following code:

```
[buildout]
parts = zope2 instance
develop-eggs =
  src/my.package
# src/my.other.package
  src/my.package2
```

Let's take a look at the following example `buildout.cfg` file that sets up a Plone-ready Zope instance:

```
[buildout]
parts = zope2 instance

find-links =
    http://dist.plone.org
    http://download.zope.org/ppix
    http://download.zope.org/distribution
    http://effbot.org/downloads

[zope2]
recipe = plone.recipe.zope2install
fake-zope-eggs = true
url = http://www.zope.org/Products/Zope/2.10.7/Zope-2.10.7-final.tgz

[instance]
recipe = plone.recipe.zope2instance
user = admin:admin
zope2-location = ${zope2:location}
eggs =
    elementtree
    Plone
```

In this example, we have two parts defined in the `buildout` section. The `zope2` part downloads and compiles Zope for us, while the `instance` part uses the `zope2` part's location and also pulls in all the eggs that are needed by Plone.

Advanced configuration

Buildout gives us some extensions to Python's `ConfigParser` syntax. Each part name can be used in variable substitution. Let's take a look at the `instance` part once again:

```
[instance]
recipe = plone.recipe.zope2instance
user = admin:admin
zope2-location = ${zope2:location}
eggs =
    elementtree
    Plone
```

The substitution syntax is ${<part name>:<option>}. In the above example, we are telling the `instance` part to use the `location` of the `zope2` part as its `zope2-location`.

The substitution syntax can be used anywhere in an option's value. In the following example, we are defining the `instance` user from two variables in the `buildout` section. We are also adding the `products` directory from inside our top-level buildout directory to the `products` option, so that we can develop on old-style Zope 2 products.

```
[buildout]
zope-user = admin
zope-password = 12345

[instance]
user = ${buildout:zope-user}:${buildout:zope-password}
products = ${buildout:directory}/products
```

Debug configuration

Buildout makes it very easy to create a repeatable development environment. The first thing that you can do is to turn on all of the debug options in the `zope.conf` for your instance.

```
[instance]
recipe = plone.recipe.zope2instance
debug-mode = on
verbose-security = on
event-log-level = debug
```

Now, you will see more messages in the console and will be able to change the template code without having to restart the environment. Note that you would not typically have the debug mode turned on in a deployment situation.

There are also some very handy packages that we can use during our development cycle:

```
[instance]
recipe = plone.recipe.zope2instance
...
eggs =
  plone.reload
  Products.PDBDebugMode
  Products.Clouseau
  Products.PrintingMailHost
  Products.DocFinderTab

zcml =
  plone.reload
```

Let's take a look at the packages we've added:

- `plone.reload` gives us a way of updating Zope with the latest Python code without restarting the environment. If you are working on some Python code, you can reload the changes without having to restart Zope. Note that this egg requires a ZCML slug for its `configure.zcml` file, which explains the additional ZCML option described in the previous section. With `plone. reload`, there is a screen registered for the Zope instance that has the UI for 'reloading' the site. This can be found at the following address: `http://localhost:8080/@@reload`.

- `Products.PDBDebugMode` will open up a post-mortem `pdb` (**Python Debugger**) prompt when Zope throws an error, so that you can inspect what is happening. It also gives you a `pdb` view class that allows you to open a `pdb` prompt on any object on the site (for example, visiting `http://localhost:8080/Plone/front-page/@@pdb` will bring you to a `pdb` prompt where `self.context` is the object you called up the view for).

- `Products.Clouseau` is a web-based Python interpreter that can be used to interact with and manipulate the site. This is a friendlier version of `bin/instance debug`.

- `Products.PrintingMailHost` is a product that disables Zope's mailhost so that email messages are sent to the console. This product will save you from those 'oops!' moments if you are working on a site that sends out emails. No real email messages will be sent out when this product is installed.

- `Products.DocFinderTab` adds a **Doc** tab to objects in the ZMI that allows you to see that object's API.

Another great debugging tool is `collective.recipe.omelette`. This tool gives us the ability to have all of our currently-used eggs set up in a folder hierarchy in `parts/omelette` for easy browsing and grepping. You won't have to dig through your whole egg cache to find the information you are looking for.

```
[buildout]
parts = instance omelette

[omelette]
eggs = ${instance:eggs}
```

Version pinning

Once our application has been set up, we need a way to make sure that all of its pieces are using the correct version. By default, buildout will seek out the latest version of a package or recipe (this is called the newest mode; use -N switch of buildout to use non-newest mode). We can tell buildout what versions we want by adding a versions option that points to a section with eggs and version numbers. This is called **pinning**.

```
[buildout]
versions = versions

[versions]
Plone = 3.2
plone.recipe.zope2instance = 2.6
```

We can also define a range of releases to use in the following manner:

```
[buildout]
parts = instance

[instance]
recipe = plone.recipe.zope2instance

eggs =
  Plone >= 3.2, < 3.3dev
```

This tells buildout to get a version of the Plone egg that is more than, or equal to 3.2, but less than 3.3 development. This will keep us in the Plone 3.2.x series.

As you can see, zc.buildout is a very flexible system. It is relatively easier to create new recipes, and you can combine existing recipes in powerful ways. It is especially useful when creating different buildouts for development and deployment environments in a team environment.

 Search PyPI for buildout (http://cheeseshop.python.org/pypi) to find more recipes, or take a look at the source code for some of Plone's own recipes, to understand how recipes are created. For more information on buildout, refer to Martin Aspeli's book, *Professional Plone Development*, or to this tutorial, which can be found at http://plone.org/documentation/tutorial/buildout.

Summary

In this chapter, we have learned:

- Why buildout is an indispensable tool
- How to use buildout from the command line
- How to customize a buildout configuration file
- How to add debugging products into our buildout

Using what we've learned in this chapter, you should be able to set up a repeatable Plone installation using buildout.

14

Find and Install Add-Ons that Expand Plone Functionality

Plone has a rich feature set and meets many needs without additional components. However, you may add new features that meet many special needs by installing add-on components called products.

In this chapter, **Steve McMahon** shows how to find and select add-on products for Plone. We'll also learn how to install them, and review some of the best and most commonly used products.

Background

It seems like every application platform uses a different name for its add-ons: modules, components, libraries, packages, extensions, plug-ins, and more. Add-on packages for the Zope web application server are generally called **products**. A Zope product is a set of Zope or Plone functionality contained in one or more Python modules. Like Plone, add-on products are distributed in source code so that you can always read and examine them. Plone itself is actually a set of tightly-connected Zope products and Python modules.

Plone add-on products can be divided into three major categories:

1. **Skins** or **themes** that change Plone's look and feel, or add visual elements such as portlets. These are typically the simplest of Plone products.
2. Products that add new content types that have specialized functionality. Some are simple extensions of built-in types, while others have custom workflows and behaviors.
3. Products that add to or change the behavior of Plone.

Where to find products

The **Products** section of Plone.org (visit `http://plone.org/products`) is the place to look for Plone products. At the time of this writing, Plone.org contained listings for 765 products and 1,901 product releases.

The Plone products section is built with a Plone product—the **Plone Software Center (PSC)**—that adds content types for projects, software releases, project roadmaps, issue trackers, and project documentation.

Using the Plone product pages

Visiting the Plone product pages for the first time may be a bewildering experience due to the number of available products. However, by specifying a product category and target Plone version, you will quickly narrow down the product selection to the point where it's worth reading the descriptions and following the links to individual product pages.

Product pages typically contain product descriptions, software releases, and a list of available documentation, an issue tracker, a version control repository, and contact resources.

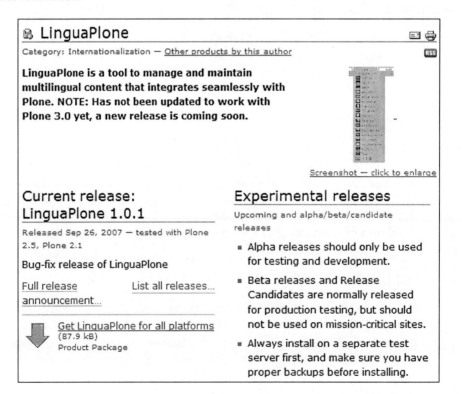

Each release will have release notes, a change log, and a list of Plone versions with which the release has been tested. If the release has a product package, it will be available for download here. Some releases do not have associated software packages. This may either be because the release is still in the planning stage and the listing is primarily meant to document the product's development roadmap, or because the development is still at an early stage and the software is available only from a version-control repository.

The release notes commonly include a list of dependencies, and you should make a special note of these, along with the compatible Plone versions. Many products require the installation of other supporting products. Some require your server or test workstation to have particular system libraries or utilities to be installed.

Product pages may also have links to a variety of additional resources: product-specific **Documentation**, other **Releases** pages, an **Issue tracker**, a **Roadmap** for future development, a contact form for the project, and a version-control repository.

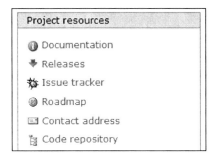

Playing it safe with add-on products

Plone 3 is probably one of the most rigorously-tested open source software packages in existence. While no software is defect-free, Plone's core development team is on the leading edge of software development methodologies, and works under a strong testing culture that requires that they prove their components work correctly before they ever become part of Plone.

Plone's library of add-on products is a very different story. Add-on products are contributed by a diverse community of developers. Some add-on products follow the same development and maintenance methodologies as Plone itself, while others are haphazard experiments. To complicate matters, today's haphazard experiment may be—if it succeeds—next year's rigorously-developed and reliable product. (Most of Plone's core codebase began as add-on products.) Moreover, this year's reliable standby may lose the devotion of its developers and not be upgraded to work with the next version of Plone.

If you're new to the world of open source software, you may be dismayed. Don't be discouraged! It is not hard to evaluate the status of a product, and the Plone community is happy to help. Be encouraged by the evidence of continuous, exciting innovation. Most importantly, stop thinking of yourself as a consumer. Take an interest in the community process, which produces good products. Test some early releases, and file bug reports and feature requests. Participate in, or help document, test, and fund the development of the products that are most important to you.

Product choice strategy

Trying out new Plone add-on products is great fun, but incorporating them into production web sites requires planning and judgment if you're going to have good long-term results.

New versions of Plone pose a particular challenge. Major new releases of Plone don't just add features. With every major version of Plone, the **Application Programming Interface (API)** and presentation templates change. This is not done arbitrarily, and there is usually a good deal of warning before a major change, but it means that the add-on products often need to be updated before they will work with a major new version of Plone.

This means that when a new version of Plone appears on the scene, you won't be able to migrate your Plone site to use it until compatible product versions are available for **all** of the add-on products in use on the site. If you're using mainstream and well-supported products, this may happen very quickly. Many products are upgraded to work with new Plone versions during the beta and release-candidate stages of Plone development. Some products may take longer, and some may not make the jump at all. The products least likely to be updated are often the ones made obsolete by the new functionality.

This creates a somewhat ironic situation when a new version of Plone arrives. The quickest adopters are often those with the least history with the platform. The slowest adopters are sometimes the sites that have invested most heavily in the new features. Consider, as a prime example, Plone.org—a very active, very large, community site—which must be conservatively managed and stick with proven versions of add-on products. Plone.org often does not migrate to a new Plone version until many months after its release.

Is this a problem? Not really—unless you need both the features of the newest Plone version and the functionality of a more slowly-developed add-on product. If that's the case, prepare yourself to make an investment in either time or money to support product development and possibly the writing some custom migration scripts.

If you want to be more conservative, try the following strategies:

- Enjoy testing many products and keeping up with new developments by trying them out on a test server
- Learn the built-in Plone functionality well, and use it in preference to add-on products wherever possible
- Make sure that you have a good understanding of the maturity level and the degree of developer support for the add-on products
- Incorporate the smallest possible number of add-on products into your production sites
- Don't be just a consumer: when you commit to a product, help support it by filing bug reports and feature requests, contributing translations, documentation or code, and answering questions about it on the Plone mailing lists or `#plone` IRC channel

Evaluating a product

Judging the maturity of a Plone product is generally easy. Start with a product's project page on Plone.org. The product page (visit `http://plone.org/products/plone`) may offer you a **Current release** and one or more **Experimental releases**. Anything marked as a current release should be stable on its tested Plone versions. If you need a release to work with an earlier version of Plone as compared to the ones supported by the current release, follow the **List all releases** link.

Releases in the experimental list will be marked as **alpha**, **beta**, or **Release Candidate**. These terms are well-defined:

- **Alpha releases** are truly experimental, and are usually posted in order to get early feedback. Interfaces and implementations are still in a state of flux. Download an alpha release only for testing in an experimental environment, and only for the purposes of previewing new features and giving feedback to developers. Do not plan to keep any content you develop using an alpha release, as there may be no upgrade path to later releases.
- With a **beta release**, feature sets and programming interfaces should be stable or should change incrementally. It's reasonable to start testing the integration of the product with the platform and with other products. Typically, there will be an upgrade path to future releases. Bug reports will be welcome and will help develop the product.
- **Release candidates (RC)** have a fixed feature set and no known major issues. Templates and messages should be complete, so that translators may work on language files with some confidence that their work won't be lost. If you encounter a bug in a release candidate product, please file an issue report immediately.

Products may be re-released repeatedly at any release state. For alpha, beta, and RC releases, each additional release changes the release count, but not the version number. Therefore, 'PloneFormGen 1.2' (Beta release 6) is the sixth beta release of version 1.2 of PloneFormGen. Once a product release reaches current release status, new releases for maintenance will increment the version number by 0.0.1. 'PloneFormGen 1.1.3' is thus the third maintenance release of version 1.1 of that product.

Don't make too much of version numbers or release counts. The release status is a better indicator of maturity.

If your site is mission-critical, don't use beta releases on it. However, if you test carefully before deploying, you may find that some products are ready for live use late in their beta development, on sites where an error or glitch wouldn't be intolerable.

Testing a product

Conscientious Plone site administrators maintain an offline mirror of their production sites on a secondary server — or even a desktop computer — that they may use for testing purposes.

Always test a new product on a test server. Before deploying a product, test it on a server that has precisely the same release level and combination of products in use on your production server. Ideally, test the new product with a copy of the database of your live server. Check the functionality of not only the new product, but also the products you're already using. The latter is particularly important if you're using products that alter the base functionality of Plone or Zope.

Looking to the future

Evaluating product maturity and testing the product will help you judge its current status. But what about the future? What are the signs of a product that's likely to be well-maintained and available for future versions of Plone? There are no guarantees, but here are some signs that experienced Plone integrators look for:

- **Developing in public**: Plone is an open source software. Check if the product is being developed with a public roadmap for the future, and with a public version control repository. Plone.org provides product authors with great tools for indicating release plans, and makes a **Subversion (SVN)** version control repository available to all product authors. Check if the product is using these facilities.

- **Issue tracker status**: Every released product should have a public issue (bug) tracker. Look for it. Check if it's being maintained, and if issues are being actively responded to. The absence of an issue tracker, or lots of old, uncategorized issues, are bad signs.

- **Support for multiple Plone versions**: If a product has been around for a while, check if versions are available for at least a couple of Plone releases. This might be the previous and current releases, or the current and next releases.

- **Internationalization**: Excellent products attract translations.

- **Good development methodologies**: This is the hardest criterion for a non-developer to judge, but a forthcoming version of the Plone Software Center will ask developers to rate themselves on compliance to a set of community standards. My guess is that product developers will be pretty honest about these ratings.

Several of these criteria have something in common. They allow the Plone community to participate in product maintenance and development. The best projects belong to the community, and not to any single author.

One of the best ways to get a quick feel for the quality of an add-on product is to hop on the `#plone` IRC channel and ask. The chances are that you'll run into someone who can share their experiences and offer insight. You may even run into the product author himself or herself!

Installing and testing products

Installing an add-on product requires two steps:

1. Installing the product files on the file system so that they become a part of the Zope instance.

2. Activating the product on a Plone site—we'll call this Plone installation.

Zope installation

The method by which add-on products are integrated into a Zope instance is by undergoing a change, and over the course of Plone 3's lifetime, you're probably going to have to install products using both the old and new techniques. We'll cover both here.

The older style of add-on is based on the original Zope product system. In this model, any specially-structured Python module that exists inside the `products` directory in your Zope instance is installed as a Zope product when Zope starts.

Newer style products are distributed as Python eggs. (Visit `http://peak.telecommunity.com/DevCenter/PythonEggs` for a discussion of eggs, and their working with Python.) The main advantage of this approach is that it encourages a modular style of development, where components are available to multiple packages as a part of the Python library.

Several products, including Plone itself, are currently hybrids: some parts are eggs while other parts are traditional Zope products.

How do you know what type of installation procedure is required? The project's description or release page may tell you, but the best information is nearly always in a `README.txt` or `INSTALL.txt` file distributed with the product.

Downloading and unpacking a product

You already know where to find product packages: in the **Products** section of Plone.org, or on **Product Releases** pages. You can generally download them with a single click. Save them in a workspace where you might store other uninstalled products.

Plone product packages are generally distributed in the form of tarballs—gzip-compressed Unix tape archive (TAR) files—and will have a `tar.gz` or `.tgz` file extension. A few products are in ZIP archive format, and have a `.zip` extension.

Windows users may use a program like WinZip or 7-Zip to unpack both formats. Linux, BSD, and OS X users may use unzip to directly unpack `.zip` files, and will use the following command to unpack `.tgz` and `.tar.gz` files:

```
tar -zxf product_file.tar.gz
```

Always unpack a product package into a working directory first, and not directly into your Zope/Plone install. You're going to want to take a look at the contents before installing the package.

Product packages will generally unpack into a directory with a name similar to that of the product package archive. Look for the `README.txt` file in this directory, and check if there is an `INSTALL.txt` file.

Even the most experienced users should not take it for granted that they know how a product installs. Always read the `README.txt` and (if available) `INSTALL.txt` files. Installation methods and product dependencies may change with product versions.

These text files may specify **dependencies**: requirements that must be satisfied for a product to work. Sometimes, these are specific Python, Zope, or Plone versions; sometimes Python or system utilities or libraries; and sometimes other products.

The texts should also let you know whether your new product requires a traditional (`products` directory) install, an egg installation, or a hybrid of the two.

Traditional product installation

Remember that a traditional Plone (or Zope) product is just a specially-structured Python module located in a special `products` directory. Typically, these products are distributed in archives that contain a single product directory. For example, you might download Ploneboard as a single archive file such as `Ploneboard-1.0.tar.gz`. The archive unpacks this into a single directory, `Ploneboard`. Zope-level installation of a product like this is simple:

1. Move the directory that you created when you unpacked the archive into the `products` directory or your Zope/Plone *instance*.

2. Check the ownership and permissions.

3. Restart the Zope server.

Finding the Instance products directory

Where is your Zope/Plone *instance*? A single Zope installation may be used with several running Zope servers, which we call **instances**. An instance directory contains the `parts`, `var`, and `products` subdirectories for a given Zope server.

If you've installed a standalone Plone with the Unified Installer, the instance directory will be:

`/opt/Plone-3.1/zinstance`

or:

`~/Plone-3.1/zinstance`

depending on whether you installed as root or as a normal user. If you installed a ZEO cluster, substitute `zinstance` with `zeocluster`.

In a Windows installation, the instance directory will usually be:

`X:\Plone 3\Data`

Where `X` is the installation drive.

In a Mac installation created with the binary OS X installer, it will be at:

`/Applications/Plone-3.1.x/Instance`

In all of these cases, you should find a `products` subdirectory within the `instance` directory. Copy your product into it.

Some 'bundle' distributions may contain multiple products in a single archive file. Check the `README.txt` or `INSTALL.txt`, but the usual procedure will be to copy all of the directories that you created when unpacking the archive into the `instance\products` directory.

Checking ownership and permissions

If you are running Zope and Plone on a Unix-like machine, and you ran a root installation (that is, you were either logged in as root, or used 'sudo' when you installed Plone), you need to make sure that the ownership and permissions of the new product directories are correct. The key is that the user identity used to run Zope must be able to write to these directories. (This is so that Zope will be able to create compiled versions of the new Python files.) If you used either the Unified Installer or the OS X binary installer, the installer will have set Zope up to run under the `plone` user identity. You may satisfy the owner/permission requirements by using `chown` to give the `plone` user ownership of the new directory. The following command will change the ownership of the Ploneboard directory and all its contents to the `plone` user:

`chown -R plone Ploneboard`

Restarting Zope

Zope only looks for new products when it starts or restarts. When you've added a new product to the file system, restart Zope to make sure that your product is registered.

Eggs

Plone 3 products may be delivered in whole, or in part, as Python eggs. Eggs are packaged Python libraries that know about their own dependencies and have simple installation procedures.

If your Zope/Plone installation is buildout-based—likely the case with Plone 3.2 and above—you may install egg-based products by adding lines to your `buildout.cfg` file and running buildout.

For example, to add LinguaPlone, which is officially named `Products.LinguaPlone`, find the eggs section near the top of your `buildout.cfg` file and add the product name on a line of its own to the indented eggs section as follows:

```
eggs =
    Plone
    Products.LinguaPlone
```

Some add-ons—usually those with names not beginning with `Products`—require an extra step: the specification of a ZCML slug in the `zcml` section. To add `plone.reload`, for example, you would add the product name in two places as follows:

```
eggs =
    Plone
    plone.reload
...
zcml =
    plone.reload
```

After making these configuration file changes, stop Zope, back up everything, and run `bin/buildout`. The add-ons and all dependencies will automatically be downloaded and installed.

Plone installation

Installing a product for Zope does not automatically install it for use with your Plone site. You must take an additional step to add the product in Plone. Although it may seem like extra work, this is actually a good thing. Remember that you may be running several Plone sites, in a single Zope instance. The Plone product installation step means that each may have its own mix of Plone products, out of a common pool of Zope products.

To add a product to a given Plone site, log in and navigate to **Site Setup**. Choose the **Add-on Products** configlet. If your Zope-level install succeeds, you should see your new product listed in the **Products available for install** section. Select the checkbox beside it, and press the **Install** button. The listing for the new product should move to the **Installed products** section within a few seconds.

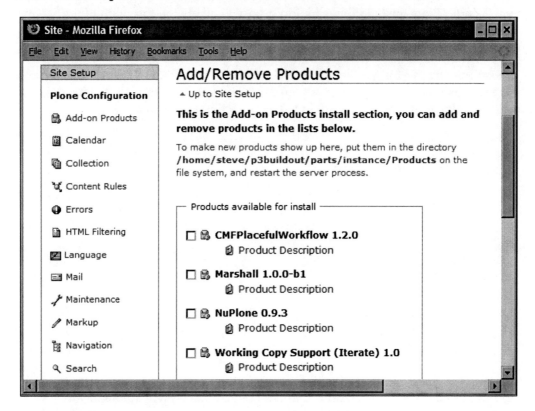

Installation problems

When something goes wrong in a product installation, the first place it's usually noticed is when you check the **Add-on Products** configlet and don't find the product listed. If this happens to you, first ask yourself a couple of questions:

- Did I remember to restart Zope after the filesystem installation? Remember, your new product won't be available until after Zope has been restarted and the Product directory has been reloaded.

- Is this actually a Plone product? Some products, for example, DocFinderTab and many field and widget products are Zope products and not Plone products. They supplement the facilities of the Zope application server, but don't need to be installed on a Plone site directly.

You can check if a product has been loaded by Zope via the **Zope Management Interface (ZMI)**. You may already know how to view the ZMI, but if not, log into Plone and go to **Site Setup**. Select the **Zope Management Interface** and navigate to the Zope application server root view by clicking on the slash (*/*) following **Plone Site at**. Then, click on **Control Panel** and **Product Management**. You'll see a long list of products. Look for the new one!

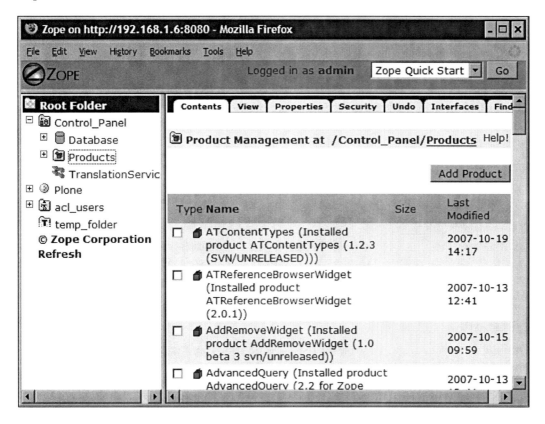

If your new product is listed, consider again the possibility that it may be a Zope-level product that does not contain a Plone-specific component. If it really is a Plone product, then some error probably occurred when the Plone product installation component (often called the **QuickInstaller**) tried to load the product installation code.

If the product is not listed, then an error nearly certainly occurred when Zope tried to load it. In either of these cases, you should first review the product requirements (or dependencies) specified in the README.txt or INSTALL.txt file.

If you'd like to debug this, start with your `event.log` log file. This will be in the `log` directory of your Zope instance. Event log files may be very noisy, though, and it may simplify your hunt to start your Zope instance running in the 'foreground' mode. This is a special operating mode, where messages are issued to the terminal window rather than just being added to the log file. The great advantage of starting in the foreground mode is that, in this mode, Zope will halt on an error loading a product. This makes it likely that your error will be the last item in the messages preceding the halt.

To start Zope in foreground mode, use the command:

```
./instance fg
```

To start Zope, the usual startup command is `instance start`. (Use `zopectl` rather than `instance` if your installer did not create an `instance` command.)

If you're using a ZEO cluster, you'll probably need to stop one of your clients, and then restart that client in foreground mode.

Widely-used Plone products

Let's take a quick look at some of Plone's most useful products, organized by the general classes of problem they address. This list leaves out many favorites and mainstays, in the interest of showing variety and new approaches.

Integration

One of the most common problems faced by a Plone integrator is sharing authentication (login IDs and passwords) with other systems. A common solution is to use **LDAP, Lightweight Directory Access Protocol**, for a shared authentication system. OpenLDAP, Microsoft's **Active Directory**, and Apple's **Open Directory** are common LDAP implementations.

PloneLDAP provides Plone integration with LDAP. You may mix users, groups, and member properties from your LDAP database with other Plone **Pluggable Authentication Service (PAS)** sources.

Plone 3 also comes with **OpenID** support ready to be enabled. Check out `OpenID.net` for more information about this distributed authentication system.

Integration with file system-based content is another common integration problem. All Plone content is typically stored in a **Zope Object Database (ZODB)**, and that presents a challenge if you need to serve content maintained on the file system (or kept out of the ZODB for other reasons, such as avoiding binary bloat). **Reflecto** is an amazingly slick solution. Like many great products, Reflecto looks simple, and is easy to install and use, and does a sophisticated job of mapping file-system file types to MIME types, and can even index many file types.

Content management

Let's look at a few products that help with common content management chores.

Press Room and **Plone Help Center** are good examples of products that provide specialized content types.

Many organizational web sites need a polished repository for press releases and clips. Press Room provides basic content types for both of these, and a `Press Room` folder that organizes them. There's nothing complex about what Press Room does; it just does it well, and saves you a lot of work in the process.

Plone Help Center is the product behind the **Documentation** section of Plone.org. It's a simple knowledge-based package with content types for FAQ items, short how-to's, multipage tutorials, multisection manuals, and tutorial videos.

If your web site's content is licensed under a single copyright or license policy, life is easy (at least in that regard). But some sites need to manage content appearing under several licenses. If that's your situation, the **ContentLicensing** product will ease your burden. This product allows you to manage multiple licensing policies and control their application, from site defaults, to particular site sections, down to individual page licenses.

As a site ages, you'll increasingly need to move content from its original location. Ideally, this should be done without breaking old URLs. Install **RedirectionTool**, and you'll be able to establish in-site aliases for content. Requests for those aliases will be automatically redirected to the new document home. This is another product in heavy use on Plone.org.

Community

A great content management system is, in its own way, the ultimate community feature because it makes it possible to build a well-structured web site from distributed contributions, and to find the content once it's on the site. In addition, Plone has many add-on products that promote community information sharing. And, don't forget that **wiki**-style markup is built-in—thanks to a product named **Wicked** that began as a popular add-on and subsequently became part of the Plone core.

PloneBoard is your best choice for bulletin-board-style structured discussion.

If you need to maintain a community calendar, consider the **Plone4Artists Calendar** product, which supplements the basic Plone event content type by adding much-improved calendar views and **iCal** import and export.

Need integrated emailing lists? Check if **Listen,** which was still in beta-release at the time of writing, has matured. Listen is being championed by Openplans.org, which makes heavy use of it, and it makes great use of Zope 3 component architecture technologies.

A truly great **blog** product has eluded the Plone community, perhaps because Plone provides so many out-of-the-box key blogging components that there's been no consistent push for more. If you're just after a simple blog with date sorting and an RSS feed, you don't need any add-on product for this, or may find the very lightweight **Scrawl** product ideal. However, if you need cool blogging functions such as trackback pings, MetaWeblogAPI, aggregation into planets, or topics with images, take a look at **Quills.** Quills has had its ups and downs as a product, but has been the beneficiary of some recent loving care that promises a good future for the product.

Feedback

For structured feedback, Plone has a couple of well-supported, solid products.

Poi is an issue-tracker product, and is used on Plone.Org for the product issue trackers in the Plone Software Center. Poi is not meant to be a replacement for database-oriented and SVN-integrated project management systems like **Trac**. Rather, Poi is lightweight, easy to use, well-integrated with Plone, and integrates easily with other products.

Well-behaved forms are some of the toughest parts of web design. They need to look good, incorporate help, validate data, do useful things with input, and be secured against easy repurposing by hackers. **PloneFormGen** is a general-purpose form generator that makes use of the form styles, widgets, and validators already built into Plone to allow you to easily create the web forms that can send via email, and/or save, user input. PloneFormGen allows you to create form folders, populate forms with fields that act like content objects, and add action handlers such as mailers, data-savers, and thank-you pages.

Page composition

One of the most common questions on the `#plone` IRC channel is about how to incorporate the presentation of multiple content items onto a single page—typically, the home page of a site. Plone 3's more flexible portlet facility will help answer this question for some, but others will still need a more flexible approach to identify page areas and fill them with content, such as site news, obtained from various parts of the site.

Products that do this sort of composite page construction are necessarily dependent on the Plone version, and there have been one or more product solutions for each of the recent major versions of Plone.

Collage appears to be the current leader for filling this role in Plone 3. It makes good use of the new component architecture and even supports in-line content editing of collage elements.

Media

The **Plone4Artists** project (visit `http://plone4artists.org/`), has been providing great leadership for integrating rich audio and video media into Plone. Two of its products, **Plone4Artists Audio** and **Plone4Artists Video**, are not only good products for handling audio and video, but also point to a new pattern for Plone products. Using Zope 3 component architecture facilities, these products add functionality without proliferating content types.

When Plone4Artists Audio is installed, for example, and you want to upload an MP3 or OGG audio file, you just upload it by creating a new Plone file object. The file object, with the P4A support, is smart enough to recognize that it's not just a file, but an audio file with metadata such as artist and album. The file is then displayed in Plone using an embedded audio player, and showing the appropriate audio metadata.

Want to create a **podcast**? Just mark a folder or collection as an audio container via a new item on the actions menu. The folder is then presented as an audio collection, complete with RSS feed.

Plone4Artists Video does the same thing for video files, but adds an extra twist. Because video files, due to their large size and bandwidth demands, are often served elsewhere, P4A Video extends the link item by allowing you to activate links to Google Video, YouTube, and other video repositories, as video links. The link items are then displayed using embedded video players.

Managing images? There are several Plone products that provide photo gallery functionality. If you don't really need their special functions, you may be better off sticking to Plone's built-in folder gallery view. **Image Repository**, though, is much more than a photo gallery: it extends the idea of content management to images. Using this product, you can organize thousands of images by keyword and then browse the keywords as if they were hierarchically-organized. Image Repository is useful throughout your site because it extends the Kupu visual editor to allow you to locate images by keyword.

E-commerce

GetPaid is unique among Plone e-commerce products, and deserves your attention if you want to sell items or site content. Visit the project web site at `http://www.plonegetpaid.com/` to get an idea of the tremendous support and community this project has drawn. GetPaid allows you to mark any of the content of your site as payable. Shopping cart and payment processors complete the transaction.

Mashups

Mashup is **Web 2.0** jargon for presenting the web content from a third-party, for example a Google Maps map view, in a web page alongside your own content. We already saw an example of a mashup when discussing Plone4Artists Video, which allows you to put a viewer for a Google or YouTube video on a page.

The **Maps** product puts a Google Maps map view on a page, complete with location pointers. Using this is as simple as putting a set of location objects in a folder and then setting the folder view to show the map. Maps zooms and centers the map based on the locations. You can also use a Plone collection to gather location objects and then show them in a map view, which makes Maps a sort of lightweight Geographic Information System. To use Maps, you'll need a Google Maps API key, which is generally free.

windowZ provides an old-fashioned sort of mashup. It shows another web page inside an XHTML iFrame in your Plone page. That may not win you any awards for Web 2.0 coolness, but it will solve a surprising variety of web integration problems quickly. windowZ will even index the content of the iFrame-linked web site.

Internationalization

One of Plone's great strengths is internationalization. With Plone interface translations for many languages, internal use of Unicode, and a default UTF-8 character set, Plone is ready to produce a web site in most languages. But, what if you need to support content in multiple languages on the same web site? **LinguaPlone** to the rescue! Chapter 19 covers the use of LinguaPlone to manage multilingual content in detail.

Development and examples

Soon, you may wish to solve problems that aren't covered by any existing Plone products. There are several add-on products that aid the would-be Plone developer. These range from code examples, to API inspection tools, to code generators.

Examples

Martin Aspeli's **RichDocument** code example accompanied a tutorial entitled *RichDocument: Creating content types the Plone 2.1 way*, and has served as a canonical example for many of us developing new content types for Plone. Don't be deceived by the 'Plone 2.1' title. Martin has been continually updating the code examples to work with new versions of Plone. The **B-Org (Base Organization)** example product has served a similar function for the use of component architecture for more complex applications such as collaborative workspaces.

API exploration

If you're developing with Plone, you know you can always read the source code to understand how a given bit of functionality works. However, it can often be a daunting chore to figure out where to start reading. Fortunately, there are a couple of excellent products that make use of the introspective power of Python to allow you to explore the methods and properties of content objects, along with their documentation strings and security declarations.

DocFinderTab adds a tab to the Zope Management Interface that allows you to explore the class hierarchy of a content object. You can expand the display for any class, to see class method declarations and their security and document strings.

Clouseau uses AJAX techniques to allow you to open an interactive Python prompt from inside Plone. As you type, Clouseau helps you with identifier completion, and shows you documentation strings and class attributes. You may even change objects and commit the changes. All of this would be a terrible security hole but for the fact that Clouseau only works when you're running Zope in debug mode.

Code generators

Although code generator projects aren't formally products, in the sense of running as a Plone extension, they are available in the `Plone.Org/products` area.

ArchGenXML allows you to model new Plone content types in **Unified Modeling Language (UML)** and generates an Archetypes-based product ready for Plone installation.

ZopeSkel is a Zope-oriented extension to the Python code skeleton generator, **paster**. One of ZopeSkel's options allows it to produce a 'plone3_theme' product skeleton that has a solid basis for starting a Plone skin or theme product project. If you've worked on skins for the earlier versions of Plone, you may have used the excellent **DIYPloneStyle** code generator to create your product skeleton. ZopeSkel fills the same niche in Plone 3.

It's amazingly easy to add international message translation features, often called **i18n**, to a Plone product. If you're developing a widely-useful Plone product, you should do so. Creating and maintaining the language translation files, though, is never easy. **i18nDude** helps a lot. It scans your Plone product code and templates and automatically generates the base translation files. It also helps to keep translation files in sync. For the editing of actual language files, take a look at **Poedit**, at `www.poedit.net`. Poedit is not a Plone product, but it has been enthusiastically embraced by the Plone i18n team.

Summary

In this chapter, we have learned:

- That Plone add-on modules or extensions are available in bundles called **products**
- How to use the Plone.org product pages to find add-on products for Plone
- Strategies for using and choosing products wisely
- How to install and test a product
- About several of the most popular and useful Plone products

By using what you have learned in this chapter, you should be ready to start enhancing the functionality of your Plone site.

15
Build Forms

Many web sites, even very simple ones, include forms for users to submit information to the site. Forms can include feedback requests, sign-up sheets, resource requests and reservations, quizzes, surveys, and SQL database updates.

PloneFormGen is an add-on product for Plone that makes it fast and easy for you to build simple forms for your web site. PloneFormGen assumes that you have a basic familiarity with standard HTML forms. For a quick refresher on HTML forms, visit: `http://www.w3schools.com/html/html_forms.asp`.

In this chapter, **Jon Stahl** will show you how to:

- Install PloneFormGen
- Build a basic form
- Configure "Action Adapters" to process submitted form data
- Create "Overrides" to make your forms more dynamic

Installing PloneFormGen

PloneFormGen is an optional add-on product for Plone, which means that you must download and install it separately from Plone itself. You can download PloneFormGen from: `http://plone.org/products/ploneformgen`, but for the purposes of this chapter, we will install PloneFormGen using buildout.

As of the time of writing, the current version of PloneFormGen for Plone 3 is version 1.2.5. Versions of PloneFormGen before version 1.2 are NOT compatible with Plone 3, and you should not use them.

PloneFormGen depends on a set of underlying products called **ScriptableFields**. If you're not using buildout, you need to download the **PloneFormGen | ScriptableFields** bundle, which includes both the PloneFormGen and the ScriptableFields products. Buildout will include them by default.

To install PloneFormGen, we need to modify the `buildout.cfg` file located in our buildout. You will find your buildout in **Applications | Plone** or **Products | Plone**, depending on your operating system or your local setup. Modify the `buildout.cfg` file by including the PloneFormGen egg, as shown in the following code:

```
# Eggs
# ----
# Add an indented line to the eggs section for any Python
# eggs or packages you wish to include.
#
eggs =
    Plone
...
    Products.PloneFormGen
```

Note that PloneFormGen lives in the magical Products namespace, which means that Plone recognizes it automatically, without requiring additional changes to our `buildout.cfg` file. Next, we need to stop Zope/Plone, and then run `buildout`, by issuing the following command:

```
./bin/buildout
```

Once `buildout` has finished running, you should restart your Zope instance, by issuing the following command:

```
./bin/instance fg
```

You should now be able to navigate to **Site Setup | Add/Remove Products** and see PloneFormGen listed there. (The ScriptableFields products are "behind the scenes" products, and won't appear in your **Add/Remove Products** menu.)

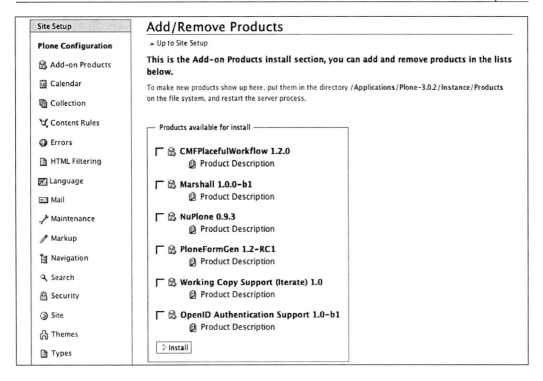

Next, select the checkbox next to PloneFormGen, and then click on the **Install** button.

Congratulations! You've now installed PloneFormGen into your Plone site, and you're ready to go ahead and build your first form.

Creating a form

One of the most appealing qualities of PloneFormGen is the way it lets you build forms using the basic Plone content creation skills that you've already learned.

The basic steps for creating a form are:

1. Add a **Form Folder**.
2. Configure the basic properties of your form.
3. Add and edit fields in your form.
4. Configure one or more action adapters to handle the data that your form collects.

Adding a Form Folder

A **Form Folder** is PloneFormGen's basic container for a form. It will contain other content objects that represent the fields that make up your form, along with objects that control how your form is processed. (In Plone, content objects that contain other content objects are referred to as "folderish" objects; hence the name **Form Folder**.)

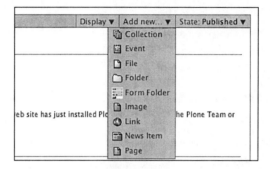

To add a **Form Folder** to your Plone site, go to the place in your site where you wish to add the form, and then click on the **Add new...** menu and choose **Form Folder** from the drop-down list.

Configure the basic properties of your form

You'll now be able to configure the basic properties of your form. This screen has very detailed help text for each field. We won't repeat them all here, but will simply note a few of the less-obvious tips.

- Like most Plone content objects, **Form Folders** have a **Title** and a **Description**.
- All forms have a **Submit** button, which submits the form for processing. Forms can have an optional **Reset** button, which clears all of the data entered into the form. In modern practice, **Reset** buttons are generally not used, and are thus disabled by default in PloneFormGen. You can give these buttons any label (human-readable text) you like.
- **Action Adapters** handle the forms after they are submitted. PloneFormGen includes a **Mailer Adapter** by default, which is capable of emailing form data to designated recipients. We'll learn more about configuring this adapter, and using other action adapters, later in this chapter.
- A **Thanks Page** is the page that users land on after successfully submitting the form. Again, PloneFormGen ships with a default Thanks Page, which you can customize, replace, or supplement.
- The **Form Prologue** and **Form Epilogue** fields let you insert chunks of HTML before and after your form.

All of the tabs are standard Plone tabs, except for one—the **Overrides** tab. We will cover this tab later.

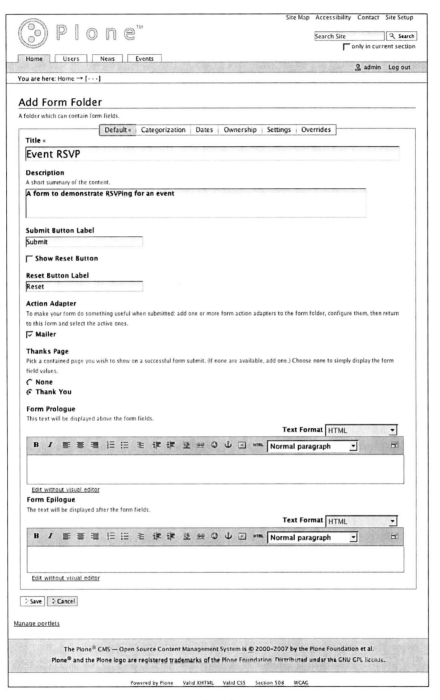

Adding and editing form fields

Once we've created our **Form Folder**, we are ready to add new fields to our form, or edit existing ones in it.

PloneFormGen pre-populates each **Form Folder** with a few fields that comprise a simple comment form. This default form, with a few minor edits to the description, appears as shown in the following screenshot:

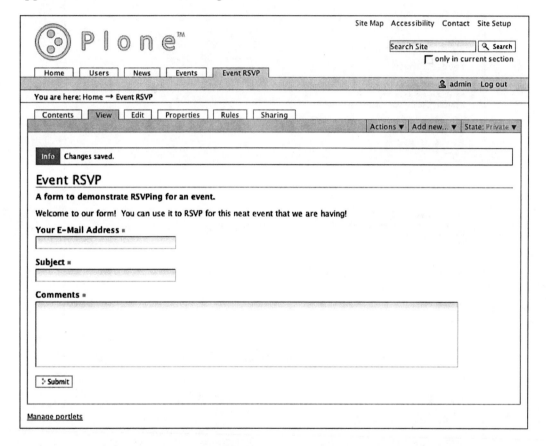

> **Key concepts for editing forms**
> - The entire form is a "folderish" object called a **Form Folder**
> - Each field in your form is a content object inside the **Form Folder**
> - You can group fields by placing them in a **Fieldset** folder
> - The action adapters for processing form data, and **Thank You** pages, are also content objects inside a **Form Folder**
> - The form renders fields based on their order in the **Form Folder**

To start editing your form, click on the **Contents** tab to see the contents of your **Form Folder**:

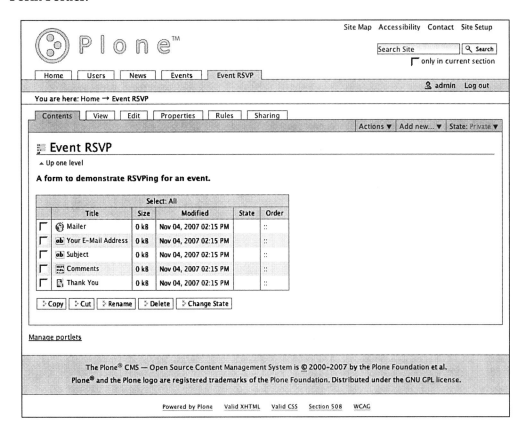

The default form contains:

- A **Mailer Adapter**: responsible for emailing form submissions to a site manager
- Three **form fields**: **Your E-Mail Address**, **Subject**, and **Comments**
- A **Thanks Page** named **Thank You**

To add a new field to your form, click the **Add New...** menu item. PloneFormGen gives you a wide array of fields and other objects that you can add to your form. Most of these are different types of data fields. The most commonly-used ones are as follows:

- **String Field**: for simple one-line text entry, for example, first name, last name, and so on
- **Text Field**: for longer blocks of text

- **Boolean Field**: for true or false responses
- **Selection Field**: for letting users choose one item from a predefined list
- **Multi-Select Field**: for letting users choose multiple items from a predefined list

The following screenshot shows all of the possible field types:

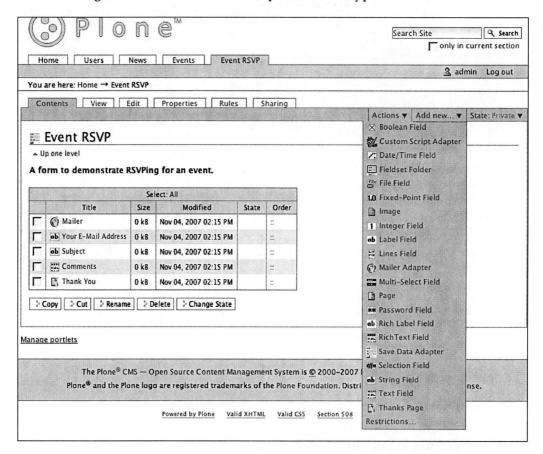

 A complete guide to all of PloneFormGen's basic field types can be found at: http://plone.org/products/ploneformgen/documentation/reference/fields-and-objects.

Choose **String Field** to add a simple text input box to your form, as shown in the following screenshot:

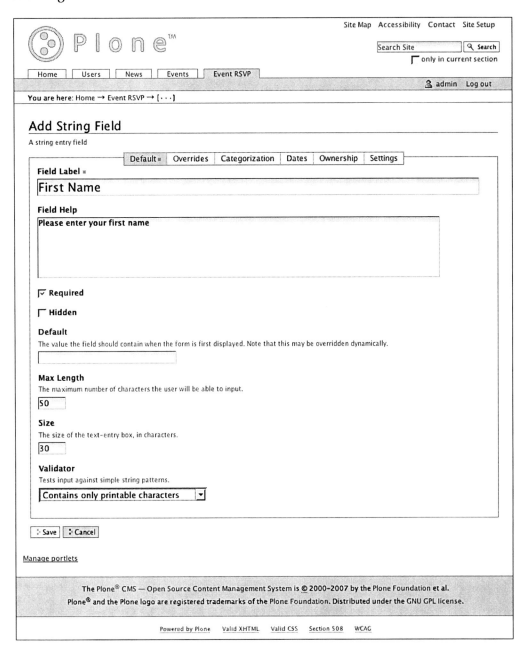

On this screen, you'll see all of the configuration options for your new string field.

You can optionally select a **validator** to ensure that the data user enters into this field matches one of the predefined validation patterns that PloneFormGen provides. This can help to ensure that users don't enter incorrectly-formatted or bogus data into your forms.

Keep the default values, or enter some new values, and then click on **Save** to save and view your new field:

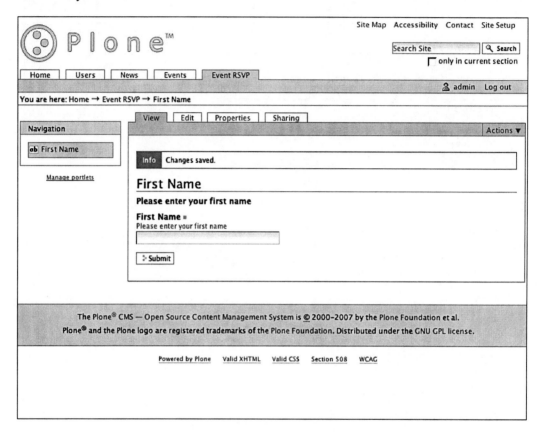

To view your entire form, click on **Event RSVP** in the breadcrumbs.

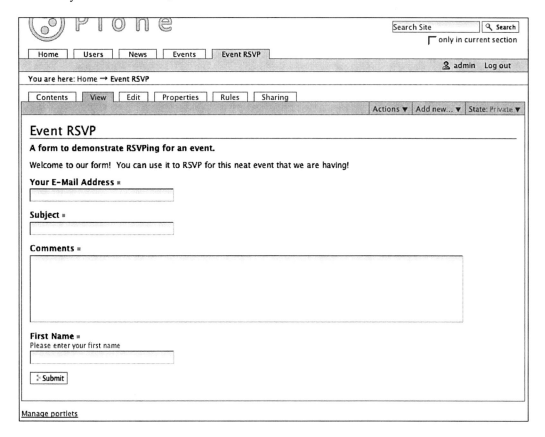

You will see that your new field, **First Name**, is visible at the bottom of the form. The red dot indicates that your field is a required field.

If you want to place the field in a different location on your form, click on **Contents**, and then drag-and-drop the field to the desired location on your form by using the arrow indicators in the rightmost column.

Adding selection fields and multi-select fields

Selection fields and **multi-select fields** are among the most commonly-used types of form fields. They allow users to select from among a predefined set of values, by using checkboxes, menus, or option buttons.

Let's try adding a selection field, which lets the user choose one value from a list. Go to your form-in-progress and choose menu option **Add New... | Selection Field**.

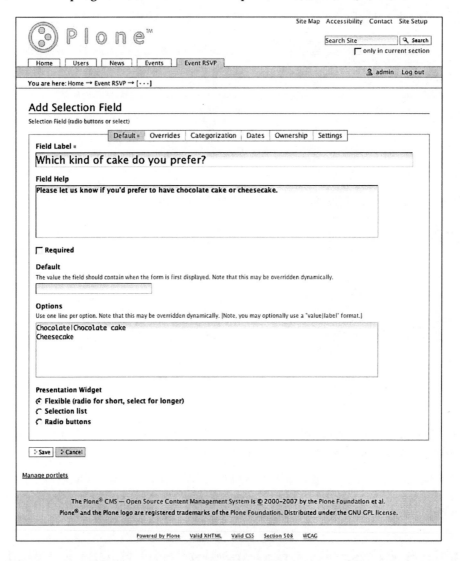

As with the string field, you can provide a title and some help text, choose whether the field is required, and set a default value for the field.

You can then enter the answer choices in the **Options** box. To have the form save a different value for the field than the value displayed to and selected by the user, enter it in the format, value | label. For example, to show the user the choice 'Chocolate Cake' but to save the value as simply 'Chocolate', you would enter **Chocolate | Chocolate Cake** as one of your options.

You can also choose which widget the form will use to render your selection field: a drop-down selection list, or a set of option buttons. You can also select **Flexible**, which will let PloneFormGen choose for you, based on the number of available options.

A **Multi-select field** lets the user choose one or more items from a predefined list of values. To include a Multi-select field, to your form-in-progress, and then select menu option **Add New… | Multi-Select Field**.

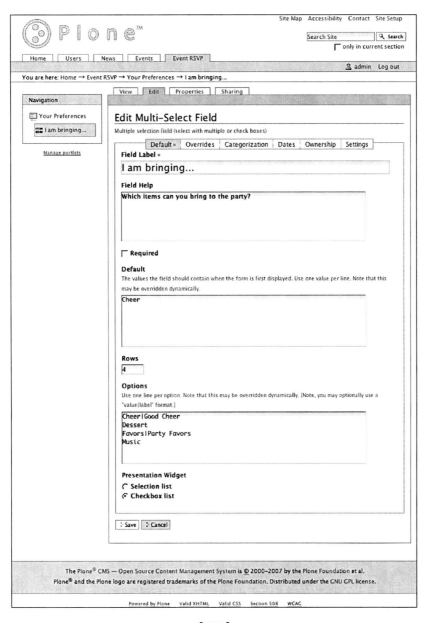

Multi-select fields are quite similar to selection lists. You can choose a selection list widget or a checkbox list; the latter tends to be easier to use.

 If you want to include a default value for which you've provided an alternative label, you should refer to it by the value, not by the label. In the previous example, we've set the default value to **Cheer**, not **Good Cheer** or **Cheer | Good Cheer**.

Click the **Save** button, and then navigate back to your form. It should now look roughly like the example in the following screenshot:

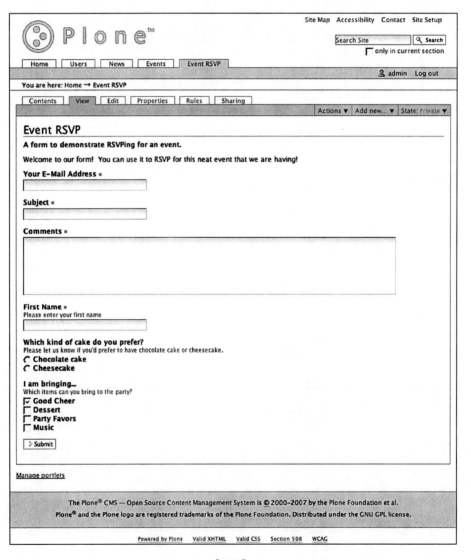

Let's go ahead and remove some of the default fields that PloneFormGen provides, and re-order the fields that remain into a more sensible order:

1. Click on the **Contents** tab, and then select the checkboxes next to the **Subject** and the **Comment** fields.

2. Click the **Delete** button at the bottom of the folder listing to delete these fields from your form.

3. Drag-and-drop the **Your E-Mail Address** field to appear immediately after the **First Name** field.

The **Contents** tab of your form should now look like this:

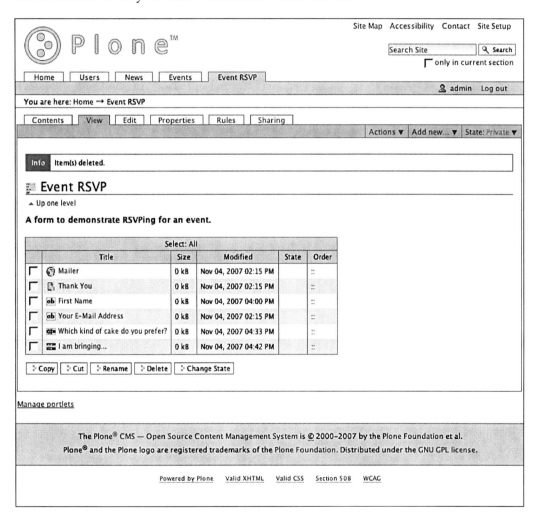

Finally, we can create a fieldset to group two of our fields together:

1. Add a **Fieldset Folder** to your form.

2. Give it the title **Your Preferences**, and then click the **Save** button.

3. Navigate back to your form and click on the **Contents** tab.

4. Select the checkboxes next to the **Which kind of cake would you prefer** field and the **I am bringing...** field, and then click the **Cut** button located below the folder listing.

5. Click on the **Your Preferences** fieldset folder that you've just created, and then click on the **Paste** button to complete the process of moving your fields inside the **Fieldset Folder**.

The **Contents** tab of your new **Fieldset Folder** should now appear as shown in the following screenshot:

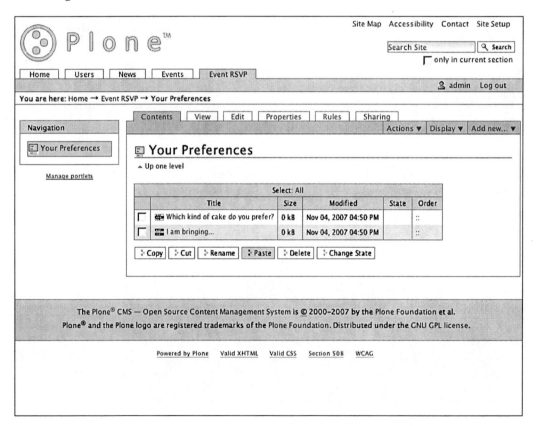

Your complete form should now look like this:

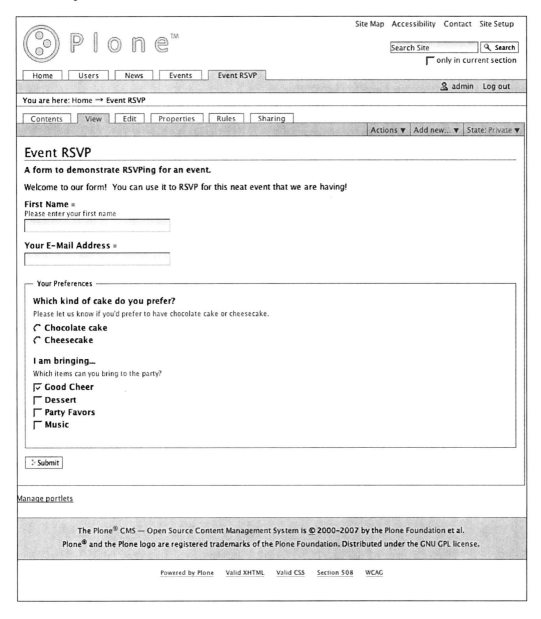

Congratulations, you've now got a simple, useful form! To make it accessible to the public, use the **State** drop-down menu to publish it.

Next, we'll demonstrate how to configure the appropriate adapters to handle form data.

Action Adapters

PloneFormGen uses **Action Adapters** to process form data. PloneFormGen ships with three kinds of adapters—a **Mailer Adapter**, which emails form data to designated users; a **Save Data Adapter**, which saves form data in Plone for later viewing and downloading; and a **Custom Script Adapter**, which lets you write short Python scripts to handle form data.

Mailer Adapter

A **Mailer Adapter** emails submitted form data to one or more recipients. If you have GPG encryption software (see http://www.gpg.org) installed on your server, you can encrypt these emails before they are sent.

The sample form that PloneFormGen automatically creates includes a simple Mailer Adapter, named **Mailer**. You can find it in the **Contents** tab of your form; click on it to view it.

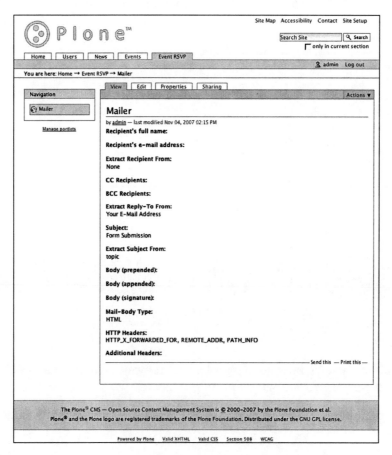

The view of a Mailer Adapter is very plain, as site users never see it. It is simply a summary of configuration settings. Click on the **Edit** tab to edit it.

As with most other PloneFormGen edit forms, the fields of a Mailer Adapter have very descriptive help text.

You can have multiple Mailer Adapter forms if you want to send different emails to different recipients. For example, you could configure one Mailer Adapter to send a confirmation email to the user, and another to send the results to a site administrator.

Make sure that you configure a recipient for any Mailer Adapters that you create, including the default Mailer Adapter!

Unless you specify a recipient, PloneFormGen will try to mail the form input to the owner of the form. If the form owner does not have an email address, the input will be mailed to the site owner. This may not be your intention.

If there're no configured recipients in a mailer, and neither the form owner nor the site owner has an email addresses, PloneFormGen will display an error message. In addition, you should make sure that you have set up a mail server in your site's Mail control panel configlet.

Save Data Adapter

PloneFormGen's **Save Data Adapter** saves form data in your Plone site, and allows you to view it and download it in either tab-delimited format or CSV format. Either of the formats can easily be used in most spreadsheet or desktop database programs.

To add a Save Data Adapter to your form, select menu option
Add New... | Save Data Adapter.

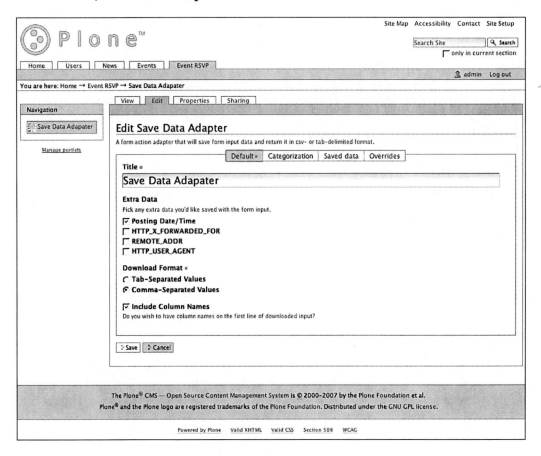

On this screen, you can choose to optionally save some additional fields from the
user's browser session, choose the download format for the saved data, and specify
whether or not to include column names with the downloaded data.

The **Saved Data** tab shows you the raw saved data from your form, if you have any.

Set some options, click the **Save** button, and you're all set!

Custom Script Adapter

A **Custom Script Adapter** is an action adapter that lets you write a short Python
script to handle form data. You'll have to have some knowledge of Python to take
advantage of this.

You can use this kind of script to create content objects, communicate with an SQL database, or manipulate the data before it is processed by other action adapters. (Action adapters are processed in the order in which they appear in the form folder.)

Custom Script Adapters are just a convenient form of **Python Scripts**. Python Scripts are usually added and edited through the Zope Management Interface, and the script adapter saves you having to carry out the ZMI steps and the need to specify a form override.

For more information on Python scripting, see the *Advanced Zope Scripting* chapter of the *Zope Book*, which is available at http://www.plope.com/Books/2_7Edition/ScriptingZope.stx.

Overrides

PloneFormGen **Overrides** allow you to add simple programming logic to form folders, fields, and action adapters. Overrides make PloneFormGen extremely versatile.

Let's take a look at field overrides first. For most fields, you can change the field's default, validation, and display. You'll find the override settings in the **Overrides** fieldset on the **Edit** tabbed page.

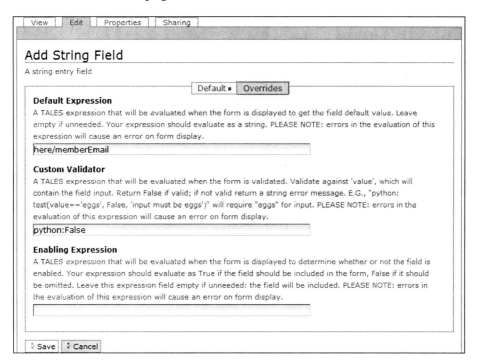

Nearly all of PloneFormGen's override settings are specified using **TALES** expressions. TALES is the same **Template Attribute Language Expression Syntax** used in Zope/Plone templates. You can find an overview of TALES in the *Zope Book*, which is available at `http://www.plope.com/Books/2_7Edition/AppendixC.stx#1-10`.

There are several excellent how-to's and tutorials on using overrides in the PloneFormGen documentation section, which is available at `http://plone.org/products/ploneformgen/documentation`, so we won't cover them in detail here.

In addition to controlling field defaults, validation, and display, override expressions can be used to control:

- **Form Folder** multi-field setup, success actions, and CSS and JavaScript headers
- **Action Adapter** execution
- **Mailer Adapter** addressing

Form folder setup and success overrides are commonly used in conjunction with Python Scripts for external database record entry and update. A popular tutorial in the PloneFormGen documentation section details the use of PloneFormGen for SQL database record creation and update. This tutorial is available at `http://plone.org/products/ploneformgen/documentation/tutorial/sql-crud`.

Configuration

PloneFormGen provides a configlet in the Plone control panel (accessible via **Site Setup**). You can allow or grant various PloneFormGen-related permissions to different user roles in your site, change the default email settings, and edit the default email template.

The permission/role mapping is a particularly important configuration option for site administrators. PloneFormGen uses these settings to hide many advanced or potentially risky options from users who don't have the site manager's role. Non-managers, for example, may not set overrides, add Custom Script Adapters, or edit templates in the default configuration. Be careful about extending permissions for the TALES template or Python Fields, as these can be abused by knowledgeable users.

References

We've just scratched the surface of what PloneFormGen can do. With small bits of copy-and-paste code, you can do the following things:

- Redirect to a custom URL based on a form field
- Read and save form data to and from a SQL database
- Dynamically populate form selection fields

For more information, see the PloneFormGen documentation, which is available at `http://plone.org/products/ploneformgen/documentation`.

Summary

In this chapter, we've learned how to:

- Use PloneFormGen to create a basic form to gather input from site visitors
- Add different types of fields to your form
- Create and configure Action Adapters to handle form results
- Override PloneFormGen settings with small chunks of custom logic
- Find more information about advanced uses of PloneFormGen

16

Create New Content Types

Not all content is the same, and it can be useful to have meaningful **content types** for storing your content in your CMS. Plone makes this task painless by offering graphical tools for generating new content types.

In this chapter, **Matt Bowen** gives you an introduction to the concepts behind Plone's content types and its battle-tested content types system, **Archetypes**. He then explains how to use **Unified Modeling Language (UML)** to draw your content types, and how to use **ArchGenXML** to turn these drawings into code. Finally, he shows you how to turn your drawing into a polished, working Plone product.

Background

One of Plone's greatest strengths is its easy extensibility. Although it comes with a great set of default content types, Plone allows you to extend its functionality. It is a particularly common need to represent a new content type in Plone, and Plone makes this task painless. Although adding new types does require some Python code, thanks to tools like ArchGenXML, most people can completely avoid actually writing even a line by themselves.

Although everyone who uses Plone is familiar with content types, it would be useful to have a baseline definition going forward. A **content type** is a representation in Plone of some data, and the behavior required to manipulate that data. Folders, Collections, News, Events, and more, are all content types that Plone ships with, out-of-the-box. Content types generally appear to the user as a collection of fields that the user can edit, combined with a few displays of those fields as a web page.

When do I actually need a custom content type?

Before we begin though, it would be good to make sure that you actually need a full-out custom content type. Although writing your own type is surprisingly easy, that doesn't mean that it doesn't take time. Additionally, once you have added a custom code to your Plone installation, you are going to have to maintain that code to keep it compatible with subsequent releases. Although the tools help with this, maintaining your product is not always totally straightforward. So, before embarking on adventures in content type creation, be sure that the built-in types can't be used to meet your needs. I'm consistently impressed with how much mileage I can get out of the built-ins and a custom view or a clever collection.

However, there are times when a person does need to customize. Generally, if what you need to represent to the system cannot be captured by the fields in the existing types, or if it has no equivalent within the out-of-the-box types, you're going to need to write your own. Additionally, you could use your new type to set up relationships between different types; for example, you may have a type that contains several others to make an easy bundle for management and consumption.

For example, Plone.org has a type that represents software projects; you have probably seen it in action in the **Products** section of the site. This type allows Plone.org to capture, search, and display lots of useful information (description, category, and compatibility) about the available products. The product type also sets up relationships between some other useful types, such as releases (a special type of file), bug trackers, and documentation centers for the products. The type captures and organizes information in a way that would be extremely difficult with the out-of-the-box types.

But I'm not a programmer!

The most common way of adding a new type to Plone is through the Python code on your file system. At this point, it's not uncommon to think, "Wait, no, that's not for me; I can't program my way out of a paper bag". However, this is usually not a problem. Although it is not part of the standard bundle, the Plone community has developed a tool called ArchGenXML, which allows integrators to develop types by drawing them in a modeling language called UML. There's little chance that you know UML any better than you know Python, but thankfully, for what we need, UML is very easy to learn—if you can click and drag, you can generate new types with ArchGenXML.

The tools—or drawing code for fun and profit

Before you start drawing, you'll need to have a basic understanding of several high-level concepts used in Plone.

Archetypes and object-oriented programming

Since Plone version 2.0, Plone has shipped with a product called Archetypes that makes it easy to create new content types. Conveniently, all of the out-of-the-box types in Plone are based on Archetypes, and because Plone is object-oriented, you can base your new types on the existing types. In this section, you'll learn the concepts that you'll need to understand in order to use ArchGenXML to create new content types.

The concept of schema

The first, and probably most important, concept for this chapter is **schema**. A schema is a description of the fields in your content type. Plone uses the schema to create the edit form when someone creates or edits a new object of your type, and the schema describes all of the directly-editable attributes of your type. Any content type that actually has fields has a schema, and you deal with them all of the time. For example, fire up your instance and create a new page. Looking at the edit form, there are fields for the **Title**, **Description**, and **Body text**. So, a page's schema would be its title, description, and body text.

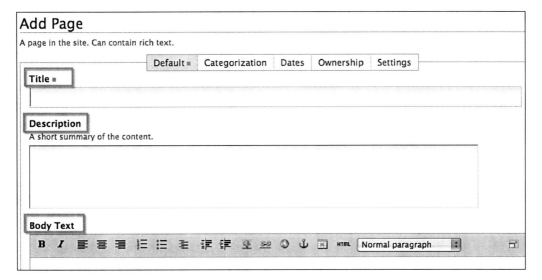

A schema also contains information about what each field is called, whether a field is required, how to validate the field, and which interface widget (text box, date picker, Kupu rich text editor, and so on) to use when displaying the edit form for that type. So, in the case of a page, the schema knows that you need a single line text widget for the title (which is required), and a multi-line text widget for the description. It also knows that Plone should use Kupu or some other WYSIWYG editor for the body text. Most of creating new content types is about describing new schemas, and we'll be covering them in more depth shortly.

Object-oriented programming concepts

Plone is built with Python, an **Object Oriented Programming (OOP)** language. OOP is a way of describing the world to the computer. With OOP, you create models of various "objects" (a document, a folder, or more abstractly, an event) and then describe to the computer how these objects interact. In Plone, all of the "content" that you are managing is represented as objects behind the scenes. These objects have schemas to describe their attributes (the data that makes a document a document). They also have behaviors associated with validating that data, making it accessible over WebDAV, and a whole host of other things that you don't have to worry about.

When designing an object-oriented system, there are a few kinds of relationships between your various objects that are important. With OOP, objects can inherit from one another, like organisms in real life. So, suppose that you have an object that describes events, and you want to describe a birthday party, which is a class of events. You might say a birthday party is a kind of an event. It has all of the attributes of a regular event (a date and time, a location, attendants, and so on), but it also has some attributes of its own—presents and a birthday cake. It also has certain constraints that would override the attributes of a regular event. For example, a birthday party can't really last for more than one day in a year. With OOP, this kind of model is easy to describe. You can make a birthday party that inherits all of the properties of the event model that you already have, and then add your own additional ones, overriding what you've inherited as appropriate. This process is called **subclassing**, and you make extensive use of it with Plone. Plone ships with a lot of good models out-of-the-box that you can inherit from, saving you lots of work and thought.

Not all relationships can be explained through inheritance, though. Sometimes, an object is composed of other objects. For example, one can think of a newspaper being "composed" of articles. In this sense, a newspaper has many articles. In OOP, this is called aggregation, and in Plone, you deal with it often; folders in Plone are objects that aggregate. And, indeed, in Plone parlance, an object that is composed of other objects is "Folderish" (and the rest are "Pageish"). Going back to our example of the products section of Plone.org, a product uses this relationship often. A product is composed of releases, a documentation section, a bug tracker, and several other independent types.

UML and a quick introduction of the symbols you'll use

UML is a symbolic language for representing object-oriented programs. If you've ever made a flow chart before, you've used a symbolic language to represent something. Although it may seem intimidating at first, you only need to know a little bit of the language to be productive in Plone, and even that little bit is comfortingly intuitive.

A quick look at the programs that make it possible

There are a variety of programs for creating UML diagrams, ranging from free and open source software to enterprise-priced packages that bring with them whole software methodologies. To use ArchGenXML, you need one that generates an **XMI** (an XML serialization of your diagram) that it can parse. In the ArchGenXML documentation on Plone.org, several are listed, but two of them have most of the mindshare in the community: **ArgoUML** (http://argouml.tigris.org/) and Gentleware's **Poseidon** (http://www.gentleware.com). Interestingly, these two projects share common roots, and are similar in functionality and interface design.

If your company already uses object domain, or if you really love KDE and want to use Umbrello, don't hesitate to test your favorite editor with AuthGenXML. If you are successful, leave a comment on the AuthGenXML manual so that others can benefit from your experience: http://Plone.org/documentation/manual/archgenxml2.

For the rest of this chapter, I'll use ArgoUML Version 0.24 for the screenshots and explanations; ArgoUML is free (as in speech and beer) and widely used, making it a good complement to Plone.

 The Version 0.24 is not the most current version of ArgoUML. Unfortunately, Version 0.26, released shortly before this book went to the press, is incompatible with ArchGenXML at the time of this writing.

Although I'm using ArgoUML for this chapter, I actually pay the $16 USD per quarter for Gentleware's Poseidon, for my own use. When developing complicated models, I find Argo's lack of undo to be crippling. On the other hand, the ArchGenXML profile for ArgoUML (created by running agx_argouml_profile from the command line and then importing the file that it generates, argouml_profile.xmi, into ArgoUML) reduces the opportunity for typos. With the monthly cost of Poseidon at only $5, it may be worthwhile experimenting with both editors to see which one you prefer.

The class, the package, composition, aggregation, and generalization

Remember when I said that you need to know very few symbols in UML to be productive? Well, it turns out that you'll really want to know about five pretty well; so I'd like to introduce you to them.

Class

The class is the heart of everything we'll be doing in this chapter. It is not a grand-looking symbol — it is a box divided into three parts:

MyClass
myAttr : text
myMethod() : void

In the top of the box is the class's name (required) and "stereotype" (optional). The name of the class is how the system will refer to your type internally (we'll cover giving your type a human-friendly name later). The stereotype tells the system what "kind of" type you are making. It specifies the "is a" relationship discussed previously.

In the second section of the class symbol, you can specify the fields that your type will need. For example, if your type needs a text field to hold a name, you can write *name:text* into this second section. We will cover fields and types in much greater detail later.

The third section of the class box is for the methods of the type. This is where you can override existing behaviors, or add new ones to your type, using Python. Although there is lots of fun to be had with methods, it is beyond the scope of this book to go into it. In ArgoUML, click the fourth button from the left on the toolbar, as shown here, and then click in the large drawing area on the screen to create a class:

Package

The package is a much simpler beast. Packages hold classes. A package has a name, and often that's all there is to it. Conventionally, Plone developers put their new content type classes in a package called `content`. This helps to keep your classes organized, and lets you keep content separate from other classes you may generate, such as tests (which are great, if slightly out of scope for this chapter).

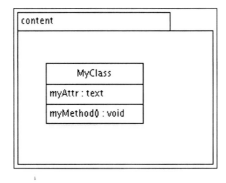

In ArgoUML, click on the third button from the left on the toolbar, as shown here, and then click in the large drawing area on the screen to create a package:

Composition and aggregation

In addition to the two symbols described above, there are three useful relationships between classes that you can model, using the various arrowish shapes in your GUI. Composition and aggregation are two ways of expressing the "has many" relationship from above.

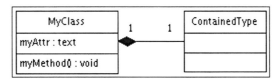

With composition, denoted by the black diamond, you can express that your type contains some other type, and the contained type will appear only as a child of your type, and not in any other type of container. Using our example from Plone Software Center, a project contains (through composition) a release; you would not expect to find a release anywhere but within a project. In ArgoUML, click on the seventh button from the left on the toolbar, as shown in the following screenshot, and then click and drag from your container type (a folderish type) to the type that's the contained (a pageish type) to create a composition relationship:

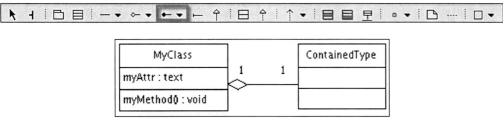

Aggregation is similar, but less strict. Your type has many of the contained types, but the contained type may appear in other contexts. In Plone Software Center, a project has an issue tracker (through aggregation). You might find an issue tracker in a project, and you might also find one somewhere else on a site (such as in a regular content folder). In ArgoUML, click the sixth button from the left on the toolbar, as shown in the following screenshot, then click and drag from your container type (a folderish type) to the type that's contained in the container (a pageish type) to create an aggregation relationship.

Generalization

Finally, to express inheritance (the 'is a' relationship from above), you use the generalization arrow, which is a white arrowhead pointing from your type to the base, or parent, class (the one that your type "is a kind of").

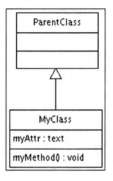

Whatever the arrow points to is more general. Whatever it is coming from is a more specific kind of what the arrow points to. In our birthday party example, the birthday party would have an arrow coming from it, pointing to an event. It would then inherit all the attributes of the event type (for free!). In ArgoUML, click the ninth button from the left on the toolbar, then click and drag from your child type (this is likely to be what you're creating) to the parent type (the type you're going to inherit from) to create a generalization.

Stereotypes and tagged values

Before we get started, there are two other important UML concepts to be covered that will help make this process a lot smoother. Stereotypes and tagged values are not symbols in themselves. Instead, they are additional information that you can use to tell ArchGenXML important information about your model.

Stereotypes are controlled through a tab in your UML editor and offer you shortcuts to several useful settings. For example, you can specify that your type is folderish through the **<<folder>>** stereotype, or that your type should not actually be generated (perhaps because it already exists in another package) through the **<<stub>>** stereotype.

To apply a stereotype in ArgoUML, the simplest way is to left-click on your class, click on **Apply Stereotypes**, and then pick the appropriate stereotype from the fly-out menu.

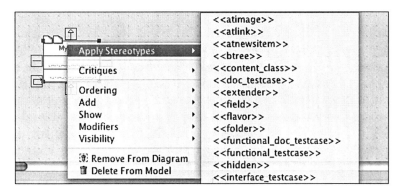

Tagged values let you associate useful information with your class and its attributes, such as human-readable names, security settings, and an incredible number of other details. To apply a tagged value in ArgoUML, use the **Tagged Values** tab in the bottom portion of the right-hand pane of the ArgoUML window. In this area, you can click on the leftmost column to pick a tagged value, and then type its value in the rightmost column.

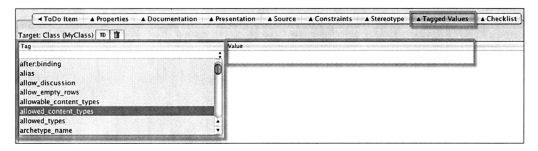

We'll be using several stereotypes and tagged values in the next section of this chapter, and you can find a complete reference to them in the online ArchGenXML manual, which is available at: `http://Plone.org/documentation/manual/archgenxml2`.

Our bridge to happiness: ArchGenXML

If all you had was UML, you would be able to draw nice models of your types, but that wouldn't be worth much without the code to implement these models. That's where ArchGenXML comes in—it translates your diagrams into working Plone products. Using it is much the same as using any other Python script. You run it from the command line by its name (`archgenxml`), specifying the name of your XMI file (the export of your UML diagram), and (optionally) a number of flags, such as where the output of the code should be saved and who you are (for documentation purposes).

You can get a full list of flags by running `archgenxml -h`. Most of the time, however, you're going to be running it with only the required argument and the path to save your code ArchGenXML. It is smart when it generates code, so if you have made changes to your generated source, it will generally preserve them. Even smarter, ArchGenXML (AGX) is well-documented online, in the manual mentioned previously, which describes its various features and settings. You should keep the manual handy as a valuable complement to this chapter. It explains several methods for installing AGX on a variety of platforms, and provides an up-to-date reference for specific technical aspects of AGX, such as supported field types or tagged values.

The most up-to-date install instructions are available in ArchGenXML's online manual. My favorite method of installing AGX is through Python's Setup Tools utility, `easy_install` (`http://peak.telecommunity.com/DevCenter/setuptools`). Using `easy_install`, you can install AGX in two easy steps. First, run `easy_install archgenxml`. This will pull down the most recently released version of the program. Then, you'll need to tell AGX where it can find Zope, so that it can find the libraries it needs. Do this by creating a file in your home directory called `.agx_zope_path`. This file contains a path to your Zope installation's libraries. If you used the unified installer, this will be `/YOUR_HOME/Plone/zinstance/parts/zope2/lib/Python`. So, for example, my `.agx_zope_path` file has one line: `/home/matt/Plone/zinstance/parts/zope2/lib/Python`.

Once you've installed AGX using `easy_install`, you get four very useful commands:

1. `archgenxml`, which is the program that you run to convert your diagrams into code.
2. `agx_argouml_profile`, which generates a profile file that you can import into ArgoUML, that brings in all of the stereotypes and tagged values that AGX needs.
3. `agx_stereotypes`, which provides a quick, command-line reference to all of the stereotypes that AGX understands.
4. `agx_taggedvalues`, which provides a quick, command-line reference to all of the tagged values that AGX understands.

Once you have installed AGX, it will be worthwhile creating an ArgoUML Profile file, which makes using ArgoUML a much more pleasant experience. To do so, run `agx_argouml_profile` from the command line. This will generate a file, `argouml_profile.xml`, which you can import into ArgoUML when you start a project. Do this by using the **File | Import ...** menu in ArgoUML. Then, I always use the **File | Save Project As...** after importing the profile, and save my blank model with the name I want it to have. This way, whenever I click **Save**, my model will be where I want it, with the correct name, and it will have all of the stereotypes and tagged values available in drop-downs.

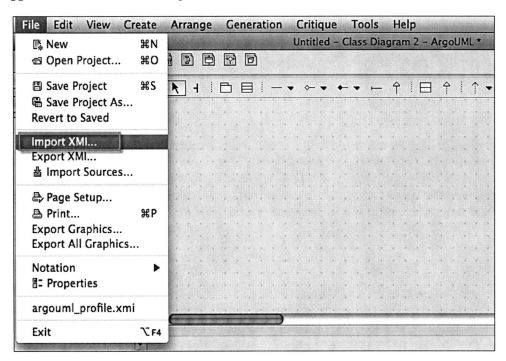

Building a custom newsroom

Now, let's apply all of that background information from above and make something. Imagine that you are a stellar Plone integrator, and your client, a tech-savvy executive director of a local nonprofit organization, has told you that she has big dreams of a newsroom on her web site. (We'll base this example off of the PressRoom product built by ONE/Northwest: `http://Plone.org/products/pressroom`.)

Your client wants top-notch, web-friendly press releases, including a compelling image, and a lot of valuable metadata associated with each one. She also wants to be able to put together "Press kits," which are sets of logos, research documents, and pre-made press releases, so that she can easily distribute her media campaigns to the field. Although you could probably stretch Plone's out-of-the-box types into something close to what she wants, there's no need to force and cajole the built-ins into tasks beyond their means. Now, it's time to create a custom content type.

A rough outline of the types we'll use

Before you dive into any software project, it's good to have an idea of what you're actually going to be building. One of the great strengths of AGX-based development is the agility it can lend you. So here, we'll roughly scope out what we need, and then refine as we develop.

Press release

The press release type sounds a lot like the built-in news item. In fact, it probably is a news item, only with a few extra fields. After passing back and forth some prototypes, it turns out that your client wants to be able to list contact information for the specific field office of her organization to which the press release applies, as well as to have a headline, a subheading, and a dateline. So, it looks like you'll be adding four or five fields to a new type that inherits from the built-in news item.

Press kit folder

The press kit is an interesting beast. On its own, it has few fields—a name, a brief description, and a field where the organization can describe the target audience. However, this type is most of value for what it puts together—a press kit folder has many research documents, press releases, and logos. In this case, it looks like you'll be making a new folder with an extra field (the target audience), and then aggregating a few of your news types as well as a few of the stock types. It's a good thing you already know about all those symbols!

Drawing your first new product

Now it's time to start drawing. Fire up your UML editor (I'll be using ArgoUML in the examples, as above) and let's get ready to draw some code! Once your editor has started, you'll first want to name your project. Do so by clicking the folder icon in the left-hand pane called **default** (if you're using the ArgoUML profile described previously) or **untitled Model** (if not), and changing its name in the Properties drawer at the bottom of your screen.

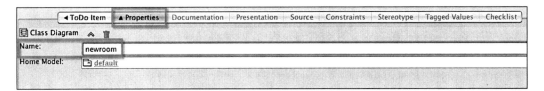

Give your model a good name (I'll call mine **newsroom**), and save it into your installation's `products` directory (the path would be `/YOUR_HOME/Plone/zinstance/products` if you used the Unified Installer), which is where we'll generate our code, later.

Creating a package for your types

First, create a package called **content** for your new types. Do this by clicking on the folder-looking icon and then clicking anywhere in the workspace on your screen. This will create a new, nameless package. Now, double-click in the tab part of the folder, or in the **Name** field in the **Properties** drawer on the bottom of your screen, and call this folder **content**. Once you've named this package, you'll probably want to drag out its lower-right corner to make it a little bigger, so that it can hold all of our classes.

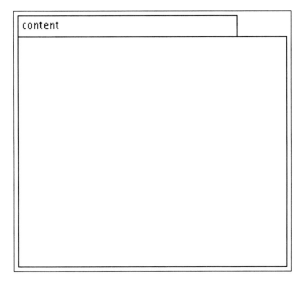

Creating your first classes

Now that you have a package, you're ready to add your first class to it. Click the Class symbol in the toolbar (this is the symbol with three sections), and then click anywhere inside your package. You'll get a new, unnamed class. So, just as the package before it, **Name** your class by double-clicking in the top section or by using the name field in the **Properties** drawer. We'll start with the press release, so name this class PressRelease (no spaces). Now that it's been created, let's tell ArchGenXML that we want this to be based on a news item. So, right-click on your class, go to the **Apply Stereotypes** fly-out menu, and then click on **<<atnewsitem>>**. (The **at** refers to ArcheTypes.)

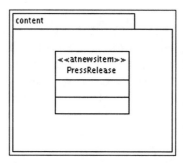

Knowing how to use **atnewsitem** might be a little opaque, but if you read the ArchGenXML documentation, you can learn a lot about which stereotypes to pick. We know from our planning that we want to create a type based on Plone's **News Item**, so that gives us a starting point. We can use stereotypes to tell ArchGenXML which Plone built-in type we want to base our new type on. So now, we just need to find which stereotype to use.

By running the agx_stereotypes command, we get a listing of all of the stereotypes that ArchGenXML understands. Near the top of the list are some surprisingly-decipherable and particularly useful stereotypes, which are listed here:

- atdocument, which translates to Plone's **Page** type; called **Document** in an earlier version of Plone
- atevent, which translates to Plone's **Event** type
- atfile, which translates to Plone's **File** type
- atfolder, which translates to Plone's **Folder** type
- atimage, which translates to Plone's **Image** type
- atlink, which translates to Plone's **Link type**
- atnewsitem, which translates to Plone's **News Item** type

These stereotypes are most of the built-in Plone types.

Generate your product!

I realize that it doesn't feel like we've done much yet, but now seems like a great time to generate our first product. So, from the command line in the `products` directory of your instance, run the following command:

```
archgenxml newsroom.xmi newsroom
```

ArchGenXML should output something that looks like the following:

```
INFO  ArchGenXML Version 2.0

(c) 2003-2007 BlueDynamics Alliance, Austria, GPL 2.0 or later

INFO  Parsing...

INFO  Directory in which we're generating the files: 'newsroom'.

INFO  Generating...

INFO  Starting new Product: 'newsroom'.

INFO  Generating package 'content'.

INFO  Generating class 'PressRelease'.
```

Now, enter the newsroom directory in your instance and take a look around. You should see the following files and directories:

- `config.py`: Product-wide settings and values. Useful for programmers.
- `configure.zcml`: Basic configuration of your product in **Zope Configuration Markup Language (ZCML)**. Useful for programmers.
- `content`: The result of your `content` package in your model contains:
    - `__init__.py`: A blank file that lets Python know that this directory is a Python package.
    - `interfaces.py`: Automatically-generated marker interfaces for your types. Useful for programmers.
    - `PressRelease.py`: The Python file that resulted from the class that you created in your diagram. Contains your schema, your class, information about where it inherits from, and any behaviors that you might have added. Generally useful for programmers, although we may dip in it ourselves.
- `__init__.py`: Like the other `__init__.py`, only this is for the whole product.

- **profiles**: GenericSetup profiles, which are a sophisticated way to control the configuration of your product. We won't cover them in much detail here, but you can learn more about them in the Plone.org documentation section (see, for example `http://Plone.org/documentation/tutorial/genericsetup`), or see Chapter 17 of this book. The following profiles will be available:

  - ○ **default**: An automatically-generated default profile for your product. This contains the following files:

    - ○ `cssregistry.xml`: GenericSetup for you to control any additional CSS that your product might require for correct display.

    - ○ `factorytool.xml`: GenericSetup that registers your new type with Plone's factory tool.

    - ○ `import_steps.xml`: GenericSetup to determine which profiles to run.

    - ○ `jsregistry.xml`: GenericSetup for you to control any additional JavaScript files that your product might require for proper display.

    - ○ `newsroom_marker.txt`: A blank text file to aid GenericSetup's functionality.

    - ○ `skins.xml`: GenericSetup that registers the skins directories (below) with Plone.

    - ○ **types**: Directory to hold profiles for your types. These profiles are:

      - ○ `PressRelease.xml`: GenericSetup registration of your type, including its name, any associated views, and other information the factory tool needs in order to be able to create a new PressRelease.

      - ○ `types.xml`: GenericSetup registration of your type with the `portal_types` tool.

- **profiles.zcml**: Registration of your GenericSetup profiles with the application server.

- **refresh.txt**: A file that triggers the application server to look for changes in your Python modules and reload them without restarting the server.

- **setuphandlers.py**: Additional setup steps that GenericSetup can run when when there are no profiles providing the required functionality. Useful for programmers.

- `skins`: A directory for skins for your product. This directory contains the following files:

    ◦ `newsroom_images`: A directory containing the images to be used in the display of your types. This directory will contain the following files:

        ◦ `PressRelease.gif`: An image that will display next PressReleases in the contents view and in the navigation portlet. This is a simple, generic icon for your type, and can be replaced with another image if so desired.

    ◦ `newsroom_styles`: Stylesheets used in the display of your types.

    ◦ `newsroom_templates`: Page templates that control the display of your types (including any additional views beyond the ones Archetypes provides out of the box).

- `version.txt`: The version information for your product. Automatically incremented by ArchGenXML for each build, and used by the `QuickInstaller` to determine when a product is eligible for reinstallation.

Now that you know which files are generated with your product, you can take comfort in knowing that you will only need to touch a few, if any, of them. The vast majority of files are fine just the way AGX generates them, while others need to be customized only in an advanced use case.

If you look at your model, you may be interested in knowing which files correspond to which parts of your model. Although nearly every file generated is customized in some way to suit your model, the ones most directly tied to it are the `content` directory, the `PressRelease.py` file, the `PressRelease.xml` file, and the humble `PressRelease.gif` image. Each of these files was generated as a direct response to something you drew.

`PressRelease.py` contains the Python code that "is" your type (its schema, behaviors, and what it inherits from, along with a little other boilerplate). `PressRelese.xml` contains the type-specific information for a `PressRelease`, which includes its human-friendly name, its icon for the drop-downs, which views are associated with it (for the "display" menu), and where it should be addable (throughout the site, or only in specific folder types). `PressRelease.gif` is a simple, generic icon for your type, so that Plone doesn't throw an exception when you view the `contents` view of a folder.

With your product generated, you should fire up your instance and install it at the **quick_installer** by visiting **Site Setup | Add/Remove Products**. Gratifyingly, if everything has gone well, you'll see it under **Products available for install**. If you don't see it there, double-check to see if your generated product has ended up in the products directory of your instance, and whether Plone has started successfully.

Install your newsroom, and go to a folder on your test instance. Click the **Add new...** drop-down and add a new press release. You will be presented with a form that unsurprisingly looks (hopefully) like the one for adding new news items (if it doesn't, double-check your stereotype in your model). This is because we've inherited all of the properties of a news item and haven't added any of our own. That means that it's time to learn the next step: adding fields.

Adding your fields

Now comes what I suspect is the reason why you're reading this chapter. Before we start typing, let's review which are the fields that we need beyond the ones that come with the out-of-the-box news item:

- **Headline**: This may not even be a new field, as we already have a **Title** field that we could rename "headline." We'll cover this change in the advanced topics section of this chapter.

- **Subheading**: This sounds a lot like the existing **Title** field, but is positioned under it. It is probably just a single line of plain text.

- **Field office contact info**: The field office contact info could be any number of things, from a line with an address to a picture of the office team and a link to that office's web site. So this will probably be safe as a rich-text field.

- **Dateline**: This is actually two fields, one taking a time and date for the date info, and one taking a single-line string for the location.

Looking at ArchGenXML's online documentation (which has the most up-to-date reference for supported fields and other features), there are a few field types that look promising. They are as follows:

- `string`, which will create a single-line text field. The "image caption" on the news item is a `StringField`, as is the title. This will be useful for the subheading field, and the location of the date line.

- `richtext`, which will create a rich-text editor widget, such as "Kupu." This will allow the client to add as much rich information about the particular field-office as necessary.

- `date`, which will create a date/time widget (complete with calendar). This is the same widget you've seen on the event type. This will be useful for the date aspect of the dateline.

Now, going back to your model, it's time to create these fields. Field names must be valid Python variable names, and therefore they can only contain letters, numbers, and underscores, and they must start with a letter. Following the Plone convention, we will camel-case words together, starting with a lower case letter. So, our fields will be called `subHeadline`, `fieldOfficeInfo`, `datelineDate`, and `datelineLocation`. We specify the field type with a colon and then the field type name.

So, enter the following into the second section of your class by clicking in the blank space until a text box appears (note that you may need to make your class larger to have space to type more fields):

- `subHeadline:string`
- `fieldOfficeInfo:richtext`
- `datelineDate:date`
- `datelineLocation:string`

Your model should now look like this:

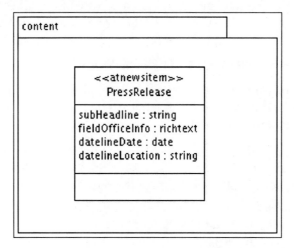

Once you've double-checked for typos and other problems, it would be a good idea to regenerate and reinstall.

 It's important to point out that you cannot round-trip from Plone back to ArgoUML. So if you've made changes on the filesystem before going back to ArgoUML, those changes will be overwritten.

Just follow the same steps as you carried out the first time you generated the model. AGX is smart enough to know what it should replace and what its should leave alone, and it will politely increment the version number so that you can use the Plone **quick_installer** to reinstall your updated model. When you go to add a new press release, the bottom of your add form should look as shown in the following screenshot:

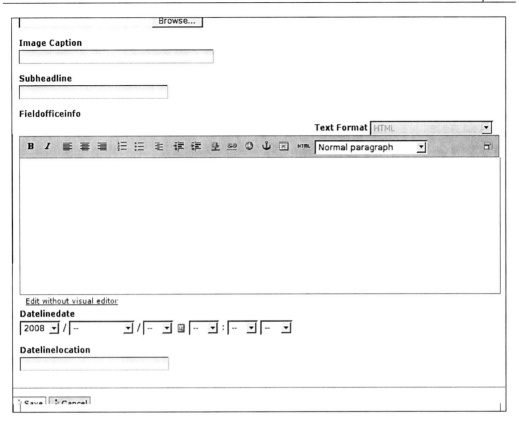

Sure enough, your new fields are now on the form, below the existing news item's fields. Their names aren't exactly human-friendly yet, and neither are they optimally-sized or positioned, but this is probably enough to start getting client feedback. Even better, you've now made your own new type, complete with custom fields.

We'll clean up the names and positions on the form. If you put information in the fields and save the object, you'll see the default display of your type—field names followed by their field values. Again, this probably isn't optimal, but it will certainly confirm that the type works, and that you're capturing the correct data.

Adding a custom folder type

Now that we've created our first custom pageish content type, it's time to move forward and add a custom folder. This will be our Press Kit type, which aggregates press releases, regular documents, and images into one convenient package. Field offices could potentially copy these objects and paste them into their sections of the site. Or, later, a Python developer could come make the folder available as a compressed file for download with PDFs of all of the folder's content. For now, we just need to capture and display the information online. Looking at the specifications above, it looks as though our folder will need the following fields:

- **A name**, for which the default title will suffice.
- **A brief description**, for which the default description will suffice.
- **A field where the organization can describe the target audience**. In this case, we'll add a new field. After talking to the client, you discover that her organization has done a lot of market research and has broken down their target audiences into a few, well-defined types. This seems like a good candidate for a selection box, where the end user can select a target audience from a list.

Moreover, this type is a folder. It needs to contain specific types. From the specification, it will need to contain the following:

- **press releases**—just like the ones that we have created
- **documents**—just the vanilla ones that come with Plone
- **logos**—for this purpose, the standard Plone image type should do fine

In each case, these types will be aggregated into our folder. They can appear both in our folder and anywhere else on the site. So, to start, let's create our new PressKit type. In your UML editor, create a new class in the `content` folder. Name your new class *PressKit*, assign the stereotype **<<atfolder>>** to it, and add a field named `targetAudience:selection`.

We know to use `atfolder` because that's what Plone's folders are based on, and we want something much like a Plone folder. Now, your model should look appear as shown in the following screenshot:

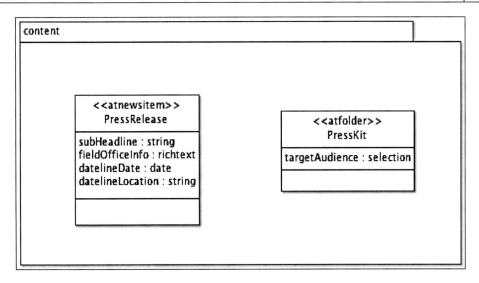

This, however, is familiar to us. To aggregate the types, they need to be in our model. **PressRelease** is there, obviously, although **Document** and **Image**, are not. We don't want to replace the default Document and Image that come with Plone. So what do we do? AGX has us covered here. We can use the **<<stub>>** stereotype to add classes to our model that we don't want to auto-generate, and thereby subclass the standard image and document types. To add stub classes for Document and Image, we do the following:

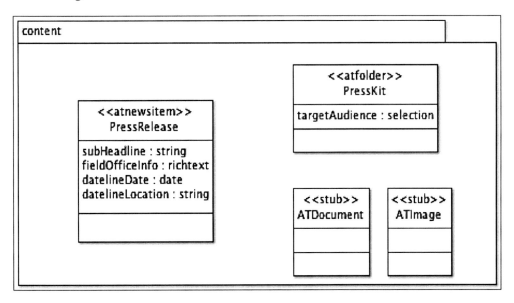

Now, all that's left to do is to draw our aggregation arrows. So, in your UML tool, look for the white diamond in the toolbar, and click on it. Then, drag from your **PressKit** to each contained type. Your model should now look like the following screenshot:

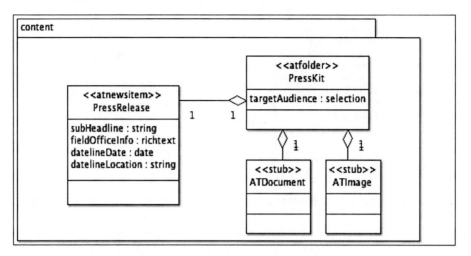

Now that we've gotten so far, this seems like a good time to regenerate our code. So, following the same steps, run AGX again, restart your Zope instance, and reinstall the product so that any changes you made are registered in your portal.

After you regenerate, you should have three new files in your product:

1. PressKit.py, which contains the Python definition for your new type.
2. PressKit.xml, which contains the factory type information (name, and where it can be added).
3. PressKit.gif, a copy of the folder icon so that displaying the contents view of folders containing your type doesn't break.

When you go to add your new type, you'll see a field for the target audience. But there's no drop-down. This is because we haven't told Plone what the potential values for the drop-down are. We'll get to this in the next section. For the moment, create a new Press Kit, and then go to **Add new...**. You should see a menu that looks like the one in this screenshot:

If it does, it means you now have a new, folderish type to which you can add images, pages, and PressReleases. This is a lot of progress for such a short amount of time, and the client is very happy. There's still plenty of cleanup to do, and so after a little break, it's time to dive into tagged values and even (just a tiny bit of) Python code.

Cleaning things up a bit

Although we've already created our new content types, we're not quite ready to hand over our work to the client. We still need to do the following:

- Give the fields and content type human-friendly names
- Set a list of values for the target audience
- Move the fields around into a more rational order, and rename some inherited fields

Additionally, the client wants to make the dateline fields and target audience values required fields, so that her charming but forgetful staff doesn't post a lot of incomplete information on the site.

Tagged values for greater precision

We can cover most of these tasks through tagged values. Tagged values are a feature of UML that lends UML great flexibility. With a tagged value, you can assign an arbitrary key and value to any aspect of your model. ArchGenXML understands many tagged values, and you can read about all of them in the ArchGenXML manual (see `http://Plone.org/documentation/manual/archgenxml2/reference/tagged-values`). For our purposes, we're only going to need to tag our classes and their attributes.

Taking things one at a time, let's start with the friendly names for our types. Looking at the ArchGenXML manual, there are a dozen of tagged values you can apply to a class to override the (sensible) defaults that AGX uses when it generates your code. For friendly names for our type, `archetype_name` looks like a good candidate. So, in the UML editor, select your PressRelease. Then, in the properties drawer, click on **Tagged values**. Under the **Tag** column, select **archetype_name,** and under the **Value** column, enter **Press release**. When you're selecting your class, be careful to select the class and not one of its attributes—this is easy to do and is hard to debug.

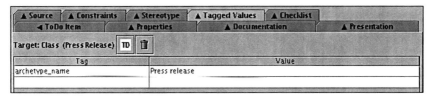

Repeat the process for PressKit, and then you will have friendly names for each of your classes.

Now, let's go on to making the field values user-friendly. Looking back at the documentation, you'll see that there are two good candidates for the field labels: the `label` tag for attributes, and the `widget:label` tag for the widget. Because the widget is what is actually displayed TTW, this is an important value to be changed. So, as an example, click on the `targetAudience` attribute of PressKit, and then go to the **Tagged Values** tab, just as earlier. This time, in the **Tag** section, select **widget: label** and in the **Value**, enter **target audience**.

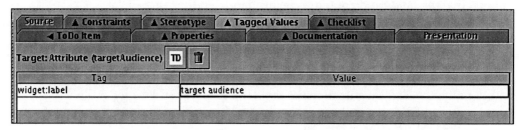

Repeat this process for all of your attributes. When you're done, you may want to double-check to see that you didn't miss anything, or make any typos. For the purposes of this chapter, we're going to keep plowing through.

With the types now more human-friendly, it's time to add some values for the target audience, so that the selection actually works. Looking at the AGX manual, there's a tag named **vocabulary**. Unfortunately, it says that it will accept "Set to a Python list, a DisplayList or a method name (quoted) which provides the vocabulary for a selection widget." All of these sound advanced.

Thankfully, a Python list is actually a very simple creature, and should be well within your comfort zone. A Python tuple (which you can think of as a list), in this case, is just a list of quoted values, separated by commas, and surrounded by parentheses. So, our list could be **('Integrators', 'Developers', 'End users',)**. Remember that the commas come after the quotes, and you should be golden.

Setting a tagged value of **vocabulary** and a list as the one above, our tagged value control looks like the following screenshot:

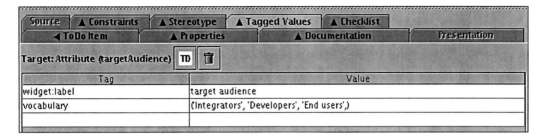

Tag	Value
widget:label	target audience
vocabulary	('Integrators', 'Developers', 'End users',)

Note that I've added a comma after **'End users'**. This isn't required, but if I need to add something later, the comma is there and I won't forget it.

If you regenerate and create a new PressKit, you should now have the option buttons to select a target audience. Plone is a highly intuitive system, and will switch to a drop-down when the list gets too long for option buttons to be practical. You can force it to use one or the other by specifying the widget:type tagged value, although flex is the default behavior, select guarantees a selection box, and radio gets you option buttons.

Finally, we'll need to set a few fields as required. This is easily done with tagged values. Under attributes in the documentation, you'll find a tagged value called, unsurprisingly, **required**, which you set to **1** (which is true in Python). Applying this value to the target audience field you'll get a screen that looks like this:

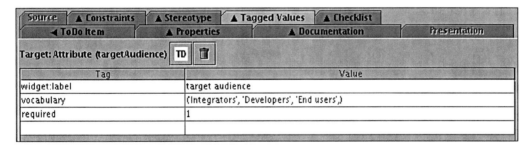

Tag	Value
widget:label	target audience
vocabulary	('Integrators', 'Developers', 'End users',)
required	1

Repeat this process for datelineDate and datelineLocation, regenerate, and pat yourself on the back. This product is becoming quite polished. Unfortunately, there's still the problem of those ill-placed fields.

Moving around in the code and renaming fields them

The product is nearly ready to be shown to the client again, but the fields are still not in an ideal order for our PressRelease. The client wants the subheading under the title, and the dateline info under the subheading. Although there are tagged values for this, because the code to make the change is very simple, I'd like to present it that way. It'd also be a good idea to get a look at the code before the product is finished. To move the headline under the title, open `content/PressRelease.py` in your favorite text editor. Then, scroll through the file until you see the following:

```
##code-section class-header #fill in your manual code here
##/code-section class-header
```

Between those two lines, insert the following:

```
schema.moveField('subHeadline', after='title')
```

Because whitespace matters in Python, make sure that your new line is indented to the same position as the `##code-section` header and footer. What this line says is, "In the schema, move the field called `subHeadline` after the `title` field." The `title` field comes from the inherited news item. So, to then move our other two fields, add two more lines:

```
schema.moveField('datelineDate', after='subHeadline')
schema.moveField('datelineLocation', after='datelineDate')
```

Changes like this don't even require you to reinstall your type. Just restart your instance, and the change should take effect.

Now that we have reordered our fields, we can regenerate our product, and we will then have a working custom content type, almost entirely without needing to know Python!

If you've enjoyed this, then you may have a promising future as a Plone developer. I'd recommend really scouring the online documentation for ArchGenXML and picking up a Python book. There's plenty to learn about AGX and Archetype content types. The high points include adding extra fields that aren't included with Plone (such as the ones in the ArchAddOn product), validating user input, and storing values in the catalog, from where they can be searched.

Once you are feeling comfortable with the generated code and with Python in general, you cannot do better than read Martin Aspeli's book *Professional Plone Development*, which covers Plone development for programmers, and teaches you tons of API and best practices along the way. You may also want to look into an alternative, evolving way of creating content types dreamed up by Martin Aspeli, known as **Dexterity**. It should be making its debut in Plone 4.0, and shows great promise. See `http://martinaspeli.net/articles/dexterity-now-has-a-project-area`.

In the meantime, model away!

Summary

In this chapter, we have learned:

- When you might need to add a new content type
- How to use Object-Oriented Programming to save yourself a lot of work
- How to draw a new model in UML and turn it into an installable Plone product
- How to take your product from a rough prototype and turn it into a polished content type, ready for your end users
- How to make simple modifications to the code generated by ArchGenXML

17
Customize Plone

You can customize Plone by changing the settings in the ZMI (through the web) or by making changes to an installable filesystem product. These customizations can serve as the scaffolding upon which a theme product can be built, if desired, although these changes are not necessarily theme-related.

In this chapter, **Veda Williams** explains how to make minor adjustments to a Plone site through the ZMI, introduces basic Zope 3 concepts, and explains how to make these same changes in a filesystem product. In particular, this chapter involves a tour of `portal_actions`, and `portal_skins` template overrides, the customization of browser resources (views, viewlets, and portlets), and GenericSetup.

Background

In order to perform most of the customizations mentioned in this chapter, you need manager rights to your site, basic programming skills, and a little common sense. For some of the changes, you will need to be comfortable working with Plone filesystem products, although this does not mean that you need to know Python in order to make these changes. A filesystem product is merely a product that can be installed; much of the boilerplate is written for you via automated scripts, known as **recipes**.

It will be helpful in some cases to have an understanding of **ZPT**, the **Plone templating language**. You can find a good description of ZPT in the *Definitive Guide to Plone* (out of date, but still valuable), which is available from: `http://plone.org/documentation/books/definitive_guide_to_plone.pdf`, and also at `http://www.zope.org/Documentation/Books/ZopeBook/2_6Edition/AppendixC.stx`.

Make changes to tabs, buttons, and menu options

On your Plone site's home page, you will notice various areas where there are menu options or buttons. A default Plone site has a top navigation area, various links for printing or emailing a page, as well as menu actions that allow you to cut, paste, or otherwise manipulate the objects within a folder. You will also see tabs that allow you to access the contents of a given folder, a history tab, a sharing tab, and various tabs along the top for **Home, Users, News,** and **Events**:

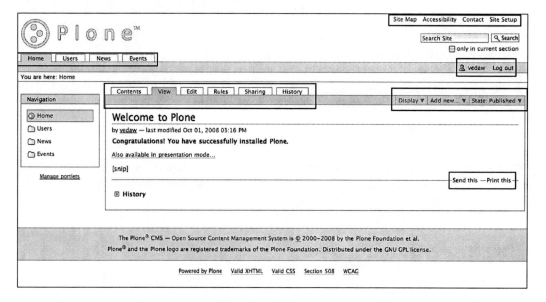

Each of these tabs, buttons, and menu objects corresponds to an action defined in `http://localhost:8080/yoursitename/portal_actions/manage`, in the ZMI. You must log in to your site in order to see the available **portal_action** categories. The following is a screenshot of the main **portal_actions** screen:

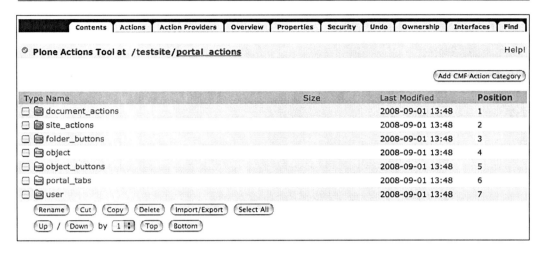

By default, there are seven CMF action categories that are listed. **CMF (Content Management Framework)** is an add-on product for Zope that is used to build content management systems. It provides some basic tools for handling metadata, members, and so on, but is not a CMS by itself. Plone is an example of a sophisticated CMS built using the CMF.

CMF Action Categories use this technology, but for practical purposes they are merely categories in which you can alter the buttons, tabs, and menu options for your site. An example scenario where action categories might come in handy is where you want to add a new action category, to drive something like a portlet with drop-down lists. Generally, though, you will only be adding or altering action items within the existing categories. The default categories include:

1. **document_actions**
2. **site_actions**
3. **folder_buttons**
4. **object**
5. **object_buttons**
6. **portal_tabs**
7. **user**

To add a new action category, choose **Add CMF Category** from the drop-down list found on the top right area of the ZMI.

To add a new action within one of these categories, click on the category and choose **Add CMF Action** from the drop-down menu. Often, all you may want to do is deselect the **Visible?** checkbox to hide the items that you do not wish to see, or change the logic slightly, say to point to a different URL. For example, the following **portal_action** is not marked as visible, and hence does not display:

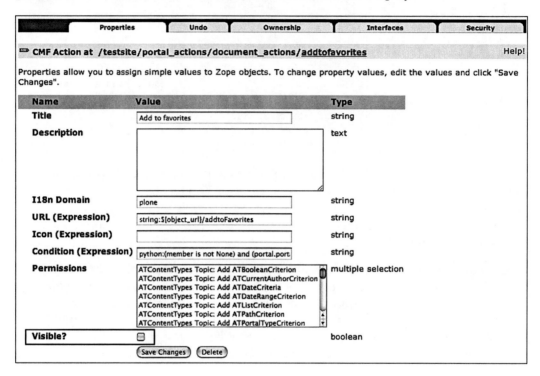

 Note that you should not delete any of the categories, or the actions within them. It is safer to simply not mark the actions as visible."

Document actions category

Within the **document_actions** category, you can alter or add to the buttons and widgets that are available on a given site. These document actions are found in the area outlined in the following screenshot:

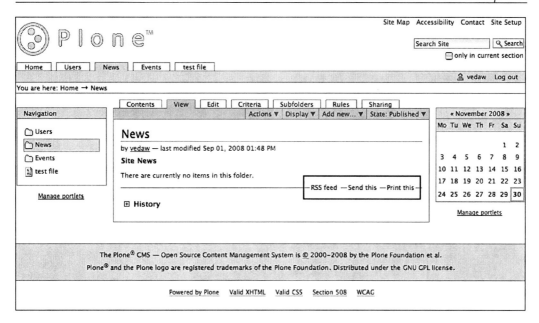

The default document actions include:

- **rss**: Displays an RSS button with a link to the aggregated page; in this case, we see this link because the **News** section is syndicated.

- **sendto**: Displays an email button with the logic needed to email a link to the page to a specified email address.

- **print**: Adds a print button and the logic needed to print the page.

- **addtofavorites**: Flags an item as a favorite; this option only appears and works if you have **user folders** enabled on the security control panel; actual support for this feature is unknown.

- **full_screen**: Expands the window to take up the full screen.

- **extedit**: Enables external editing, if an editor is specified.

Only the first three of these actions are visible by default; the others are not marked as "not visible" in the ZMI and have additional constraints, as defined in their condition expression. **Add to Favorites**, for example, requires a **Members** folder to be installed on the site in order to be functional, and **Toggle Full Screen Mode** requires the user to be logged in.

Site actions category

Within the **site_actions** category, you will find the menu options that correspond to the top navigation on a default Plone installation. By default, these include: **Site Map**, **Accessibility**, **Contact**, and **Site Setup**, as shown in the following screenshot:

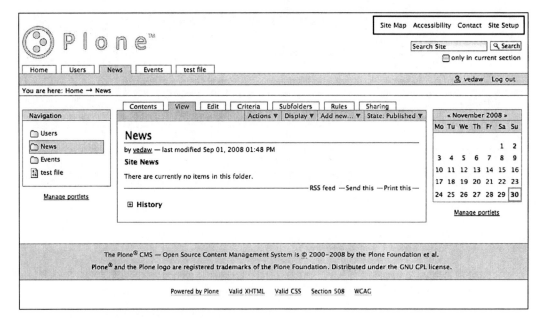

If you want to include an additional menu option here, (for example, a **Site Help** option that is available only to persons with managerial rights) you can add a new CMF action. You will need to specify the **Title**, **Description**, **I18n (internationalization)** domain if you wish to use Plone's translation services, and the URL to which the link will point, utilizing a TALES expression.

Next, you will need to specify the URL of an icon to correspond to the action if one exists, any specific conditions, using a TALES expression, and then select the permissions required for that action. In this case, that permission would be **Manage portal**.

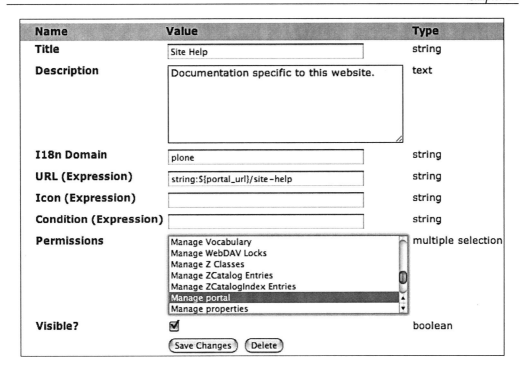

Name	Value	Type
Title	Site Help	string
Description	Documentation specific to this website.	text
I18n Domain	plone	string
URL (Expression)	string:${portal_url}/site-help	string
Icon (Expression)		string
Condition (Expression)		string
Permissions	Manage Vocabulary / Manage WebDAV Locks / Manage Z Classes / Manage ZCatalog Entries / Manage ZCatalogIndex Entries / Manage portal / Manage properties	multiple selection
Visible?	✓	boolean

Save Changes   Delete

Saving the new site action definition shown above will result in the following:

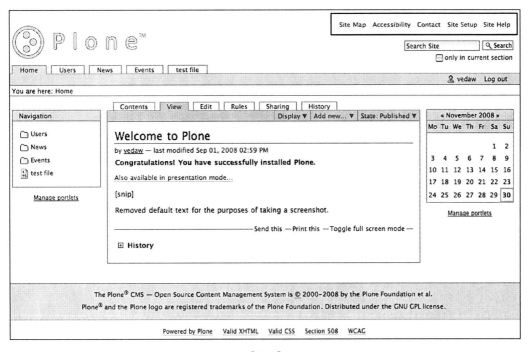

Note the additional menu item on the top. This menu item will only display if the user is logged in, due to the permission specified.

In this fashion, we can add menu options to or remove menu options from this area.

Folder buttons category

Within the **folder_buttons** category, you will find a listing of all of the buttons that are available when a user is on the **Contents** tab of any folder on the site. These include actions that can be taken against a piece of content, such as copy, cut, rename, paste, delete, and change state. You will rarely need to customize these items, but the principle is the same.

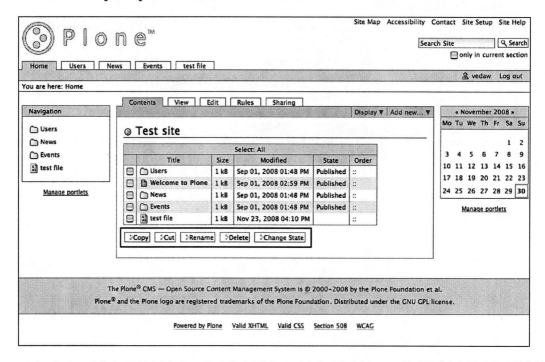

As seen in the following screenshot, the difference between folder buttons and site actions is that a method is passed in the **URL (expression)** field that causes an action to occur, in this case, the copying of an object when the **Copy** button is clicked:

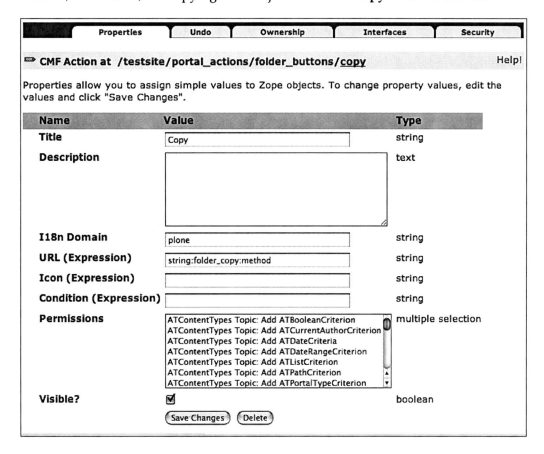

Object category

This category contains actions that appear as the tabs above the content area, as seen in the following screenshot:

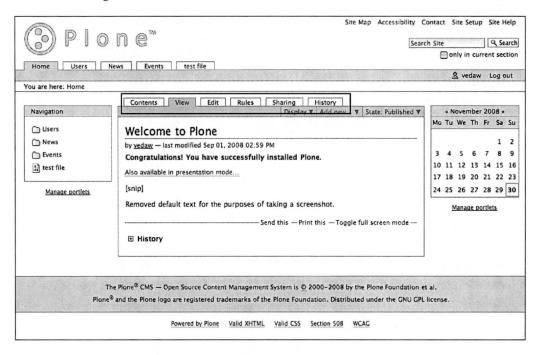

This area includes the following actions:

- **folderContents**: Provides the logic for displaying the **Contents** tab itself, and not the view that you get when you click on it; for this item and the following items, the actual views can either be skin-layer templates or browser views that are configured elsewhere.

- **syndication** : Provides the logic for determining if an object can be syndicated.

- **content rules**: Provides the logic for displaying the view for the **Content Rules** tab.

- **local_roles**: Provides the logic for accessing the **Sharing** tab.

- **history**: Provides the logic for displaying the viewlet for viewing an object's history.

Not all of these actions appear all of the time, as each of them has a special logic that controls their behavior. The **Contents** tab, for example, can only be accessed if you are on a "folderish" item, and the **Syndication** option is generally only turned on for folders such as **News** and **Events**, although the option can be adjusted if desired.

This mechanism does not control the **View** and **Edit** tabs.

Object buttons category

Within this category are the actions that can be taken against a piece of content. These include **Cut**, **Copy**, **Paste**, **Delete** and **Rename**. These items are seen in the drop-down list when you are working with a piece of content:

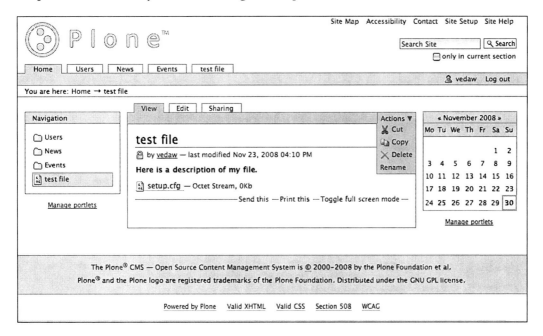

Again, you will rarely need to modify these.

Portal tabs category

This category contains a single action that causes a **Home** tab to be displayed at the top of a default Plone site:

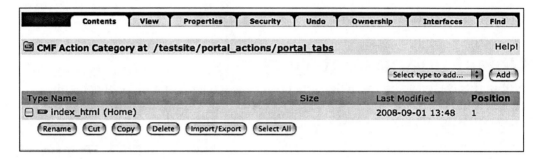

You might see additional items appearing next to the **Home** tab, but these items are controlled by the navigation code. If you alter the navigation settings in the **plone_control_panel** to disable **Automatically generate tabs**, only those tabs defined in the **portal_tabs** category will be displayed.

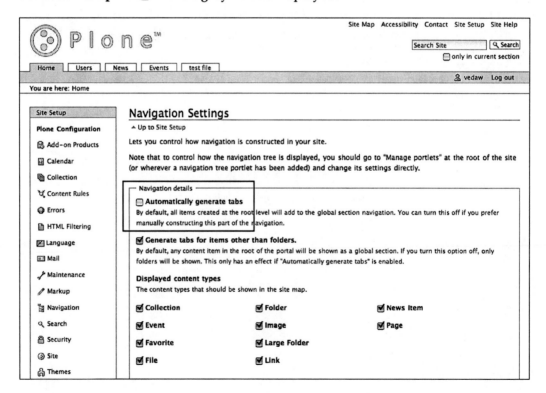

Disabling the automatic generation of tabs will allow you to control your navigation more tightly.

User category

This category contains all of the actions that are displayed in the `portal-personaltools` area of your site. This is the bar with the log out link, as seen in the following screenshot:

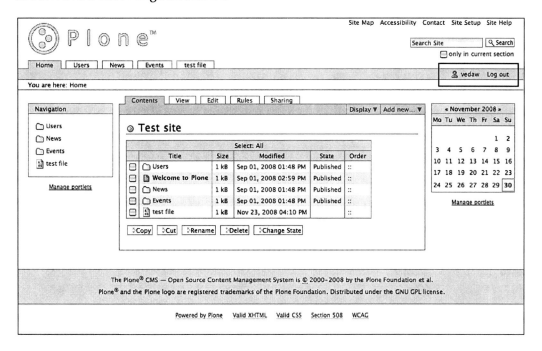

These items are generally displayed only when the user is logged in to the site. They contain all of the functions specific to the logged-in user, many of which are not enabled by default.

These actions include the following:

- A link to the logged in user's **Member** folder (`http://localhost:8080/yoursitename/dashboard`)

- A **preferences** link (`http://localhost:8080/yoursitename/plone_memberprefs_panel`)

- A **login** link (`http://localhost:8080/yoursitename/login_form`; disappears once the user is logged in)

- A **logout** link (`http://localhost:8080/yoursitename/logout`)
- A **join** link (`http://localhost:8080/yoursitename/join_form`)
- An **undo** link (`http://localhost:8080/yoursitename/undo_form`)
- An **Add to Favorites** link
- A **My Favorites** link

Additional items in this area that you could add include the following:

- Link to a Site Help section specific to a client
- Link to Plone documentation
- Link to a Support page

Now that we've looked at how to adjust the buttons, navigation, and other menu items on our site, let's take a look at how we can make larger changes through the customization of templates.

Customization using templates

Site administrators can customize templates within the ZMI by using either the **portal_skins** tool (for traditional CMF skin layer resources), or the **portal_view_customizations** tool (for Zope 3 views, viewlets, and portlets). This chapter will clarify how you can identify which of these you are working with. Although **through-the-web** (TTW) customization is acceptable for making quick fixes, it is not ideal for building or deploying a robust, maintainable project.

First, we will explain how to make changes **through-the-web**, and then explain how these changes can be implemented in a better way in a filesystem-based product.

Skin layer customization—The old fashioned way

Prior to Plone 3.x, most customizations performed in the ZMI relied on the concept of a single, global namespace such that the resources for a given product could not easily be shared between products. This was a fairly limiting idea. Plone before 3.x also used Zope's concept of acquisition. Essentially, this means that when looking for an item, Plone finds the closest object that contains the property. For example, when looking for a logo specific to a given section, Plone first looks in the folder for that section, and if it does not find it, it moves up the folder hierarchy until it finds one.

A Zope object can acquire any object or property from any of its parents. That is, if you have a folder called A containing two resources (a document called homepage and another folder called B), then an URL pointing to `http://.../A/B/homepage` would work even though B is empty. This is because Zope starts to look for homepage in B, doesn't find it, and goes back up to A, where it's found. The reality, inevitably, is more complex than this. For more information, read the chapter on acquisition in the Zope book, which can found at `http://www.zope.org`

A tool called **portal_skins** was created to help manage the resources within Plone and to control the order of acquisition. If you enter the **portal_skins** tool, which is located in the ZMI at `http://localhost:8080/mysite/portal_skins/manage_main` (where `mysite` is the name of your site), and click on the **Properties** tab, you will see a skin called **Plone Default**, and next to it a listing of skin layers. A "skin," often referred to as a "theme," is just an ordered list of skin layers. Don't worry too much about the distinction between skins and themes — there isn't one.

The following is a screenshot of the **portal_skins** tool:

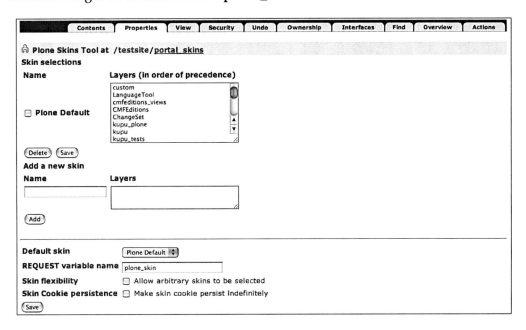

The skin layers listed on the **Properties** tab correspond to folders inside the **portal_skins** tool. A skin's appearance depends heavily on the order in which these skin layers are listed. Plone uses acquisition to look through this list of skin layers, giving precedence to the skin layers at the top of the list. If Plone requests a resource, such as `logo.jpg`, it will look for it by starting at the top of the list and going down until it finds this resource in one of the directories. The **Find** tab in **portal_skins** provides the ability to search for a resource within a selected skin.

Note that there is a drop-down list below the skin layers, called **Default skin**. This area allows you to switch to a different theme product. (A skin product must first be installed via the **portal_quickinstaller** option in the ZMI for it to appear in this list. So it ultimately makes more sense to simply install your skin product in **portal_quickinstaller** for your site rather than use this drop-down option.)

The **custom** skin layer should always appear at the top of the list of skin layers, generally followed by skin layers for a theme or product's images, stylesheets, and templates. This configuration might change in the event that you have a product installed with which you want to override the installed products beneath it. In this case, the product with the most precedence should be listed at the top.

 Skin layers often get out of order when a new product is installed, and this can cause some confusing behavior to occur. It would be helpful to monitor this area during product development, and especially prior to going live with a Plone site.

In the following screenshot, the selected skin is the **Dogwood Theme**. This theme looks first at the **custom** skin layer, then goes down to **dogwood_templates**, **dogwood_styles**, **dogwood_scripts**, **dogwood_images**, **dogwood_content_templates**, and so on, down thorugh the list. Items in the custom layer take precedence over all of the other resources in the skin layers below, as long as **custom** is at the top of the list.

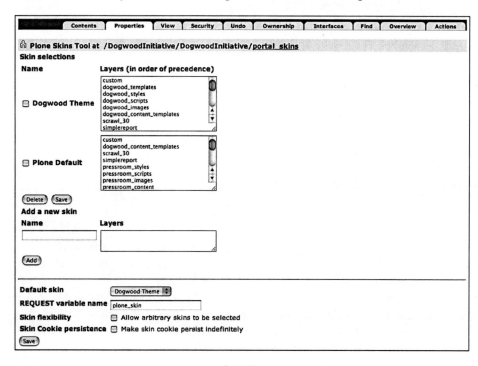

Click on **portal_skins** again to get to the main page that displays all of the available pages, templates, and other resources. To modify one of these resources, locate an item listed there, for example `plone_images/logo.jpg`, and click on it. You will then be given the opportunity to customize that item in the **custom** folder. This is a copy of the original item provided by Zope. Removing that item from the **custom** folder after customizing it means that the site will use the original, non-customized version.

Note that you cannot customize items within their own folders, as they are not folders in the traditional sense. They are filesystem directory views, or folders that correspond to the files inside a particular folder on the filesystem. However, they are not the filesystem themselves. The **custom** folder, in contrast, lives in the **ZODB** (**Zope Object Database**), and its contents cannot be found in the filesystem.

Registering and installing a new filesystem-based skin layer

Let's look now at how we can register a new skin layer in the ZMI. The basic steps involve generating a theme product (or other product), altering some boilerplate code, and then letting Plone know that the skin layer exists.

Getting started

Creating a product that overrides a resource in a skin layer involves carrying out the following steps:

1. Installing **paster** and **ZopeSkel**.
2. Running the appropriate paster recipe to generate a filesystem product.
3. Placing the product in the correct location and registering it in your buildout (see Chapter 13 on buildout for more information, or see the tutorial at `http://plone.org/documentation/tutorial/buildout/installing-a-third-party-product.`)
4. Registering a new filesystem directory view for that product.
5. Placing this view in the list of available skin layers.
6. Copying the relevant resource into the new skin directory layer.
7. Customizing it. Occasionally, a resource also has a metadata file associated with it that must be copied in addition to the resource itself.

There is a good bit of documentation on Plone.org for learning how to create a filesystem product. You may want to look visit the following site if you are unfamiliar with the process: `http://plone.org/documentation/how-to/use-paster/`. You can also refer to the tutorial at: `http://plone.org/documentation/how-to/how-to-create-a-plone-3-theme-product-on-the-filesystem`.

In a nutshell, in Plone 3.x you can now create Zope 2 products that install in your `$PYTHONPATH` in neatly ordered packages, rather than in the flat namespace of the `Products/` directory. Moreover, you can create packages that are not Zope 2 products at all, but which your other products can depend on.

Zope and Plone are steadily moving towards greater dependency on **eggs**—self-contained distributions of code and extensions that can manage dependencies automatically, containing useful metadata. The **buildout** structure of setting up a development environment makes it easier to use these eggs. To support this new structure in your own code, however, you need to provide some boilerplate.

To make creating this boilerplate easier, you can use `ZopeSkel`, a set of `PasteScript` templates for the `paster` command that generates common Plone boilerplate.

Plone 3.2+ installations give you `ZopeSkel` and `paster` by default. To install ZopeSkel in the older versions of 3.x, you first need to have `easy_install` installed on your system. If you don't have it already, download and then run `ez_setup.py`, for example:

```
$ wget peak.telecommunity.com/dist/ez_setup.py
$ python ez_setup.py (where "python" is the version of you are using
  with Plone, e.g. python2.4)
```

Then, to install the `ZopeSkel` egg and its dependencies (including `PasteScript`), run:

```
$ easy_install -U ZopeSkel
```

This will install the `paster` command in the place where your Python binaries go. Keep an eye on the output of `easy_install`, in case you can't find it afterwards. If it's not in your `$PATH`, you may want to symlink it in there.

For now, create a filesystem product using one of the standard `paster` recipes such as:

```
$ paster create -t plone
$ paster create -t plone_app  or
$ paster create -t plone3_theme
```

There are a number of other recipes available. To see the available options, you can run:

```
$ paster create --list-templates
```

If you are creating a Plone-based product, you will need the `plone` recipe; if you are creating a product for the core of plone, you will have to use `plone_app`; if you are creating a theme product, you will want to use the `plone3_theme` recipe. Integrators will probably want to use either the `plone` or `plone3_theme` recipe.

Once the package has been created, you will be given a boilerplate product that holds a **skins** subdirectory with a skin layer directory contained within it. There may be similar folders within the package's `browser/` folder. To register the product with your development environment and make it available for installation, please see Chapter 13. (You will need to return your buildout and restart your Zope in order to see any changes to your `buildout.cfg` file.) We'll cover the buildout setup very briefly in a moment, after we have seen how to generate a product.

Once your product is correctly registered, you should install the product through the ZMI using **portal_quickinstaller**. If your product is not displayed in this list, it is likely that you did not register it correctly in your buildout.

For the purpose of this chapter, we are using the `plone3_theme` recipe to demonstrate what a Plone 3 product looks like, although the theory is the same for policy products as well. Where differences occur between themes and policy products, these will be described. Here, we will create a Plone theme called `plonetheme.example` (it's best to not create an egg with spaces in the name, and the word `plonetheme` distinguishes it from other kinds of eggs). In this case, I am creating the product in my personal buildout, named `rockaway` in this example:

```
[bash: /opt/zope/buildouts/rockaway/src] paster create -t plone3_theme
Selected and implied templates:
  ZopeSkel#basic_namespace  A project with a namespace package
  ZopeSkel#plone            A Plone project
  ZopeSkel#plone3_theme     A Theme for Plone 3.0
Enter project name: plonetheme.example
Variables:
  egg:      plonetheme.example
  package:  plonetheme.example
  project:  plonetheme.example
Enter namespace_package (Namespace package (like plonetheme))
['plonetheme']:
Enter package (The package contained namespace package (like example))
['example']:
Enter skinname (The skin selection to be added to 'portal_skins' (like
'My Theme')) ['']: example
Enter skinbase (Name of the skin selection from which the new one will
be copied) ['Plone Default']:
Enter empty styles (Override default public stylesheets with empty
ones?) [True]: False
```

```
Enter include_doc (Include in-line documentation in generated code?)
[False]:
Enter zope2product (Are you creating a Zope 2 Product?) [True]:
Enter version (Version) ['0.1']:
Enter description (One-line description of the package) ['An
installable theme for Plone 3.0']:
Enter long_description (Multi-line description (in reST)) ['']:
Enter author (Author name) ['Plone Collective']:
Enter author_email (Author email) ['product-developers@lists.plone.
org']:
Enter keywords (Space-separated keywords/tags) ['web zope plone
theme']:
Enter url (URL of homepage) ['http://svn.plone.org/svn/collective/']:
Enter license_name (License name) ['GPL']:
Enter zip_safe (True/False: if the package can be distributed as a
.zip file) [False]:
```

In the case of the `plonetheme.example` shown here, which has been installed on a Plone site, you can see that the skins subdirectory contains three folders that are the same skin layers found in the ZMI. These are `plonetheme_example_custom_images`, `plonetheme_example_styles`, and `plonetheme_example_custom_templates`.

Optionally, you could create additional folders/skin layers that holds scripts or other resources. You simply need to configure the boilerplate to address this need. Follow the example that the generated filesystem product gives you for the folder structure, and modify it in a similar fashion if you wish. The following is a screenshot of the output given to us by the `plone3_theme` paster recipe:

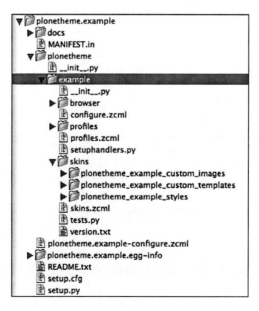

To register this product as a filesystem directory view, we must modify
the __init__.py file so that Plone can see it:

```
def initialize(context):
    "Initializer called when used as a Zope 2 product."
```

By default, this is done for us.

Additionally, we must ensure that this package is a Zope 2 product. If it is in the
magical Products.* namespace (for example, a traditional product placed in the
Products directory in a Zope instance), this happens automatically. If we are using
an egg-based product in a different namespace, we need to add this to the package's
configure.zcml file, as follows:

```
<configure
    xmlns="http://namespaces.zope.org/zope"
    xmlns:five="http://namespaces.zope.org/five"
    xmlns:cmf="http://namespaces.zope.org/cmf"
    i18n_domain="plonetheme.example">
    <five:registerPackage package="." initialize=".initialize" />
    <include package=".browser" />
    <include file="skins.zcml" />
    <include file="profiles.zcml" />
</configure>
```

The line registering our package with the product Five allows the **portal_
quickinstaller** to see our theme product. Again, this is available by default.

We then need to create the directory view and install it for the current skin, when
the product is installed on a Plone site. We do this using GenericSetup, which we
will cover in depth later. First, we must register a new **extension profile** so that the
product is installable. An extension profile is a profile that extends the configuration
of an existing site. This is done in the profiles.zcml file, as follows:

```
<configure
    xmlns="http://namespaces.zope.org/zope"
    xmlns:genericsetup="http://namespaces.zope.org/genericsetup"
    i18n_domain="plonetheme.example">
  <genericsetup:registerProfile
      name="default"
      title="example"
      directory="profiles/default"
      description='Extension profile for the "example" Plone theme.'
      provides="Products.GenericSetup.interfaces.EXTENSION"
      />
</configure>
```

Once again, this is done for us by default.

Next, we need to configure the `skins.xml` file located in the `profiles` directory to indicate which directories are to be treated as skin layer folders — in this case, `plonetheme_example_custom_images`, `plonetheme_example_custom_templates` and `plonetheme_example_styles`.

```
<?xml version="1.0"?>
<object name="portal_skins" allow_any="False"
      cookie_persistence="False"
   default_skin="example">
 <object name="plonetheme_example_custom_images"
    meta_type="Filesystem Directory View"
    directory="plonetheme.example:skins/
                 plonetheme_example_custom_images"/>
 <object name="plonetheme_example_custom_templates"
    meta_type="Filesystem Directory View"
    directory="plonetheme.example:skins/
                 plonetheme_example_custom_templates"/>
 <object name="plonetheme_example_styles"
    meta_type="Filesystem Directory View"
    directory="plonetheme.example:skins/plonetheme_example_styles"/>
 <skin-path name="example" based-on="Plone Default">
  <layer name="plonetheme_example_custom_images"
     insert-after="custom"/>
  <layer name="plonetheme_example_custom_templates"
     insert-after="plonetheme_example_custom_images"/>
  <layer name="plonetheme_example_styles"
     insert-after="plonetheme_example_custom_templates"/>
 </skin-path>
</object>
```

This code is generated automatically for us. You can register as many additional directory views as you wish, as long as you follow the boilerplate example.

To test that the boilerplate is properly configured, we must then register the product for installation. To do so, we need to modify our `buildout.cfg` file to specify the theme product, as discussed previously.

```
[buildout]
 ...
 develop =
    src/plonetheme.example
[instance]
 eggs =
 ...
    plonetheme.example
 zcml =
 ...
    plonetheme.example
```

Then, we need to re-run buildout:

`./bin/buildout`

Once buildout finishes running, restart Zope:

`./bin/instance fg`

Next, go to the ZMI via `http://localhost:8080/manage_main/` and create a Plone site via the drop-down list on the top right, giving it a portal name and a description.

Then, through the ZMI, drill down to the option called **portal_quickinstaller** and find the name of your theme product. Select the checkbox next to the product and then click on **Install**.

☐ **Working Copy Support (Iterate)**	1.1.5
☐ **dogwood.content**	0.1
☑ **example**	0.1
☐ **guria**	0.1
☐ **qPloneComments**	2.3.1
☐ **slideshowfolder**	4.0

(Install)

Installed Products

Product	Version at Install time Product version

(Uninstall) (Reinstall)

It is important to remember that when making any skin changes, it helps to put your **portal_css** in **debug** mode so that you can see your changes. You can do this by drilling into your web site through the ZMI and looking for the option named **portal_css**: `http://www.mysite.com/portal_css/manage_workspace`.

Do not leave a production site in debug mode. It will cause performance issues because the CSS will be uncompressed and uncached.

Next, try to override the standard Plone logo. To do this, put any `logo.jpg` in the theme product's images folder (we know that `base_properties` for Plone defaults to `logo.jpg` for the logo, although this can be adjusted). In this case, the image needs to go in the `plonetheme/example/skins/plonetheme_example_custom_images` folder.

You should also make sure that your cache is cleared. Firefox's Web Developer Toolbar may come in handy here, as it has a **disable cache** option that can be set. See the help text for the toolbar add-on to locate this option.

Again, if you have made changes to your ZCML or your GenericSetup profile, you need to restart Zope and install the product if you have not already done so:

```
./bin/instance fg
```

The rules for restarts/reinstalls are as follows:

- If you change your `buildout.cfg` file, you must re-run your buildout.
- If you change ZCML, you must restart Zope. You can use the `plone.reload` product discussed in Chapter 13 to avoid the need for full Zope restarts: `http:// pypi.python.org/pypi/plone.reload`
- If you change GenericSetup, you must reinstall your product or import the specific GenericSetup steps you need.
- If you change your CSS or Script (Python) files, just refresh your browser, assuming that **portal_css** is in debug mode.

Again, remember that anything located in the `skins/` directory can be modified TTW via **portal_skins**.

In the past, all Plone resources could be managed via **portal_skins**, including images, style sheets, JavaScript files, page templates, and Python scripts. However, this framework has been revised to make it more flexible. Many of the resources that Plone needs following the 3.x release are not immediately available through the **portal_skins** interface because they are Zope 3 views, not templates.

In general, if a resource is mentioned in the Plone UI (for example, from a URL, an action in **portal_actions**, or an alias in **portal_types**) and it is not prefixed with either `@@` (for example, `@@view`) or `++resource++` (for example, `++resource++stylesheet.css`), then it is likely to be found in a skin layer available via **portal_skins**.

Portlet templates may or may not be in **portal_skins**, depending on whether the portlet is a Classic (pre-Plone 3.x) portlet or a Plone 3 portlet. If you wish to edit a portlet and you are not sure if it is a Classic portlet or not, click on the portlet in the `@@manage-portlets` interface (available via the **Manage Portlets** link at the bottom of the left and right columns). Additionally, if your portlet contains all of its code in a single page template file, it's likely that you're working with a Classic portlet.

Similarly, if you are working with a **viewlet**, then that item will not be modifiable via **portal_skins**, but via **portal_view_customizations** or through filesystem development (preferred). Most of the structural pieces of Plone are now considered viewlets. We will cover these shortly.

Zope 3 basics

How do you tell the difference between Zope 2 and Zope 3 code? And what is Zope 3 anyway?

Plone 3 sits on top of a combination of Zope 2 and Zope 3 architectures. It is not a pure Zope 3 implementation, in spite of the ongoing perception that it is. You might recognize the name **Five**, which is a product that helped bridge the gap from Zope 2 and Zope 3 (2+3=5). Five is now baked into Plone and is the basis of the Plone 3 architecture, but you will still hear it referred to as Zope 3 most of the time. Pure Zope 3 doesn't have acquisition, but Five does, and Plone still relies on it.

Plone's Zope 3 implementation differs from Zope 2 in a number of ways. Plone 3 introduces the concept of a Component Architecture that encourages the reusability of existing components. Essentially, components need to know what the other components promise or provide. This information can be gleaned through the use of interfaces and adapters. Interfaces describe the methods and attributes that an object provides. They describe *what* a component can do, but not *how*. Adapters provide a link to the *how* piece of the puzzle.

Adapters extend the existing components without changing the code of the original component. They connect the request and the context to a third object (the browser view). The request is the web browser request (the get command), and the context is where you are on your Plone site. A browser view is simply an adapter of the context and a request (usually for a context with a particular interface and a request with a particular layer), and is dependent on both. But there are many other types of adapters in Zope 3 besides browser views, including views, viewlets, and portlets.

Think of an adapter like this: you're looking for an interpreter to translate between two people who speak different languages. One person represents the request, and one person represents the context. The interpreter is the browser view that connects them. You might need to get a different interpreter if the request or the context provides IJapanese instead of IEnglish. For example, you can't ask someone who speaks IJapanese to translate ISpanish for someone who speaks IEnglish.

If you want to identify a particular interpreter, you also need to specify his or her name (for example, David, the English-German interpreter vs. Andrew, the English-German interpreter), because there might be various interpreters for any given pair of languages. (This corresponds to the name of a browser view — you can have different named views of the same context/request pair.)

Zope 3 only knows how to find an adapter if you tell it about the available adapters. We do that using **ZCML**, the **Zope Configuration Markup Language**. This is an XML dialect that is used to configure many aspects of Zope 3 code, such as permissions and component registration. You can do what ZCML does by using Python code as well, but typically it's more convenient to use ZCML because it allows you to separate your logic from your configuration.

ZCML directives are stored in a file called `configure.zcml`, which in turn may include other files. A `configure.zcml` file in your products directory (`Products/myproduct/configure.zcml`) will be picked up automatically as long as the product is in the Products namespace. Packages in other namespaces need to have a ZCML **slug** (a slug is a ZCML line that includes another file; it's usually generated by buildout these days, or else is included from another product's ZCML) so that their `configure.zcml` can be read.

Another concept that has been borrowed from Zope 3 involves eliminating the idea of a single, global namespace. Now, resources can be registered in ZCML based on their context, so a view called `@@view` can be used in more than one location and displayed differently each time. The benefit of this is that you can be much more specific about what sort of an object a view might be valid for, whereas, with templates in skin layers, you can navigate to the template from any object (but it's not likely to work or be useful for most of them).

These resources can optionally be registered as a **browser layer** and exposed to outside your immediate package. A Zope 3 browser layer is similar in purpose to a CMF skin layer that is accessible via **portal_skins**, or the skins directory of your product, but it is implemented very differently.

Zope 3 browser layers

The next two paragraphs may be daunting, but don't worry. Again, think about the idea of the adapter as a translator. The intricacies of the concepts here are not as important as understanding that Zope 3 components rely on each other in order to produce a result, and that they are not modified in the **portal_skins** tool.

Technically speaking, a **portal_skins** layer is a container of templates and resources, whereas a browser layer is an empty, marker interface that is applied to the request upon traversal, and for which views (and templates, resources, viewlets, and portlet renderers, which are all special types of views) can be registered. A marker interface is simply a flag that says "I have a special purpose," and is expressed as an empty interface. Views and their derivatives attach to that flagged item and respond appropriately when they are called.

A Zope 3 browser resource is a multi-adapter on the context and the request. When the request is marked with a particular interface, the Component Architecture may find a more specific adapter in a view registered for that particular layer.

It's a complex concept, but an important one to understand. Essentially, the browser layer technology keeps your ZCML registrations from applying to all of the Plone sites on a given instance. If it wasn't for the browser layer support, a `logo.jpg` that is registered as a browser resource might show up for *all* of the sites on a given Plone instance. It can be very difficult to diagnose how or where one Plone site is stepping on another Plone site, so it's important to be proactive and use the browser layer technology before problems occur.

Note that it is good practice to use the browser layer technology in almost all circumstances, except when you are writing a package that needs to be used by all of the products on a site, such as in a diagnostic utility.

Using plone.theme to enable a custom browser layer interface

There is an implementation of the browser layer concept that is specific to themes. This technology is gleaned from the `plone.theme`, which is a package that ships with Plone. It's commonly referred to as **IThemeSpecific**.

The `plone.theme` package lets you mark the request with a `layer` interface conditional on the currently-selected skin (theme) in the **portal_skins** tool. This means that when that theme is installed, all items in the browser space need to use the `IThemeSpecific` layer designation to keep them from clashing with other themes (not sites) that might exist in the same Zope instance.

In the following example, we are customizing the global sections viewlet, or top navigation. In addition to other steps that will be covered in Chapter 18, you need to edit your `browser/configuration.zcml` file as follows:

```
<!-- Viewlets registration -->
    <browser:viewlet
        name="example.global_sections"
        manager="plone.app.layout.viewlets.interfaces.IPortalHeader"
        layer=".interfaces.IThemeSpecific"
        class=".viewlets.GlobalSectionsViewlet"
        permission="zope2.View"
        />
```

Note that the dotted names begin with a dot, which means "relative to the current directory."

There are two problems with this implementation. First, every time you customize an object in your browser space, you must remember to tell it to use the `IThemeSpecific` layer. This is easily forgotten, which can lead to theme clashes.

The second problem with the `plone.theme` implementation is that although this functionality is useful for products that install a whole new theme in Plone, it's less useful for general (non-theme) products, as only one `plone.theme-installed` layer is active at any given point in time. For maximum flexibility, layer installation needs to be additive, so that we can install any number of products, each providing its own layer. We'll cover that next.

Using browser layer technology to allow additive layers

The most common way to enable a custom browser layer interface is to use the `plone.browserlayer` package. This package works somewhat differently behind the scenes to the `plone.theme`. This package is not part of Plone 3.x out-of-the-box, but its functionality ships with Plone 3.1. For 3.x products, we must install it along with our package.

To make use of a `plone.browerslayer` layer in a Plone add-on product, we need to:

1. Define a marker interface representing the browser layer. A marker interface is simply a class with no body, deriving from `zope.interface.Interface`. Put another way, a marker interface is nothing more than a dummy interface that gets added to your `interfaces.py` file.

2. Ensure that the interface is applied to the request automatically, enabling the browser layer for our site. Registering the layer in `browserlayer.xml` will take care of this.

3. Register our browser resources, views, viewlets, and portlets for the new layer by using the ZCML directives. This allows the resources to override the defaults.

Add the marker interface to your package by adding the following line to the `interfaces.py` file:

```
from zope.interface import Interface
from zope.publisher.interfaces.browser import IDefaultBrowserLayer
from zope.viewlet.interfaces import IViewletManager
```

In the same file, you must then tell your class to use the interface, as follows:

```
class IMyBrowserLayer(IDefaultBrowserLayer):
    " Marker interface for this product's browser layer."
```

For an egg-based product, we can get `plone.browserlayer` by requiring it in the `mypackage/configure.zcml` file. We simply add the following line to the file:

```
<include package="plone.browserlayer" />
```

The ZCML line above makes sure that `plone.browserlayer`'s ZCML is read. This could also be done by creating a ZCML slug (or having buildout do that for you), but it's probably better to explicitly declare the dependency, as above, so that users of the add-on product can get by without needing to create the slug themselves. It's better to build this into your product.

The following code is different, and is also needed. It tells `easy_install` (and thus also buildout, which uses `easy_install`) that this add-on product depends on `plone.browserlayer`, and that this should also be installed.

To summarize the difference, the line above relates to loading ZCML every time Zope starts, and the lines below relate to installing the products in the first place (often a one-time thing).

```
install_requires=[
        'setuptools',
        'plone.browserlayer',
        # -*- Extra requirements: -*-
    ],
```

Additionally, you will need to use buildout or `easy_install` to download and install the package: `http://pypi.python.org/pypi/plone.browserlayer`.

If the dependency is declared correctly in the add-on product's `setup.py` file, this should happen automatically.

 Plone 3.x requires a version of `plone.browserlayer` that is no later than version 1.0rc3 (because subsequent versions depend on GenericSetup support for registering setup steps in ZCML, and this wasn't introduced until Plone 3.1.x).

Next, we need to ensure that the interface is applied to the request automatically, enabling the browser layer in our site. We also need to install `plone.browserlayer` as a product. In the absence of GenericSetup dependency support (scheduled for Plone 3.1), we do so by using an `Extensions/Install.py` file inside our package, using the boilerplate code found in Martin Aspeli's tutorial on browser layers: `http://plone.org/documentation/tutorial/customization-for-developers/browser-layers`.

Note that this is the best way to do this in Plone 3.x.

Alternatively, you can skip the code above, and just install the **Local browser layer support** profile before installing your add-on product. In Plone 3.1.x, the `plone.browserlayer` profile does not exist and does not need to be installed in order to use `plone.browserlayer`.

With this, `plone.browserlayer` (**Local browser layer support**) will be installed when we install our product, and it's now safe to load your package onto your Zope instance without fear of your product interacting negatively with another package.

The final step is to register our browser resources, views, viewlets, and portlets for the new layer by using ZCML directives. For example, if we wish to customize the personal bar for a product, the following code would need to be added to the `browser/configure.zcml` file, and the local browser layer would need to be applied:

```
<browser:viewlet
        name="mypackage.personal_bar"
        manager="plone.app.layout.viewlets.interfaces.IPortalTop"
        layer="..interfaces.IMyPackageLayer"
        class=".viewlets.PersonalBarViewlet"
        permission="zope2.View"
        />
```

This is only one part of what is needed to customize viewlets. Advanced customization of viewlets is covered in more detail in Chapter 18.

About Zope 3 browser resources

Zope 3 browser resources can encompass images, stylesheets, views, viewlets, and portlets. Each one of these is managed in a similar fashion, via ZCML registrations.

Before we dive in, it's important to remember that any time you alter your ZCML, in order to see your changes you must restart Zope. In the beginning, as you get used to using ZCML, this can be a time-consuming process. Over the time, you will do fewer restarts, and the process will get faster.

It is also very important, when developing a filesystem product, to run Zope in the foreground by using `./bin/instance fg` when you start your Zope, so that you can detect bugs in your ZCML code more easily, through traceback errors that may occur.

Images and stylesheets

Zope 3 allows browser resources, notably images and stylesheets, to be registered under a special namespace. For example, if you register an image resource in your browser folder with the name `myimage.gif`, the browser resource would be addressable as `http://yoursite.com/++resource++myimage.gif`.

This serves to get the resource out of the flat global namespace. This allows a resource to be used more flexibly. Browser resources don't do much by themselves. They are typically installed in a registry such as **portal_css**, **portal_javascripts**, or **portal_kss**, or used in actions or other links.

Similar to all Zope 3 browser components, browser resources are registered with a ZCML directive in the browser namespace that takes, among other things, a layer attribute. The layer should resolve to an interface.

For an example of a browser resource, take the `plone.app.iterate` package. In its `browser/configure.zcml` file, you will find the following definition:

```
<browser:resource
      name="checkin.png"
      image="checkin.png"
      />
```

This defines a resource, `++resource++checkin.png`, which is used in the check-in action when `iterate` is installed. If we wanted to alter this button, we could customize it using the `IMyPackageLayer`. With a custom image called `new_checkin.png` in our own `browser/` directory, we would add the following code to the `browser/configure.zcml` file:

```
<configure
    xmlns="http://namespaces.zope.org/zope"
    xmlns:browser="http://namespaces.zope.org/browser"
    i18n_domain="my.product">
    <browser:resource
        name="checkin.png"
        image="new_checkin.png"
        layer=".interfaces.IMyPackageLayer"
        />
</configure>
```

Note that without the layer attribute, we would get a configuration conflict with the original `++resource++checkin.png` definition.

For registering images and stylesheets in a Python package, it's best to register them one at a time, and not in a folder. This is because overriding a single item within that folder would mean overriding every item in the folder. The `plone3_theme` recipe incorrectly implies that a folder should be used to hold these resources.

Browser views and pages

It is possible to customize browser view and pages either through the ZMI or through the filesystem, although it is advisable to make changes through the filesystem wherever possible. We'll cover both the methods.

Browser views are similar to page templates (`.pt` files) in skin layers. However, they are registered in ZCML for a particular type of context. They can also be associated with a class that provides extra functionality implemented in Python.) Here is an example from a theme product that has a custom homepage view:

```
<!-- Browser views -->
    <browser:page
        for="*"
        name="@@hp_view"
        class=".homepage.Homepage"
        layer=".interfaces.IThemeSpecific"
        permission="zope2.View"
        />
```

In this example, a browser resource is defined for a homepage view, `@@hp_view`, and is available for any context (`for="*"`). Although the `@@` disambiguator is not strictly necessary, it makes it clear that this is a view and not, say, a content item or a skin layer template. The implementation is held in a class called `hp_view` in a file named `homepage.py` in the current directory. You can either use a skin layer template named `homepage.pt` (not shown in the previous example) which navigates to the view as `context/@@hp_view` and then calls methods on it, or you can use a class-based viewlet which pulls in the template via its render attribute and refers to the view instance as a view.

Similarly, here is an example of a browser page from `plone.app.content.browser`:

```
<browser:page
        for="*"
        class=".reviewlist.FullReviewListView"
        name="full_review_list"
        permission="cmf.ReviewPortalContent"
    />
```

For this example, a browser page is defined for a view called `full_review_list`, which is available to all users with Review Portal Content rights. It's available in any context, and is held in a class called `FullReviewListView.py`, which is defined in `reviewlist.py`, in the current folder, and rendered by a template named `full_review_list.pt`.

One way to customize this resource is to provide an override for a more specific (or different) context. The * context is the most general (under the hood, this means `zope.interface.Interface`). If we had our own implementation for a standard Page (as identified by the `Products.ATContentTypes.interface.document.IATDocument` interface), we could do so with the following declaration in our own package's ZCML:

```
<browser:page
        for="Products.ATContentTypes.interface.document.IATDocument"
        class="plone.app.content.browser.
              reviewlist.FullReviewListView"
        name="full_review_list"
        template="document_full_review_list.pt"
        permission="cmf.ReviewPortalContent" />
```

Here, we have chosen to use the default layer (that is, we haven't specified a layer), but a new context type (by using the `for` attribute, which points to the interface of the context type in question). We could have provided a new class (or none at all), but here, we use the default view class from `plone.app.content`.

Note that we have converted this from a relative module path to an absolute one, as we are now in a different package! This is extremely important. We also change the template, which again is relative to the directory in which the ZCML file can be found. We could have chosen to use only a class or a template if that made more sense.

Alternatively, we could customize it by layer (and thus ensure that the customization only takes effect when the product is installed). Here is another example, this time replacing the default view with a new one, using the old class with a new template:

```
<browser:page
        for="*"
        class="plone.app.content.browser.
              reviewlist.FullReviewListView"
        name="full_review_list"
        template="standard_full_review_list.pt"
        layer=".interfaces.IExampleCustomization"
        permission="cmf.ReviewPortalContent" />
```

Note that these two declarations can co-exist. In this case, the default will use standard_full_review_list.pt, but the view on a Page will use document_full_review_list.pt, as it is more specific. Of course, we could do both—use a context override, and a layer. Thus, the context override would take effect only if the layer is installed.

Another example could be that you want to modify the **Events** portlet to be specific to your own theme product and you have customized the template of the events portlet, events.pt.

```
<plone:portletRenderer
    portlet="plone.app.portlets.portlets.events.IEventsPortlet"
    template="mytheme_events.pt"
    layer=".interfaces.IThemeSpecific"
    />
```

Here, the portlet points to the interface defined in plone.app.portlets, but it uses a different, local template in this case, mytheme_events.pt. It's not necessary to rename the portlet template, but renaming makes it easier to find the correct template in **portal_view_customizations** in the ZMI. We'll cover this in a moment.

Using portal_view_customizations

Assuming that you have a product that has browser resources in place, you can modify these resources through the ZMI in **portal_view_customizations**, which is available from the http://mysite.com/manage_main page. These browser resources may be resources that are exposed from base Plone, or they may be resources that you've created, added, and registered in your filesystem package.

You can only *modify* browser resources here; you cannot add new browser resources. This is a serious limitation of the **portal_view_customizations** tool. Addition of new browser resources must first be done on the filesystem so that the appropriate ZCML configurations can be defined. Customization of Python code must also be done on the filesystem.

The **portal_view_customizations** page appears as shown in the following screenshot:

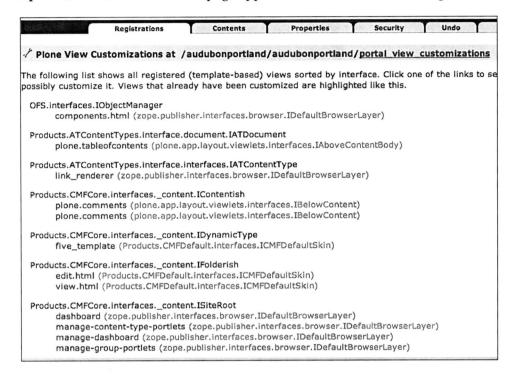

Finding views

As of Plone 3.1, if you have multiple products with customized resources (that is, you have three themes living on the same Zope instance that have `portal_footer.pt` customized), you will find all of these items exposed in **portal_view_customizations**.

> Note the multiple versions of `audience_navigation.pt`, `collection.pt` and `events.pt` in the following screenshot. For the last two, all three links end up editing the same file, and there's no way to edit the others. It's more of a bug, and not just poor design, and has been resolved as of Plone 3.1.4.

```
zope.interface.Interface
    addform_macros (zope.publisher.interfaces.browser.IDefaultBrowserLayer)
    audience_navigation.pt (Products.GreenSeattleTheme.browser.audience_navigation.IAudienceNavigationPortlet)
    audience_navigation.pt (plonetheme.tilth.browser.audience_navigation.IAudienceNavigationPortlet)
    audubonportland.path_bar (plone.app.layout.viewlets.interfaces.IContentViews)
    base-pageform.html (zope.publisher.interfaces.browser.IDefaultBrowserLayer)
    base-subpageform.html (zope.publisher.interfaces.browser.IDefaultBrowserLayer)
    batch_widget (Products.CMFDefault.interfaces.ICMFDefaultSkin)
    calendar.pt (plone.app.portlets.portlets.calendar.ICalendarPortlet)
    calendar_day.html (Products.CMFDefault.interfaces.ICMFDefaultSkin)
    calendar_widget (Products.CMFDefault.interfaces.ICMFDefaultSkin)
    classic.pt (plone.app.portlets.portlets.classic.IClassicPortlet)
    collection.pt (plone.portlet.collection.collection.ICollectionPortlet)
    collection.pt (plone.portlet.collection.collection.ICollectionPortlet)
    collection.pt (plone.portlet.collection.collection.ICollectionPortlet)
    consbio.logo (plone.app.layout.viewlets.interfaces.IPortalHeader)
    consbio.searchbox (plone.app.layout.viewlets.interfaces.IPortalHeader)
    customizezpt.html (zope.publisher.interfaces.browser.IDefaultBrowserLayer)
    edit-markers.html (zope.publisher.interfaces.browser.IDefaultBrowserLayer)
    events.pt (plone.app.portlets.portlets.events.IEventsPortlet)
    events.pt (plone.app.portlets.portlets.events.IEventsPortlet)
    events.pt (plone.app.portlets.portlets.events.IEventsPortlet)
```

As of version 3.1.4, all of the browser resources available for the current product will be displayed in **portal_view_customizations**. But the grey text is a browser layer in all cases, rather than a portlet schema, or a viewlet manager interface in some cases. So it will be possible to know which one you're editing. And it will also work when you click on it!

For the meantime, if you expect your web site integrators to use **portal_view_ customizations**, it is always best to create a new name for your browser resource, such as audubonportland.path_bar or consbio.logo, as listed above. Just remember to bring those customizations out to the filesystem if you ever want to use the changes in a distributed product.

You can also do either of the following to locate the desired browser resources:

1. Go to **portal_view_customizations** in the ZMI, where you will find views, viewlets, and portlet renderers, grouped together according to their context type. Hover your mouse over the view title, and you should see a package name and a template name in a tool tip. This, unfortunately, does not resolve the problem mentioned above. Naming your browser resources specific to your product can help here.

2. Append /@@zptviews.html to the end of a particular URL, for example, http://localhost:8080/plone/@@zptviews.html. This shows views with templates (but not viewlets or portlet renderers, unfortunately), along with their template, context type interface, and source ZCML file.

Viewlets

Now, it is time to look at viewlets, which are small bits of code that represent pieces of functionality on a Plone site. Examples of viewlets are the breadcrumbs, the searchbox, the footer, and the logo.

These snippets can be customized and moved around in order to make changes to Plone's default appearance. Rather than make changes to `main_template.pt`, we will rely on XML and ZCML declarations to make these changes. Previously, `main_template.pt` consisted of code that referenced page templates using lengthy TAL statements. For example:

```
<div id="portal-top" i18n:domain="plone">

    <div id="portal-header">
      <p class="hiddenStructure">
        <a accesskey="2"
           tal:attributes="href string:${current_page_url}
                            #documentContent"
           i18n:translate="label_skiptocontent">
          Skip to content.
        </a>

        <a accesskey="6"
           tal:attributes="href string:${current_page_url}
                            #portlet-navigation-tree"
           i18n:translate="label_skiptonavigation">
            Skip to navigation
        </a>
      </p>

        <div metal:use-macro="here/global_siteactions/
                            macros/site_actions">
          Site-wide actions (Contact, Sitemap, Help, Style
                            Switcher etc)
        </div>

        <div metal:use-macro="here/global_searchbox/
                            macros/quick_search">
          The quicksearch box, normally placed at the top right
        </div>

        <a metal:use-macro="here/global_logo/
                            macros/portal_logo">
          The portal logo, linked to the portal root
        </a>

        <div metal:use-macro="here/global_skinswitcher/
                            macros/skin_tabs">
```

```
                    The skin switcher tabs. Based on which role you have,
                    you get a selection of skins that you can switch
                    between.
                </div>

                <div metal:use-macro="here/global_sections/
                                      macros/portal_tabs">
                    The global sections tabs. (Welcome, News etc)
                </div>
            </div>

            <div metal:use-macro="here/global_personalbar/
                                  macros/personal_bar">
                The personal bar. (log in, logout etc...)
            </div>

             <div metal:use-macro="here/global_pathbar/
                                   macros/path_bar">
                The breadcrumb navigation ("you are here")
            </div>
        </div>
```

The preceding code has now been rewritten to look much slimmer, as shown here:

```
<div id="portal-top" i18n:domain="plone">
        <div tal:replace="structure provider:plone.portaltop" />
</div>
```

Moving parts around means modifying the `main_template.pt`, which presents upgrade problems and can be messy at times. For Plone 3.x, if you look at the `main_template.pt` found in `parts/plone/CMFPlone/skins/plone_templates/ main_template.pt`, you will find various bits of code that indicate where a viewlet is displayed in the `main_template.pt`, in a much cleaner fashion.

 Although it is still discouraged to make changes to `main_template. pt`, it is sometimes necessary, but only if modifying and moving viewlets is not the solution. Modifying `main_template.pt` may introduce migration issues that will need to be addressed when a migration is attempted.

Note that the `main_template.pt` does not show the actual viewlets themselves. The **provider** TAL expression above is a Zope 3 expression that looks up a content provider from a page template. In Zope 3, a content provider is a component that generates a portion of an HTML page. Similar to Zope 3 views, content providers are multi-adapters that adapt to the context and the request. Content providers additionally adapt the view from which they were invoked.

Viewlets are a type of content provider; they are small components of a page that render a small piece of HTML code. In Plone templates, viewlets are not looked up directly, though. In order to be able to organize viewlets with maximum flexibility, they are aggregated in **viewlet managers**. A viewlet manager is also a Zope 3 content provider, which renders a set of viewlets that are registered to it.

Viewlet registration happens in ZCML, and this will be covered in detail in the next chapter. You can then move, reorder, and hide viewlets in myproduct/profiles/default/viewlets.xml. To find the base Plone viewlets.xml file, go to: parts/plone/CMFPlone/profiles/default/viewlets.xml. This file looks like as follows:

```xml
<?xml version="1.0"?>
<object>
  <order manager="plone.portaltop" skinname="Plone Default">
    <viewlet name="plone.header" />
    <viewlet name="plone.personal_bar" />
    <viewlet name="plone.app.i18n.locales.languageselector" />
    <viewlet name="plone.path_bar" />
  </order>
  <order manager="plone.portalheader" skinname="Plone Default">
    <viewlet name="plone.skip_links" />
    <viewlet name="plone.site_actions" />
    <viewlet name="plone.searchbox" />
    <viewlet name="plone.logo" />
    <viewlet name="plone.global_sections" />
  </order>
  <order manager="plone.contentviews" skinname="Plone Default">
    <viewlet name="plone.contentviews" />
    <viewlet name="plone.contentactions" />
  </order>
  <order manager="plone.portalfooter" skinname="Plone Default">
    <viewlet name="plone.footer" />
    <viewlet name="plone.colophon" />
  </order>
</object>
```

As you can see, the viewlets are all grouped into managers. The viewlet manager is responsible for finding, ordering, filtering, and rendering its viewlets. In the portaltop area, you will find the header, the personal bar, the language selector, and the path bar. You can move these items around by altering the XML and the ZCML of the browser/configure.zcml file.

Next, we want to look at the viewlet registration in ZCML. The default Plone `configure.zcml` file is located in `eggs/plone.app.layout[version number]/ plone/app/layout/viewlets`. The following is a sample of what the default `configure.zcml` file contains:

```
<!-- The logo -->
    <browser:viewlet
        name="plone.logo"
        manager=".interfaces.IPortalHeader"
        class=".common.LogoViewlet"
        permission="zope2.View"
        />
```

This code tells us that the Plone logo is managed by the `IPortalHeader` viewlet manager, its class is `LogoViewlet`, and it is available to users with the `View` permission.

If you go to `http://localhost:8080/plone/@@manage-viewlets`, you will see a graphical representation of what the viewlets structure looks like in a default Plone theme. This interface can be used for quickly identifying where a viewlet is assigned, and from a TTW perspective, you can use the **show** and **hide** links to display or suppress certain viewlets.

 `@@manage-viewlets` loses value as your theme is built out, because your rendered CSS often obscures the information that you are trying to see.

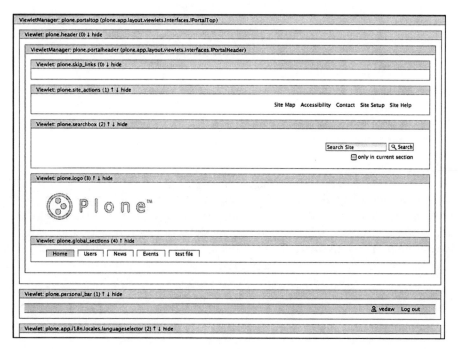

Viewlets can consist of the following:

- Page templates
- Classes
- Page templates combined with classes

You can see all of the viewlets available on a default Plone site by going to: `parts/omelette/plone/app/layout/viewlets` (this works only if you have the `plone.collective.omelette` egg installed, which creates symlinks to all of the pertinent egg directories). If you do not have the omelette installed, you can find the viewlets by going to: `eggs/plone.app.layout...some version number.../plone/app/layout/viewlets`. Omelette is a tool that makes it much easier to locate the pieces and parts needed to build a Plone site, by symlinking eggs into a single folder, and also makes grepping easier.

In order to determine what kind of viewlet it is, open the `common.py` file. If you find a class defined for a viewlet here, it means that you are working with a class-based viewlet. Alternatively, you can look in the `configure.zcml` file in `plone/app/layout/viewlets` and see if it has a `class` declaration next to the viewlet. Customization of these will be discussed in the next chapter.

An example of a class-based viewlet is as follows:

```
class PathBarViewlet(ViewletBase):
    render = ViewPageTemplateFile('path_bar.pt')
```

You can see that this viewlet uses a class named `PathBarViewlet`, and it also uses a page template named `path_bar.pt`. In other words, if a viewlet uses a class at all, it is considered to be class-based.

Conversely, if you search for the footer, you will not find a class definition here. The footer only uses a page template named `footer.pt`. It's important to know what kind of viewlet you are dealing with, as the steps for customizing these differ slightly.

The next chapter will address how to move, hide, and add new viewlets by adjusting the boilerplate code using ZCML and XML.

Portlets

Portlets are similar to viewlets in terms of their basic functionality. Portlets can be designated to appear in either the left column or the right column—formerly known as **left_slots** and **right_slots**—but they cannot yet appear elsewhere in a site's structure without an additional code. You can adjust the portlet settings using the `@@manage-portlets` page, which is accessible via the **Manage portlets** links in the right or left columns. See Chapter 10 for more information on how to configure portlets on your site.

There are several key differences between portlets and viewlets. With portlets, the portlet is always registered in ZCML with `renderer=` pointing at a renderer class. The `renderer` class has a `render` method in Python that returns the HTML for the portlet. Most commonly, this is just a `ViewPageTemplateFile` that parses a template from the filesystem. The `portletRenderer` ZCML tag can be used to replace the render method for an existing portlet renderer class with a `ViewPageTemplateFile` associated with a different template on the filesystem.

Portlets are rendered by a portlet renderer directive using ZCML, written as: `<plone:portletRenderer />`. The `portletRenderer` directive is used only to override the portlet's initial template and is thus generally seen only in theme products. The initial registration of portlets is done via the `plone:portlet` ZCML tag. Conversely, a template-only custom portlet renderer will use the renderer view class (as its view variable) that was used to register the original portlet renderer.

In the case of the news portlet located in `plone.app.portlets.portlets`, the `configure.zcml` code reads as follows:

```
<plone:portlet
        name="portlets.News"
        interface=".news.INewsPortlet"
        assignment=".news.Assignment"
        renderer=".news.Renderer"
        addview=".news.AddForm"
        editview=".news.EditForm"
        />
```

If we want to customize the **News** portlet, we can do so by copying `news.py`, which exists in the same folder, to our filesystem product's `browser/` folder. You don't need to copy `news.py` unless you are going to make significant changes to the Python code. Generally speaking, you don't need to copy the Python file at all. Instead, just copy the template and then use `portletRenderer` to override (for a particular layer) the portlet renderer's template, which is what you actually do with the following ZCML in the `browser/configure.zcml` file:

```
<configure
    xmlns="http://namespaces.zope.org/zope"
    xmlns:browser="http://namespaces.zope.org/browser"
    xmlns:plone="http://namespaces.plone.org/plone"
    i18n_domain="example.mypackage">

    <!-- We must include the package of the portlets we are
       customizing and place this before our ZCML declarations -->
    <include package="plone.app.portlets" />

    <plone:portletRenderer
        portlet="plone.app.portlets.portlets.news.INewsPortlet"
        layer=".interfaces.IExampleCustomization"
        template="mypackage_news.pt"
    />

</configure>
```

We must explicitly include the `plone.app.portlets` package in ZCML processing—before we attempt to override any portlets—as we are now using its `portletRenderer` class implicitly. You also need to make sure that you define the plone XML namespace in the opening of `configure.zcml`, or you'll get "Unknown prefix" errors.

We now define a new portlet renderer with a custom template, `mypackage_news.pt`, for our new layer. Instead of using a custom template, we could use a whole new `renderer` class. You can see that the code for the renderer is contained in `news.py`.

It is also possible to use the `for` attribute to customize for a particular context, or the `view` attribute to customize for a particular view, as with viewlets. Note that only `plone:portletRenderer` understands `for` and `view`; `plone:portlet` does not.

 If we are editing an existing portlet, we use the `plone:portletRenderer` syntax, but if we are creating a new portlet, we use the standard `plone:portlet` syntax, at the beginning of our ZCML declaration.

From the perspective of a filesystem-based product, if you have created a new (not modified) Plone 3 style portlet, and it appears in the `browser/` directory for your product, that portlet will automatically be available via the **Add new... Portlet** drop-down list once you refresh or reload. If you create a Classic portlet, or one that does not use Zope 3 views and which, therefore, lives in a `skins/templates` directory (not in the browser space), you must add that portlet as a Classic portlet using the syntax, `my_portlet` (corresponding to the name of the page template that you are using). There is no need to add a `.pt` extension when adding a Classic portlet via `@@manage-portlets`.

As a final note, there are two portlet-related packages that do not ship with Plone 3.x yet, but ship with Plone 3.1 as part of the core. These packages are `plone.portlet.static` and `plone.portlet.collection`. Refer to Chapter 10 for more information on these portlet products.

Writing a filesystem product

Clearly, there is much to be done in order to make modifications to a Python package or theme product that cannot be accomplished TTW. **GenericSetup** helps us to automate some of our configuration settings, to make them repeatable and easily adjustable.

About GenericSetup

GenericSetup is a major step forward in managing Plone site configuration, and is a core part of how Plone handles its own site creation process. If you find that you are doing a lot of tweaks in the ZMI, GenericSetup may save you some time in terms of getting lots of settings the way you want them, quickly and easily. And, it's not just a time-saver; it reduces the possibility of you forgetting some important part of the site configuration if you ever have to rebuild the site!

GenericSetup introduces the idea of the **configuration profile**. A profile is essentially a set of steps defined using XML. Each `.xml` file defines what happens in one of those steps. Note the fundamental difference between a **profile** and an **install method**; install methods define a set of steps that must be run to get a result, whereas a profile actually describes the result itself. If you export all of the steps from **portal_setup**, you end up with XML defining the steps to get back to a defined state of the site, so it seems as if an install method describes an end result, but that's not generally true, particularly not for the partial profiles that run when a product is installed.

Practically all of the various knobs and twiddling that occurs in the ZMI can be exported to the filesystem via XML files. Additionally, this XML can be tweaked by hand to create an import profile so that when the product is installed, or the GenericSetup profile is imported by hand, the settings will take effect. An example would be where you want to turn on a new **portal_tab** for your site and have it displayed when your filesystem product is installed. You could easily define this in GenericSetup and import the modified profile (this is the safest method) or reinstall the product (this is slightly more dangerous, as your site grows). It is easy to get GenericSetup conflicts because it is sometimes unintuitive, although it is quite powerful.

An important point to note about profiles is that there are two types of profiles that GenericSetup understands: **base profiles** and **extension profiles**.

Base profile

Base profiles provide the base-level information that a site needs, in order to be created. Plone's default setup is itself a GenericSetup base profile. Base profiles contain configuration information such as tools, workflows, types, and register plug-ins for some packages. Most people building custom sites with GenericSetup will never need to create a base profile, and you should not create or alter your base profile until you have had some practice.

Extension profiles

Extension profiles are intended to be applied after the base profiles. Any number of extension profiles can be applied to a site, whereas only a single base profile will ever be applied. Extension profiles are meant to describe new content types, custom skins, custom workflows, or custom tools, and to add configuration to the already set up base profile. All of these are additive actions that do not make any changes to currently-existing products. This is an important concept.

Changing the configuration in existing tools, modifying content types to respond to different workflow, or any other modifications of the base profiles, are less-safe actions, and should only be undertaken when you have a solid understanding of GenericSetup.

An example extension profile

The great thing about GenericSetup is that it's written in a human-readable format in order to make edits quick and easy. The profiles typically live in a `profiles/` folder in a filesystem product. Note that your product might have different files listed than the ones shown in the following screenshot:

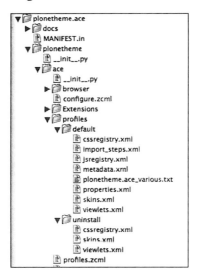

The default/ folder contains all of the information on which knobs and switches need to be twisted when the product is installed, and the uninstall/ folder contains the information on which knobs should be untwisted when the product is uninstalled. Note that the **quick_installer** takes care of this untwisting for a number of the things that a product installation normally does, but does not take care of everything. Hence, simply uninstalling a product may not bring you back to zero.

Common examples of the files you might see include:

- cssregistry.xml: Contains the information needed to install stylesheets for a filesystem product
- jsregistry.xml: Contains the information needed to install JavaScripts for a filesystem product
- viewlets.xml: Contains ordering, hiding, and moving information about viewlets for a product
- portlets.xml: Contains information that defines new portlets or modifies existing portlets for a product
- toolset.xml: Registers all of the tools available to the site; this must happen before the tools are configured
- skins.xml: A list of all of the skin paths that should be added to the skins tool when your site is configured
- types.xml: A list of all of the types that should be defined in the site's portal_types tool
- workflows.xml: Registers all of the workflows for the product (those in the workflows folder)

If we open the cssregistry.xml file for the previous example, a project called plonetheme.ace, we see the following code:

```
<?xml version="1.0"?>
<object name="portal_css">
 <stylesheet title=""
    id="ace.css"
    media="screen" rel="stylesheet" rendering="import"
    cacheable="True" compression="safe" cookable="True"
    enabled="1" expression=""/>
</object>
```

In this case, the file states that upon install, a stylesheet called `ace.css` will be imported. Here, the additional information is not necessary for comprehension, but it might be helpful in investigating whether you use GenericSetup frequently.

CMFPlone, which contains the base profile for a Plone site, also contains a `profiles/` directory. Within its `cssregistry.xml` file is a much larger XML file that defines exactly which CSS files will be loaded when a base Plone site is installed. This means that as your site uses base Plone, and your site has its own profiles, the profiles are additive. This is where **snapshots** come in handy.

Taking snapshots

When working with GenericSetup, it's important to know what your site's profile looks like before you start making your changes. This is especially important if you are trying to resolve a GenericSetup conflict. Within the ZMI for your site, click on **portal_setup**. There are three tabs that are important to point out here: **Import**, **Export**, and **Snapshots**:

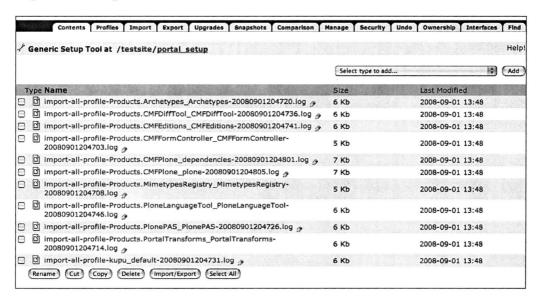

Before making any changes to your site's profile, you should always take a snapshot of your site, as this will give you the opportunity to evaluate the XML at various points in time by using the `diff` command. Alternatively, you could do a comparison via the **portal_setup** tool under the **Comparison** tab. It is very important to take a snapshot before making changes so that you can backtrack to the original profile if you need to. Click on the **Create a Snapshot** button. The site will appear to spin for a while, and will actually never stop spinning, due to a flaw in this area. Wait for about 30 seconds, and then click on the **Snapshots** tab again, and you will see the following snapshot:

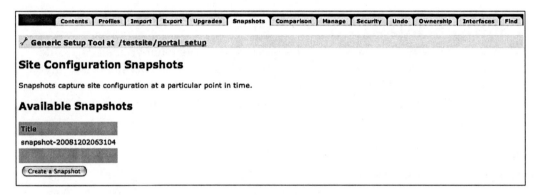

The snapshot that is generated is given a name that may not be indicative. Click on the **Snapshots** tab again, select the checkbox next to the snapshot, and give it a more meaningful name.

If you make additional changes to your GenericSetup, either through the filesystem or through the ZMI, you can create a second snapshot, export both profiles to your desktop using the **Import/Export** button, and then use a different tool, or the **Comparison** tab, to examine the differences.

Export profile

Occasionally, you may just want to know what your current profile looks like for a selected set of items. For example, you might want to know what the profile is for your **portal_tabs**. In this case, click on the **Export** tab, select the checkbox next to **Action Providers**, and click on the **Export Selected Steps** button. Extract the `.tar` file and you will see a file called `actions.xml`, which outlines the current state of affairs for your product. This file may be quite lengthy, so if you want to make a small change to your profile, remove all of the pieces that you don't want, taking care to close the lines correctly.

Import profile

Assuming that you wish to import a few minor changes to your site, first export the profile that you want to alter, and then make your changes as needed. Then, click on the **Import** tab to import the selected steps.

Once the profile has been imported or the product has been reinstalled, the new profile steps will be processed. In this example, we want to alter the order and placement of several of the viewlets. Plone provides a `viewlets.xml` file that provides the default ordering of all new Plone sites. Use this as the base for your own `viewlets.xml` file:

```xml
<?xml version="1.0"?>
<object>
  <order manager="plone.portaltop" skinname="Plone Default">
    <viewlet name="plone.header" />
    <viewlet name="plone.personal_bar" />
    <viewlet name="plone.app.i18n.locales.languageselector" />
    <viewlet name="plone.path_bar" />
  </order>
  <order manager="plone.portalheader" skinname="Plone Default">
    <viewlet name="plone.skip_links" />
    <viewlet name="plone.site_actions" />
    <viewlet name="plone.searchbox" />
    <viewlet name="plone.logo" />
    <viewlet name="plone.global_sections" />
  </order>
  <order manager="plone.contentviews" skinname="Plone Default">
    <viewlet name="plone.contentviews" />
    <viewlet name="plone.contentactions" />
  </order>
  <order manager="plone.portalfooter" skinname="Plone Default">
    <viewlet name="plone.footer" />
    <viewlet name="plone.colophon" />
  </order>
</object>
```

The key is to insert only those pieces that are different from the base profile, and not rewrite the entire profile. Be vigilant here, as including more information than you actually want can cause unexpected behavior when your profile is installed, and can result in your site becoming unmanageable.

Here is the `viewlets.xml` from a sample theme product. In the case of viewlets, what you really want to do is register them for your own skin product, rather than for `Plone Default`, and also say `based-on="Plone Default"`.

Note that there are two pieces here: order managers, which contain viewlets, and hidden managers, which hide select viewlets.

```xml
<?xml version="1.0"?>
<!-- This file holds the setup configuration of the viewlet managers
     for the "example" skin.
     -->
<object>
  <order manager="plone.portaltop" skinname="example"
    based-on="Plone Default">
    <viewlet name="plone.header" />
    <viewlet name="plone.personal_bar" />
    <viewlet name="plone.app.i18n.locales.languageselector" />
  </order>

  <order manager="plone.portalheader" skinname="example" based-
   on="Plone Default">
    <viewlet name="plone.skip_links" />
    <viewlet name="plone.logo" />
    <viewlet name="plone.site_actions" />
    <viewlet name="plone.searchbox" />
    <viewlet name="plone.global_sections" />
  </order>

  <order manager="plone.contentviews" skinname="example" based-
   on="Plone Default">
    <viewlet name="example.path_bar" insert-
    before="plone.contentviews"/>
  </order>

  <hidden manager="plone.portaltop" skinname="example" based-
   on="Plone Default">
    <viewlet name="plone.path_bar" />
  </hidden>

</object>
```

This file indicates that the various viewlets are assigned to different viewlet managers, and some of the original viewlets are being suppressed in order to allow custom viewlets to take their place.

The actual mechanics behind this will be covered more in more detail, with practical examples, in the next chapter. For examples of the necessary syntax, check the profiles/ directory of CMFPlone, or rely on an exported profile step.

Summary

In this chapter, we have learned:

- How to make minor adjustments to a Plone site through the ZMI
- How to create a filesystem product, and then register and install it
- About skin layer elements, and (optionally) stylesheets and images
- About Zope 3 components, including browser views, pages, viewlets, portlets, and stylesheets and images
- How to make these same adjustments in a filesystem product via **portal_view_customizations**, GenericSetup, and light coding

Using what you have learned in this chapter, you should now be able to create a product for a web site, register it, install it, make changes through the web and on the filesystem, and create a repeatable profile of the product. This ties in nicely with the next chapter on theming for Plone, which relies on many of the technologies described in this chapter.

Change the Look and Feel

A common task that needs to be performed before putting a web site online is to give it a proper look and feel. Unfortunately, performing this task in Plone 3 is not easy for designers. It requires having much more than web design skills. It requires understanding many of the concepts explained in the previous chapter.

In this chapter, **David Convent**, with assistance from **Veda Williams**, will demonstrate, through step-by-step instructions, how to develop and implement a theme in Plone, ultimately creating a Python theme product that can be distributed and installed easily on any Plone 3 web site.

The theme is attributed to Andreas Viklund, who created this open source theme, Andreas09.

Developing on the filesystem

One of the strengths of Zope (and therefore Plone) is the ability it gives users to set it up and customize it through the web interface, as explained in the previous chapter. When it comes to making massive changes and customizations, it is more practical to develop a theme on the filesystem by using code.

Theming a Plone site often requires making fairly complex customizations. Many elements including images, stylesheets, templates, viewlets, and portlets may potentially need to be overridden in a custom theme. It would be a good idea to keep all of these customizations in a central place, in a stable and repeatable state. A package on the filesystem is ideal for that purpose. We can easily move it from a development environment to a production server, or distribute it for use among other web integrators.

The process used for developing theme products relies heavily on a tool known as **buildout**, which helps you to set up a controlled and repeatable Python development or production environment. In this chapter, we will use buildout to quickly set up a Zope instance that will be used for our theme development needs. For more information on buildout, refer to Chapter 13.

As the development of a web site's look and feel often leads to some experimentation (for example, while making a design compatible across browsers), it would be a good idea to keep a history of your development steps and keep your code in a location other than your own development machine. Using a revision control system such as **Subversion** is extremely valuable in this case. Subversion can be downloaded from the following location: `http://subversion.tigris.org/project_packages.html`.

When installing Subversion on your local machine, be careful to choose a version that is compatible with your subversion repository. As of the time of writing, Subversion 1.4 was the safest bet.

It helps to check a theme into Subversion immediately after creating the theme product, check in it again after you complete the major steps, and then once more after the theme has been completed. In a production scenario, it is best to never check broken code. If it doesn't work on your local instance, it could potentially break other sites on your production server; so be diligent.

Assumptions

Developing a theme for Plone has many challenges. It differs radically from the old 2.0x architecture where all of the elements needed for building a theme generally lived in the same place and could be modified fairly easily. In the world of Plone 3, you must now be able to tell the difference between the "old style" templates and the new Zope 3 browser views. You must also understand that there are multiple ways in which a theme can be built.

You will need to know HTML, CSS, basic Zope 3 technologies, Zope Page Templates (**ZPT**, described at: `http://www.zope.org/Documentation/Books/ZopeBook/2_6Edition/AppendixC.stx`), and some Python. You will also need to know how to make minor adjustments to a Plone site through the ZMI (**portal_actions, portal_skins**, and **portal_view_customizations**). GenericSetup customizations are essential here as well.

You'll need to learn how to set up your development environment for filesystem development (via `easy_install`, `ZopeSkel`, and `paster`). As of the time of writing, these items are provided by default with the Plone installer. You will also need to do light coding using ZCML and Python. It's a lot to understand initially, but once you get the hang of it, the process is fairly straightforward. Much of what you learned in the previous chapter will be of use here.

As you develop a theme, you might also need to make decisions about the structure of your filesystem product, or determine if you need to expose certain items such as stylesheets and images to the browser layer for use by other Python packages. Additionally, you might need to decide whether you want to start from scratch with your CSS rather than build on top of base Plone stylesheets. Lastly, we'll explain how to tell the difference between the Zope 2 and Zope 3 elements of a theme, and will also make suggestions on best practices.

If you are in doubt about best practices for how a theme product should look, you can refer to the default Plone implementation called CMFPlone. This theme product is located in the `parts` directory of your buildout, though it may be distributed as an egg in the later versions of Plone. Instead, you may find it in your buildout's `eggs` directory. Occasionally, you may need to modify the base templates provided by CMFPlone in the `skins/plone_templates/` directory, although this is an advanced topic that we will not cover here. Refer to the documentation on `www.plone.org` for information on how to modify page templates.

For most of your theming needs, the key pieces that you will use to modify your themes will be found in the `eggs/` directory of your buildout (or your `Plone` folder, if you are using a more recent version of Plone). These two eggs are referred to as `plone.app.layout` and `plone.app.portlets`. As of the time of writing, the egg for `plone.app.layout` is `plone.app.layout-1.1.5-py2.4.egg`, and the egg of `plone.app.portlets` is `plone.app.portlets-1.1.5.1-py2.4.egg`. You can drill down into these eggs to see their contents. For the purposes of this chapter, we will focus specifically on the components located in `plone.app.layout`.

Setting up a development environment

The "official way forward" for Plone 3 theme and product development is to use the system known as buildout. Buildout is a self-contained environment that allows you to manage dependencies (including those for Zope and Plone and any third-party products or libraries that you need) and custom code for your project.

To create a buildout, download Plone from `http://www.plone.org/products/plone`. Once the installer is downloaded, double-click to install it. Your installer will install a buildout and **bootstrap** it for you, which means that your buildout will be ready immediately. Bootstrapping finishes the buildout installation process and makes buildout ready for use.

> The later versions of the installer (3.2+) create a buildout environment by default. For the earlier versions of Plone, we recommend that you refer to this tutorial: `http://plone.org/documentation/tutorial/buildout/tutorial-all-pages`, or to Chapter 13 of this book. Refer to the previous chapter for information on how to install `ez_setup`, `easy_install`, and `ZopeSkel` if you are not using a recent version of Plone. You can also ask questions on the user group lists or on #plone, the Plone IRC channel.

Your Zope/Plone instance will be created in your `Products` or `Applications` directory, depending on your operating system, in a folder named `Plone`.

In a moment, we will create a base theme product using `paster`, a scripting tool that generates a skeleton Python package (in this case, a theme) when it is run.

Windows users

If you are using Windows, there are a few additional things that you need to do to satisfy Plone's dependencies. Additional information is available from the following web page: `http://plone.org/documentation/how-to/buildout-using-windows-installer`

First, install the Python Win32 extensions for Python 2.4, from: `http://downloads.sourceforge.net/pywin32/pywin32-210.win32-py2.4.exe?modtime=1159009237&big_mirror=0`

If you intend to compile Zope yourself rather than use a binary installer, or if you would ever need to compile an egg with C extensions, you will need the mingw32 compiler. Make sure that you choose the `base` and `make` modules as a minimum, when the installer asks you which modules to install. By default, this installs into `C:\MingW32`. Inside the `installation` directory, there will be a `bin/` directory, for example, `C:\MingW32\bin`. Add this to your system path.

Finally, you need to configure Python's `distutils` package to use the mingw32 compiler. Create a file called `distutils.cfg` in the directory `C:\Python24\Lib\distutils` (assuming that Python was installed in `C:\Python24`, as it is by default). Edit this with Notepad, and add the following lines to it:

```
[build]
compiler=mingw32
```

Generating your theme product

Assuming that all the dependencies are now satisfied, we will create our skeleton theme product. Navigate to your Plone product via your Terminal tool. You will see a directory called `src/`. Navigate into this folder. Next, type the following text into your terminal:

`$ paster create -t plone3_theme`

You may need to be in your buildout's `src/` directory for this command to work, depending on how your Plone instance is set up.

The `paster` recipe will ask you a series of questions about the template you are creating. You usually want to accept the defaults, here.

The questions are likely to resemble the following output:

```
[bash: /opt] paster create -t plone3_theme
Selected and implied templates:
  ZopeSkel#basic_namespace  A project with a namespace package
  ZopeSkel#plone            A Plone project
  ZopeSkel#plone3_theme     A Theme for Plone 3
Enter project name: plonetheme.mytheme
Variables:
  egg:      My_Theme
  package:  mytheme
  project:  plonetheme.mytheme
Enter namespace_package (Namespace package (like plonetheme))
['plonetheme']:
Enter package (The package contained namespace package (like example))
['example']: mytheme
Enter skinname (The skin selection to be added to 'portal_skins' (like
'My Theme')) ['']: mytheme
Enter skinbase (Name of the skin selection from which the new one will be
copied) ['Plone Default']:
```

```
Enter empty_styles (Override default public stylesheets with empty ones?)
[True]: False

Enter include_doc (Include in-line documentation in generated code?)
[False]:

Enter zope2product (Are you creating a Zope 2 Product?) [True]:

Enter version (Version) ['1.0']:

Enter description (One-line description of the package) ['An installable
theme for Plone 3']:

Enter long_description (Multi-line description (in reST)) ['']:

Enter author (Author name) ['Plone Collective']: David Convent

Enter author_email (Author email) ['product-developers@lists.plone.org']:
me@email.com

Enter keywords (Space-separated keywords/tags) ['web zope plone theme']:

Enter url (URL of homepage) ['http://svn.plone.org/svn/collective/']:

Enter license_name (License name) ['GPL']:

Enter zip_safe (True/False: if the package can be distributed as a .zip
file) [False]:
```

A few key points on these questions are as follows:

- `Project name` corresponds to the name of your theme. This might be your client's name or the name of the web site for which you are building a theme. It's generally best to name your project something along the lines of `plonetheme.mytheme` or `mytheme.plonetheme`, as eggs tend to have problems with spaces within their names. Using `plonetheme` in the name also helps to distinguish your project from a **policy product**, which might be named something like `mytheme.content`. Pick a convention and stick to it.

- `Namespace package` is usually `plonetheme`; but you could name it after your company if you wished to brand your theme.

- `Package name` is usually a short name for your theme, and one word is generally advisable here.

- One question that requires thought is `empty styles`, which determines whether you wish to override the default public styles with blank stylesheets. Users new to Plone, and users new to CSS, are likely to want to say `False`. Also, if you always prefer to build on top of the stylesheets that Plone provides you with (which are quite robust), you might want to say `False` rather than start from scratch.

- Lastly, `include_doc` determines whether certain documentation will be included with your product. This can be helpful, especially in the beginning.

Installing a theme product on a Plone site

Next, we will add our newly created theme to our buildout. Our theme is `eggified` by default, which means that it can be easily distributed. Because we are still in development, we want to put our new skeleton theme product into the `src/` directory of our buildout. Next, open your `buildout.cfg` file, which is located in the root of your buildout, and we will modify it so that Plone can see your theme product.

Updating your buildout to recognize your theme product

Open your `buildout.cfg` file and make the following modifications in the `develop` instance, `eggs`, and `zcml` sections, based on how you answered the questions when you ran the `paster` recipe. In a typical buildout, this would look like:

```
[buildout]
...
eggs =
    ...
    plonetheme.mytheme
develop =
    src/plonetheme.mytheme
zcml =
    plonetheme.mytheme
```

> The buildout structure for the Andreas09 theme product is different from the above, as it uses two configuration files, thereby "extending" the default buildout configuration file. This is an advanced topic. Refer to Chapter 13 or the documentation on Plone.org for more information. Additionally, if your theme product uses the top level namespace 'Products', as is the case with the Andreas09 buildout, you will not need the ZCML directive mentioned above.
>
> Most new themes created with the plone3_theme recipe will require the ZCML directive.

As we have made changes to our buildout (such as adding new Python eggs and packages, reconfiguring your Zope instance, and so on), we now need to re-run our buildout for these changes to be read by Zope. These changes include adding your Plone theme to the buildout, and any other ZCML changes. Go to your buildout's root (Plone directory) and type the following:

```
$ ./bin/buildout
```

After running your buildout (it may take a few minutes), start your Zope instance in the foreground. This is extremely helpful during development, as it displays errors in your terminal window. Type the following:

```
./bin/instance fg
```

Once Zope is up and running, you can connect to its management interface from any web browser. We'll assume in this chapter that Zope is running on port `8080`. In your browser, go to `http://localhost:8080/manage_main` and log in using **admin/admin,** or using the default login that was assigned when your Zope instance was created.

 Optionally, at this point, you can create a new user in the **acl_users** area of the ZMI, so that you can login using a different user name.

Creating a Plone site

Now, let's create our Plone site.

From the ZMI accessed via the URL above, we choose **Plone Site** from the **Add** pop-up list. You will not need to select a profile at this time, although you could do so if you knew that you would be building on top of a policy product that will control generic settings.

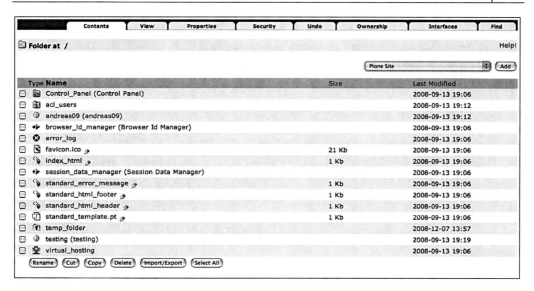

Now, if you point your browser to the root of your brand new site (and you chose not to override Plone's default stylesheets), you should see the following screen:

Putting your site into debug mode

Before going any further, we will put our site's stylesheets into **debug** mode. This allows you to see the changes to your theme product's CSS stylesheets immediately upon refreshing the page, and without requiring a Zope restart.

In order to put **portal_css** in debug mode, go to the **portal_css** tool in the ZMI, by pointing your browser to an address that should look like this: `http://localhost:8080/mysite/portal/css/manage_main`, where `mysite` is the name of your Plone site. Then select the **Debug/development mode** checkbox and click on the **Save** button. You can also access this page by drilling down into **portal_css** through the ZMI.

Rarely will you need to put your entire Zope instance into a debug mode just to theme a web site (this is done through buildout configuration), but you may occasionally also need to put your **portal_javascripts** and **portal_kss** into debug mode. These files are also accessible through the ZMI.

Installing your product

Typically, at this point, we would install our theme product on our Plone site. There are two ways to install a theme product: through the **Site Setup** or through the ZMI. To install via **Site Setup**, click on the **Site Setup** link at the top right of your site, and then click on the **Add-on Products** link:

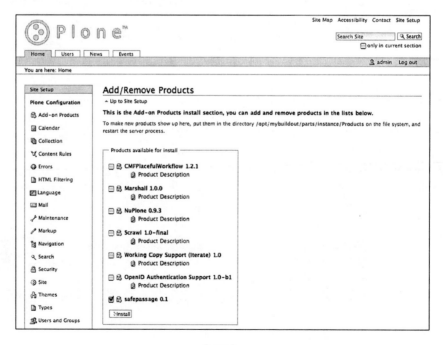

Alternatively, you can do this by going into the ZMI to the **portal_quickinstaller** tool, available at a URL such as: `http://localhost:8080/mysite/portal_quickinstaller/manage_installProductsForm`, where `mysite` is the name of your Plone site.

Assuming that you've modified your `buildout.cfg` file correctly, re-run your buildout, and restart Zope. Your theme product should now be listed on this page. You can select the checkbox next to it and install it, as seen in the following screenshot, for a Plone site and a Plone theme product called **safepassage**.

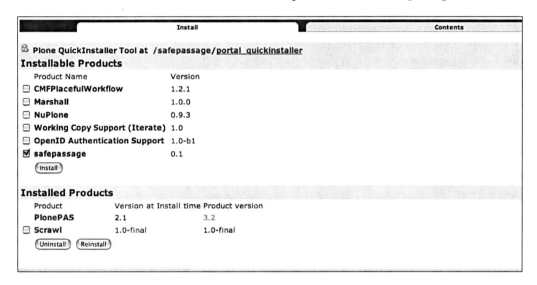

When viewing your web site, you should see the **Installed Products**.

As with any software product, you should always check version compatibility before trying to install products on your site. A typical Plone 2.x theme product will not be installable on a Plone 3 site, for example.

Getting started with an example theme product

The process described above generates a new theme product that you can then fill in with images, stylesheets, and more. For the purposes of explaining how this will work in practice, we have set up an actual theme and will walk through the steps that were involved in creating this theme. This theme is called **Andreas09**.

First, we have created a buildout specific to this theme, to ensure that all dependencies are met. The theme product itself has been created in steps to make it easier to understand.

Download the entire buildout here by navigating to your /opt, Programs, or Applications directory, depending on your operating system:

```
svn co https://svn.plone.org/svn/collective/Products.Andreas09Theme/
buildout/ AndreasBuildout
```

 Make sure that you include the space directly before the word "AndreasBuildout" above.

Once the buildout has been downloaded, we need to bootstrap it because the Plone installer didn't create it, and as a result, bootstrapping doesn't happen automatically. Type the following code in your terminal window:

```
python2.4 bootstrap.py
```

Then, run your buildout:

```
./bin/buildout
```

After the buildout finishes running, you can then start your Zope instance:

```
./bin/instance fg
```

Next, log in to your Zope instance using the login name **admin**, and password, **admin**. Create a new Plone site using the drop-down list on the upper right (choose **Plone Site**). Do not install Andreas09 as an extension profile; instead, do it via **Site Setup/Add-on Products** or the **portal_quickinstaller** option in the ZMI as described above. We're able to see the theme as available in the **quick_installer** because it has already been registered in our buildout's buildout.cfg file.

To view your site, go to: http://localhost:8080/andreas09 (or whatever you've named your site). The theme you will see is based on a design by Andreas Viklund, named Andreas09. How the theme will look, when it is completed, is shown here: http://andreasviklund.com/files/demo/andreas09. For the purposes of this demo, however, you will not yet see the completed theme product, as the buildout is set up to demonstrate in steps the process involved in getting to the finished product.

If you compare the finished theme against a default Plone site, you will notice that basic styling is applied. But we are also concerned with items that have been moved or customized with more than CSS. For example:

- The logo displays the title of the page and the description of the page instead of the standard logo.jpg.

- The footer has been customized to have a wrapper around it so that it can be styled.

- The breadcrumbs appear above the center content instead of floating over the portal columns. You can see this if you customize your navigation settings in @@manage-portlets to display a navigation portlet on the home page.

- Credits appear at the bottom of the page, and much more...

We will walk through the various changes made in the Andreas09 theme product, one step at a time. First, let's take a look at the overall file structure in our theme product. You'll notice that the final theme lives in the src/ directory and that there is also a tutorial_steps folder:

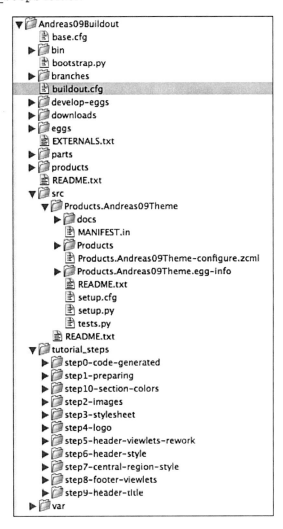

By commenting and uncommenting lines in your buildout.cfg using the # sign, you can move from one step to the next:

```
[buildout]
extends = base.cfg

develop +=
        tutorial_steps/step0-code-generated
#       tutorial_steps/step1-preparing
#       tutorial_steps/step2-images
#       tutorial_steps/step3-stylesheet
#       tutorial_steps/step4-logo
#       tutorial_steps/step5-header-viewlets-rework
#       tutorial_steps/step6-header-style
#       tutorial_steps/step7-central-region-style
#       tutorial_steps/step8-footer-viewlets
#       tutorial_steps/step9-header-title
#       tutorial_steps/step10-section-colors

[instance]
debug-mode = on
eggs +=
    Products.Andreas09Theme
```

In the code above, we can see that step0-code-generated is activated.

This is a fairly unusual buildout.cfg. But all you need to know is that you can add or remove a # (comment) sign, and each time you do that for the following steps, you will need to re-run your buildout using:

./bin/buildout -No

The -No switch forces buildout to re-run in non-network mode and does not search for new eggs, thus speeding up the process of re-running your buildout.

Then, reinstall your product. Plone will know that you have an updated product because the version number has been incremented in each of these steps.

Generating the theme product

Let's look now at the changes generated in the setup of the branch located at AndreasBuildout/Products.Andreas09Theme/tutorial_steps/step0-code-generated/.

Using Mac's Finder, Windows Explorer, or an editor such as TextMate, open the entire code tree in this folder. You will see the following tree structure:

You can browse through the contents of the various files in this step, but nothing has been changed at this point. The purpose of this intial setup step is to have a vanilla theme that can be checked into the subversion as a starting point, which you can trace back to if needed.

Altering important boilerplate code

Let's now look at the changes generated in the first step of the branch located at `AndreasBuildout/Products.Andreas09Theme/tutorial_steps/step1-preparing`.

 Reminder: Don't forget to update your `buildout.cfg` file to show the next step of our theme product, and re-run your buildout. Then, reinstall your product, as the version number of the product has changed.

The changes made in this step should be performed immediately after checking the vanilla theme into subversion, and should be done before starting Zope. In any case, a Zope restart will be needed after applying them.

 In the cases where you have modified your ZCML, you can often avoid re-running your buildout, by including an egg called `plone.reload` in your buildout, and going to `http://localhost:8080/reload` and choosing the **ZCML** option. `plone.reload` can be downloaded from the following location, and installed just like any other egg: `http://pypi.python.org/pypi/plone.reload`.

Fixing the installer bug

The `plone3_theme` recipe of ZopeSkel (versions prior to 2.10) previously generated code that included a bug which made packages in the **Products** top-level Python namespace appear twice in the Quick Installer Tool (in the ZMI, listed as **quick_installer**) as well as in the **Add/Remove Products** control panel (in the **Site Setup** interface).

This bug only affects the themes built using the Products namespace (using the now obsolete `DIYPloneStyle`, or one of the other plone `paster` recipes). So if you use the `plone3_theme` recipe, which is now considered best practice, you will not need to make this fix.

So, before generating your theme base code with ZopeSkel, confirm that you have the most recent version of ZopeSkel installed on your machine. Then, make sure that your code contains the bug: go to the **Add/Remove Products** configuration panel in the **Site Setup** area of your Plone site and check whether your package shows up twice in the listed installable products.

If it does, then open `Products.Andreas09Theme/Products/Andreas09Theme/_ _init__.py` and replace all of its content with a # (comment). Removing or commenting out the code in `__init__.py` is not needed for the bug to disappear, though it is better to clean it.

Then, we will remove the code that declares the product with **Five**. In `Products. Andreas09Theme/Products/Andreas09Theme/configure.zcml`, remove the highlighted line:

```
<configure
    xmlns="http://namespaces.zope.org/zope"
    xmlns:five="http://namespaces.zope.org/five"
    xmlns:cmf="http://namespaces.zope.org/cmf"
    i18n_domain="Products.Andreas09Theme">

    <five:registerPackage package="." initialize=".initialize" />

    <include package=".browser" />

    <include file="skins.zcml" />
    <include file="profiles.zcml" />

</configure>
```

If your theme product has already been created, you can fix this bug through the ZMI. In the ZMI, go to the Zope **Products** control panel. Be careful! This is not the **Add/Remove Products** page of Plone that you have to go to, nor the **portal_ quickinstaller** tool management page, but the **Product Management** page of your Zope instance itself. From the root of your Zope instance, in the ZMI, you will find that the page by following this path: `/Control_Panel/Products/manage_main`.

If your package is named **Products.Andreas09Theme**, you will see that it is registered twice as a Zope product: once with the name **Andreas09Theme**, and once again with its full name, **Products.Andreas09Theme**.

Simply select the checkbox for the one with the full name (the one whose name starts with **Products.**), go to the bottom of the page, and then click on the **Delete** button.

Now, if you refresh or go to the **Add/Remove Products** page of your Plone site, you can confirm that your theme product shows up only once. Your code should now be clean, and your Zope product registration should be back to normal.

Naming the theme meaningfully

For all the themes, you should alter your theme product's GenericSetup profile to give it a name that makes it obvious to the installer that it is indeed a theme. In cases where you are working with additional products that may be named similarly, this becomes increasingly important.

In `Products.Andreas09Theme/Products/Andreas09Theme/profiles.zcml`, change the title of the default profile, and name it `Andreas09 Theme` (in the highlighted line):

```
<configure
    xmlns="http://namespaces.zope.org/zope"
    xmlns:genericsetup="http://namespaces.zope.org/genericsetup"
    i18n_domain="Products.Andreas09Theme">
    <genericsetup:registerProfile
      name="default"
      title="Andreas09 Theme"
      directory="profiles/default"
      description='Extension profile for the "Andreas09" Plone
                   theme.'
      provides="Products.GenericSetup.interfaces.EXTENSION"
      />
</configure>
```

This makes it obvious when installing your theme product that you are actually installing a theme, and not, for instance, a policy product. This is discussed by Martin Aspeli in his book, *Professional Plone Development*. When you view your site in the **portal_quickinstaller** in the ZMI, you will see the revised name of the product (listed once, as we fixed the bug mentioned above):

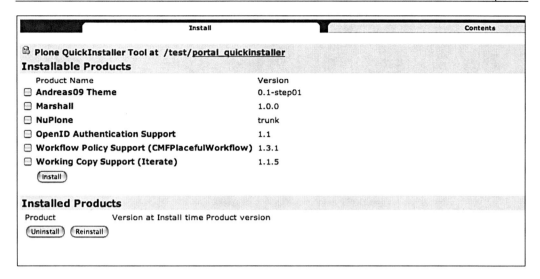

Policy products, in short, are the products that could add content to a web site, flip a few switches in the ZMI, or orchestrate various dependencies. These products abstract logic away from presentation. Theme products and policy products tend to be applied to a single Plone site; so naming them intelligently in this manner makes it easier to see which product you are installing.

Adjusting the names of skin layer folders

The ZopeSkel paster template names the skin layer folders in a somewhat cumbersome fashion. The names generated by paster are as follows:

```
Products_Andreas09Theme_custom_images
Products_Andreas09Theme_custom_templates
Products_Andreas09Theme_styles
```

We want to alter these to be named as follows:

```
Andreas09Theme_custom_images
Andreas09Theme_custom_templates
Andreas09Theme_styles
```

In `Products.Andreas09Theme/Products/Andreas09Theme/skins.zcml`, alter the code to read:

```
<configure
    xmlns="http://namespaces.zope.org/zope"
    xmlns:cmf="http://namespaces.zope.org/cmf"
    i18n_domain="Products.Andreas09Theme">

<!-- File System Directory Views registration -->
<cmf:registerDirectory
    name="Andreas09Theme_custom_images"/>
<cmf:registerDirectory
    name="Andreas09Theme_custom_templates"/>
<cmf:registerDirectory
    name="Andreas09Theme_styles"/>

</configure>
```

You can see that your skin layers' names have changed if you view them in the ZMI, via the **portal_skins/properties** tool:

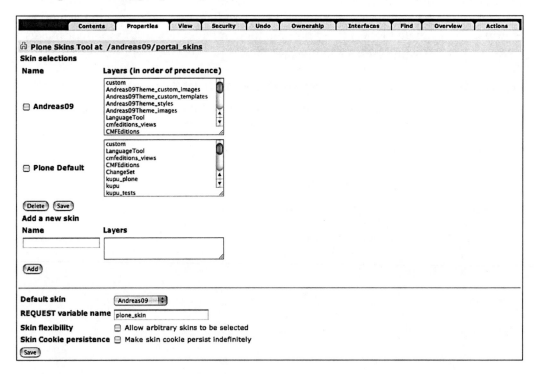

We'll explain how these folders (and their skin layers) are used in the next step. For now, let's take a quick look at our theme product that is installed, so that we can see what we are starting with. You can do this by going to: `http://localhost:8080/mytheme/`, where `mytheme` is the name of your Plone site. You should see something ugly and unstyle, as shown in the following screenshot:

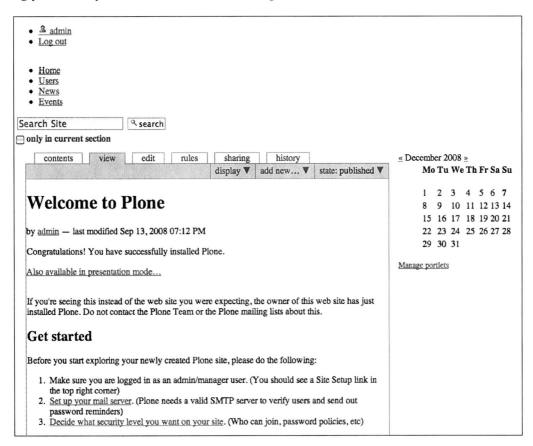

Working with images

Next, we will look at the code contained in the second step of the Andreas09 theme:

```
AndreasBuildout/Products.Andreas09Theme/tutorial_steps/step2-
images/
```

Reminder: Don't forget to update your `buildout.cfg` file to show the next step of our theme product, and re-run your buildout. Then, reinstall your product, as the version number of the product has changed.

Now we are ready to look at how to work with images in our theme product.

Overriding the default Plone icons

Small images are used all over the Plone interface in order to help the user identify basic elements contained within a web site, such as documents or folders. These small images are 16x16 pixels images that we can find in the search button (the 'magnifier' icon in the search button), in the personal bar (the 'member' icon), in the navigation menu, in the edit page titles (the 'content type' icons), in the page content (the external link 'globe' icon), and so on.

All of these icons are stored in, and accessed from, the **portal_skins** tool. There are ways to access images as Zope 3 resources, but these are still exceptions, and will be covered later in the chapter.

Images stored in the **portal_skins** tool are pretty easy to customize using a filesystem-based product or package. It is merely a question of storing the custom image in a folder that is registered as a **portal_skins** layer, which takes precedence over the one that contains the original image.

For example, let's customize the 'magnifier' icon used in the quick search box, and the 'member' icon that is displayed in the personal tools section. Log in to your Plone site to see the member icon.

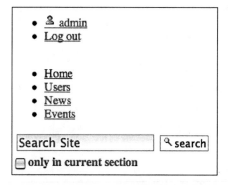

In order to customize these images, we'll first need to identify the ones that we will override, and then place the overridden images into the correct folder of our product. Finally, we will make sure that this folder is registered as a skin layer for our theme in the **portal_skins** tool.

First, we need to know the names of the images that we are about to override. The 'member' icon is easy to identify: display a page where the icon is present in your browser, right-click on the icon and choose **View Image** (using Firefox) from the pop-up menu that shows up. You are then redirected to a page that only shows the 16x16 pixels wide image. In the URL bar, you see the name of the image file at the end of the path: **user.gif**. The 'magnifier' (search) icon is a bit more difficult to identify. It is used as a background image for the search button, and we can use Firebug to see the name of this image.

Using Firebug to inspect CSS code

Firebug is an extension of the Mozilla Firefox browser that allows you to inspect any element of a web page and scan its style properties. Download Firebug from `http://www.getfirebug.com`. First, install Firebug if it's not there already, making sure that you use the correct version for your version of Firefox. Then, display any Plone page in Firefox (even Plone.org will work here), choose **Inspect element** from the Firebug submenu in the Tools menu of Firefox, and click on the search button in the quick search box in the Plone page. In a typical Plone site, the icons look like this:

Using Firebug, we can see in the right-hand style box that the background image used for the search button is called **search_icon.gif**.

Now that we know the names of the images that we want to override, let's customize these in our theme product. We first need two icons that will replace the original ones. Choose the ones you like, or draw them, or take them from this chapter's example code, and place them in the folder called `Andreas09Theme_custom_images`. In our example, the folder is located in our buildout at `$buildout_path/src/Products.Andreas09Theme/Products/Andreas09Theme/skins/Andreas09Theme_custom_images`. Because we are looking at our completed theme products, the **user.gif** and **search_icon.gif** are already located in this folder. But you can certainly override them with different images.

Because the folder in the `skins` directory was created when we created the base code of our package, we can be assured that it has been registered as a skin layer in the **portal_skins** tool, and Plone can see it.

Reload the welcome page of your Plone site with the Andreas09 theme, after dropping the two replacement icons in the images folder. You should now get a page with icons replacing two of the original Plone icons, and the updated images should look like this:

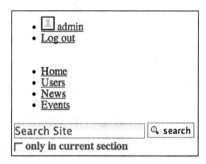

Examining the images in our theme product

Open the file structure for Step 2. In this case, we will expand the two images folders to see the following:

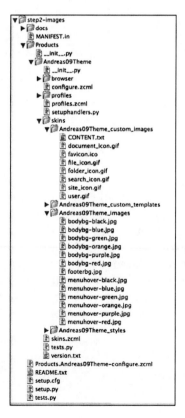

Images are located in the `Andreas09Theme_custom_images` folder and in a second folder named `Andreas09Theme_images`. The images located in the first folder are Plone-specific images that have been modified during the development of this theme. The `Andreas09Theme_images` folder, meanwhile, is used for new images, if any, that are not given to us by Plone (specifically, images not included in the **CMFPlone** product located in your `parts/` directory).

Optionally, you could put all of your images into a single folder. However, the default best practice is helpful in case you need to track back and specifically see which parts are modified over the default Plone settings, and which are new images.

Modifying your folder structure to add an additional skin layer

To create the additional images folder seen here, go to `Products.Andreas09Theme/Products/Andreas09Theme/skins/` and add a new folder named `Andreas09Theme_images`.

Then, in `Products.Andreas09Theme/Products/Andreas09Theme/skins.zcml`, we will modify the code to add a few lines:

```
<configure
    xmlns="http://namespaces.zope.org/zope"
    xmlns:cmf="http://namespaces.zope.org/cmf"
    i18n_domain="Products.Andreas09Theme">

    <!-- File System Directory Views registration -->
    <cmf:registerDirectory
        name="Andreas09Theme_custom_images"/>
    <cmf:registerDirectory
        name="Andreas09Theme_custom_templates"/>
    <cmf:registerDirectory
        name="Andreas09Theme_styles"/>
    <cmf:registerDirectory
        name="Andreas09Theme_images"/>

</configure>
```

This is a mere two-line addition from the previous step, where we did our first general boilerplate modifications.

Then, in `Products.Andreas09Theme/Products/Andreas09Theme/profiles/default/skins.xml`, we want to add a few more lines:

```xml
<?xml version="1.0"?>
<object name="portal_skins" allow_any="False" cookie_
persistence="False"
   default_skin="Andreas09">
 <object name="Andreas09Theme_custom_images"
    meta_type="Filesystem Directory View"
    directory="Products.Andreas09Theme:skins/
               Andreas09Theme_custom_images"/>
 <object name="Andreas09Theme_custom_templates"
    meta_type="Filesystem Directory View"
    directory="Products.Andreas09Theme:skins/
               Andreas09Theme_custom_templates"/>
 <object name="Andreas09Theme_styles"
    meta_type="Filesystem Directory View"
    directory="Products.Andreas09Theme:skins/Andreas09Theme_styles"/>
 <object name="Andreas09Theme_images"
    meta_type="Filesystem Directory View"
    directory="Products.Andreas09Theme:skins/Andreas09Theme_images"/>

 <skin-path name="Andreas09" based-on="Plone Default">
  <layer name="Andreas09Theme_custom_images"
     insert-after="custom"/>
  <layer name="Andreas09Theme_custom_templates"
     insert-after="Andreas09Theme_custom_images"/>
  <layer name="Andreas09Theme_styles"
     insert-after="Andreas09Theme_custom_templates"/>
  <layer name="Andreas09Theme_images"
     insert-after="Andreas09Theme_styles"/>
 </skin-path>
</object>
```

At this point, as we have changed our boilerplate code (in the `skins.zcml` file), we need to restart Zope. Moreover, because we have changed our GenericSetup in `skins.xml`, we need to either reinstall our product, or import the GenericSetup step specific to `skins.xml`. Reinstalling is likely to be the easiest thing to do, as we are dealing with a fairly simple theme product at this point.

If you're using a revision control system for your own theme, now is a good to time to add and commit this newly created folder to your repository.

Adding a favicon

Next, we will look at the favicon added to this theme. A favicon is the small icon that appears in the URL bar in most browsers and gives a graphical identity to a web site. It also shows up in the page tabs, in those browsers that are able to organize web pages as tabbed pages. In a default Plone site, the favicon looks like this:

The favicon is a small file in the Windows Icon format (`.ico`), and must be named `favicon.ico`. If you display the HTML code of a Plone page, you should see in its header section a declaration similar to the following one:

```
<link rel="shortcut icon" type="image/x-icon"
      href="http://127.0.0.1:8080/mytheme/favicon.ico" />
```

This is so because it is a skin layer object. For example, if it is an image that is found in `parts/CMFPlone/skins/plone_images`, it belongs in the `Andreas09Theme_custom_images` folder. Simply drop a file named `favicon.ico` into this folder, making sure that it is in Windows `.ico` format. Other formats (`.gif`, `.jpg`, `.png`) are not widely-supported by other browsers. The result should look like this:

Modifying other skin layer images

Any images found in `parts/CMFPlone/skins/plone_images` can be modified in the same way. The key is to make sure that the modified file has exactly the same file name as the default Plone image found in **portal_skins**. For example, in `Andreas09Theme_custom_images`, we dropped two images, named `user.gif` and `search_icon.gif`. Plone already knows about the images with these names and will automatically update your skin product with these images.

Content icons, such as the folder icon, the document icon, the news item icon, and many others can be modified in the same fashion. You can drop 16x16 pixel images named `site_icon.gif`, `folder_icon.gif`, `document_icon.gif` and `file_icon.gif` into `Andreas09Theme_custom_images`.

Again, your Plone site will automatically update these icons site-wide, because it already knows about their existence in base Plone.

Adding new images to our theme product

Next, we will add images to our product that Plone does not yet know about. As these images do not ship with CMFPlone, we need to put them in `Andreas09Theme_images`. In the case of this theme, these images are named as follows:

- `bodybg-black.jpg`
- `bodybg-blue.jpg`
- `bodybg-green.jpg`
- `bodybg-orange.jpg`
- `bodybg-purple.jpg`
- `bodybg-red.jpg`
- `footerbg.jpg`
- `menuhover-black.jpg`
- `menuhover-blue.jpg`
- `menuhover-green.jpg`
- `menuhover-orange.jpg`
- `menuhover-purple.jpg`
- `menuhover-red.jpg`

For these images to be visible in our theme product, we will need to write CSS for your theme that makes use of these images. Before we get to that point, it's also important to realize that the images can be used in a different, more global (across your Zope instance) fashion. Let's cover this briefly.

Images as Zope 3 browser resources

Since Plone 2.5, it is possible to use Zope 3 image resources in Plone, instead of accessing images through the **portal_skins** tool. Although it is possible, very few products do so, and in the case of basic themes, it's quite rare that you will want to declare your images as Zope resources.

The base code that was originally generated by the `plone3_theme` template of ZopeSkel contains a folder that can be used for storing Zope 3 resource images. This folder is located at `Products.Andreas09Theme/Products/Andreas09Theme/browser/images`. It is declared as a resource directory in the `configure.zcml` file in `Products.Andreas09Theme/Products/Andreas09Theme/browser/`:

```
<!-- Resource directory for images -->
<browser:resource
    name="Products.Andreas09Theme.images"
```

```
directory="images"
layer=".interfaces.IThemeSpecific"
/>
```

This means that if we place an image called `my_image.jpg` in this folder, it will be accessible from the URL: `http://127.0.0.1:8080/mysite/++resource++Products.Andreas09Theme.images/my_image.jpg`. In this case, "mysite" is the name of your Plone site.

It is also possible to declare an image as a Zope 3 resource file separately, without needing to put it in the images directory of the `browser/` folder in our theme. For instance, we can add an image file called `my_image.jpg` to the `Products.Andreas09Theme/Products/Andreas09Theme/browser/` folder of our product on the file system (not in the images folder), and add the following lines to `Products.Andreas09Theme/Products/Andreas09Theme/browser/configure.zcml`, immediately after the resource directory declarations:

```
<!-- Images declared separately -->
<browser:resource
    name="my_image.jpg"
    file="my_image.jpg"
    layer=".interfaces.IThemeSpecific"
    />
```

Note that an image declared separately is not a `resourceDirectory` any more, but is just a `resource`.

This image is now accessible from the URL: `http://127.0.0.1:8080/mytheme/++resource++my_image.jpg`

 Don't forget to restart Zope after modifying a ZCML file, or the changes won't be taken into account.

The advantage of declaring images separately, versus storing them in a Zope 3 browser resource directory, is that they can be overridden separately from ZCML (otherwise, you will have to customize the resource directory and all of its contained images). For example, if there is an image named `myimage.jpg` located in the `browser/images` folder, you cannot override it without customizing everything in that folder.

Images declared as Zope 3 resources can't be overridden by using the **portal_skins** tool machinery, either. And images accessed from the **portal_skins** tool have handy methods that can be used for setting their height and width, which Zope 3 browser resources don't have. Additionally, Zope 3 resource images must be accessed from ugly, unfriendly URLs. These are among the many reasons why you would not want to use Zope 3 resource images in your product, unless you have a very good reason to do so. Most themers will not use the `browser/images` folder.

Working with stylesheets

Let's look now at the changes generated in the third step of the branch, located here:

```
AndreasBuildout/Products.Andreas09Theme/tutorial_steps/step3-
stylesheet
```

 Reminder: Don't forget to update your `buildout.cfg` file to show the next step of our theme product, and re-run your buildout. Then, reinstall your product, as the version number of the product has changed.

Next, we will look at how to work with stylesheets in Plone. The ZopeSkel paster recipe does not generate a stylesheet specifically named for our theme product, and we will want to create a new stylesheet to avoid confusion between this and other stylesheets.

Stylesheets as Zope 3 resources

As with the images folder found in the theme product's `browser/` folder, ZopeSkel added an empty CSS file that is registered as a Zope 3 resource, named `main.css`. For the same reasons as we have just learned about images, it is unlikely that you will want to use stylesheets that are registered as Zope 3 resources.

The paster `plone3_theme` template gives us a CSS file named `main.css`. This stylesheet is located on the filesystem in the `Products.Andreas09Theme/Products/Andreas09Theme/browser/stylesheets` folder also. The registration of that folder as a Zope 3 Resource Directory is done in the `configure.zcml` file contained in the `browser/` folder of our package (at the same level as the `stylesheets/` folder itself).

From the ZCML declarations, we can see that the `stylesheets/` folder has been registered as a Zope 3 Browser Resource Directory named `Products.Andreas09Theme.stylesheets`.

```
<!-- Resource directory for stylesheets -->
    <browser:resourceDirectory
        name="Products.Andreas09Theme.stylesheets"
```

```
directory="stylesheets"
layer=".interfaces.IThemeSpecific"
/>
```

In the `Profiles/default/cssregistry.xml` file to we find the `main.css` registered:

```
<stylesheet title=""
    id="++resource++Products.Andreas09Theme.stylesheets/main.css"
    media="screen" rel="stylesheet" rendering="import"
    cacheable="True" compression="safe" cookable="True"
    enabled="1" expression=""/>
```

Registering a stylesheet as a browser resource file may be sufficient if we want to edit a pure CSS file. For the purpose of this example though, we want to be able to use Plone's `base_properties.props` definition sheet, which is the file that is used when we need to make global changes to our theme by using variables. To use `base_properties.props`, we must add a new stylesheet to our package that will be accessed from the **portal_skins** tool, and not as a browser resource file.

Working with base properties

Plone provides a properties stylesheet named `base_properties.props` that allows us to make global changes using what are known as DTML variables. The base properties file consists of code that looks like this:

```
title:string=Andreas09's color, font, logo and border defaults

plone_skin:string=Andreas09

logoName:string=logo.jpg

fontFamily:string="Lucida Grande", Verdana, Lucida, Helvetica, Arial,
sans-serif
fontBaseSize:string=69%
fontColor:string=Black
fontSmallSize:string=85%

backgroundColor:string=White

linkColor:string=#436976
linkActiveColor:string=Red
linkVisitedColor:string=Purple

borderWidth:string=1px
borderStyle:string=solid
borderStyleAnnotations:string=dashed

[snip]
```

Within base Plone's stylesheets, there is a CSS that hooks into these base properties, for example:

```
.documentContent {
    font-size: 110%;
    padding: 1em 1em 2em 1em !important;
    background-color: &dtml-backgroundColor;;
}
```

In this example, the class named .documentContent will use a background color that corresponds to the &dtml-backgroundColor definition in the base properties.

This DTML code works only if certain code is put in place. First, the stylesheet that you create specific to your theme product, in this case, andreas09.css.dtml, must have the .dtml extension. Additionally, the stylesheet must contain the following code at the beginning and in the end:

```
/* <dtml-with base_properties> (do not remove this)
  <dtml-call "REQUEST.set('portal_url', portal_url())"> (not this
either)
*/

Your stylesheet rules go here

/* YOUR CSS RULES STOP HERE */

/* </dtml-with> */
```

Adding the extension and including this code ensures that any DTML is recognized.

To get the boilerplate code for enabling DTML, you can copy the following file into your own theme product's styles directory: parts/CMFPlone/skins/plone_styles/ ploneCustom.css.dtml and then rename the stylesheet to something meaningful, in this case andreas09.css.dtml, and place the file in your theme product's Andreas09Theme_styles folder.

Registering a new stylesheet for your theme product

For your theme product to recognize a new stylesheet, we must tell Plone that it exists. In Products.Andreas09Theme/Products/Andreas09Theme/profiles/ default/cssregistry.xml, we will register the stylesheet like this:

```
<?xml version="1.0"?>
<object name="portal_css">
 <stylesheet title=""
```

```
            id="++resource++Products.Andreas09Theme.stylesheets/main.css"
            media="screen" rel="stylesheet" rendering="import"
            cacheable="True" compression="safe" cookable="True"
            enabled="1" expression=""/>
      <stylesheet title=""
            id="andreas09.css"
            media="screen" rel="stylesheet" rendering="import"
            cacheable="True" compression="safe" cookable="True"
            enabled="1" expression=""/>
  </object>
```

Note that we do not use the `.dtml` extension here. Moreover, we've also left the code intact which will allow us to use stylesheets as browser resources, in the event that it is ever needed. We also do not use the ++ designation here.

At this point, if you want to see your stylesheet take effect, you do not have to restart Zope. You either need to reinstall the theme product or import the GenericSetup step that is specific to the CSS registry. You should increment the product version of your theme in `version.txt` if you want to reinstall from the **Add-on Products** page.

Stylesheets located in our theme product

In this theme, we have several stylesheets that have been placed in the `skins/Andreas09Theme_styles` folder. For the purposes of this theme, we answered "True" to the `paster` question regarding whether we wanted to override Plone's base stylesheets. These include the base properties file that we have already discussed, as well as three empty stylesheets named `base.css.dtml`, `portlets.css.dtml`, and `public.css.dtml`. These files are empty in order to override Plone's base styling. These stylesheets have the same names as the default ones in Plone, and are accessed from a skin layer that comes before the Plone layers in our skin definition in the **portal_skins** tool. This means that you could, as an example, take pieces of Plone's original `base.css.dtml` file and customize only pieces of it in the empty `base.css.dtml` stylesheet provided by the theme recipe.

It's quite acceptable to override these default Plone CSS files and start from scratch. However, you could delete these files and build onto Plone's default stylesheets, which are quite robust. Particularly, if you are new to CSS, you may wish to build on top of Plone's existing stylesheets rather than create your own from scratch. Even experienced themers often leave Plone's default stylesheets intact.

Using empty stylesheets is the only way to override default ones for a specific theme, without impacting other themes that may be applied to a Plone site. Disabling stylesheets using the **portal_css** tool will impact all the themes. If the goal is to create a Python package that will be distributed as a theme, it's best not to disable stylesheets by using XML (GenericSetup), simply because it could possibly create side-effects. These side-effects will occur rarely, as the usual case is to have only one theme applied to a Plone site. However, it is a cleaner practice from an end user/site administrator perspective not to have themes affect each other adversely.

In any case, if you knew that more than one theme product will not be applied to a site, and you were aware of the potential side effects, you could disable stylesheets in `profiles/cssregistry.xml` using the following code:

```
<stylesheet title=""
    id="public.css"
    media="screen" rel="stylesheet" rendering="import"
    cacheable="True" compression="safe" cookable="True"
    enabled="0" expression=""/>
```

In this case, we will leave the empty stylesheets (the ones that our `plone3_theme` template gave us) alone, and we will start from scratch with our own stylesheet. Similarly, we will leave the `main.css`, located in the `browser/stylesheets` folder, alone for now, although you could certainly remove it and any related boilerplate if you wanted to.

Basic theming of a Plone site

At this point, we will make some very minor stylistic changes to our site. You can open the file located in step three, `skins/Andreas09Theme_styles/andreas09.css.dtml`, to see what changes we expect to see here. These changes include some basic changes to the background color of the site, some font changes that do not make use of the base properties file, changes to link colors, and some other miscellaneous changes.

In order to apply these changes to your site and make your new stylesheet available in the **portal_css** tool, go to the **quick_installer** from the ZMI (**portal_quickinstaller** at the root of your Plone site), select **Andreas09 Theme**, and click **Reinstall** if you have not already done so.

We can make sure that our new stylesheet is applied to our Plone site by editing it. Edit `andreas09.css.dtml` and make sure that it contains the following code, which will add some very basic styling to our site. Don't forget to verify whether your Plone site is in debug mode, so that the new changes can be seen immediately.

If you are unfamiliar with how to use CSS stylesheets, please refer to a CSS style guide. The **CSS Mastery Guide** is highly recommended: `http://www.cssmastery.com/`

```
/*
  Original design: andreas09 (v2.2 - July 07, 2008) - A free
  xhtml/css website
  template by Andreas Viklund.
  For more information, see
  http://andreasviklund.com/templates/andreas09/

  This file is based on the ploneCustom.css.dtml file shipped with
  Plone.

  <dtml-with base_properties> (do not remove this)
  <dtml-call "REQUEST.set('portal_url', portal_url())"> (not this
    either)
*/
/* YOUR CSS RULES START HERE */

/* Main tags */

body {
    background: #8b8b8b;
    color: #303030;
    font: 76% Verdana,Tahoma,Arial,sans-serif;
    margin: 0;
}

a {
    color: #505050;
}

a:hover {
    color: #808080;
}

img    {
    border: none;
}

/* Main container */

div#visual-portal-wrapper {
    background-color: #f0f0f0;
    color: #303030;
}

/* Personal Actions */

div#portal-personaltools-wrapper ul {
```

```
        list-style-type: none;
        clear: both;
    }
    div#portal-personaltools-wrapper ul li {
        display: inline;
    }
    /* Horizontal menu */
    ul#portal-globalnav, ul#portal-globalnav * {
        list-style: none;
        display: block;
    }
    ul#portal-globalnav li {
        float: left;
        position: relative;
    }
    ul#portal-globalnav li a {
        padding: 10px;
    }
    ul#portal-siteactions {
        list-style-type: none;
    }
    ul#portal-siteactions li {
        display: inline;
        padding: 10px;
    }

    /* YOUR CSS RULES STOP HERE */

    /* </dtml-with> */

    /* Latest version of the documentation on pre-defined properties from
    Plone
        can be found in CMFPlone/skins/plone_styles/ploneCustom.css.dtml */
```

Once you have edited the file according to the code shown above, refresh your site to see the new styling.

You now have a web site that looks a bit more like what Plone used to look like, and which is now a better base for your styling work.

Altering the logo

Next, we will look at the code contained in the fourth step of the Andreas09 theme:

```
AndreasBuildout/Products.Andreas09Theme/tutorial_steps/step4-logo
```

Reminder: Don't forget to update your `buildout.cfg` file to show the next step of our theme product, and re-run your buildout. Then, reinstall your product, as the version number of the product has changed.

Changing the logo is the most common task done when making changes to a web site. There are a couple of ways in which to accomplish this, the easiest of which is by overriding images using the image customization technique explained above in step two. As we've already covered this technique, we'll look at a more interesting implementation.

Altering the image using base properties

Altering base properties makes it easy to alter the image and the image name, without having to change the logo template.

In `Products.Andreas09Theme/Products/Andreas09Theme/skins/ Andreas09Theme_images`, we will drop the image **plone-logo-56.png**, which is available from the Logo Pack located at `http://plone.org/about/logo/`.

Then, in `Products.Andreas09Theme/Products/Andreas09Theme/skins/ Andreas09Theme_styles/base_properties.props`, change the logo name as follows:

```
title:string=Andreas09's color, font, logo and border defaults

plone_skin:string=Andreas09

logoName:string=plone-logo-56.png

fontFamily:string="Lucida Grande", Verdana, Lucida, Helvetica, Arial,
sans-serif
fontBaseSize:string=69%
fontColor:string=Black
fontSmallSize:string=85%

[snip]
```

If you refreshed your browser, you should see the new logo displayed. Our theme product does not demonstrate this method of displaying a new logo, which we'll discuss in a moment.

Altering the Logo viewlet

A second implementation option is to alter the logo template itself to render different HTML. This means that we need to look more closely at the viewlet that renders the logo.

In general, the first step towards overriding a viewlet is to determine if the viewlet is class-based or template-based. What this means in practice is that the steps for overriding viewlets differ slightly based on this distinction.

All viewlets that are used by default Plone are declared in the `viewlets.xml` file located in CMFPlone (on the filesystem in the `Products` folder of your zope instance, or in the `parts/plone/CMFPlone/profiles` path of your buildout).

In order to override class-based viewlets, the steps are as follows:

1. Customize the template or create a new one.
2. Override or reference the class that controls the viewlet.
3. Register the custom viewlet (only if you've created a new viewlet).

Instead, if the viewlet is template-based, the steps are as follows:

1. Identify which viewlet to override.
2. Write the code in the template that renders the viewlet.

Identifying if the Logo is template-based or class-based

In this example, we want to customize the logo so that we can apply a `<div></div>` around it that we can style. We need to look first at the `configuration.zcml` file in `plone.app.layout.viewlets`. The dot-delimited path here means that we are looking at the egg located in your buildout's `eggs/` folder named `plone.app.layout`, in a folder named `viewlets/`, then in a file named `configuration.zcml`.

Search the file for the word `logo` to locate the LogoViewlet, and you will see a line that indicates that the viewlet is class-based:

```
<!-- The logo -->
    <browser:viewlet
        name="plone.logo"
        manager=".interfaces.IPortalHeader"
        class=".common.LogoViewlet"
        permission="zope2.View"
        />
```

Customize the template that renders the Logo or create a new one

Next, we locate the logo template at `plone/app/layout/viewlets/logo.pt`, and copy that to `Products.Andreas09Theme/Products/Andreas09Theme/browser/`. All viewlet templates belong in the browser space.

Rename the page template to `logo_modified.pt`. The default code looks like this:

```
<a metal:define-macro="portal_logo"
   id="portal-logo"
   accesskey="1"
   tal:attributes="href view/navigation_root_url"
   i18n:domain="plone">
    <img src="logo.jpg" alt=""
         tal:replace="structure view/logo_tag" /></a>
```

Hypothetically, at this point, we would check the logo template into subversion, so that we have a vanilla version to track back to, if needed.

Next, in `Products.Andreas09Theme/Products/Andreas09Theme/browser/logo_modified.pt`, we wrap the existing code with a `<div></div>` tag to style it:

```
<div metal:define-macro="portal_logo"
     i18n:domain="plone"
     id="sitename">

   <a id="portal-logo"
      accesskey="1"
      tal:attributes="href view/navigation_root_url">
       <img src="logo.jpg" alt=""
            tal:replace="structure view/logo_tag" /></a>

</div>
```

The rendered code will have a `<div></div>` with an ID, `sitename`, wrapped around it.

Overriding or referencing the class that controls the Logo viewlet

Then, in `Products.Andreas09Theme/Products/Andreas09Theme/browser/configure.zcml`, we will declare the viewlet that replaces the default logo viewlet. In this case, both the class and the template must be declared, even if we only want to change the template. We will still use the logic of the original viewlet class, rather than override it.

Open `plone.app.layout.viewlets.configure.zcml`. The relevant code is as follows:

```
<!-- The logo -->
    <browser:viewlet
        name="plone.logo"
        manager=".interfaces.IPortalHeader"
        class=".common.LogoViewlet"
        permission="zope2.View"
        />
```

Copy this code into the `configure.zcml` file located in the theme product's `browser/` folder. The code should then be altered as follows:

```
<!-- Viewlets registration -->
    <browser:viewlet
        name="plone.logo"
        manager="plone.app.layout.viewlets.interfaces.IPortalHeader"
        class="plone.app.layout.viewlets.common.LogoViewlet"
        template="logo_modified.pt"
        layer=".interfaces.IThemeSpecific"
        permission="zope2.View"
        />
```

The manager will use the dot-delimited path to locate the default code that controls the `IPortalHeader` interface located in `interfaces.py`. This interface code in turn renders the `LogoViewlet`.

In this case, we will not alter the code involved in rendering the logo. We only want to alter the template. Thus, the class line also uses a dot-delimited path back to the original class.

The template link points to the file located in our `browser/` folder, specifically `logo_modified.pt`, and the layer applies the change only to the theme with which we are currently working using the `IThemeSpecific` designation.

Registering the viewlet for the Logo

We are not creating a new viewlet here, so there is no need to modify `viewlets.xml`. The theme relies on the Plone Default `viewlets.xml` definition of `plone.logo` for now. If you renamed your viewlet something along the lines of `mytheme.logo`, you would need to register a new viewlet in `viewlets.xml`. This is mainly a stylistic choice.

Now, we need to restart our Zope to see our changes, as we have changed the ZCML code. To check what is being rendered, view the source code of the rendered page to verify that the `<div></div>` surrounding the logo is present:

```
<div id="sitename">

    <a id="portal-logo" accesskey="1"
       href="http://localhost:8080/andreas09">
        <img src="http://localhost:8080/andreas09/plone-logo-56.png"
alt="" title="" height="56" width="216" /></a>

</div>
```

Note that the modifications made to the viewlet here are not changes that we will make in our final theme product, so we are not showing the rendered code for this example. We've simply investigated our options here so that you understand the different ways in which you can modify your site's logo. For the purposes of the final theme product, we will suppress the logo entirely and create a new viewlet that has a radically different behavior from that of a logo image display.

For now, our site will appear as shown in the following example, displaying the `plone-logo-56.png` specified in `base_properties.props`, wrapped with the extra CSS ID:

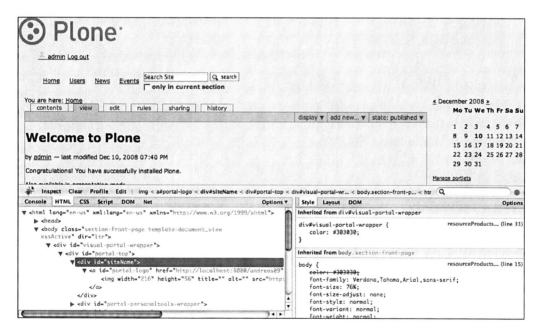

Reworking the header area viewlets

Next, we will look at the code contained in the fifth step of the Andreas09 theme:

```
AndreasBuildout/Products.Andreas09Theme/tutorial_steps/step5-
header-viewlets-rework
```

[**Reminder**: Don't forget to update your `buildout.cfg` file to show the next step of our theme product, and re-run your buildout. Then, reinstall your product, as the version number of the product has changed.]

Now that we have seen our options for modifying the logo, we will look at some of the other viewlets framing the page.

As explained in the previous chapter, elements of a Plone page (search box, breadcrumbs, logo, footer, section tabs, and so on) are rendered by viewlets. In turn, a viewlet manager renders these viewlets in a specific order. The order of viewlets inside a viewlet manager is defined in the GenericSetup profile of our package, specifically in the `viewlets.xml` file.

This `viewlets.xml` file is initially empty, as it has been generated by ZopeSkel, but is not yet modified. However, if you generated your package with the inline documentation (`include_doc` option set to `True`), it will contain some sample boilerplate.

Moving the breadcrumbs to a new viewlet

In this example, we want to move our breadcrumbs to a different viewlet manager so that they will be displayed in a different location on the page. The default code provided by Plone assigns the breadcrumbs to the `IPortalTop` viewlet manager, but because we want to move it, we assign it to a different viewlet manager, `IContentViews`. We won't really be "moving" a viewlet from a viewlet manager, though. What we are really doing is hiding the viewlet from the viewlet manager it is currently registered to, and ordering it in the viewlet manager in which we want it to appear.

To know which viewlet manager you want to move a viewlet into, it helps to visit `http://localhost:8080/mysite/@@manage-viewlets`, where `mysite` is the name of your site. This interface allows you to see how viewlets are nested inside their viewlet managers, and manually control the ordering of viewlets. But for the purposes of this theme product, we will rely solely on configuring the assignment and placing the viewlets using only code. A screenshot of the `@@manage-viewlets` view is shown here:

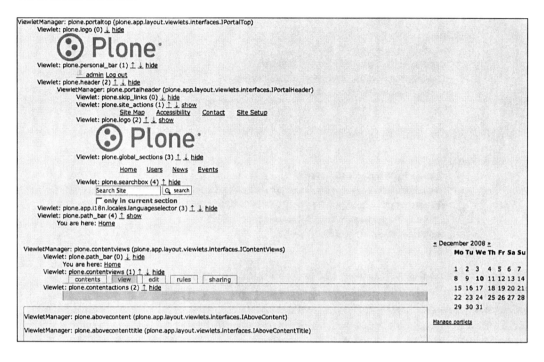

`@@manage-viewlets` is especially helpful if you have incorrectly specified your GenericSetup in `viewlets.xml`, and it has become difficult to **hide** or **show** viewlets simply by using code. Optionally, you can use the **show** or **hide** links and the arrow options to manage your viewlets TTW.

Generally, though, changes made in this view should only be temporary tweaks, as the next time you install your theme product, you may undo any manual changes that were made through this view; so be careful!

Register the breadcrumbs viewlet for the correct viewlet manager

To move our breadcrumbs, we will first register our breadcrumbs viewlet in `Products.Andreas09Theme/Products/Andreas09Theme/browser/configure.zcml`. The default Plone code, located in `plone.app.layout.viewlets.configure.zcml`, is as follows:

```
<!-- The breadcrumbs -->
    <browser:viewlet
        name="plone.path_bar"
        manager=".interfaces.IPortalTop"
        class=".common.PathBarViewlet"
        permission="zope2.View"
        />
```

We will alter the code as follows:

```
<browser:viewlet
        name="plone.path_bar"
        manager="plone.app.layout.viewlets.interfaces.IContentViews"
        class="plone.app.layout.viewlets.common.PathBarViewlet"
        layer=".interfaces.IThemeSpecific"
        permission="zope2.View"
        />
```

We specify the name with the standard Plone designation, `plone.path_bar`. We then provide the full dot-delimited path to the manager that controls the `IContentViews` viewlets, the manager to which we are assigning our breadcrumbs. Additionally, we provide the full dot-delimited path to the class that controls the path bar viewlet, as we don't want to change the default behavior of the breadcrumbs; we only want to move them. Lastly, we assign the viewlet to the current theme by using the `IThemeSpecific` designation.

Ordering the viewlet in the correct location in our profiles

In `CMFPlone/profiles/viewlets.xml`, Plone provides a default configuration for ordering, hiding, or showing viewlets. We will alter this configuration, but use only the pieces that pertain to how our site differs from the base Plone implementation. In our theme product's `profiles/` directory, place the following code in `viewlets.xml`:

```
<?xml version="1.0"?>
<object>
  <order manager="plone.portaltop" skinname="Andreas09"
         based-on="Plone Default">
```

```
      <viewlet name="plone.logo"
              insert-before="*" />
      <viewlet name="plone.personal_bar"
              insert-after="plone.logo" />
  </order>

  <hidden manager="plone.portaltop" skinname="Andreas09">
    <viewlet name="plone.path_bar" />
  </hidden>

  <order manager="plone.portalheader" skinname="Andreas09"
        based-on="Plone Default">
    <viewlet name="plone.searchbox"
              insert-after="*" />
  </order>

  <hidden manager="plone.portalheader" skinname="Andreas09">
    <viewlet name="plone.site_actions" />
    <viewlet name="plone.logo" />
  </hidden>

  <order manager="plone.contentviews" skinname="Andreas09"
        based-on="Plone Default">
    <viewlet name="plone.path_bar"
              insert-before="*" />
  </order>

</object>
```

The `hidden manager` designation hides the `plone.path_bar` from the `portaltop` manager, and then moves it to a new order manager, `plone.contentviews`. We need to specify the `based-on` value as `Plone Default` for the order manager, so that Plone knows to reference the default Plone configuration and alter it accordingly. We also order the `path_bar` above all of the other viewlets in this section by using the '`*`' designation.

Now, reinstall your product to see your changes. If you display a Plone page in your browser, you will see the changes applied. You can also verify the changes by visiting the `@@manage-viewlets` page.

Moving the Logo viewlet to a new viewlet manager

While we're here, we can also move the logo viewlet from the `plone.portalheader` manager to the `plone.portaltop` viewlet manager, and above all of the other viewlets. In `Products.Andreas09Theme/Products/Andreas09Theme/browser/configure.zcml`, we specify the following code:

```
<!-- Viewlets registration -->
    <browser:viewlet
        name="plone.logo"
        manager="plone.app.layout.viewlets.interfaces.IPortalTop"
        class="plone.app.layout.viewlets.common.LogoViewlet"
        template="logo_modified.pt"
        layer=".interfaces.IThemeSpecific"
        permission="zope2.View"
        />
```

Here, we change the name of the viewlet manager from the default `IPortalHeader` to `IPortalTop`, provide a dot-delimited path to the standard class that renders the logo viewlet, specify a new logo template, and assign the viewlet change to the current theme product. We use dot-delimited paths as we don't want to change the default behavior of either the manager or the class.

Then, in `Products.Andreas09Theme/Products/Andreas09Theme/profiles/default/viewlets.xml`, we want to hide the `plone.logo` viewlet from the `plone.portalheader` viewlet manager, and order it in the `plone.portaltop` viewlet manager. If we were not moving the viewlet to a new manager, we could skip this step.

```
<?xml version="1.0"?>
<object>
  <order manager="plone.portaltop" skinname="Andreas09"
        based-on="Plone Default">
    <viewlet name="plone.logo"
            insert-before="*" />
    <viewlet name="plone.personal_bar"
            insert-after="plone.logo" />
  </order>
  <hidden manager="plone.portaltop" skinname="Andreas09">
    <viewlet name="plone.path_bar" />
  </hidden>
  <order manager="plone.portalheader" skinname="Andreas09"
        based-on="Plone Default">
    <viewlet name="plone.searchbox"
            insert-after="*" />
  </order>
  <hidden manager="plone.portalheader" skinname="Andreas09">
```

```
    <viewlet name="plone.site_actions" />
    <viewlet name="plone.logo" />
  </hidden>

  <order manager="plone.contentviews" skinname="Andreas09"
        based-on="Plone Default">
    <viewlet name="plone.path_bar"
            insert-before="*" />
  </order>
</object>
```

Moving the site actions viewlet to a new viewlet manager

We also want to hide `plone.site_actions` from `plone.portalheader` in `viewlets.xml`, as it will be registered with the footer later on:

```
<hidden manager="plone.portalheader" skinname="Andreas09">
    <viewlet name="plone.site_actions" />
    <viewlet name="plone.logo" />
  </hidden>
```

Reordering the personal bar viewlet

Next, we reorder the `plone.personal_bar` viewlet inside the `plone.portaltop` viewlet manager so that it appears directly after the logo section.

```
<order manager="plone.portaltop" skinname="Andreas09"
        based-on="Plone Default">
    <viewlet name="plone.logo"
            insert-before="*" />
    <viewlet name="plone.personal_bar"
            insert-after="plone.logo" />
  </order>
```

A Zope restart is needed at this point, and we must also reinstall the product, as we changed the GenericSetup profile in `viewlets.xml`.

Styling the header

Next, we will look at the code contained in the sixth step of the Andreas09 theme:

```
AndreasBuildout/Products.Andreas09Theme/tutorial_steps/step6-
header-style
```

Reminder: Don't forget to update your `buildout.cfg` file to show the next step of our theme product, and re-run your buildout. Then, reinstall your product, as the version number of the product has changed.

Our next objective is to style the header area so that it has a background image—in this case, `bodybg-black.jpg`. Because we are only working with CSS changes for this step, reloading your browser as you make changes will enable you to see the effect of those changes. There is no need to restart your Zope instance.

The very first modification to the stylesheet is to make some basic changes to how anchors (links) display. The original code is:

```
a {
    color: #505050;
}
a:hover {
    color: #808080;
}
```

We will modify the code to change the font weight and to ensure that underlines or other text-decoration properties are not applied.

```
a {
    color: #505050;
    font-weight: bold;
    text-decoration: none;
}
a:hover {
    color: #808080;
    text-decoration: underline;
}
```

Next, we will apply a background image to the div with an ID of `#visual-portal-wrapper`. This wrapper contains everything within the body tag of your page, and essentially wraps around all of the elements on the page, but is located within the body area.

In `Products.Andreas09Theme/Products/Andreas09Theme/skins/ Andreas09Theme_styles/andreas09.css.dtml`, we will change the styling of `#visual-portal-wrapper` from the styling specified in step five. The previous code that we have in our theme product looks like this:

```
/* Main container */
div#visual-portal-wrapper {
```

```
    background-color: #f0f0f0;
    color: #303030;
}
```

We remove the background color designation and replace it with the name of the image that we want to use, and set it up to tile horizontally.

```
/* Main container */
div#visual-portal-wrapper {
    background: #f0f0f0 url(bodybg-black.jpg) repeat-x;
    color: #303030;
}
```

Next, we want to align the site name and personal actions (user name, login link, and so on), so that the site name floats to the left, and the personal actions float to the right. Padding and margins are also adjusted slightly. The clear property is used to ensure that items play nicely with each other, and to set the sides of an element where other floating elements are not allowed.

```
/* Header section */
#sitename {
    float: left;
    clear: right;
    width: 50%;
    padding: 20px;
    height: 62px;
}
/* Personal Actions */
div#portal-personaltools-wrapper {
    float: right;
    clear: right;
    text-align: right;
    padding-top: 75px;
    margin: 0;
}
div#portal-personaltools-wrapper ul {
    list-style-type: none;
    margin: 0;
    padding: 0;
    width: 100%;
}
div#portal-personaltools-wrapper ul li {
    line-height: 18px;
    display: inline;
}
```

We also change the color of the `personalbar` items to white so that they are in contrast against the background image; we adjust the font style and size slightly. Alignment is specified so that the items appear neatly in the `personalbar` wrapper area.

```
div#portal-personaltools-wrapper a {
    color: white;
    font-style: none;
    font-size: 10px;
    vertical-align: middle !important;
    padding: 0 10px;
}

div#portal-personaltools-wrapper a img {
    vertical-align: middle !important;
}
```

Then, we write some CSS statements to position the global navigation and the search box, and apply some basic height, size, and padding properties. `portal globalnav` items also receive styling to apply a right-hand border after each list item. They are styled in uppercase, have their default color changed, have a background color applied for the hover state, and have a background color and image applied for the selected state.

```
/* Horizontal menu */

ul#portal-globalnav {
    height: 35px;
    font-size: 12px;
    margin-bottom: 20px;
    float: left;
    clear: both;
}

ul#portal-globalnav, ul#portal-globalnav * {
    margin: 0;
    padding: 0;
    list-style: none;
}

ul#portal-globalnav li {
    float: left;
    position: relative;
    width: auto;
    border-right: 1px solid #b0b0b0;
    display: block;
    height: 35px;
    text-transform: uppercase;
```

```
    }

ul#portal-globalnav li a {
    display: block;
    color: #606060;
    padding: 10px 10px;
    text-decoration: none;
}

#portal-globalnav li a:hover {
    background: #f0f0f0 url(menuhover-black.jpg) top left repeat-x;
    color: #505050;
    text-decoration: none;
}

#portal-globalnav li.selected a {
    background: #f0f0f0 url(menuhover-black.jpg) top left repeat-x;
    color: #505050;
}
```

The search box is then styled to have a specific height. This helps when viewing the site in IE7, which occasionally places a scrollbar in the search box area if the height is not specified. It may also help to include an `overflow:visible` property here, though we have not included it in our CSS.

Next, the coloring of the border of the search box is adjusted, a font size specified, and a background image applied to the search button. Basic padding and width/height settings are also included.

```
    /* Search box */

div#portal-searchbox {
    height: 35px!important;
    float: right;
}

div#portal-searchbox form {
    padding-top: 7px;
    padding-right: 10px;
}

div#portal-searchbox .searchSection {
    display: none;
}

div#portal-searchbox input {
    border: 1px solid #b0b0b0;
    font-size: 12px !important;
    vertical-align: middle;
}
```

```
div#portal-searchbox input.searchButton {
    background: transparent url(search_icon.gif) no-repeat left top;
    border: 0px !important;
    cursor: pointer;
    padding: 18px 0px 0px;
    width: 18px !important;
    height: 18px !important;
    overflow: hidden;
}
```

Refresh your browser to see the new styling. The result should appear as shown in the example in the following screenshot:

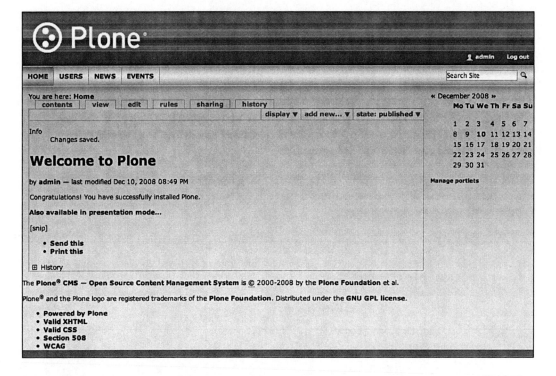

Styling the central region of the page

Next, we will look at the code contained in the seventh step of the Andreas09 theme:

```
AndreasBuildout/Products.Andreas09Theme/tutorial_steps/step7-
central-region-style
```

Reminder: Don't forget to update your `buildout.cfg` file to show the next step of our theme product, and re-run your buildout. Then, reinstall your product, as the version number of the product has changed.

Our next mission is to style the elements located in the center content area. In some cases, we are borrowing code directly from `CMFPlone/skins/plone_styles` and just modifying it slightly. This is particularly true in the case of navigation styling.

We will add sections for wrapping the content, sidebars, various portlets, breadcrumbs, content, and content actions (print, email, and so on). Let's first look at the code for the center content:

```
/* Content wrap */

#portal-columns {
    width: 99% !important;
    margin-top: 20px;
    margin-bottom: 20px;
    margin-left: auto;
    margin-right: auto;
}

td#portal-column-content {
    background-color: #fafcff;
    border: 1px solid #909090;
    color: #2a2a2a;
    font-size: 0.9em;
    padding-bottom: 10px;
}
```

This code defines the styles for all of the columns on our Plone site (there are three, `#portal-column-one`, `#portal-column-two`, and `#portal-column-content`, which is the middle column). Then, we apply some styling to the center column to give it a background color, a border, a color for the base text that will be displayed in the column, a slightly reduced font size, and some padding at the bottom.

Next, let's add some code to support the sidebars, by adjusting the the left and right columns to specify the column width and some basic padding within the columns.

```
/* Sidebars */
#portal-column-one, #portal-column-two {
    width: 200px !important;
}
#portal-column-one .visualPadding, #portal-column-two .visualPadding {
    padding: 0 10px;
}
```

Next, we apply some base portlet code that all of our portlets will use, specifying a color behind the portlet header area, some minor text manipulation, text color for hyperlinks in the portal header area, and some basic line height and margin buffers.

Additionally, the portlet is given list-style of none. Basically, there may be times when you have a list, but you don't want it to include any bullets, or you want to use some other character in place of the bullet. Simply add list-style: none; to your rule.

```
.portlet .portletHeader {
    color: #505050;
    font-size: 1.6em;
    font-weight: bold;
    letter-spacing: -1px;
    margin: 0 0 12px;
}
.portlet .portletHeader a {
    color: #303030;
}
.portlet {
    list-style: none;
}
.portletItem {
    font-size: 0.9em;
    line-height: 1.4em;
    margin: 0 0 16px 10px;
}
```

Next, we style the login portlet with some more specific code. To see these changes, open a new browser so that you can view the site in logged-out style, as shown in the following example:

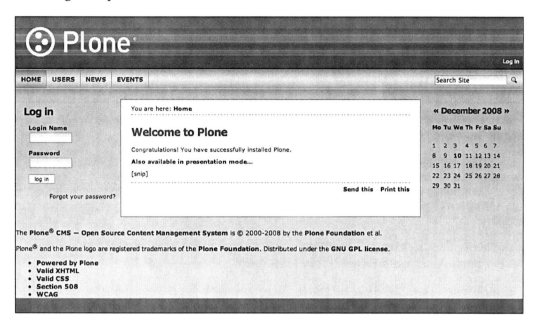

If you are logged in, the login portlet is automatically suppressed, so you need to be logged out to see the change in styles. In the portlet, we will set a text alignment of right, so that the **Forgot your password** text aligns to the right.

```
/* Login portlet */
.portlet.portletLogin .portletItem.even {
    text-align: right;
}
```

We also apply some basic font weight and color settings to the anchor tags, hide the images that ordinarily display in the login box, add a border with a different color around the **Login Name** and **Password** boxes, and specify a font size and alignment for the input fields. Then, the **Login Button** receives some styling, a background color, some padding, and a smaller font size.

```
.portlet.portletLogin .portletItem.even a {
    font-weight: normal;
    color: #505050;
}
.portlet.portletLogin .portletItem.even a img {
    display: none;
}
```

```
.portlet.portletLogin input {
    border: 1px solid #b0b0b0;
    font-size: 12px !important;
    vertical-align: middle;
}
.portlet.portletLogin input.context {
    background: #fafcff none;
    padding: 2px 10px;
    font-size: 90% !important;
}
```

The next bit of code is for styling the calendar portlet, enlarging the size of the header text and centering the alignment of the header.

```
/* Calendar portlet */
.portletCalendar .portletHeader {
  font-size: 1.2em;
  text-align: center;
}
```

Next, we will look at how to modify the navigation section of our site. Most of this code is borrowed from the base Plone stylesheet, `navtree.css.dtml`.

The best way to see the effect of this code is to modify the portlet that controls the navigation via `http://localhost:8080/mysite/manage-portlets`, and change the settings so that it includes the top node and has a start level of 0:

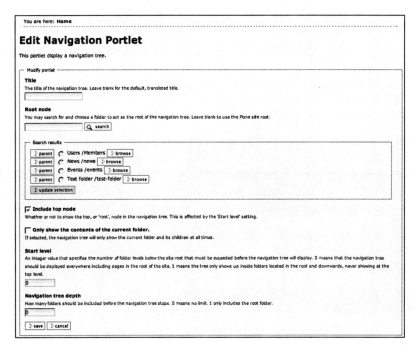

Next, add some test content to your site (folders are the best content to be added, as you can nest your folders and see how secondary and tertiary levels of navigation are displayed). Don't forget to save your settings to the navigation portlet and the settings to the `@@manage-portlets view` as well.

Here, we are applying some padding properties, removing any list decorations or styling, and adjusting the margins of each navigation item:

```
/* Navigation portlet */
/* Adapted from original plone one */
.portletNavigationTree {
    padding: 0;
    list-style: none !important;
    list-style-image: none !important;
    line-height: 1em;
}

.navTree {
    list-style: none;
    list-style-image: none;
    padding-left: 0px;
}

.navTreeItem {
    margin-top: 5px;
}
```

Next, we adjust the styling of each individual navigation link, giving them a background color, a different color border, a block property to display each item as a box, no link styles (such as an underlines), and some basic padding and alignment.

Additionally, we adjust the alignment of the folder icons to center them vertically.

```
.navTreeItem a,
dd.portletItem .navTreeItem a {
    background: #e8e9ea;
    border: 1px solid #b0b0b0;
    display: block;
    text-decoration: none;
    padding: 3px;
    vertical-align: middle;
}

.navTreeItem a img,
dd.portletItem .navTreeItem a img {
    vertical-align: middle;
}
```

```
.navTreeItem a:hover,
dd.portletItem .navTreeItem a:hover {
    background-color: #f8f9fa;
    border: 1px solid #909090;
    text-decoration: none;
    color: #606060 !important;
}
```

For the selected navigation items, we alter the background color slightly, adjust the border coloring, remove any underlining or similar styles, and apply a font color. For published navigation items, we use a different font color.

```
.navTreeCurrentItem,
.navTreeCurrentItem:hover {
    background-color: #f8f9fa !important;
    border: 1px solid #909090 !important;
    text-decoration: none !important;
    color: #303030 !important;
}
.navTreeItem a.state-published,
dd.portletItem .navTreeItem a.state-published {
    color: #606060 !important;
}
.navTreeItem a.state-published.navTreeCurrentItem,
dd.portletItem .navTreeItem a.state-published.navTreeCurrentItem {
    color: #303030 !important;
}
```

Plone's default `navtree` stylesheet contains some boilerplate CSS to alter the height of the current navigation item's anchor tag for Internet Explorer 6.

```
/* Another workaround for broken Internet Explorer */
* html li.navTreeCurrentItem a,
* html li.navTreeCurrentItem a:hover {
    height: 1.6em;
}
```

Then, for each sublevel of the navigation, we adjust the indentation slightly. Each navigation item is nested within the next; so they are indented by 20 pixels every time you drill down further.

```
.navTreeLevel0 { margin: 0; }
.navTreeLevel1 { margin-left: 20px; }
.navTreeLevel2 { margin-left: 20px; }
.navTreeLevel3 { margin-left: 20px; }
.navTreeLevel4 { margin-left: 20px; }
.navTreeLevel5 { margin-left: 20px; }
```

Next, we style our breadcrumbs to alter the bottom border styling and some of the basic margin and padding settings.

```
/* Breadcrumbs */

div#portal-breadcrumbs {
    border-bottom: 1px dashed #B0B0B0;
    margin: 0 10px 10px;
    padding: 0 0 5px;
}
```

Our content area also requires some small changes such as some increased padding. Additionally, the h1 and h2 tags receive some basic color, size, font weight and compression styling, plus margin and padding settings. Additionally, they are set to inherit the background color of their parent container, for example, the #content div.

```
/* Content */

#content {
    padding: 10px;
}

#content h1,#content h2 {
    background-color: inherit;
    color: #606060;
    font-size: 1.8em;
    font-weight: bold;
    letter-spacing: -1px;
    margin: 0 0 15px;
    padding: 0;
}
```

Lastly, we add styling to the content actions, for example, the email and print icons, adding a dotted border along the top, some padding, and margin spacing. The list items are set as inline, which takes up only as much width as it needs, and does not force new lines.

```
/* Document Actions */

div.documentActions {
    border-top: 1px dashed #B0B0B0;
    margin: 10px 0 0;
    padding: 5px 0 0;
    text-align: right;
}

div.documentActions ul {
    list-style-type: none;
```

```
        padding: 0;
        margin: 0;
    }
    div.documentActions ul li {
        display: inline;
    }
    div.documentActions ul li a {
        display: inline;
        padding-left: 10px;
    }
```

These styles give us the basic styling we need for the content area. Refresh your browser to see the effect of these changes. Your screen should now look similar to the example shown here:

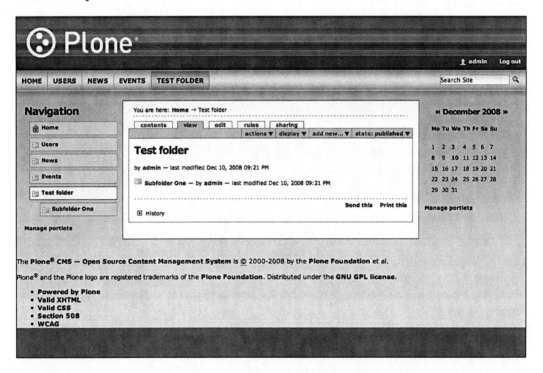

Altering the footer area viewlets

Next, we will look at the code contained in the eighth step of the Andreas09 theme:

```
AndreasBuildout/Products.Andreas09Theme/tutorial_steps/step8-
footer-viewlets
```

Reminder: Don't forget to update your `buildout.cfg` file to show the next step of our theme product, and re-run your buildout. Then, reinstall your product, as the version number of the product has changed.

In this step, we need to wrap the footer inside a `<div></div>` section with a specific CSS ID in order to apply a background image. Only two viewlets will be displayed in the footer: a viewlet with credits for the original design, and the portal actions (site map, accessibility, contact, and site setup).

Those two viewlets will be called from a custom manager that contains a template with a `<div></div>` wrapper. To make this happen, we need to create a new viewlet manager and override the original footer viewlet. Generally speaking, Plone contains enough viewlet managers that you should not need to add new viewlet managers. But it's important to understand how this process works in the event that you do need to do so.

Firstly, in `Products.Andreas09Theme/Products/Andreas09Theme/browser/interfaces.py`, we will add a new viewlet manager called `IAndreas09Footer` that will be used for registering the viewlets.

```
from plone.theme.interfaces import IDefaultPloneLayer
from zope.viewlet.interfaces import IViewletManager

class IThemeSpecific(IDefaultPloneLayer):
    "Marker interface that defines a Zope 3 browser layer."

class IAndreas09Footer(IViewletManager):
    "A viewlet manager for wrapping the footer into a <div
    id="footer"> tag."
```

Don't forget to add the line that imports the `IViewletManager`.

Then, in `Products.Andreas09Theme/Products/Andreas09Theme/browser/configure.zcml`, we want to register the interface that we have just declared and give the new manager the name, `andreas09.portalfooter` and provide a dot-delimited path back to the class that manages this viewlet.

```
<browser:viewletManager
        name="andreas09.portalfooter"
        provides=".interfaces.IAndreas09Footer"
        permission="zope2.View"
        class="plone.app.viewletmanager.manager.
            BaseOrderedViewletManager"
        />
```

Next, in `Products.Andreas09Theme/Products/Andreas09Theme/browser/`, we will add a new page template called `footer_viewlet.pt` that will contain the code that calls the viewlet manager inside a `<div></div>` wrapper:

```
<div xmlns="http://www.w3.org/1999/xhtml"
     xmlns:tal="http://xml.zope.org/namespaces/tal"
     id="footer">
   <div tal:replace="structure provider:andreas09.portalfooter" />
</div>
```

In `Products.Andreas09Theme/Products/Andreas09Theme/browser/configure.zcml`, we will add the declaration for the `andreas09.portalfooter` manager. We will also add the overriding declaration for `plone.footer` that will use the template that was just added, and declare the viewlet itself:

```
<browser:viewlet
        name="plone.footer"
        manager="plone.app.layout.viewlets.interfaces.IPortalFooter"
        template="footer_viewlet.pt"
        layer=".interfaces.IThemeSpecific"
        permission="zope2.View"
        />
```

Note that we use the dot-delimited path to the standard `IPortalFooter` manager, specify the new template, and declare the viewlet as applicable to this theme only.

We then configure the viewlet for the `plone.site_actions`, so that it also uses the new manager:

```
<browser:viewlet
        name="plone.site_actions"
        manager=".interfaces.IAndreas09Footer"
        class="plone.app.layout.viewlets.common.SiteActionsViewlet"
        layer=".interfaces.IThemeSpecific"
        permission="zope2.View"
        />
```

Again, we use the dot-delimited path to the `SiteActionsViewlet` class, as we are not modifying this class, and we configure this viewlet so that it is applicable only to the current theme.

At this stage, we still have the colophon displayed. We can hide it by using the GenericSetup profile, `viewlets.xml`:

```
<hidden manager="plone.portalfooter" skinname="Andreas09">
    <viewlet name="plone.colophon" />
   </hidden>
```

Then, we can add a viewlet that contains credits to the original author of the design, Andreas Viklund. We will do this by adding a new page template called `credits_viewlet.pt`, and enter the following code in it:

```
<p id="design-credits">
  <a href="http://andreasviklund.com/files/demo/andreas09/
">Andreas09</a> Theme
  for <a href="http://plone.org">Plone</a> |
  Original design by <a href="http://andreasviklund.com/">Andreas
Viklund</a>
</p>
```

We then need to register the viewlet in `Products.Andreas09Theme/Products/Andreas09Theme/browser/configure.zcml`:

```
<browser:viewlet
        name="andreas09.design_credits"
        manager=".interfaces.IAndreas09Footer"
        template="credits_viewlet.pt"
        layer=".interfaces.IThemeSpecific"
        permission="zope2.View"
        />
```

This viewlet uses the new viewlet manager, `IAndreas09Footer`, a template named `credits_viewlet.pt`, and is specific to the current theme product.

Now that we have configured both viewlets to use the correct manager, we need to order them in the `andreas09.portalfooter` manager in `Products.Andreas09Theme/Products/Andreas09Theme/profiles/default/viewlets.xml`:

```
<order manager="andreas09.portalfooter" skinname="Andreas09">
    <viewlet name="andreas09.design_credits" />
    <viewlet name="plone.site_actions" />
</order>
```

Restart your Zope and reinstall the theme product to see the changes. Then, we can apply some CSS around the newly configured viewlets in `andreas09.css.dtml`. The footer area is given a background color and a background image that tiles horizontally. The footer area should have a "clear" setting to make sure that it does not clash with other elements on the page, and has some basic font, margin, and padding settings applied to it. The text is centered in the viewlet, and the viewlet stretches across the entire width of the page. Additionally, the anchor tags are styled with a color and a font weight, and the credits are given some padding at the bottom.

```
/* Footer */
#footer {
```

```
    background: #8b8b8b url(footerbg.jpg) top left repeat-x;
    clear: both;
    color: #d0d0d0;
    font-size: 0.9em;
    font-weight: bold;
    margin: 0;
    padding: 0;
    padding-top: 20px;
    text-align: center;
    width: 100%;
}
#footer a {
    color: #d0d0d0;
    font-weight: bold;
}
p#design-credits {
    margin-bottom: 30px;
}
```

We also need to add the styling rules for the portal-site actions that appear in the page footer. The list items have all list styling removed, stretch across the width of the page, have a customized top border, and have some margin and padding settings defined for them. The list items have a line height set, are set for inline display, and have additional padding defined. Finally, the anchor tags are white, font styling is removed so that it is displayed as normal, and the size is set to 10 pixels.

```
ul#portal-siteactions {
    list-style-type: none;
    width: 100%;
    border-top: 1px dashed #d0d0d0;
    margin: 0;
    padding: 5px 0 5px;
}
ul#portal-siteactions li {
    line-height: 1.0em;
    display: inline;
    padding: 10px;
}
ul#portal-siteactions li a {
    color: white;
    font-style: none;
    font-size: 10px;
}
```

This code completes the modifications needed for this section of our site. Refreshing the site displays the following result:

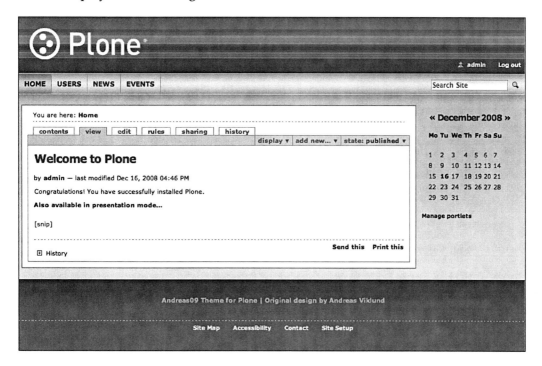

Altering the header area title

Next, we will look at the code contained in the ninth step of the Andreas09 theme:

```
AndreasBuildout/Products.Andreas09Theme/tutorial_steps/
step9-header-title
```

 Reminder: Don't forget to update your `buildout.cfg` file to show the next step of our theme product, and re-run your buildout. Then, reinstall your product, as the version number of the product has changed.

Occasionally, you may wish to add to a part of the default Plone page or replace it with one that uses some additional logic (or logic that is different from the original one). In this example, the logo viewlet we configured earlier will be replaced with a new one that displays the title and the description of the portal, as the original design implies.

This is not heavy logic, but we will still need a little bit of Python code to fetch the portal title and description, in order to display them.

First, we will create the viewlet class that will contain the logic.

In `Products.Andreas09Theme/Products/Andreas09Theme/browser/viewlets.py`, we will add the following class declaration:

```
from zope.component import getMultiAdapter
from Products.Five.browser.pagetemplatefile import
ViewPageTemplateFile
from plone.app.layout.viewlets.common import ViewletBase

class PortalTitleViewlet(ViewletBase):
    render = ViewPageTemplateFile('portal_title_viewlet.pt')

    def update(self):
        self.portal_state = getMultiAdapter((self.context, self.
request),
                                            name=u'plone_portal_state')
        self.portal_title = self.portal_state.portal_title
        self.portal_description = self.portal_state.portal().
Description()
```

Do not forget to import `getMultiAdapter` at the top of the file. We need this because the new logo viewlet class needs to fetch the `portal_state` Zope 3 utility to get one of its attributes and use one of its methods.

Backward-Compatibility of 3.x themes

Note that the render statement mentioned above has been replaced with an "index" directive in the later versions of Plone 3.x. Version 1.1.3 of the `plone.app.layout` egg was released in July of 2008. As of this version, the viewlet template is controlled via the `index` attribute rather than via `render`, because `index` can be overridden by using the ZCML `template` attribute, removing the need for a special viewlet subclass.

If you need to make a subclass anyway, you can continue to use the `render` directive as mentioned above or you can use `index` instead, as shown here:

```
from Products.Five.browser.pagetemplatefile import
ViewPageTemplateFile

from plone.app.layout.viewlets import common

class PathBarViewlet(common.PathBarViewlet):
    "A custom version of the path bar class"
    index = ViewPageTemplateFile('path_bar.pt')
```

If you're going to distribute your theme, and need to maintain backward-compatibility with the Plone 3.0.x series, additional code needs to be included. You should add the following lines that make the render method defer to the index attribute. (This is done in ViewletBase in Plone 3.1.x, but not in Plone 3.0.x):

```python
from plone.app.layout.viewlets import common

class PathBarViewlet(common.PathBarViewlet):
    "A custom version of the path bar class"

    def render(self):
        # defer to index method, because that's what gets overridden
          by the template ZCML attribute
        return self.index()

    index = ViewPageTemplateFile('path_bar.pt')
```

Otherwise, themes created with the newer versions of plone.app.layout will not be compatible with the older versions of Plone. Now, back to where we left off…

Creating the template

Next, we will create the template that will pull in this logic. Create a new page template called portal_title_viewlets.pt and place it in the browser/ folder, and enter the following code in this template file:

```html
<div id="sitename">
  <h1 tal:content="view/portal_title">
    Title of the portal
  </h1>
  <h2 tal:content="view/portal_description">
    Description of the portal
  </h2>
</div>
```

We then need to add a description to the portal that will make it display both the title of the portal (your site) and the description of the site. Do this in the ZMI via the **Properties** tab or via the Site configlet in the Plone Control Panel (**Site Setup**).

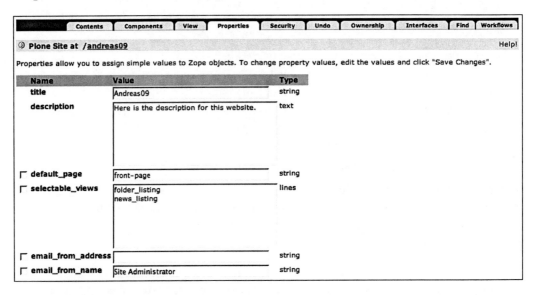

We also want to register the viewlet as a replacement for the logo. The logo code from the previous step looks like this:

```
<browser:viewlet
        name="plone.logo"
        manager="plone.app.layout.viewlets.interfaces.IPortalTop"
        class="plone.app.layout.viewlets.common.LogoViewlet"
        template="logo_modified.pt"
        layer=".interfaces.IThemeSpecific"
        permission="zope2.View"
        />
```

In `Products.Andreas09Theme/Products/Andreas09Theme/browser/configure.zcml`, we add the following code:

```
<browser:viewlet
        name="plone.logo"
        manager="plone.app.layout.viewlets.interfaces.IPortalTop"
        class=".viewlets.PortalTitleViewlet"
        layer=".interfaces.IThemeSpecific"
        permission="zope2.View"
        />
```

Notice that this viewlet is also designated as `plone.logo`, and uses the standard `IPortalTop` viewlet manager. However, now, it uses a locally-defined viewlet class named `PortalTitleViewlet`, and we remove the template designation because the class already tells us which template to use. As always, it is applied only to the current theme.

Now, we restart our Zope and style the header using the CSS described below.

The styles serve to float the name of the site to the left, clear it from the boundaries of the other elements, stretch it halfway across the page, give it white text, a fixed height, left alignment and some margin settings.

Then, the `h1` and `h2` tags are given a weight of 400%, a compressed spacing, and margin and padding settings of zero. Additional styles for font-size and padding are applied to the `h1` and `h2` tags to distinguish them from each other.

```css
/* Header section */
#sitename {
    float: left;
    clear: right;
    width: 50%;
    color: #ffffff;
    height: 92px;
    margin: 0 20px 10px;
    text-align: left;
}

#sitename h1,#sitename h2 {
    font-weight: 400;
    letter-spacing: -2px;
    margin: 0;
    padding: 0;
}

#sitename h1 {
    font-size: 2.4em;
    padding-top: 20px;
}

#sitename h2 {
    font-size: 1.6em;
}
```

If you refreshed your browser, the resulting screen would look as shown in the example in the following screenshot:

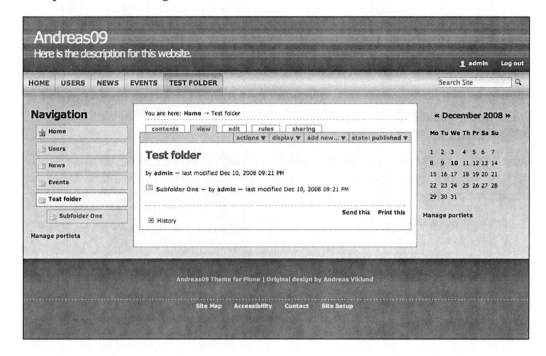

Working with section colors

Next, we will look at the code contained in the tenth step of the Andreas09 theme:

```
AndreasBuildout/Products.Andreas09Theme/tutorial_steps/step10-
section-colors
```

 Reminder: Don't forget to update your `buildout.cfg` file to show the next step of our theme product, and re-run your buildout. Then, reinstall your product, as the version number of the product has changed.

If you look at the original Andreas09 Theme (`http://andreasviklund.com/files/demo/andreas09/`), you will see that when you move to a new section, the header background image changes. We are going to add the same behavior using only CSS. The default Plone HTML allows us to do this easily.

If you use Firebug, it is easier to see this in action, but you can also just refer to the URL of the section you are on. Essentially, each page in Plone is given a unique ID based on its shortname, preceded by `section-`. The following screenshot illustrates how when you are in a given section, the body tag picks up a special `section` style tag, in this case, `.section-front-page`:

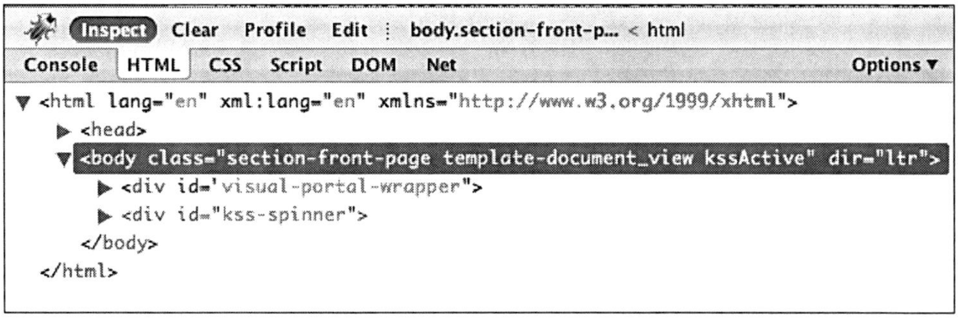

The following code uses a different image for the header, tiled horizontally. It also applies background colors and images to buttons for their hover state.

```
/* Section Colors */

.section-front-page div#visual-portal-wrapper {
    background: #f0f0f0 url(bodybg-blue.jpg) repeat-x;
}

#portaltab-index_html a:hover {
    background: #f0f0f0 url(menuhover-blue.jpg) top left repeat-x
!important;
}

#portaltab-index_html.selected a {
    background: #f0f0f0 url(menuhover-blue.jpg) top left repeat-x
!important;
}

.section-Members div#visual-portal-wrapper {
    background: #f0f0f0 url(bodybg-red.jpg) repeat-x;
}

#portaltab-Members a:hover {
    background: #f0f0f0 url(menuhover-red.jpg) top left repeat-x
!important;
}

#portaltab-Members.selected a {
    background: #f0f0f0 url(menuhover-red.jpg) top left repeat-x
!important;
}
```

```
.section-news div#visual-portal-wrapper {
    background: #f0f0f0 url(bodybg-green.jpg) repeat-x;
}

#portaltab-news a:hover {
    background: #f0f0f0 url(menuhover-green.jpg) top left repeat-x
!important;
}

#portaltab-news.selected a {
    background: #f0f0f0 url(menuhover-green.jpg) top left repeat-x
!important;
}

.section-events div#visual-portal-wrapper {
    background: #f0f0f0 url(bodybg-purple.jpg) repeat-x;
}

#portaltab-events a:hover {
    background: #f0f0f0 url(menuhover-purple.jpg) top left repeat-x
!important;
}

#portaltab-events.selected a {
    background: #f0f0f0 url(menuhover-purple.jpg) top left repeat-x
!important;
}
```

Now, when you navigate to another section, it will automatically pick up the new background image. Note that this technique is a little brittle (if someone changes the shortname of a section, the CSS will break), implying that you have to do more hand-coding. There are other options for customizing Plone sites by section, but this is the most common method.

This concludes the bulk of the styling needed in our theme product. Certainly, this is a fairly lightweight theme; a more difficult theme will require significantly more CSS.

In terms of best practices to be followed for styling, it helps to be diligent about commenting your code appropriately, to designate which section of the page your CSS statements apply to, and by following the same order of sections each time. This can make it easier to find your code, and will provide some consistency.

Going forward, if you are new to Plone, you should start with trying to recreate some of the themes located at oswd.org, the open source site where we found the Andreas09 theme. Happy theming!

Summary

In this chapter, we have learned:

- How to set up a development environment, and start a Zope instance
- How to generate a theme product
- How to configure your buildout to recognize a theme product, install the theme on a Plone site, and put it into debug mode
- How to modify the boilerplate code of your theme product
- How to work with stylesheets and images in Plone
- How to change your site's logo
- How to move, order, and hide viewlets
- How to create new viewlet managers and page templates
- How to do basic styling, and how to customize styles based on the section of your site that is being displayed

Using what you have learned in this chapter and the previous chapter, you should now be able to create a skin product using only filesystem development.

Part 4

My boss wants me to...

...take my site live

...make it go faster

...connect to your LDAP/Active Directory repository

19

Take My Site Live

Plone is easy to install and run, but launching a site on a production server with a robust and secure configuration takes some extra work.

In this chapter, **Steve McMahon** covers the fundamentals of deploying Plone on a production server. We'll cover a wide range of practical topics including proxying, security, backup, and log files. Finally, we'll discuss staging your work from a development server to a live server.

Reverse proxying

Zope has a built-in web server. You could use that web server to directly serve content to the Internet, but you probably shouldn't. Instead, you should consider the advantages of installing a **reverse proxy server** between the Zope server and the Internet.

What is a reverse proxy and why do you need one?

A **proxy server** is a server that stands between a client computer and the larger network. Proxy servers forward requests from the client computer, capture the response, and return it to the client. They are often used as a type of firewall. A reverse proxy does the opposite: it forwards requests from client computers on the larger network (usually the Internet) to a local server, captures the response, and returns the response to the outside client.

Installing a reverse proxy server between Zope and the Internet means that the proxy server will receive all of the requests from the Internet, forward them to Zope, capture the responses, and return the responses to the Internet. This may seem inefficient, but let's look at the advantages, which are as follows:

- **Easy Virtual Hosting**: Virtual hosting is the mechanism by which a single host computer may appear to be many, virtual hosts. In practice, this means that a single Zope instance may provide web content for several host names or domains. It's possible to do virtual hosting via Zope alone, but it's much easier with a reverse proxy.

- **Mixing Application Servers**: Zope and Plone may do everything that you need to do. But, maybe you want to use several best-of-breed applications in conjunction with Zope. Some of these may be served via Apache modules or even from other application servers. A versatile reverse-proxy server makes it possible to integrate all of these services seamlessly, under the same host/domain name.

- **Caching, Compression, and Encryption**: A good reverse proxy provides fast-response caching of commonly requested objects, GZIP and deflate compression, and SSL encryption. These are all possible with Zope, but it is typically better and easier with a good proxy.

- **Efficiency**: Each thread of the Zope process maintains its own object cache, and is consequently very memory-intensive. It's common to run Zope with two to four threads. Now, consider what happens when a very poorly-connected web client (for example, a slow modem user) makes four simultaneous requests. Suddenly, a few of your Zope threads may be spending several seconds serving a few hundred bytes per second. Wouldn't you rather have a light-weight proxy process handle that network traffic while Zope moves on to other requests?

There are many excellent reverse proxy servers. A few open-source packages, with their respective strengths, are as follows:

- **Apache HTTP Server**, `http://httpd.apache.org/`: A versatile web server; well-understood and documented

- **Pound**, `http://www.apsis.ch/pound/`: A dedicated reverse-proxy, particularly good at load balancing

- **Varnish**, `http://varnish.projects.linpro.no/`: A high-performance caching reverse proxy

- **Squid**, `http://www.squid-cache.org/`: A caching proxy that can also reverse proxy

- **Nginx**, `http://www.nginx.net/`: A lightweight web server/reverse proxy, often used for load balancing

But I have to use IIS!

Windows server users must have noted that **Microsoft's Internet Information Server** (IIS) isn't on the list (although several of the listed packages run on Windows servers). IIS doesn't have reverse-proxying abilities, and Microsoft's package that does—the **Microsoft Internet Security and Acceleration (ISA)** Server—is shockingly expensive. This poses a problem for those who may need to mix IIS-hosted applications with Zope/Plone. There are several packages available to remedy IIS's deficiencies, ranging from unreliable hacks to polished and well-supported solutions. Enfold Systems' **Enfold Proxy Server**, available from `http://www.enfoldsystems.com/Products/Proxy`, plays well with Zope and Plone and is well-regarded within the Plone community. (Enfold Systems' founder, Alan Runyan is a co-founder of Plone.)

Reverse proxying with Apache

Of all the ways available to provide a reverse-proxy for Zope and Plone, the most commonly employed tool is the Apache web server. It is also well understood and supported by the Plone community. We won't cover Apache installation here; there are several great books and web sites that cover it in detail, and it's pre-installed on many server platforms.

You should check to make sure that several optional Apache modules are installed and activated. On Apache 1.1.x, you'll need `mod_proxy` and `mod_rewrite` for basic reverse proxying. With Apache 2.x, you'll need `mod_proxy`, `mod_proxy_http`, and `mod_rewrite`. These may be built as static parts of the web daemon, or as loadable modules. These modules are included with most Apache packages these days, although you may need to activate them by editing your `httpd.conf` file or symbolically linking a module file into an active modules directory. A typical format for module load instructions is:

```
LoadModule rewrite_module /usr/lib/apache2/modules/mod_rewrite.so
```

Using Apache 2, you should be able to check the active modules with the `apache2 -M` command. You want to see something like this:

```
Loaded Modules:
...
proxy_module (shared)
proxy_http_module (shared)
rewrite_module (shared)
...
```

While you're checking and activating modules, you should also consider setting up `mod_ssl` (to provide the **HTTPS** protocol) and `mod_deflate` (for GZIP compression). You may also activate `mod_cache` for caching, though there are better options for HTTP caching.

Apache virtual hosting

Virtual hosting is the process of getting a single physical server to provide services for multiple host names. You may, for example, want a single computer to provide web services for `www.PloneSiteOne.com`, `www.PloneSiteTwo.org`, and so on. (Host names are not case-sensitive.) There are two major components to virtual hosting:

1. Getting traffic for a particular host name directed to a particular machine. This is solved by using your **domain name servers** to provide host (A) or canonical name (CNAME) records that associate the host name with an IP address. This is not difficult, but is way outside the scope of this book.

2. Getting the server to associate the correct host name with the correct resource. We're going to use the Apache web server to associate particular host names with particular Plone site objects in Zope.

Let's take a quick look at how the Apache virtual hosting setup looks, without reverse proxying. A typical virtual hosting fragment of an Apache configuration file looks like this:

```
NameVirtualHost 192.168.1.5
...
<VirtualHost 192.168.1.5>
    ServerName www.mynonplonesite.com
    DocumentRoot /var/htdocs
</VirtualHost>
```

The `NameVirtualHost` directive tells Apache to do name-based virtual hosting for a particular IP address (you may also use an * for all addresses). Name-based virtual hosting takes advantage of the fact that the HTTP 1.1 protocol sends a host name with each request, to allow multiple host names to be served from the same public IP address.

The `VirtualHost` stanza in the example then specifies that this section of the configuration file applies to requests for `www.mynonplonesite.com` received on `192.168.1.5`. In this case, we're just telling Apache to serve static documents from a particular part of our file system.

Rewrite rules for fun and profit

Now, let's make Apache act as a reverse proxy, getting its resources from Zope instead of the file system. Let's assume that you want your virtual host operating on the IP address `192.168.1.5`, and that your Zope instance is answering on port `8080` (the default) and has a Plone site at `/Plone`.

```
<VirtualHost 192.168.1.5>
    ServerName www.MyPloneSite.com
    RewriteEngine on
    RewriteRule ^/(.*) http://localhost:8080/Plone/$1 [P]
</VirtualHost>
```

The `RewriteRule` is going to cause Apache to transform URLs such as `http://www.MyPloneSite/SomePath` into `http://localhost:8080/Plone/SomePath`. The `^/(.*)` regular expression matches every path beginning with `/` and gobbles up the rest of the pathname and saves it. The `$1` puts the saved information into the rewritten URL.

The final magic in this rule is the `[P]` option for the rewrite rule, which tells Apache to use its proxying abilities to fetch the requested item and return it.

If you try using this recipe to serve a Plone site, though, you'll get an unpleasant surprise. You'll get the requested pages, but with no stylesheets or images. And, all the links on the page will be useless! That's because all of the resource URLs in the page will point to items such as `http://localhost:8080/Plone/stylesheet.css`. When a remote browser asks for that, it'll get nothing.

Introducing a friendly monster

This is where the Zope **Virtual Host Monster (VHM)** comes in. It can automatically translate request and response URLs to meet the requirements of virtual hosting.

 The Virtual Host Monster is actually an object in the Zope database. In fact, your Zope database always comes preconfigured with a Virtual Host Monster in the root of the object tree. You only need one to meet all your virtual hosting needs, so, you may generally rely on it without notice or worry.

You use the Virtual Host Monster by crafting special URLs with information meant for consumption by the monster. This crafting is usually done via an Apache `RewriteRule`.

The pattern for VHM's special URLs is as follows:

```
http://zope_host:zope_port/VirtualHostBase/http/vhost_name:
      vhost_port/zodb_path/VirtualHostRoot/remaining_path
```

In this formula:

- `zope_host` is the hostname or IP address of the Zope server (usually `localhost`)
- `zope_port` is the Zope port number (usually `8080`)
- `vhost_name` is the virtual host name
- `vhost_port` is the port number for your virtual host (usually `80`)
- `zodb_path` is the path of your Plone site inside the ZODB
- `remaining_path` is the rest of the URL
- `VirtualHostBase` is a marker text used to tell VHM that the virtual host base address and path follow this marker
- `VirtualHostRoot` indicates that what follows is the part of the URL after the virtual host's document root

This is a complex, convoluted, and error-prone formula, although a few examples will help. In all of these examples, our Zope instance is listening on local port `8080` and our server is listening on port `80` at IP address `192.168.1.5`.

Let's say we have a Zope instance with a Plone site at `/Plone` in the ZODB, and that we wish to serve it as `www.myplonesite.com`. We'll want an Apache virtual hosting configuration file section that looks like this:

```
<VirtualHost 192.168.1.5>
    ServerName www.myplonesite.com
    RewriteEngine on
    RewriteRule ^/(.*) http://localhost:8080/VirtualHostBase/
      http/www.myplonesite.com:80/Plone/VirtualHostRoot/$1 [P]
</VirtualHost>
```

Now, let's say that the same Zope instance has another Plone site at `/Plone2` in its ZODB, and that we wish to serve it from `www.anotherplonesite.org`:

```
<VirtualHost 192.168.1.5>
    ServerName www.anotherplonesite.org
    RewriteEngine on
    RewriteRule ^/(.*) http://localhost:8080/VirtualHostBase/
      http/www.anotherplonesite.org:80/Plone2/VirtualHostRoot/$1 [P]
</VirtualHost>
```

The key things to look for here are where the virtual host name, `www.anotherplonesite.org`, and the ZODB site of the Plone site, `/Plone2`, fit in. The rest is pretty much boilerplate.

Selective rewriting

Ready for a realistic example? See if you can figure out what the following code is doing:

```
<VirtualHost 192.168.1.5>
    ServerName aplonesite.com
    RedirectPermanent / http://www.aplonesite.com/
</VirtualHost>
<VirtualHost 192.168.1.5>
    ServerName www.aplonesite.com
    DocumentRoot /var/htdocs/

    RewriteEngine on
    RewriteRule ^/mailman - [L]
    RewriteRule ^/pipermail - [L]
    RewriteRule ^/apache - [L]
    RewriteRule /(.*) http://localhost:8080/VirtualHostBase/http/
www.aplonesite.com:80/Plone/VirtualHostRoot/$1 [P]
</VirtualHost>
```

The first `VirtualHost` stanza sets up an automatic permanent redirect that will send requests for the host `aplonesite.com` to the host `www.aplonesite.com`. You may wish to reverse the formula (have the `www.` form redirect to the bare form). Apache's `RedirectPermanent` automatically takes care of the part of the URL after the hostname.

The second `VirtualHost` section has a `DocumentRoot` directive. Why? Because we're going to serve content both from Zope and the file system.

The specification of the first three rewrite rules will prevent reverse-proxying of requests with pathnames beginning with `/mailman`, `/pipermail`, or `/apache`. When "-" is specified for the substitution string, the rewrite engine will make no substitution. The final `[L]` flag specifies that this is a "last rule"—no further rewriting will take place.

As requests beginning with these three paths aren't rewritten, they're going to be served as normal by Apache, by the static files and CGI for the popular **Mailman** list server and the Apache icon set.

SSL hosting

Now, let's set up an SSL-encrypted (**HTTPS**) web site. Most of the virtual host directives will be based on the Apache examples, with your certificate files specified. The rewrite rule changes are simple: just substitute port 443 (the standard `https` port) for 80 and `https` for `http` in the virtual host portion of the URL.

```
Listen 443
<VirtualHost 192.168.1.6:443>
    ServerName www.mysslplonesite.com
    SSLEngine on
    [Lots of Apache SSL boilerplate setting certificates, etc.]
    RewriteEngine On
    RewriteRule ^/(.*)
    http://localhost:8080/VirtualHostBase/https/www.mysslplonesite.
        com:443/Plone/VirtualHostRoot/$1 [P]
</VirtualHost>
```

> You won't use a `NameVirtualHost` directive for HTTPS virtual hosts because name-based virtual hosting is not possible under the HTTPS protocol. HTTPS virtual hosts have to be IP address-based, and each will require its own IP address.

Putting Plone inside a larger site

In all the above examples, the Plone site was being served at the root path of a host's web site. What if you want to put a Plone site at a particular path, while the rest of the web site is served by other mechanisms? This is called **inside-out hosting** in the Virtual Host Monster documentation.

Let's say, for example, that we have an existing web site, served by Apache from the file system, operating at www.ahybridsite.com and that we wish to incorporate a Plone CMS at www.ahybridsite.com/ourcms. Take a very close look at the following rewrite rule, then I'll explain it:

```
<VirtualHost 192.168.1.5>
    ServerName www.ahybridsitesite.com
    DocumentRoot /var/htdocs/

    RewriteEngine on
    RewriteRule /ourcms/(.*) http://localhost:8080/VirtualHostBase/
        http/www.ahybridsite.com:80/Plone/VirtualHostRoot/
        _vh_ourcms/$1 [P]
</VirtualHost>
```

_vh_ is a magic marker for Zope's Virtual Host Monster. It signals that the current path element (in this case, /_vh_ourcms) should be ignored when determining the ZODB location to serve. But, it will be added back in (except for the _vh_) to the generated URLs in the page.

Securing a production server

The Python/Zope/Plone software stack has an excellent security record, but you should not rely on that fact alone for server security. Good system administration practices require that you protect software services from unauthorized connections and run long-lived processes with the minimum level of permissions required for their function.

Securing the ports

If you've set up a reverse proxy between your Zope instance and the larger network, you should make sure that outside users can't step around it by directly connecting to Zope. The best way to do this is to use a **firewall** to block remote access to the ports used by Zope and ZEO.

In a standalone Zope install, this usually means blocking remote access to port 8080. For a ZEO installation, you must block the ZEO server (often port 8100) and all ZEO client ports (often 8080 and 8081). Check your Zope or buildout configuration files to determine the exact port numbers.

The firewall itself may be a software firewall on the server, or a firewall host or switch that stands between the server and the larger network.

 Do not make the mistake of thinking that a departmental or organizational firewall will be sufficient, or that you don't need a firewall because you're providing Intranet services. Experienced security professionals will tell you (again and again, if you'll listen) that as many threats originate from inside the organizational firewall as from outside.

If your reverse proxy only allows access to virtual hosts that are associated with Plone sites, then a good firewall solution will also effectively block remote access to the ZODB root. So then how will you administer Zope? The answer is that you should learn to use **secure port-forwarding** in order to remotely access protected ports on firewalled machines. This is a basic computer security skill that should be mastered by all web professionals.

On Linux, OS X, Solaris, BSD, and other Unix work-alikes, this is generally done via **SSH (Secure Shell Program)** tunnels. Windows servers have their own remote access solutions, but you may also run an SSH server on a Windows server. SSH clients are available for all significant operating systems.

If this isn't practical, a good alternative is to set up an HTTPS virtual host that connects to the root-level Zope.

Locking down the service

Network services are frequent avenues of attack on servers. Long-lived server software is usually written with great attention to security, but it's never wise to rely on the service's own security. Instead, you should use your operating system's security mechanisms to limit the damage that may be done if the service is subverted. This is one form of **defense-in-depth**, a key security concept.

In practical terms, this means that you want Zope to run under a user account that has only the minimum system privileges required to do its job. Ideally, this is an account specifically created to run Zope, and that is not used for any other purposes. Using a user account named **zope** or **plone** is common.

If you're using the Unified Installer on a Unix-work-alike platform, much of this is taken care of for you provided that you use the **root** install method. This will cause the creation of a **plone** user ID with minimal permissions. It also sets up the Zope and ZEO instances so that they're set to use **plone** as an effective user, if you start them as the super user.

If you're installing on another platform, or from source, or via a custom buildout, you'll need to take care of much of this yourself. The key elements are:

- Create a user account that's used only for this purpose
- Give that user account the minimum permissions needed to run Zope and Plone
- Start the Zope service so that it runs under the special account

So, what are the **minimum permissions** required to run a Zope instance or ZEO cluster? At a minimum, the Zope service will need write permission for the following directories:

- All var directories and their subdirectories. This includes the var directories used by both the ZEO and Zope client instances. In a simple source install, it will just be the instance var directory. In a buildout-style install, it will be the var and parts/instance/var directories. (Any directory named var in the install is a likely candidate.)

- Instance directories containing old-style **Zope products:** In a simple source install, it is the instance `Products` directory. In a buildout-style install, it will be the `products`, `parts/productdistros`, and `parts/plone` directories.

The latter requirement — that the Zope/Plone user be able to write into product directories — is unfortunate, and arises from the need for Zope to be able to write **Python byte-code** (`.pyc` and `.pyo`) and i18n compiled message (`.mo`) files into these directories. (Zope, by the way, compiles its own files on installation; it's just the add-on products that need the extra step.) There is, fortunately, a way to avoid this requirement:

1. Give the Zope/Plone user account the rights to write into product directories.

2. Start Zope once and then stop it again. This will write out all of the byte-code and translation files.

3. Change permissions so that the Zope/Plone user account can no longer write into the product directories.

Unfortunately, you'll need to repeat this procedure whenever you add a new product or update an old one.

 The Plone 3.1 version of the Unified Installer takes care of all of this for you, as long as you use buildout to configure your changes, by setting the required permissions and pre-compiling Python scripts.

Running Zope as a special user

The procedure for running Zope under a particular user ID varies with the platform it is running on.

Linux, OS X, BSD

On Unix work-alikes, you'll use the super-user account (**root**) to start Zope, and then use one of the following two approaches to have it run under a limited, effective user account:

- Use the `su` command to start the Zope process via another user ID. A typical startup command might be:

```
sudo su plone -c "/opt/Plone-3.0/zinstance/bin/zopectl start"
-s /bin/sh
```

`sudo` indicates that the command executes with super-user authority while the `su plone -c` command causes command to be executed under the `plone` user account. Finally, the `-s /bin/sh` specifies that `/bin/sh` be used for a shell, as the plone user account ideally should have no shell of its own. Check the man pages for `su`, if you're not experienced with this sort of command.

- Specify an effective user via the Zope configuration files. This will cause the startup routine to change the effective user on startup. In a client `zope.conf` file, this is specified by adding the directive:

```
effective-user plone
```

In the `zeo.conf` ZEO server configuration file, add:

```
user plone
```

to the `<runner>...</runner>` section. Then, use `sudo` to start Zope (or `su` to root, and then start Zope).

Both of these examples assume that you're using the `plone` user account.

Windows servers

The setting of ownership and permissions is typically done interactively for a Windows server.

- Open your **Computer Management** application (usually found on the **Administrative Tools** menu).

- From menu path **System Tools | Local Users and Groups | Users**, create a new user. Set your new user so that the user can't change the password, and the password never expires. After creation, remove the new user from **Users** so that this won't be a login account.

- Set minimal directory permissions for your new user, as described in the *Locking Down the Service* section.

- With your **Computer Management** application, open **Services and Applications | Services** and edit the properties of **Zope instance at ....** Use the **Log On** tab to specify that the service should log on as your new user rather than the system account, which has way too many privileges for good security.

- Start or restart the service.

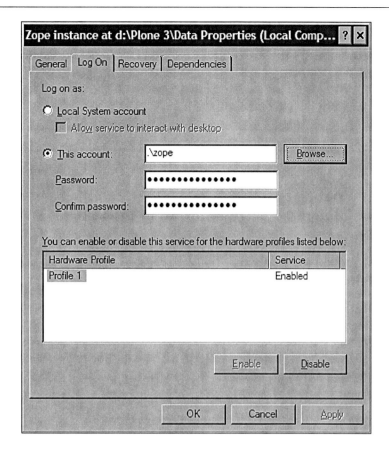

Turning off debug modes

Every few days, somebody stops by the #plone IRC channel complaining about poor performance. Sometimes, they're trying to run Zope and Plone on inadequate hardware; sometimes, they need help tuning caching or implementing load balancing. But, far more often, they're unwittingly running in one of the Zope or Plone debug modes. The various debug modes are very useful for product and theme development, but they can have an appalling impact on performance. Make sure that they're turned off on your production server. Here's how to do this.

Checking Zope debug mode

Zope's debug mode causes the Zope server to reload various file system components (mostly skin related) for every request. It also increases diagnostics. Check if Zope is in debug mode by visiting Plone's **Site Setup**. Look at the bottom of the page for a message that indicates the current status.

Plone Version Overview

- Plone 3.0.4

- CMF-2.1.0

- Zope (Zope 2.10.5-final, python 2.4.4, linux2)

- Python 2.4.4 (#1, Oct 28 2007, 15:07:56) [GCC 4.1.2 (Ubuntu 4.1.2-0ubuntu4)]

- PIL 1.1.6

Note: You are running in "debug mode". This mode is intended for sites that are under development. This allows many configuration changes to be immediately visible, but will make your site run more slowly. To turn off debug mode, edit your zope.conf file to say 'debug-mode off' — then restart the server process.

If you're in debug mode, you may change this by editing configuration files. Edit `buildout.cfg` and comment out the `debug-mode = on` line if you've used buildout (then re-run `bin/buildout`), or edit `etc/zope.conf` and set `debug-mode` to `off` if you're using any other kind of install.

Resource registry debug modes

Plone maintains **resource registries** for its CSS, JavaScript, and KSS (CSS/JavaScript integration) components. Resource registries allow the development of very finely grained, well-formatted, and well-commented CSS, JSS, and KSS components, without a loss in performance. They do this by grouping and compressing these components for delivery to the browser, and by sending appropriate caching headers. That is, unless you've turned on a resource registry's debug mode, in which case, the components are sent individually, uncompressed, and with no cache headers.

Consider, for example, the CSS registry. With the debug mode turned off, this typically delivers five or fewer merged and compressed stylesheet files, all of which are cached by the browser. With debug on, it may deliver 24 uncompressed stylesheet files with every page view. This may have a huge impact on page load times.

Check your registry debug modes by using the ZMI to visit the `portal_css`, `portal_javascripts`, and `portal_kss` objects in your site's root. You may toggle debug mode on or off for these registries via the web interface.

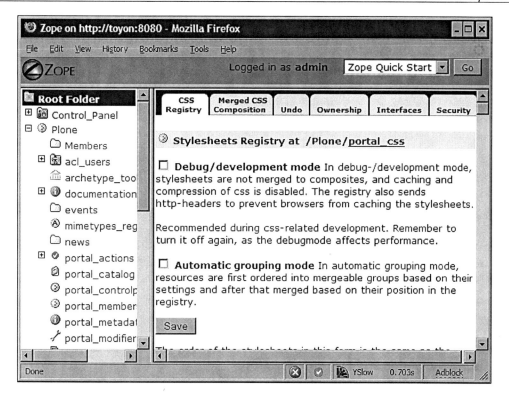

Starting Zope automatically

If you're running a production server, you've got to make sure that Zope will start automatically when your server starts or restarts, and that it stops gracefully when the server stops or restarts. The procedure for this varies from platform to platform.

Linux

If you've used a platform package-based installer (rpm or apt-get), this may have been taken care of for you already. However, the Unified Installer, source installs, and buildout-based installs don't set up Zope for automatic start/stops. Unfortunately, the mechanism for setting up automatic starts varies quite a bit between various Linux, BSD, and other Unix distributions such as Solaris. A common element is that most require the creation of a special start/stop/restart script in a special directory. The format of that script file is specific to platforms/distributions. It may then be necessary to symbolically link that script into various run-level resource control script directories. Often, there are mechanisms for automating the symbolic link creation.

If you're using the Unified Installer, look for an `init_scripts` subdirectory in the installer distribution. That directory contains sample initialization scripts and instructions for FreeBSD, OS X, Red Hat / Fedora Core, Ubuntu, and a "generic" set that you'll can adapt to any other platform.

If you didn't use the Unified Installer, you may wish to download it just to get the initialization scripts and their associated `README.txt` files. You can also check them out of `svn` separately, by using the following command:

```
svn co http://svn.plone.org/svn/plone/Installers/UnifiedInstaller/
    trunk/init_scripts/ init_scripts
```

Windows

If you've used the Windows installer, you're in luck. It installs Zope as a service that automatically starts and stops with the server. You may check this via the **Services** applet.

OS X

If you're using the OS X binary installer, make sure that you take advantage of its customization option to set up a startup item.

Backing up Plone and packing down the database

It's critical to have a good strategy for backing up your Plone database and compacting the object database.

What to back up

The easy answer to the question "What should I back up?" is "everything." Backing up the Zope database file alone is not enough. It can be very difficult to reproduce a working configuration, complete with custom settings, Python libraries, and add-on products, when pressed for time. So, make sure that you always have a good, up-to-date backup of your entire Zope/Plone instance.

That said, the Python and configuration file components of a production installation typically change very infrequently, while the object database may be changing every few seconds.

Backing up the Zope database

The **Zope Object DataBase, ZODB**, is typically stored in a single file, usually named `Data.fs`. You'll find this file in your instance's `var` subdirectory on a simple install. On a Windows installer installation, look in `Data/var`; on a typical buildout install, you'll find this file in `var/filestorage`. It is possible to have a Zope installation use multiple ZODBs at multiple mount points, and these may be stored in separate directories, or given names other than `Data.fs` (although the use of the `.fs` filename extension is a common convention).

It's this `Data.fs` file (and its equivalents, if you're using multiple mount points) that needs special attention for backups. It is kept open while Zope is running, and thus some standard backup systems will never back it up.

So, how do you back it up? Various strategies are available, many described in the documentation section of the Plone.org website. But the easiest and best to use is **Repozo**, a utility included with Zope, to back up the live ZODB, and then use your standard archiving scheme to back up the Repozo backup files.

If you don't need to back up while live, just stop Zope, copy the `Data.fs` file, and then start Zope again.

 In your data directory, you'll find the `.lock`, `.index`, and `.tmp` files. You may largely ignore these when designing your backup strategy, as Zope can recreate them from the main `.fs` file. An old file may also be present if you've packed the database; it's a pre-packing copy of the data.

Repozo

Repozo is a Python script, `repozo.py`, included with Zope. You'll find a copy in the Zope installation's `utilities/ZODBTools` directory. A typical buildout install creates a handy script at `bin/repozo`. If you're using the buildout script, you may run it directly; if you're using Zope 2 `utilities/ZODBTools/repozo.py`, make sure that you invoke it with the same Python interpreter that you use to run Zope.

Repozo, at its simplest, just makes or restores a copy of the ZODB file storage. It works with Zope's transaction-integrity system so that the copy represents a stable snapshot, even though the database may be changing. In more advanced usage, Repozo may be used to maintain incremental backups, writing out only what's new since the last run.

Run the Repozo script with no command-line arguments to get a full list of options. The key options for backing up are:

- --backup, to specify a backup.

- --repository=backup_directory, to specify the destination directory for the backup. You must use a different destination directory for each data storage that you back up. The directory must exist before you run Repozo.

- --file=Data.fs, to specify the filename of the .fs file storage to be backed up.

- --full, to specify a full, rather than incremental, backup.

- --gzip, to specify GZIP compression of the backup.

A typical command for running a backup may appear as follows:

```
$ cd /opt/p3buildout/var/filestorage
$ /opt/p3buildout/bin/repozo --backup --repository=backup --file=Data.
fs --full -gzip
```

This assumes that a repository directory named backup already exists under var/filestorage. It will generate a full, compressed backup. If you want to do an incremental backup, just omit the --full argument, and Repozo will write out only the changes made since its last operation. If you've packed your database (more on packing in the next section) since you last ran Repozo, it will automatically do a full backup.

 Repozo's incremental backup facility makes it feasible to back up a live database very frequently. In some situations where up-to-date backups are critical, Repozo may be run even on an hourly basis. It's common to use a utility such as rsync to mirror a repozo repository to a backup server, so that only new data is transferred.

Even when you do a full Repozo backup, the program will not delete old backup files from your repository directory. So, it's a good idea to clean it out occasionally, typically before running with the --full flag.

Restoring backups

Repozo can back up a live ZODB. In whichever way you back up your database, you will need to shut down Zope (and ZEO if you're clustering) before restoring a backup.

Moreover, you'll typically wish to delete the .lock, .index, and .tmp files from the ZODB storage directory. Zope will recreate these as necessary.

The key Repozo options for restoring are:

- `--recover`, to specify a recover operation.
- `--repository=backup_directory`, to specify a repozo repository directory that already contains backups.
- `--output=Data.fs`, to specify the target file for recovery. If it exists, this file will be overwritten.

There is also an advanced option that allows recovery by date/time.

A typical command for recovering a Repozo backup may look like this:

```
$ cd /opt/p3buildout/var/filestorage
$ /opt/p3buildout/bin/repozo --recover --repository=backup --
output=Data.fs
```

Packing the ZODB

When Zope is adding or changing objects, it always appends the content to the ZODB file storage. So, unlike some record-oriented databases, the ZODB grows with every edit, even if you aren't adding new objects. The good news is that this design makes it possible for Zope to undo recent transactions. The bad news is that your `Data.fs` file will grow constantly until you pack it. The packing operation allows you to remove old object revisions from the database. Fortunately, you don't have to stop Zope to pack your data. Packing is an I/O-intensive operation for a large database, though, and will raise your system load while it is running. You may wish to schedule packing for times when you expect a low system load.

You must periodically pack your Zope database. Make this a regular part of your maintenance. The ideal packing frequency for a given Zope database is very site specific, and will depend on the frequency of update and the size of your data objects. This operation is typically carried out on a weekly or monthly basis.

Packing interactively

You may pack your database via the web either from the Plone **Site Setup | Maintenance** control panel applet or via the ZMI. Packing requires a Manager's role at the ZODB root. Both the control panel applet and the **ZMI Database Management** option allow you to set the number of days of undo history that you wish to retain after packing.

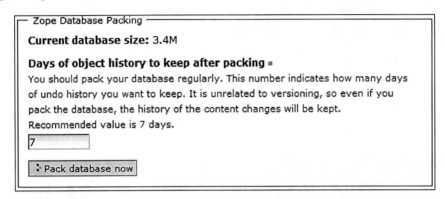

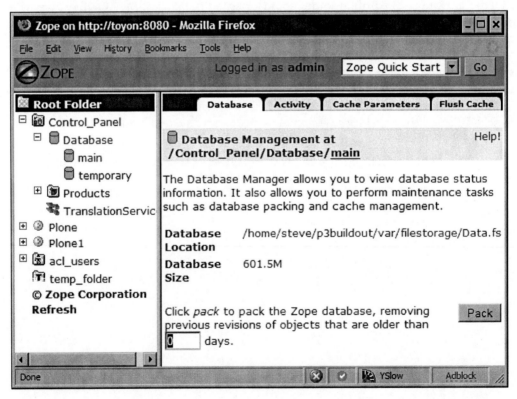

Automated packing

Nobody wants to wake up at two in the morning to pack their ZODBs. Fortunately, it is easy to automate the packing process. Typically, Plone system administrators use a `cron` (Linux, BSD, and so on) or `at` (Windows command line) script to run the packing operations automatically and unattended.

If you're using a ZEO cluster with a buildout install, you may use the **zeopack** utility to connect to the ZEO server and ask for a packing. Run `bin/zeopack -h` for an option list, but operation is usually as simple as:

```
sudo bin/zeopack -p 8100 -d 7
```

This connects to the ZEO server listening on `localhost` port `8100` and packs, removing all but the last seven days of revision information.

It's also easy to script the web commands for a pack, and this will work with or without ZEO. Using the popular `wget` utility, a command line for a pack would read as follows:

```
wget --http-user=admin --http-password=admin_password \
  http://localhost:8080/Control_Panel/Database/main/manage_pack \
  --post-data="days%3Afloat=3&submit=Pack"
```

Substitute your own administrative password, and change the `3` in `days%3Afloat=3` to the number of days of history that you need to retain.

Log rotation

Like the ZODB, the Zope server's log files will grow indefinitely if you don't do something about it. On a development server, you'll probably just delete them occasionally. On a production server, you'll typically want to rotate them, saving a few past logs, and possibly compressing the archived copies.

On source installs, you'll typically find your log files in a `log` subdirectory of your instance. Buildout installs typically keep them in `var/log`. In any case, they'll have `.log` filename extensions.

Log file rotation poses one problem: the files are typically kept open while the Zope server runs. On any platform, you should be able to stop Zope, rename the log files, and restart Zope. On Linux and other Unix work-alikes you have a slightly better option. You may send a USR2 signal to the Zope process, and it will close and reopen log files. This is a fairly common behavior for services that maintain their own logs.

`newsyslog` and `logrotate` are two popular log rotation mechanisms on Linux, FreeBSD, and similar platforms.

A configuration stanza for `newsyslog.conf` is as follows:

```
# logfilename            [owner:group]     mode count size when  flags
    [/pid_file] [sig_num]
...
# Zope logs; use SIGUSR2 to close and re-open all Zope log files
/var/db/primary_zope/log/Z2.log      zope:zope 644 10    *    $W0D0
    Z  /var/db/primary_zope/var/Z2.pid   31
/var/db/primary_zope/log/event.log  zope:zope 644 10    *    $W0D0
    Z  /var/db/primary_zope/var/Z2.pid   31
```

In this example, the log files are in the `/var/db/primary_zope/log` directory and the daemon is running with the effective user and group of `zope`. The `10` retains ten generations of history; the rotation is weekly and compressed (`Z`). The `31` is the numeric ID for `SIGUSR2`. Use `man newsyslog.conf` to check the details.

A fragment of the `logrotate.conf` file is as follows:

```
# Zope instance 1, rotate weekly, save 5
/var/zope/zope_1/log/Z2.log /var/zope/zope_1/log/event.log {
        rotate 5
        weekly
        sharedscripts
        postrotate
                kill -USR2 `cat /var/zope/zope_1/var/Z2.pid`
        endscript
}
```

Here, the logs are in the `/var/zope/zope_1/log` directory, five generations are maintained, and the backup is weekly. Use `man logrotate.conf` to check the details.

Staging from development to a live server

It's a key skill for Plone integrators to know how to stage work from development machines to live servers. Often, development machines aren't even on the same platform as the destination live servers.

The typical procedure for transferring from a development server to a production server is:

1. Install matching versions of Zope/Plone on the production server.
2. Make sure that the production server's add-on and custom products and supplementary code meet the requirements of your site.
3. Transfer the site object itself.

If you're an accomplished Plone developer, it's possible that you may be doing all of your site customization in code. If that's the case, you may be able to omit the last step, and instead simply create your site fresh on the production server using your custom products and profiles. However, it's common for integrators to do some (possibly all) of their customization work through the web. These changes will be saved in the site itself, in the ZODB. In that case, you'll need to transfer the site itself by moving the site object. (Even if you develop entirely in code, you may sometimes need to test your changes against the live content in the site.)

Synchronizing add-on products and code

Your site probably makes use of some add-on products. These may be products that you have downloaded from www.plone.org/products, or they may be custom code. They may take the form of Python libraries, in eggs or otherwise, or traditional Product directory products. There may be supplementary .zcml slug files that tell Zope about Python libraries.

No matter what the form, you'll need to match them up between the development and production sites. It's possible that you may be developing multiple sites on your development machine, and that not all of them are to be used with the production site. You only need to transfer what's to be used on the production site.

If you're using buildout on both development and production servers, and are using only the add-ons distributed via the **Python Package Index** (PyPI), then you may only need to copy your buildout.cfg file (or the pertinent sections of this) and then run bin/buildout on the production server. If there is custom code, you'll need to copy it to the products or the src directories of the production buildout.

If you're not using a buildout-based install, it's common to simply copy the product and the lib/python directories from your development instance to your production instance. You may also need to copy the .zcml slug files.

Moving object data

There are two approaches to moving a site object (and all of its contents) from a development server to a production server:

- Copy the entire ZODB file store, usually a Data.fs file. Make sure that you stop the Zope server on the destination machine before copying. (Note that Zope can manage an object database composed of different file stores mounted on different paths. We aren't covering this technique here, but it's an excellent way to copy a single site's data from a Zope that is hosting multiple Plone sites.)

- **Export** the site object from the source database, and **Import** it into the destination. The Zope/Plone versions, and all of the product versions, must match *exactly* for this to be reliable. There are generally three steps:

    1. Via the ZMI, select the Plone site, press the **Export/Import** button and export it to a local drive. *Do not use the* **XML** *option.*

    2. Copy the resulting `.zexp` file to the `import` directory on the destination instance.

    3. Use the ZMI on the destination machine to import the `.zexp`.

    If you're working with a substantial site, steps one and two can be resource-intensive. If you're low on memory, or the server load is high, plan this for a light-use time.

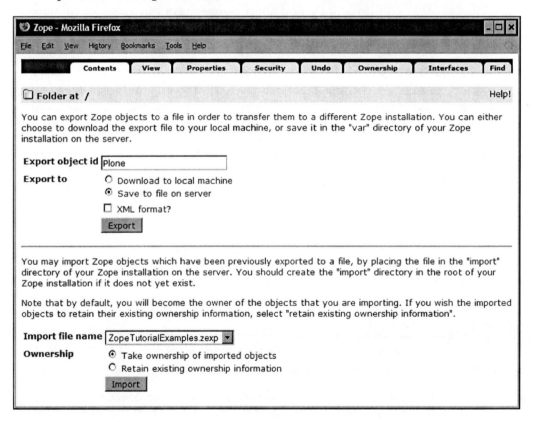

Summary

In this chapter, we have learned the fundamental skills of setting up and administering a live Plone server:

- Basic reverse proxying concepts and setup
- Security fundamentals
- Making Zope start and stop with the server
- How to back up your database
- Log rotation
- Staging from a development server to a live server

Using what you have learned in this chapter, you should be ready to deploy Plone on a production server. The next chapter will help you make sure it will be both fast and scalable.

20
Make it Go Faster

Plone is a dynamic content server, which means that it puts together the pieces of a page the moment that a request for the page comes in. One way to make a dynamic content server like Plone go faster is to intelligently cache the processed content, to reduce some of the delay and overhead of repeatedly regenerating it.

In this chapter, **Ricardo Newbery** goes deeper into some of the concepts covered in Chapter 19, showing how to cache Plone content with the help of a community-maintained Plone add-on product bundle called **CacheFu**.

CacheFu is a collection of products that aggregate and simplify various caching settings, speeding up Plone sites by using a combination of memory, proxy, and browser caching. Just installing CacheFu alone will help you speed up your site, but you will see the greatest performance benefit by using it in conjunction with a caching proxy.

We will walk through the installation and enabling of the CacheFu products, and then walk through the installation and configuration of a caching proxy. Finally, we'll discuss the various CacheFu configuration settings that you can adjust to get the best performance from your site.

Getting and installing CacheFu

Starting with version 1.2, the CacheFu products are distributed as Python eggs (see Chapter 14 for a discussion of product versus egg installations). The central product is `Products.CacheSetup` which, when installed via buildout, takes care of pulling in the rest of the products from the bundle. Check `http://plone.org/products/cachefu` to find the latest distribution. For this walkthrough, we'll be using the latest version, which, as of the time of writing, is Products.CacheSetup 1.2.

There are three different ways to install an add-on product packaged as an egg such as `Products.CacheSetup`:

- Installing into the local Zope instance with buildout
- Installing into the local Zope instance as an old-style Zope 2 product
- Installing into the Python environment using `easy_install`

The first two installation methods are the most often recommended, so we'll describe these two in more detail

Installing locally with buildout

If you're using `buildout` to manage your Zope instance, then installation is easy. Just add `Products.CacheSetup` to the list of eggs to install in `buildout.cfg`:

```
[buildout]
...
eggs =
    ...
    Products.CacheSetup
```

Then re-run the `buildout`. This will fetch the egg from the Python Package Index and install it and all of its dependencies into the buildout.

Installing locally as an old-style Zope 2 product

Packages using the special top-level **Products** namespace, such as `Products.CacheSetup`, can also be installed in Zope 2 as old-style Zope 2 products. This is another local install option if you have an older non-buildout installation.

First, you need to download the `Products.CacheSetup` package from `http://pypi.python.org/pypi/Products.CacheSetup`.

Then, move or symlink the `CacheSetup` folder that is nested within this package (at `Products.CacheSetup/Products/CacheSetup`) into the `Products` directory of the Zope instance. In this case, dependencies are not automatically installed, so you will have to do the same for each of the following products:

- `http://pypi.python.org/pypi/Products.CMFSquidTool`
- `http://pypi.python.org/pypi/Products.PageCacheManager`
- `http://pypi.python.org/pypi/Products.PolicyHTTPCacheManager`

Enabling CacheFu

To install CacheFu in your Plone instance, you need to perform one more installation step. Log into your Plone site, navigate to **Site Setup** and choose the **Add-on Products** control panel. You should see two new products in the list of **Products available for install**: CMFSquid and **CacheSetup**. Selected the checkbox next to **CacheSetup**, and then click on the **Install** button.

Upon installation, **CacheSetup** will also automatically install (and then hide) **CMFSquid**. You should now see a new link in the **Site Setup** navigation column labeled **Cache Configuration Tool**. This is the CacheFu control panel.

By default, CacheFu is disabled, so our next step is to turn it on. Go to the control panel of CacheFu, select the checkbox next to **Enable CacheFu**, and then click on the **Save** button (at the very bottom of the page).

CacheFu is now running, and you should immediately see a significant improvement in speed (up to four or ten times as fast, depending on your setup).

For now, let's ignore the rest of the options in this control panel and move on to the installation and configuration of a caching proxy server.

Picking a proxy

To gain the greatest benefit from CacheFu, you need to install a caching proxy. The most common choices in the Plone community are **Squid** and **Varnish**. For developers using a Microsoft Windows server, another popular choice is **Enfold Proxy**, a commercial solution by Enfold Systems. The **Apache** web server can also be configured as a caching proxy.

- **Squid**: `http://squid-cache.org`
- **Varnish**: `http://varnish-cache.org`
- **Apache**: `http://httpd.apache.org`
- **Enfold Proxy**: `http://enfoldsystems.com/Products/Proxy`

Squid, Varnish, and Enfold Proxy are **purgeable**, while Apache is **non-purgeable**. A purgeable cache lets CacheFu remove specific items from the cache as content changes, allowing you to cache some types of non-static items as if they were static views. It's thus best to use a purgeable proxy rather than Apache, unless your site changes very rarely.

The simplest production Zope setup is a single Zope instance behind an Apache server (without caching). Once you include a proxy, many other permutations are possible. Common variations include:

- Zope-only (no reverse proxy)
- Zope-behind-Apache
- Zope-behind-Squid/Varnish
- Zope-behind-Squid/Varnish-behind-Apache
- Zope-behind-Apache-behind-Squid/Varnish

So why would anyone use Apache in combination with a proxy?

The main benefit of using Apache is to support services in addition to Zope from the same IP/domain. Although Squid and Varnish can be configured to support multiple services, complex configuration is much easier with Apache, and some services are engineered specifically to be served by Apache.

Putting Apache *behind* your caching proxy means that you can cache the output more easily from those multiple services that your Apache server is hosting.

Putting Apache *in front of* your caching proxy means you can more easily exclude some services from being cached by your proxy.

Putting Apache (or Squid) *in front* also means that you can support SSL connections. Varnish doesn't support SSL directly, so if this is a requirement, you need to front it with Apache or use Squid instead.

Apache, Squid, and Varnish are all capable of being configured to load-balance requests across multiple Zope clients in the ZEO configuration.

If the only service you need to host is Plone, then the **Zope-behind-Squid/Varnish** setup may be all that you need. In this chapter, we will walk you through how to configure both **Zope-behind-Squid** and **Zope-behind-Varnish**. You can choose which is most appropriate for your circumstances, and you'll be able to apply what you learn to a wide range of other configurations.

Squid or Varnish?

Which caching proxy should you choose? It doesn't really matter much. Both Squid and Varnish can be installed on most Linux and Unix-type operating systems (including OS X) while Squid can also be installed on Windows.

Squid has a longer history, a larger installed base, and as a result, a larger user community. Varnish is the new kid on the block, and some claim that its more modern design results in a much faster proxy.

Some people in the Plone community feel that Squid is too heavy and complicated (although the CacheFu-generated Squid configuration is actually fairly trim and simple). Some feel that Varnish is not yet ready for production deployments (although it's currently in use by a few notable high-traffic sites, including Plone.org).

The truth is that for most use cases, either Squid or Varnish will work just fine, and both have their own idiosyncrasies. This author chooses not to take sides in this debate.

Installing a caching proxy with buildout

If you're using a buildout-based installation of Plone, buildout recipes are available for installing and configuring either Squid or Varnish. If you're not using buildout, feel free to skip to the traditional installation instructions in the next section.

In this example, we'll build a simple **Zope-Squid/Varnish** setup. In this setup, Squid or Varnish will listen for requests on port 80 and proxy all requests for the `example.com` hostname to the backend at port 8080, while rewriting the incoming URLs into VirtualHostMonster-style URLs to direct the requests to the `/Plone` folder on the Zope instance (see the section *Introducing a friendly monster* in Chapter 19).

Squid buildout recipe

The Squid recipe can be found at `http://pypi.python.org/pypi/plone.recipe.squid`

As of the time of writing, the latest release was Squid-2.7.STABLE2; earlier versions are not recommended. CacheFu has not been tested with the Squid 3.0 series, so unless you want to be the guinea pig, stick with the pre-3.0 versions.

For a **Zope-Squid** setup, let's add the following to `buildout.cfg`:

```
[squid-build]
recipe = zc.recipe.cmmi
url = http://www.squid-cache.org/Versions/v2/2.7/squid-2.7.STABLE2.
tar.gz

[squid-instance]
#user = nobody
recipe = plone.recipe.squid
```

```
daemon = ${squid-build:location}/sbin/squid
cache-size = 1000
bind = 80
backends =
    example.com:127.0.0.1:8080
zope2_vhm_map =
    example.com:/Plone
```

A note about user: To bind to a port lower than 1024, Squid must start up as root and then drop down to a less-privileged effective user, by default nobody. This user must have enough privileges to read and write to the ./var directory of the buildout. To designate a different effective user, uncomment the user directive above and substitute an appropriate user name.

Now, re-run the buildout. This will download and build Squid (in ./parts/squid-build), create a squid configuration for your instance (in ./parts/squid-instance), and then add some squid startup scripts (in ./bin).

To start up a Squid instance with this configuration, use the following command:

% sudo ./bin/squid-instance

(Note that sudo is only necessary if you are binding to a port lower than 1024)

To stop the Squid instance, use the following command:

% sudo ./bin/squid-instance -k shutdown

Again, this is a simple **Zope-Squid** proxy setup with Squid in front, where Squid is rewriting the URLs via a Python helper script.

For other setups, such as **Zope-Squid-Apache** or **Zope-Apache-Squid** (where, in both the cases, Apache may be doing the VirtualHostMonster-style URL rewrites), consult the README.txt in the plone.recipe.squid download or the instructions at http://pypi.python.org/pypi/plone.recipe.squid.

Varnish buildout recipe

The Varnish recipe can be found at http://pypi.python.org/pypi/plone.recipe.varnish.

For a **Zope-Varnish** setup, let's add the following to `buildout.cfg`:

```
[varnish-build]
recipe = zc.recipe.cmmi
url = http://downloads.sourceforge.net/varnish/varnish-2.0.1.tar.gz

[varnish-instance]
recipe = plone.recipe.varnish
daemon = ${varnish-build:location}/sbin/varnishd
cache-size = 1G
bind = 80
backends =
    example.com:127.0.0.1:8080
zope2_vhm_map =
    example.com:/Plone
```

Now, re-run the `buildout`. This will download and build Varnish (in `./parts/varnish-build`), create a Varnish configuration for your instance (in `./parts/varnish-instance`), and then add some Varnish startup and management scripts (in `./bin`).

To start up a Varnish instance with your configuration, just run the following `varnish-instance` script:

```
% sudo   ./bin/varnish-instance
```

> Again, this is a simple **Zope-Varnish** proxy setup with Varnish in front, where Varnish is rewriting the URLs.
>
> For other setups, such as **Zope-Varnish-Apache** or **Zope-Apache-Varnish** (where, in both cases, Apache may be doing the VirtualHostMonster-style URL rewrites), consult the `README.txt` in the plone.recipe.varnish download or the instructions at `http://pypi.python.org/pypi/plone.recipe.varnish`.

Installing a caching proxy without buildout

If you're not using a buildout-based installation, then you need to download and build Squid/Varnish from source (or use one of the binary distributions), and then generate the necessary configuration files from the templates provided by CacheFu.

Traditional Squid build

Squid can be found at `http://squid-cache.org`. Binary distributions are available for FreeBSD, NetBSD, Debian, Fedora, and Windows. Many operating systems also include Squid in their ports/packages system, but for this example we'll walk through a standard source code installation.

First, download and unpack the latest stable Squid-2.7 release; then do the usual `configure`/`make` dance to compile from source, as follows:

```
% cd squid-2.7.STABLE2
% ./configure --prefix=/usr/local/squid
% make all
% make install
```

This last step should install everything that you need, under `/usr/local/squid` (unless you specified a different location). The default installation also includes an extensively documented sample configuration file at `/usr/local/squid/etc/squid.conf`, but we won't be using this (a backup for reference purposes is also available at `squid.conf.default`).

Traditional Varnish build

Up-to-date packages of Varnish are available for Red Hat Enterprise Linux, CentOS, and Debian (Lenny and later, as you'll want Varnish 1.1 or higher). Other platforms should probably install from source, as we will do in this example.

First, download and unpack the latest Varnish release; then do the usual `configure`/`make` dance to compile from source, as follows:

```
% cd varnish-2.0.1
% ./configure --prefix=/usr/local/varnish
% make all
% make install
```

This last step should install everything that you need, under `/usr/local/varnish` (unless you specified a different location).

Generating proxy configuration from CacheFu templates

After a non-buildout installation of Squid or Varnish, our next step is to generate a custom proxy configuration and any necessary helpers. CacheFu makes this easy, with some auto-generated configurations being available as a separate download (CacheFu-1.2-extras) at `http://plone.org/products/cachefu`.

The configuration that you choose depends on your proxy setup. The available options are:

- `old-style`
- `apache`
- `squid`
- `squid-apache`
- `varnish`
- `varnish-apache`

The `old-style` option is just included for historical purposes. You should ignore it for a new installation. The next five options are fairly self-explanatory. If you have a Squid-only proxy setup, use the `squid` option. If you have a Varnish-only setup, use the `varnish` option, and so on.

As with the buildout examples, let's configure a simple **Zope-Squid/Varnish** setup. In this setup, Squid/Varnish will listen for requests on port 80 and proxy all requests for the `example.com` hostname to the backend at port 8080. It will also rewrite the incoming URLs to VirtualHostMonster-style ones in order to direct the requests to the `/Plone` folder (see the section *Introducing a friendly monster* in Chapter 19).

CacheFu squid template

For our **Zope-Squid** example, we'll choose the `squid` option. In this directory, you'll find the following four items:

1. `makeconfig`
2. `makeconfig.cfg`
3. `README.txt`
4. `templates`

First, edit `makeconfig.cfg` to match your desired setup. In our case, it should look something like this:

```
[python]
binary: /usr/bin/python

[squid]
#user: nobody
hostname: squid.example.com
admin_email: manager@example.com
cache_size_mb: 1000
binary:      /usr/local/squid/sbin/squid
config_dir: /usr/local/squid/etc
log_dir:     /usr/local/squid/var/logs
cache_dir:   /usr/local/squid/var/cache

[supported-protocols]
http: 80

[accelerated-hosts]
example.com:       127.0.0.1:8080/Plone
```

A note about `user`: To bind to a port lower than 1024, Squid must start up as `root` and then drop down to a less-privileged effective user, by default nobody. This user must have enough privileges to read and write to the directory defined in `cache_dir`. To designate a different effective user, uncomment the `user` directive above and substitute an appropriate user name. As nobody is typically reserved for non-privileged uses, it's best to create a dedicated `squid` user for this.

Now, set up your environment, so the script can find the libraries it needs, and then run the `makeconfig` script (adjust the following path appropriately):

```
% export PYTHONPATH=$PYTHONPATH:/path/to/zope/lib/python
% python makeconfig
```

Accept all of the defaults, and the script will create a folder called `output`. In this folder, you will find the following five files:

1. `deploy`
2. `purge_squid`
3. `squid.conf`
4. `iRedirector.py`
5. `squidRewriteRules.py`

The `deploy` shell script is provided in order to automate the process of moving these files to the `/usr/local/squid/etc` directory and setting the appropriate file ownership and permissions. Just run the following script to finish the configuration installation:

```
% ./deploy
```

Before you start Squid with this new configuration, you need to first build the cache storage structure on the file system, as shown here:

```
% sudo  /usr/local/squid/sbin/squid -z
```

(Note that `sudo` is only necessary if you are binding to a port lower than 1024)

When this is completed, you can start Squid, as shown here:

```
% sudo  /usr/local/squid/sbin/squid
```

CacheFu varnish template

For our **Zope-Varnish** example, we'll choose the `varnish` option. In this directory, you'll find the following four items:

1. `makeconfig`
2. `makeconfig.cfg`
3. `README.txt`
4. `templates`

First, edit `makeconfig.cfg` to match your desired setup. In our case, it should look something like this:

```
[varnish]
address: 127.0.0.1
port: 80
cache_size: 1000
binary:     /usr/local/varnish/sbin/varnishd
config_dir: /usr/local/varnish
cache_dir:  /usr/local/varnish/var/varnish

[virtualhosts]
example.com:    127.0.0.1:8080/Plone
```

Now, set up your environment so the script can find the libraries it needs, and then run the `makeconfig` script (adjust the path below appropriately):

```
% export PYTHONPATH=$PYTHONPATH:/path/to/zope/lib/python
% python makeconfig
```

Accept all the defaults, and the script will create a folder called `output`. In this folder, you will find the following four files:

1. `deploy`
2. `varnish-start`
3. `varnish-stop`
4. `varnish.vcl`

The `deploy` shell script is provided in order to automate the process of moving these files to the `/usr/local/varnish` directory and setting the appropriate file permissions. Just run the following script to finish the configuration installation:

```
% ./deploy
```

Start Varnish with your new configuration:

```
% sudo  /usr/local/varnish/varnish-start
```

(Again `sudo` is necessary only if it is binding to ports lower than 1024.)

Then, stop Varnish by using the following command:

```
% sudo  /usr/local/varnish/varnish-stop
```

Setting up proxy purging

Some proxies, including Squid and Varnish, support **PURGE** requests that are just ordinary HTTP requests of the type PURGE, instead of the standard GET or POST types. When the proxy receives an authorized purge request, it removes the requested page from the cache. This makes it possible to cache certain types of content more aggressively, as we can remove them from the cache on demand.

CacheFu can be configured to generate purge requests when Plone content is edited. Some proxies also allow you to purge the entire cache, but CacheFu doesn't yet support this. So if you wish to purge the entire cache, you will need to do so manually. A sample purge script for Squid is included with our auto-generated configuration files.

In order for CacheFu to generate purge requests, it needs to know two things: where to find your proxy, and the URL of the page stored in the cache.

Return to the CacheFu control panel (**Site Setup | Cache Configuration Tool**) and choose the **Proxy Cache Purge Configuration** appropriate for your proxy setup. Which purge configuration you should choose depends on the location of your proxy in the server chain, and on whether the URLs are being rewritten before or after the request hits the proxy. You have the following four choices:

- **No Purge (zope-only or zope-behind-apache)**

- **Simple Purge (squid/varnish in front)**

- **Purge with VHM URLs (squid/varnish behind apache, VHM virtual hosting)**

- **Purge with custom URLs (squid/varnish behind apache, custom virtual hosting)**

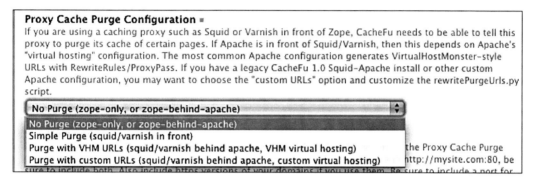

The default **No Purge** option simply turns off the generation of purge requests. The next two options generate different URLs to send the purge request to, depending on where in the server chain the proxy is found. The last option is a catch-all for special setups requiring custom purge URLs. In this case, you can customize the `rewritePurgeUrls.py` script in the `cache_setup` skin folder, as required.

For a purgeable proxy with Apache in front of the proxy, the best choice is probably **Purge with VHM URLs** (**VHM** is an abbreviation for **VirtualHostMonster**. See the section, *Introducing a friendly monster* in Chapter 19). For a purgeable proxy with the proxy in front, the best choice is probably **Simple Purge**. For a non-purge setup, choose **No Purge**.

If you choose **No Purge**, then you can skip the next two fields. Otherwise, your next step is to determine the list of **Site Domains** and **Proxy Cache Domains** for your site. These two fields are used to modify the URL for the purge requests.

Proxy Cache Purge Configuration ▪
If you are using a caching proxy such as Squid or Varnish in front of Zope, CacheFu needs to be able to tell this proxy to purge its cache of certain pages. If Apache is in front of Squid/Varnish, then this depends on Apache's "virtual hosting" configuration. The most common Apache configuration generates VirtualHostMonster-style URLs with RewriteRules/ProxyPass. If you have a legacy CacheFu 1.0 Squid-Apache install or other custom Apache configuration, you may want to choose the "custom URLs" option and customize the rewritePurgeUrls.py script.

    [No Purge (zope-only, or zope-behind-apache)   ▼]

Site Domains
Enter a list of domains for your site. This is not needed if you chose "No Purge" under the Proxy Cache Purge Configuration option above. If your site handles both http://www.mysite.com:80 and http://mysite.com:80, be sure to include both. Also include https versions of your domains if you use them. Be sure to include a port for each site.

Proxy Cache Domains
Enter a list of domains for any purgeable proxy caches. This is not needed if you chose "No Purge" or "Simple Purge" under "Proxy Cache Purge Configuration" above. For example, if you are using Squid with Apache in front, there will commonly be a single squid instance at http://127.0.0.1:3128

The **Site Domains** are the public-facing domains used to reach your site, including the port number.

The **Proxy Cache Domains** are the domains (or IPs) that can be used by the Zope server to reach your proxy. If you chose **Simple Purge** in the previous step, your public-facing domain is also your Proxy Cache Domain, so you can leave the second field blank.

For the example proxy configurations that we generated earlier, our setup is **squid/varnish in front** with a public-facing domain of http://example.com, with all servers on the same local IP address. In this case, we select **Simple Purge** for our purge configuration, leave **Proxy Cache Domains** blank, and enter the following under **Site Domains**:

```
http://example.com:80
```

If we had Apache in front, and this was rewriting URLs and sending requests through Squid or Varnish on port 3128, then our setup would be **squid/varnish behind apache** with a public-facing domain of `http://example.com`, typically with all of the servers again on the same local IP address. In this case, we select **Purge with VHM URLs** for our purge configuration and again enter the following under **Site Domains**:

`http://example.com:80`

And then add the following under **Proxy Cache Domains**:

`http://127.0.0.1:3128`

Note that we include the port number in all cases; this is required. Also note that for the Proxy Cache Domain, we simply used the localhost IP, as both the Zope server and the proxy cache server are on the same host.

Now click on the **Submit** button at the bottom of the page, and your site is ready to send appropriately-formatted purge requests whenever a content item changes.

Setting up compression and Vary headers

Another way to speed up your site is to compress your pages before serving them. It turns out that the delay required to compress a page is more than offset by the speed gained by pushing fewer bits across the Internet.

Most modern browsers support viewing content that has been compressed this way. But because some may not, you need to take a few steps to ensure that the compressed content is not forced onto non-supporting browsers. In the CacheFu default configuration, this is done for you automatically, but if necessary, you can adjust the default settings via the last two fields on the CacheFu control panel.

Compression
Should Zope compress pages before serving them, and if so, what criteria should be used to determine whether pages should be gzipped? The most common settings are "Never" (no compression) or "Use Accept-Encoding header" (only compress content if the browser explicitly declared support for compression).

`Use Accept-Encoding header`

Vary Header
Value for the Vary header. If you are using gzipping, you may need to include "Accept-Encoding" and possibly "User-Agent". If you are running a multi-lingual site, you may also need "Accept-Language". Values should be separated by commas.

`Accept-Encoding`

The **Compression** field lets you choose whether you want Zope to compress pages before serving them. The most common settings here are **Never** (to turn off compression) or **Use Accept-Encoding header** (to compress only if the browser declares support for compressed files). The default setting for a new install is **Use Accept-Encoding header**.

The **Vary Header** field is used to define a set of default values to be included in the Vary header of responses. The Vary header is used by caches to differentiate between multiple pages with the same URL. The header tells the cache to use the listed request headers in addition to the URL when determining whether to serve from cache.

If you've chosen to compress pages with **Use Accept-Encoding header** in the previous step, then you should have included **Accept-Encoding** in the Vary header. Otherwise, a browser that doesn't support GZIP compression might incorrectly receive a compressed cached copy from the proxy.

Similarly, if the content on the page can vary based on other request headers, then you should add those headers to the Vary header also. Multiple values should be separated by commas.

For example, some multi lingual sites generate different pages depending on the value of the **Accept-Language** request header. So in this case, the **Accept-Language** header should be added to the Vary header.

 Caution: It's best to be very conservative about adding more headers to Vary. The more variations the proxy cache needs to keep separate, the less efficient it gets. In general, you should rarely need to add any more headers here than Accept-Encoding.

Caches and cache control

Before diving into advanced configuration of CacheFu, let's briefly review the types of caches that we will be using, and the mechanisms that are available to control these caches.

For our purposes, there are roughly three types of caches: **memory caches, proxy caches**, and **browser caches**.

Memory caches are maintained directly by Zope within your server's memory. Zope stores all Plone content as objects within the **Zope Object Database (ZODB)**, and maintains a cache of recently accessed objects in the memory. In general, these cached objects are just "raw" objects, before any processing or skinning is applied to them. A special type of Zope memory cache, called a **RAMCache**, can be used to cache processed and skinned content, although its main use is to cache the output of expensive scripts. CacheFu uses a variant of **RAMCache** called a **PageCache**, which caches the entire page generated by Plone, including any HTTP headers.

Proxy caches are found between the origin server and the browser. As discussed in Chapter 19, proxy servers come in two different flavors: **forward proxies** and **reverse proxies**. Unless we're setting up an Intranet, we have little control over the deployment of forward proxies. So for this walkthrough, we're going to focus mostly on using caching reverse proxies.

A variant of a caching reverse proxy is a **Content Delivery Network (CDN)**, which is basically a large number of caching reverse proxies distributed across the Internet. CDNs are available as commercial services and are generally used only by very popular sites with very demanding performance needs.

Browser caches live within individual web browsers. Browser caches are what make your "back" button work so quickly. Rather than request the same page again, the page is just pulled from the browser cache.

In general, the closer the cache is to the end user, the faster is the response but the less control you, as the server administrator, have over the cache. Consequently, from the end user's perspective, content already in the browser cache is displayed faster but is potentially less "fresh" when compared to content in the reverse proxy. And similarly, content in the reverse proxy is displayed faster but again potentially less "fresh" when compared to the content residing in a Zope memory cache.

An aggressive cache strategy is likely to involve some compromise between speed and freshness. The default cache policy you get when you first enable CacheFu implements a conservative cache strategy that is weighted more toward freshness than speed. To cache more aggressively, we need to understand how to control cache behavior.

Controlling your caches

To cache anything, at a minimum, we need a **cache control** mechanism to tell the cache servers and browsers which content to put into the cache, and to refresh this content when it becomes out-of-date (or "stale").

Most cache control is done via special HTTP response headers sent along with the content. These headers include:

- Expires
- Cache-Control
- Last-Modified
- ETag

The first two, Expires and Cache-Control, are **freshness headers**. The last two, Last-Modified and ETag are **validation headers**.

 Technically, Last-Modified is both a freshness header and a validation header. In the old HTTP 1.0 standard, Expires and Last-Modified were the only freshness headers available for cache control. But for our purposes, with HTTP 1.1, we only care about the use of Last-Modified as a validation header.

We will be using all four of these cache control headers, plus a couple of more cache control mechanisms, all centrally managed via the CacheFu.

Freshness headers

Freshness request headers tell caches how long the content can be considered fresh before a new version can be requested.

The Expires header is simple. It just contains the date on which the content "expires" or becomes stale. After this date, browsers and proxies must request a new version rather than use the cached version.

The Cache-Control header, first introduced with HTTP 1.1, pretty much supersedes and overrules the older Expires header, as it gives much better control over the freshness parameters. But just in case there are still more browsers or proxies out in the wild that don't support the new Cache-Control header yet, it may be useful to set the Expires header as well. (CacheFu automatically sets the Expires header based on the cache-control settings.)

The Cache-Control header can do a bit more than control freshness. It's actually a general-purpose header that can also be used to modify general cache behavior. This header can contain multiple tokens, including the following:

- `max-age=[seconds]`: The amount of time that a page can be cached without revalidation
- `s-maxage=[seconds]`: This is the same as `max-age`, but meant to apply only to proxy caches

- `no-cache`: Indicates that revalidation must be done before serving from cache

- `no-store`: Indicates that the content must not be stored in a cache

- `public`: Indicates that content should always be cached even if an authorization header is present

- `private`: Indicates that it is fine to cache in the browser, but not in the proxies

- `must-revalidate`: Indicates that the cache must revalidate after an expire (telling the cache to strictly follow your rules)

- `proxy-revalidate`: This is the same as `must-revalidate`, but applies only to proxy caches

- `post-check=[seconds]`: A proprietary Microsoft-only extension, similar to max-age, but on expiry shows the cache copy and updates the cache in the background

- `pre-check=[seconds]`: A proprietary Microsoft-only extension, roughly equivalent to max-age

- `stale-while-revalidate=[seconds]`: An experimental extension to signal a cache to serve stale content, while sending an asynchronous revalidation request back to the origin server

- `stale-while-error=[seconds]`: An experimental extension to signal a cache to serve stale content from the cache if the backend response fails

The Varnish cache proxy does not currently support all of these cache-control header tokens (and according to the developers, probably will never do so). If you're designing a cache strategy for use with Varnish, stick with just `max-age` and `s-maxage`. However, the other tokens may still be useful for controlling other caches downstream of your Varnish proxy.

All these freshness settings are determined by CacheFu settings that we can adjust to suit our use case.

Validation headers

Validation headers provide a way for browsers (and some proxies) to revalidate their cached content by submitting a **conditional request**. A conditional request asks the server to send the new content only if the condition is true.

If the cached version contains a Last-Modified header, then an If-Modified-Since header with the Last-Modified date can be included with the request.

If the cached version contains an ETag header, then an If-None-Match header with the ETag value can be included with the request.

If the server determines that any of these conditions are true, then the updated content is returned. Otherwise, an empty response with a **304 Not Modified** HTTP status is returned, and the content is then served directly out of the cache.

Again, the values for both Last-Modified and ETag are determined by CacheFu settings that we can adjust to suit our use case.

> **LiveHTTPHeaders** (`http://livehttpheaders.mozdev.org`) is a handy Firefox browser extension for viewing HTTP headers and troubleshooting cache issues.
>
> Other useful Firefox extensions include **Firebug** (`http://www.getfirebug.com`), **Web Developer** (`http://chrispederick.com/work/web-developer`), and the **Clear Cache Button** (`https://addons.mozilla.org/en-US/firefox/addon/1801`).
>
> Note that the Firebug headers display doesn't clearly differentiate between browser-cached and non-browser-cached content, so LiveHTTPHeaders is generally more "honest" in this regard.

Zope memory cache control

The Zope memory caches are controlled differently as compared to proxy and browser caches.

The ZODB cache is managed automatically by the Zope framework and is never stale. The maximum size of this cache, adjusted via the `cache-size` directive in `zope.conf`, is measured in a number of objects, and that number is a total across all threads. If you find that your server has unused RAM, you can increase the size of this cache until your machine begins to swap, and then back off a bit.

A RAMCache requires a little more attention. Multiple RAMCaches can be added to the Plone root folder and managed via the ZMI. Available settings include limiting the number and age of cached entries, and adjusting the cleanup interval. By default, the stale entries are cleaned out every five minutes. If memory usage fluctuates too much, this cleanup interval should probably be decreased. Any object that uses `OFS.Cache.Cacheable` to provide caching services can be associated with a RAMCache. Multiple cached entries from the same object can be distinguished from each other by setting an appropriate list of request variable keys. RAMCaches can be a very effective tool to accelerate a Plone site, but they should not be used to cache images and files (as these are already cached in the ZODB cache) or complete web pages (as HTTP headers are not included).

The PageCache is managed from the CacheFu control panel, and can be used to cache complete web pages. PageCache behavior is very similar to a RAMCache, but has a more flexible ability to define complex cache keys. Plone pages are often put together from many different pieces, which makes it difficult to determine quickly whether the final cached product is still fresh without redoing all of the work to regenerate it again. The PageCache solution to this problem requires an ETag. When a request comes in for an item that exists in the PageCache, the ETag can be recalculated and compared against the cached value. If it matches, then the cached version is still fresh. If it does not match, then the content is regenerated.

Other cache control mechanisms

Another cache control mechanism involves simply removing (or purging) content from the cache. We've already discussed purging proxy caches via PURGE requests.

The PageCache also supports purging, and CacheFu takes care of individual PageCache purges at the same time that a proxy PURGE request is generated. You can also purge the entire PageCache from the **Memory** section of the CacheFu control panel (**Site Setup | Cache Configuration Tool | Memory**)

Another cache control mechanism is the direct configuration of the proxy itself to cache certain requests, even in the absence of cache control headers. But as proxy configuration is difficult and cumbersome to adjust for complex use cases, it is best not to rely too heavily on proxy configuration for complex cache control.

And finally, yet another cache control mechanism involves simply changing the URL every time the content changes. This is the strategy used by Plone's Resource Registries when generating the bundled CSS, JavaScript, and KSS files. Changing the URL is a very effective technique, and makes the item aggressively cacheable all the way down to the browser. But this technique works well only with supplemental resources such as CSS and JavaScript files, as in most cases, we don't want to change the URL of the page itself.

 Be careful with the Resource Registries' debug/development mode. Caching these resources is disabled in debug mode, so make sure that you turn this mode off when you're done with it.

Exploring the CacheFu control panel

CacheFu provides a centralized control panel that can be used to set the cache control and validation headers, based on a configurable set of rules defined by **cache policies**, **cache rules**, and **header sets**.

A **cache policy** is simply a container that holds a set of cache rules and header sets that determines how CacheFu will treat a request. You can define multiple policies, though only one policy can be active at a time.

A **cache rule** is a set of tests that is matched against the request. When a request comes in, CacheFu checks the cache rules for the active policy one by one, until it finds one that matches the request. The cache rule then delegates to one of the header sets.

A **header set** contains specific instructions on which headers should be set, and also whether the content should be stored in the PageCache. Some of these values may depend on values set in the referring cache rule.

Let's revisit the CacheFu control panel and see how all of this is organized.

The control panel contains five tabbed sections:

- **Main**
- **Policies**
- **Rules**
- **Headers**
- **Memory**

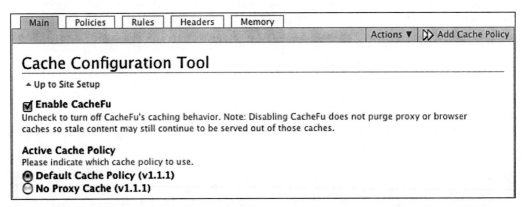

So far, we've spent all of our time in the **Main** section. We've already covered everything here except for the **Active Cache Policy** field. This field is where you select which policy to use when a request comes in. Remember, only one cache policy may be active at a time. Now, let's check out the other sections.

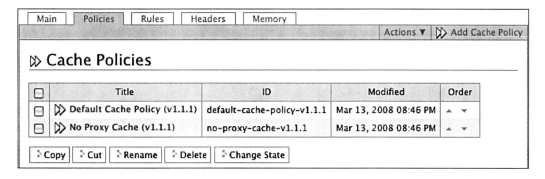

The **Policies** section contains a listing of the available cache policies. This is where you can add new policies, or delete or create a duplicate of existing cache policies.

Two cache policies are included in the default install of CacheFu 1.2: **Default Cache Policy** and **No Proxy Cache**. **No Proxy Cache** is a cache policy that is slightly more conservative than the **Default Cache Policy**, and is designed for use with a simple Zope setup without a caching proxy.

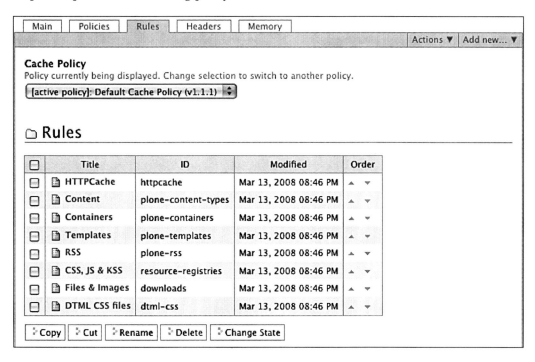

The **Rules** section contains the cache rules defined by the currently-active cache policy. Here, you can add new rules, delete or duplicate existing rules. The drop-down menu allows you to switch the "displayed" policy, if you wish to view the rules for an inactive policy.

There are three different types of cache rules.

A **Content Cache Rule** is used to match a request for a content type view.

A **Template Cache Rule** is used to match a request for a template not associated with a content type.

A **PolicyHTTPCacheManager Cache Rule** is a special rule used to match a request for an item associated with a PolicyHTTPCacheManager, which is CacheFu's replacement for Zope's AcceleratedHTTPCacheManager. Content that implements Zope's "Cacheable" interface can be associated to this cache manager, which will then automatically set the HTTP headers as necessary. This is one of the many different ways to set cache headers that CacheFu replaces and consolidates. The replacement delegates the responsibility for setting the headers for these items to CacheFu. CacheFu installs two PolicyHTTPCacheManagers: one as a replacement for Plone's HTTPCache and another to act as a default cache manager for "old-style" files and images (OFS.Image and OFS.File).

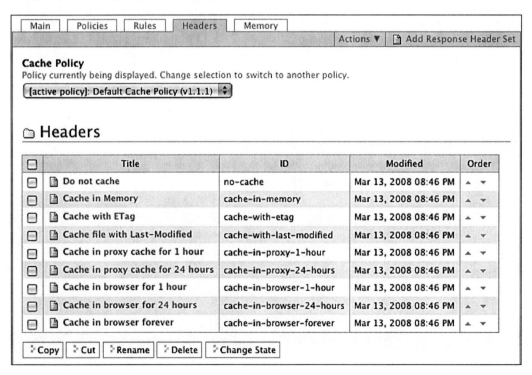

The **Headers** section contains the header sets defined by the currently-active cache policy. Again, you can add, delete, or duplicate header sets here. And again, a drop-down menu lets you switch the "displayed" policy, in case you wish to view the header sets for an inactive policy.

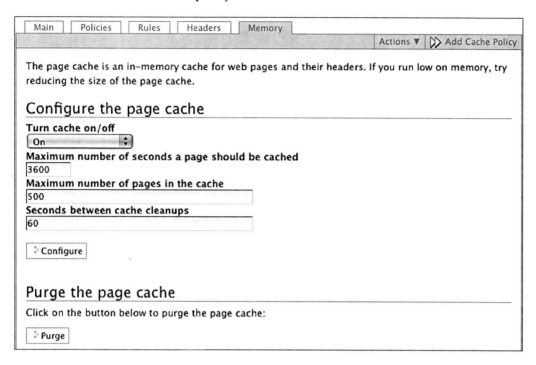

Finally, the **Memory** section contains the controls for the in-memory PageCache. From here, you can purge the entire cache or turn the cache off or on. You can also change the amount of time for which a page should be cached, the size of the cache, and the interval between cache cleanups.

In general, the default PageCache settings will work well for most setups. If you have extra memory, you might try increasing the size of the cache.

With the default cache policies, the PageCache is mostly used to cache anonymous container views such as **Folders** and **Collections**, along with a couple of template views, as these views can be difficult to keep fresh in external caches. If you have many such container views, it might be helpful to increase the size of the cache, or move some of these container views into proxy caches if they don't often change.

Making it go even faster

In general, you won't need to mess with any other tabs in the CacheFu control panel other than **Main**. The default cache policy, although a bit conservative, will work just fine in most cases.

However, depending on your use case, you may find that you can get away with making CacheFu more aggressive. You may also find that you need to tweak the cache settings to accommodate add-on products that create new content types, which the default policy doesn't know how to cache.

Thankfully, CacheFu makes it easy to tinker with the cache settings without messing up the default configuration. So you can always revert if you don't like the results.

Starting with the default

In most cases, rather than create a new policy from scratch, it would probably be a good idea to start with a clone of the default cache policy (this is easy to do with a copy and paste on the **Policies** tab). So, let's review the default cache policy and see where it can be improved.

The default cache policy includes eight cache rules and nine header sets (although two header sets aren't actually used by any of the default rules). These can be roughly categorized by how aggressively the matching items are cached.

Aggressively-cached items

These cache rules target items that rarely change, or never change without changing their URL. So all of these can be cached very aggressively all the way to the browser, for both anonymous and authenticated requests.

The cache rules are as follows:

- **httpcache** (HTTPCache): This is a rule for content associated with the HTTPCache. These are mostly filesystem images and images found in the skin folders. This content is cached in the proxy and in the browser. ETags are not useful because these files have no personalization.

  Header set: *cache-in-browser-24-hours*

- **resource-registries** (CSS, JS & KSS): This is a rule for CSS, JS, and KSS generated by Plone's Resource Registries. These files are cached "forever" (one year) in proxy caches and in browsers. There is no need to purge these files because when they are changed their URLs change. Again, ETags are not useful because these files have no personalization.

  Header set: *cache-in-browser-forever* (or *no-cache* if in debug mode)

- **dtml-css** (DTML CSS files): This is a rule for CSS files generated with DTML. Currently, this only matches the special IE-specific `IEFixes.css`. ETags are not useful because this file has no personalization.
  Header set: *cache-in-browser-24-hours*

The header sets are as follows:

- **cache-in-browser-forever**: This attempts to cache the items in both the proxy and the browser for a year. In Zope, neither memory cache nor `304 Not Modified` responses are enabled. The most relevant header is:
  `Cache-Control: max-age=31536000`.

- **cache-in-browser-24-hours**: This attempts to cache the items in both the proxy and the browser for 24 hours. In Zope, neither memory cache nor `304 Not Modified` responses are enabled. The most relevant header is:
  `Cache-Control: max-age=86400`.

Moderately-cached items

These cache rules target items that can be safely cached in the proxy, either because freshness is not critical, or because they can be easily purged from the proxy when necessary.

The following are the cache rules:

- **plone-rss** (RSS): This is a rule for RSS feeds.
  Header set for anonymous users: *cache-in-proxy-1-hour*
  Header set for authenticated users: *cache-with-etag*
- **downloads** (Files & Images): This is a rule for ATFile and ATImage downloads. Files that are viewable by anonymous users are cached in the proxy cache. ETags are not useful because these files have no personalization.
  Header set: *cache-in-proxy-24-hours* (or *no-cache* if no anonymous view)

The header sets are as follows:

- **cache-in-proxy-24-hours**: This attempts to cache the items in both the proxy and the browser. The proxy should get a new copy after 24 hours. The browser should revalidate the Last-Modified date against the version in the proxy cache on every request. In Zope, neither the memory cache, nor `304 Not Modified` responses are enabled. The most relevant headers are:
  `Last-Modified: <date>`
  `Cache-Control: max-age=0, s-maxage=86400`
- **cache-in-proxy-1-hour**: This is the same as above except that the proxy should get a new copy after 1 hour. The most relevant headers are:
  `Last-Modified: <date>`
  `Cache-Control: max-age=0, s-maxage=3600`

Weakly-cached items

These cache rules target items that are difficult to (reliably) purge from the proxy because changes to the item display may occur without any changes to the item itself. So, except for authenticated requests, we cache these items in memory.

The cache rules are as follows:

- **plone-content-types** (Content): This is a rule for views of Plone content types. Anonymous users are served content object views from memory, and not the proxy cache (because the navigation tree displayed might change without triggering a proxy cache purge). Responses for authenticated users are not cached in memory or the proxy (because caching personalized pages is inefficient), but an ETag is added to enable proper 304 responses. Member ID is used in the ETag because content is personalized; the time of the last catalog change is included, so the navigation tree stays up-to-date.
  Header set for anonymous users: *cache-in-memory*
  Header set for authenticated users: *cache-with-etag*

- **plone-containers** (Containers): This is a rule for the views of Plone containers. Its behavior is the same as that of the *plone-content-types* cache rule, although the reasons are slightly different. We can't easily purge container views when they change, as the container views depend on all of their contained objects, and contained objects do not necessarily purge their containers' views when they change.

- **plone-templates** (Templates): This is a rule for various non-form templates. Again, its behavior is the same as the *plone-content-types* cache rule, although the reasons are slightly different. Some of these templates depend on catalog queries, the results of which might change without triggering a proxy cache purge.

The header sets are as follows:

- **cache-in-memory**: This attempts to keep the item from being cached in the proxy. Browsers should revalidate the item's `Etag` before displaying a browser-cached version. In Zope, both the memory cache and `304 Not Modified` responses are enabled.

  The most relevant headers are:
  ```
  ETag: <etag value>
  Cache-Control: max-age=0, private
  ```

- **cache-with-etag**: This attempts to keep the item from being cached in proxy. Browsers should revalidate the item's Etag before displaying a browser-cached version. In Zope, the memory cache is not enabled, but 304 Not Modified responses are enabled. The header set is used primarily to protect personalized items from being cached in a shared cache.

    The most relevant headers are:
    ```
    ETag: <etag value>
    Cache-Control: max-age=0, private
    ```

- **no-cache**: This attempts to keep the item from being cached in the proxy, and forces browsers to get a new copy with each request. In Zope, neither the memory cache nor 304 Not Modified responses are enabled. This header set is used by the *resource-registries* cache rule if the registry is in debug mode. It is also used by the *downloads* cache rule if the download disallows anonymous views.

    The most relevant header is:
    ```
    Cache-Control: max-age=0, private
    ```

CacheFu will also add additional headers to the response to identify which cache rules and header sets were matched. This can be a useful troubleshooting aid when using something like the *LiveHTTPheaders* extension.

For example, a request for the default front page of a new Plone instance with CacheFu installed will include the following two headers in the response:

```
X-Caching-Rule-Id:  plone-content-types
X-Header-Set-Id:  cache-in-memory
```

Speed tip 1: Speed up weakly-cached items

The biggest speed bottlenecks are likely to be the weakly-cached items. A simple and very effective performance modification is to simply move items from the weakly-cached group to the moderately-cached group. This is easily done by changing the anonymous header set for the weakly-caching rule to one of the cache-in-proxy sets (but first read *Speed Tip #3*).

But before you do this, first review the reasons why these items are weakly cached in the default policy. If these reasons are not relevant for your site, or if you can tolerate stale content being served for some time, then go for it.

You may decide that that you can only move some items matched by the cache rule. In this case, just duplicate the relevant rule, make it specific to these items, and then move it above the old rule, so that your new rule matches first.

Caution: It's very tempting to accelerate all of the views that match the Containers and Content cache rules, by creating a special "Cache in proxy cache for 1 minute" header set and changing the anonymous header set settings in both cache rules to point to this new header set. This can indeed give your site a huge speed increase, but again, before you attempt this, first read *Speed Tip #3*.

Speed tip 2: Speed up non-cached items

In a stock Plone install, almost everything is matched by one of the cache rules in CacheFu's default cache policy. Some exceptions include several incidental templates not listed in the template rule, a couple of minor icons, and the special URLs generated by Kupu's UID link feature (at least in the latest version of CacheFu available at the time of writing). Except for the Kupu UID links, none of these is likely to significantly impact the performance of the site.

Prior to Plone 3.1, Kupu UID links worked by returning a redirect response to the current URL of the linked item. This added a small but measurable delay to the overall response time. If you have used UID links extensively enough to start impacting performance, you may want to convert them to non-UID links by using the conversion feature available via Kupu's **Links** tab (**Site Setup | Visual Editor | Links**). In Plone 3.1, Kupu has added a transform to automatically convert UID links prior to display, so this may no longer be an issue.

If you install products that add new content types or template views to your site, then you may need to edit or add new cache rules to make sure that these new content types are cached appropriately. If you need a new rule, it's often easiest to start by first cloning an existing cache rule that comes closest to matching your requirements, and then tweaking it as needed.

Again, the *LiveHTTPheaders* extension mentioned previously is a handy tool for finding out which items on your site are not being caught by any of the cache rules. Note that even if CacheFu is not adding headers, your browser may still cache a local copy, so you may also need the *Clear Cache Button* or the *Web Developer* extensions to make sure that your browser cache is clear (Firefox's **Clear Private Data** function is not always reliable).

Speed tip 3: Watch out for authenticated versus anonymous users

An easy mistake to make is to try to cache an anonymous response in the proxy or the browser, while expecting requests for the authenticated version to bypass the cache. Even if an authenticated response is excluded from the cache (via `Cache-Control: private` or some other header), a proxy or browser cache is still allowed to serve an anonymous version from cache to an authenticated request. This is often not the desired result.

The solutions are simple but not always practical. As Plone authentication is cookie-based, adding "Cookie" to the Vary header will prevent an authenticated request from getting the anonymous version from cache. However, if, in your use case, the anonymous requests also contain session/tracker cookies (for example, to make each anonymous user unique), then this solution may not be practical, as it would result in a very inefficient cache.

Some other possible solutions are either to ensure that the anonymous response is acceptable for the authenticated request (this is the default assumption for most images, CSS, and JavaScript) or to enforce a different URL or domain for authenticated requests. Enforcing a different URL can be as simple as enforcing HTTP for anonymous and HTTPS for authenticated users, as these require different VHM-style URLs. However in this case, care must be taken to disallow browser caching for both variants.

A historical note: Older versions of the proxy configurations generated by CacheFu and the proxy recipes used to allow for separate handling of authenticated and anonymous requests, without the workarounds described previously, by applying special behavior if the request included any Plone authentication cookies. This special handling has since been deprecated because there is no way to impose similar behavior on any forward proxies that may be encountered in the real world, thus potentially disabling the ability of logged-in users behind such proxies to view authenticated pages.

The last option suggested above (enforcing HTTP for anonymous users and HTTPS for authenticated users) emulates the old behavior, but in a more reliable way, as HTTPS is not cached by forward proxies.

Another option, also emulating the old behavior in a more reliable way, is discussed in the following email thread: `http://thread.gmane.org/gmane.comp.web.zope.plone.user/94644`

Speed tip 4: Set a short lifetime on purgeable content

When moving items from weakly-cached (or non-cached) to moderately-cached, another easy mistake to make is to forget that while PURGE requests may ensure the freshness of your proxy cache, they do not ensure the freshness of any other proxy caches that may be downstream from your server. So in most cases, do not set a long lifetime on purgeable content, as you can expect some stale content to be served to some clients even after you've purged your local proxy.

Another special header, called **Surrogate-Control**, is designed to handle this issue—allowing cache control directives to target specific proxy servers—but to date, only Squid 3 supports this header. The next major version of CacheFu may add support for Surrogate-Control.

More tips on advanced CacheFu configuration can be found at
`http://plone.org/products/cachefu`.

Summary

In this chapter, we have learned:

- How to download and install the CacheFu add-on
- How to install and configure a Squid proxy server
- How to install and configure a Varnish proxy server
- How to configure CacheFu to generate purge requests for a purgeable proxy cache
- How to configure CacheFu to compress pages and add the appropriate Vary headers
- How memory, proxy, and browser caches can be used to speed up a site, and how they can be managed via various cache control mechanisms
- What CacheFu cache policies, cache rules, and header sets are
- How to control the PageCache via the CacheFu control panel
- Why the default cache policy caches some items more aggressively than others
- How to speed up your site even more by tweaking the default cache policy to aggressively cache more weakly-cached or non-cached items

21

Connect to Your LDAP/Active Directory Repository

Now that your Plone site is up, running, and "live," and you've improved your site's performance by enabling content caching, you're ready to have your users browse the site and start creating content. However, you'll first need a method to enable users to authenticate themselves and log into the site. You could create generic Plone accounts for each of your users, but this can become a tedious task if your organization comprises of more than just a few users. And what if your company is already using an organizational database to manage user and group information? How can you save yourself the time and trouble of recreating and maintaining organizational information that already exists in a perfectly good, centralized source?

In this chapter, **John DeStefano** shows how, with a few tweaks, Plone can take advantage of these external sources of organizational data, and how to use them to create and manage user account entries, groups, and permissions on your Plone site.

LDAP and Active Directory

The **Lightweight Directory Access Protocol (LDAP)** is a mechanism that enables applications to query information from a centralized source. Typically, LDAP databases are used for storing and sharing organizational information about users, such as names, telephone numbers, locations, and group affiliations. The structure and the content of these databases are often referred to as the **directories** or **trees**, due to their hierarchical nature. An LDAP search query can return information about all of the users in a directory (often involving a great deal of data), it can target a specific user, group, or some other attribute, in order to narrow the scope of its search. In addition to storing information about people, LDAP can also contain other data, including permissions that can aid other applications in authenticating users.

Active Directory is Microsoft's LDAP-like implementation of a directory service, designed mostly for Windows networks. Similar to LDAP, Active Directory employs a **schema** to define directory objects, as well as a set of rules for organizing object attributes and structure.

Differences between LDAP and Active Directory support

As far as your Plone site is concerned, the main difference between LDAP and Active Directory is that, due to the nature of their interfaces, Plone sites can both read from and write to LDAP databases, but they can only **read** from Active Directory sources. Plone does not support writing to (for example, making changes in) an Active Directory database. Thus, while you'll be able to add, edit, and delete LDAP user and group objects, you will not be able to manipulate such objects in Active Directory through Plone.

For more detailed information and documentation on LDAP and Active Directory, refer to *Mastering OpenLDAP* by Matt Butcher and *Windows Server 2003 Active Directory Design and Implementation* by John Savill, respectively.

Installing LDAP/Active Directory support

In order to add LDAP or Active Directory functionality to your site, you'll need to add the following software and supporting packages to your buildout-based Plone installation:

- Install the required prerequisite packages
- Install the **PloneLDAP** product and its requirements
- Install the `plone.app.ldap` package

A few software packages are necessary in order to get your Python instance to use the LDAP protocol to speak with your LDAP or Active Directory server. PloneLDAP is the core Plone product necessary to enable LDAP or Active Directory connections to and from your Plone site. The `plone.app.ldap` package is a user interface that will ease and enhance your ability to configure the interaction between your Plone site and your centralized directory.

The most difficult part of this process may be installing the prerequisite packages for PloneLDAP and its companion packages, as this is somewhat different for each operating system and can be tricky depending on the existing packages and environment configurations. Once these packages are installed, the rest simply involves editing a text file and re-running your Plone site's buildout, which will be a breeze.

Installing prerequisites

The main software components that need to be installed before we can move on to LDAP itself for Plone are as follows:

- **OpenLDAP** is an open source implementation of the LDAP protocol. Information and downloads can be found at `http://www.openldap.org`. The latest 2.3.x version (where 'x' is the latest version number) is recommended.

- **python-ldap** is a module that allows Python to gain access to LDAP information by providing it with an API. Information and downloads can be found at `http://python-ldap.sourceforge.net`. Version 2.0.6 or later is recommended.

> Depending on your system and existing environment, installing OpenLDAP may also require the installation of additional packages, such as **Berkeley DB** and a **Simple Authentication and Security Layer** (**SASL**) framework.
>
> Similarly, depending on your environment and existing Plone configuration, `python-ldap` may be installed automatically during your buildout as a required package for PloneLDAP.

Although it is beyond the scope of this chapter to cover the installation of open source software packages on multiple platforms, we would like to offer some tips and suggestions on installing these packages on different platforms, which we hope will help ease the process.

Installing on Linux

If you don't already have LDAP and its related packages installed on your system, the best method is to install them using your built-in software package manager (`yum`, `apt`, `up2date`, and so on). If this option is not available, you can download and install their source archives:

- The Cyrus SASL library: `http://asg.web.cmu.edu/sasl/sasl-library.html`
- Berkeley DB: `http://www.oracle.com/technology/software/products/berkeley-db/index.html`
- OpenLDAP: `http://www.openldap.org`

If you experience library-related errors when installing OpenLDAP, even after the successful installation of the other packages, try setting the value of the environment variable `LD_LIBRARY_PATH` to include the location of your new Berkeley DB libraries.

For example, if you've installed Berkeley DB version 4.7 via source in `/usr/local/`, you might enter the following command (in one line) before configuring OpenLDAP for installation:

```
export LD_LIBRARY_PATH=$LD_LIBRARY_PATH:/usr/local/BerkeleyDB.4.7/lib
```

`python-ldap` may also be configured and installed via source, from `http://python-ldap.sourceforge.net`, or via the `easy_install` script from your Python's `setuptools` utility:

```
easy_install python-ldap
```

When using `easy_install`, take care to use the same binary associated with your Plone buildout, which must be associated with a Python version 2.4 installation.

Installing on OS X

Mac users have two installation options: either using source archives as described above in the Linux section, or using the MacPorts system to install specific packages. The following command will install the MacPorts versions of OpenLDAP, Cyrus SASL, and the `python-ldap` module:

```
sudo port install openldap cyrus-sasl2 py-ldap
```

As with the Linux scenario, the suggestion for installing `python-ldap` via MacPorts is based on the assumption that the active Python installation is version 2.4, and that this Python installation has also been carried out via MacPorts.

 For more information on MacPorts and the installation and use of port packages, visit `http://www.macports.org`.

It may also be helpful to set the variable `LD_LIBRARY_PATH`, as well as `DYLD_LIBRARY_PATH`, when installing packages from source.

Installing on Windows

Of the three platforms covered here, Windows is possibly the most difficult operating system on which these prerequisites have to be installed, as it does not inherently feature the ability to compile packages from source, and official binary installation packages are often not available. However, for those stubborn enough to try anyway, or for those who have little choice, we offer a few suggestions:

- Zope developer Volker Wend maintains a third-party combined installer for both OpenLDAP and python-ldap at: http://www.zope.org/Members/volkerw/LdapWin32

- Third-party binary installers for OpenLDAP are available from: http://mguessan.free.fr/nt/openldap_en.html

- python-ldap can be installed via either easy_install or a third-party installer from: http://www.agescibs.org/mauro/

> Although the author experienced little difficulty in using these installers, they are neither created nor supported by their official projects, and they should be used cautiously at your own risk.

As mentioned earlier, for Linux and OS X, keep in mind that only packages for Python version 2.4 should be used when working with Plone.

> **Getting help**
>
> If you experience trouble while installing any of these packages, the best sources of information and assistance for most open source software are usually available from their respective web sites, in the form of documentation, **frequently asked questions (FAQs)**, mailing lists, and support forums.

Installing PloneLDAP

Once the prerequisites have been installed, we can begin installing the PloneLDAP product on your Plone site.

First, open the buildout.cfg file for your Plone site project, which should begin with a [buildout] section. Within this section is a group of lines that begin with eggs. We need to add our PloneLDAP product package and its requirement products to this section, by adding the following lines:

```
eggs =
    elementtree
    Products.LDAPUserFolder
    Products.LDAPMultiPlugins
    Products.PloneLDAP
```

There may or may not be additional lines before or after these lines as well. Don't worry if your file looks a bit different. We're only concerned with adding a few lines to what is already there.

The Products.PloneLDAP line may not be necessary, as this package is a prerequisite to the other packages and is usually resolved automatically through buildout. However, it doesn't hurt to include it explicitly in your configuration.

Installing plone.app.ldap

Next, we need to install the plone.app.ldap package. Look towards the end of the buildout.cfg file, for a section called [instance], and, within this section, for another eggs section. Here, we need to add a single line, comprised of the name of our plone.app.ldap package, so it looks like this:

```
eggs =
    ${buildout:eggs}
    ${plone:eggs}
    plone.app.ldap
```

Don't worry if your section appears a bit different from this one. We're only concerned with adding a few lines in the correct place, and not with changing anything else.

If you've used an installation method other than the default (such as a unified Plone installer, or a clustered buildout configuration), your section may be titled something other than [instance], such as [client1] or a customized name for the instance.

We also need to add an additional ZCML line to tell our buildout to create a small piece of code called a **ZCML slug**, in order to have Plone (technically, Zope) recognize and activate our new package. The zcml = line in your file may initially be empty. We need to add our plone.app.ldap package again here, so it looks like this:

```
zcml =
    plone.app.ldap
```

That's it! No further editing of your configuration file is necessary. Simply re-run your buildout command from within your project folder, by using the following command:

```
bin\buildout -v
```

If the command completes successfully, congratulations! Your Plone site is now equipped with the software necessary to connect to your LDAP or Active Directory server.

Troubleshooting buildout failures

If the buildout command should fail, examine the error output, and the tail end of this in particular, for clues or references to the prerequisite packages mentioned previously. Such failures are often due to a package configuration error or an incompatibility between packages. Solutions to such issues are often requested and delivered in FAQs, support forums, and mailing lists maintained by the relevant software projects.

Activate LDAP support

In your Plone site, go to your **Site Setup** and click on **Add-on Products**.

Select the **LDAP support** option, and then click on **Install**.

Once the installation has completed, at the bottom of the **Site Setup** bar to the left of the screen, a new **Add-on Product Configuration** applet called **LDAP Connection** will appear. Click on this new link:

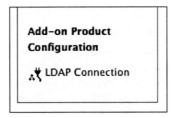

Configuring LDAP connections

Now that you've activated LDAP support, you can configure your Plone site to connect to your LDAP or Active Directory database.

The **LDAP Configuration** applet is comprised of three main sections:

- Global Settings
- LDAP Schema
- LDAP Servers

Getting the information you need

If you are not the LDAP or Active Directory administrator for your organization, you may have to coordinate with that individual or group in order to obtain the information necessary to connect to your LDAP server and obtain organizational information from the database.

Use the information described in the following sections to obtain from your LDAP administrator the parameters necessary for connecting to your database.

Configure Global Settings

The **Global Settings** section defines the global structure and organization of your LDAP or Active Directory database, and it must be completed before the other two sections can be addressed.

Let's have a look at the fields on this page, and briefly describe their meanings and common settings:

Global Settings	LDAP Schema	LDAP Servers

The following settings affect rules globally.

LDAP server type
Plone supports both Active Directory and standard LDAP servers. For Active Directory the read-only LDAP interface which is enabled for all Active Directory servers can be used.

[LDAP]

rDN attribute
This is attribute is used to build the distinguished name (DN) for users that are being created in your LDAP directory. This is commonly either the users full name ('cn' property) or the userid ('uid' property).

[cn]

user id attribute
This attribute is used as the userid inside Plone for LDAP users. It has to be unique for all users.

[cn]

login name attribute
The attribute is used as the login name for LDAP users logging into your site. In most cases this should be the same as the user id attribute.

[cn]

LDAP object classes
Each object in the LDAP database has a structural object class and optionally several supplemental object classes. These classes define the required and optional properties that can be present on an object. Classes can be entered in a comma seperated list.

[pilotPerson]

Bind DN
The DN of a manager account in the LDAP directory. This must be allowed to access all user and group information as well as be able to update and create users and groups. Please note that Plone only supports simple binds. SASL is not supported.

[ ]

Bind password
Password to use when binding to the LDAP server.

[ ]

Base DN for users
This is the location in your LDAP directory where all users are stored.

[ ]

Search scope for users
The search scope determines where the LDAP server will search for users. With BASE it will only look for users who directly in the user base location. SUBTREE will allow the server to also look in subfolders of the user base location.

[subtree]

Base DN for groups
This is the location in your LDAP directory where all groups are stored. There are several options for object class and members possible: the groupOfNames, accessGroup or group object classes can be used with members given in the member property, or the groupOfUniqueNames object class can be used with uniqueMember property. In Active Directory systems only the group object class is supported.

[ ]

Search scope for groups
The search scope determines where the LDAP server will search for groups. With BASE it will only look for users who directly in the group base location. SUBTREE will allow the server to also look in subfolders of the group base location.

[subtree]

[Save]

The contents of the **Global Settings** tab are described in the following table:

Content	Description
LDAP server type	This is the field in which you can indicate whether you need to connect to an **LDAP** (the default value) or an **Active Directory** server.
rDN attribute	This field establishes the **relative distinguished name** (rDN) for your organization's users in LDAP. You can choose one of the four attributes: a user's full or "common" name (**cn**), email address (**email**), surname (**sn**), or user ID (**uid**), which is the most common setting of the four.
user id attribute	This sets the attribute that will serve as your Plone site users' ID values; while any of the four attributes mentioned in the rDN description above may be used, this setting often matches the value set in the **rDN attribute** field, which is often set to **uid**. These values are created initially on the **LDAP Schema** tab, where they must first be set before they can be selected here. For Active Directory databases, use either sAMAccountName (for single domain configurations) or userPrincipleName (for multiple domain configurations). objectGUID is a binary property and is therefore not supported by Plone.
login name attribute	This attribute is the identifier used during authentication to your Plone site (or, literally, the user name a user will need to enter when logging into the site), and is commonly set to the same value as that of the **rDN** and **user id attribute** fields.
LDAP object classes	This field defines the structural object class, as well as any additional classes, to which any new user accounts created in Plone should be assigned. In an LDAP database, these are assigned to user entries via the property objectClass. If your users get more than one object class, separate them with a comma, as shown in this example: pilotPerson,uidObject.
Bind DN	In this field, you must specify the **distinguished name** (**DN**) of the Manager (or root) entry in your remote LDAP database in order to enable Plone to access and change user and group records as needed. Use the following format, replacing [bracketed-text] with the actual values from your Manager DN record: cn=Manager,dc=[YOUR-DOMAIN],dc=[COM].
Bind password	Enter the Manager or root, password for your LDAP or Active Directory database.
Base DN for users	This field defines the distinguished name for the **organizational unit** (**OU**) of the users in your database. If your users were defined within a main OU called people, this value would look like this: ou=people,dc=[YOUR-DOMAIN],dc=[COM].

Content	Description
Search scope for users	If your user entries are defined directly under the organizational unit defined above (in the above example, `people`), or if you want to restrict searches to only that level, the correct search scope value for this field would be **one level**; instead, if the organization defined additional sub-levels beneath the main organizational unit, the value **subtree** would enable Plone to search these sub-levels as well. If you're unsure which one to choose, try **subtree**.
Base DN for groups	Much like the **Base DN for users**, this field defines the distinguished name for the organizational unit for groups in your database. For a group OU called `groups`, you would enter: `ou=groups,dc=[YOUR-DOMAIN],dc=[COM]`.
Search scope for groups	Configure this value much like that of the similar field for users: if your organization is defined by a single, flat level, select **one level** to limit the search scope to directly beneath the specified base group. Otherwise, select **subtree** to enable searches among sub-levels of groups.

Once you've completed all of the fields in this form, click on **Save**, and move on to the **LDAP Schema** configuration tab.

Configure LDAP Schema

The **LDAP Schema** displays the properties assigned to your database user entries, and the mapping between these LDAP entry properties and user properties in Plone.

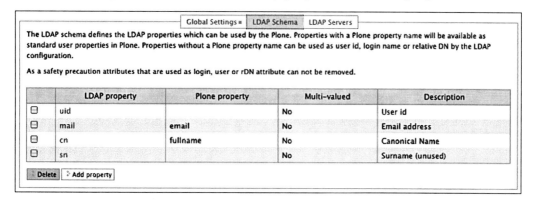

For most of the part, the default settings here should be suitable: the LDAP **mail** property is mapped to the Plone **email** property, and the LDAP **cn** property to the Plone **fullname** property. The LDAP **uid** attribute is not mapped to a Plone property by default, but Plone will use it as the **login name** property unless an alternative property is specified.

The contents of the **LDAP Schema** tab are described in the following table:

Content	Description
LDAP property	The literal name of a property from the LDAP or Active Directory database
Plone property	The Plone user property to which the LDAP property is mapped
Multi-valued	Establishes whether this property can possess multiple values, such as additional aliases for individual users; enable this option only if you need to expose the complete sequence of values for a **Multi-valued** attribute field
Description	An expanded name for the LDAP property; any property not assigned to a Plone property displays **(unused)** in its **Description** field

To edit a schema property, click on its name in the **LDAP property** column.

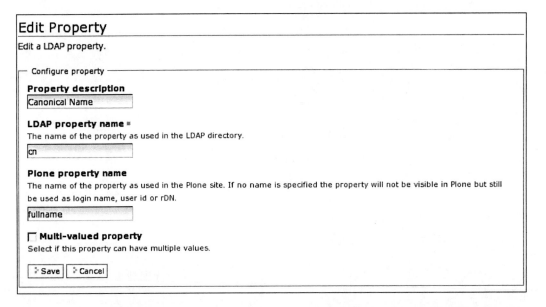

You can also add a new property in a similar fashion—by clicking on **Add property** on the **LDAP Schema** screen, and filling in the above values for the new property.

 Note that the **uid** property can be modified, but not deleted, in order to maintain the integrity of the object structure of your LDAP database.

Once you're satisfied with your LDAP schema mappings and settings, move to the third and final LDAP configuration tab, the **LDAP Servers**.

Configure LDAP Servers

Finally, before you can connect your Plone site to your LDAP or Active Directory server, you must click on **Add LDAP Server** and complete the **LDAP Servers** section.

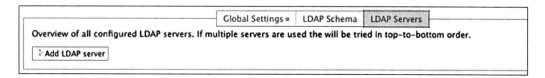

The **Add Server** form is comprised of a single section: the **Configure server** area, in which you can define an entry for your LDAP or Active Directory server, and instantly enable LDAP connections.

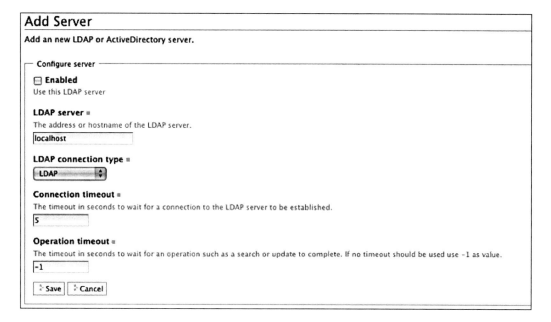

The contents of an **Add Server** form are described in the following table:

Content	Description
Enabled	If you want Plone to connect to, and begin using, the server you're adding, enable this option. You can change the value later if you need to disable connections to this server.
LDAP server	Enter the address of your LDAP or Active Directory server.
LDAP connection type	Select whether to connect to your server using generic LDAP, the LDAP over **Secure Sockets Layer (SSL)** protocol, or LDAP over **interprocess communication (IPC)**.
	By default, LDAP servers communicate using port 389, LDAP over SSL uses port 636, and LDAP over IPC obviates the need for a port, as it establishes connections via sockets instead.
Connection timeout	Enter the time interval (in seconds) that should be permitted when establishing a connection to the remote server before Plone deems the server unreachable; five **(5)** seconds is the default.
Operation timeout	Enter the time interval (in seconds) that should be permitted when performing a remote server operation, such as a record update, addition, or search, before Plone reports a connection error. The default value is **-1**, which disables operational time-outs and permits Plone to continue operation attempts indefinitely.

Once the server has been added, the **LDAP Servers** screen will display basic information about the server and Plone's connection to it, including the settings you've entered, and whether Plone is actively using the server.

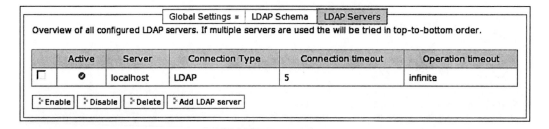

You can also enable, disable, or delete existing servers, or add additional server entries, from this screen.

Testing your LDAP connection

With your settings in place and verified, you can test the connection to your LDAP or Active Directory server, and ensure that the user and group objects are being shared properly between your database and your Plone site.

In your site's **Site Setup** area, click on **Users and Groups**.

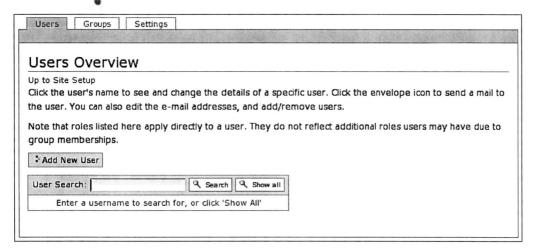

By default, the **Users** tab is selected. To see all of the users with accounts on your Plone site, click on **Show all** in the **User Search** area.

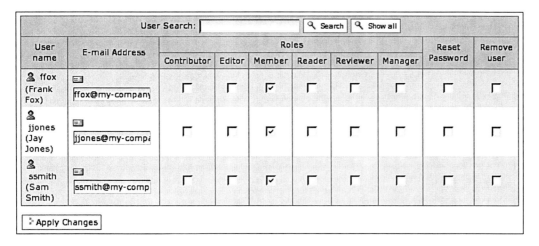

With any luck, you'll see a list of all of the users in your LDAP or Active Directory database, within the scope of the settings that you specified in the **LDAP Connection** configuration.

 As this information is usually kept in the temporary memory cache, you may need to restart your Zope in order to ensure that you're seeing the latest incarnation of LDAP data according to your new settings.

Here, you can change the users' email addresses and passwords, delete users, map specific users to Plone roles, or add new users to your Plone site and to your LDAP database by clicking on **Add New User**. You can edit the properties of specific users by clicking on their user names in the results, and editing their **User Properties**. The users themselves can also do the same to edit their own account details.

 Remember: Direct editing of your remote database via Plone is supported only for LDAP connections; Active Directory support in Plone is limited to read-only operations.

You can verify that your LDAP or Active Directory groups have been propagated in your Plone site in this **Users and Groups** section as well, by clicking on the **Groups** tab.

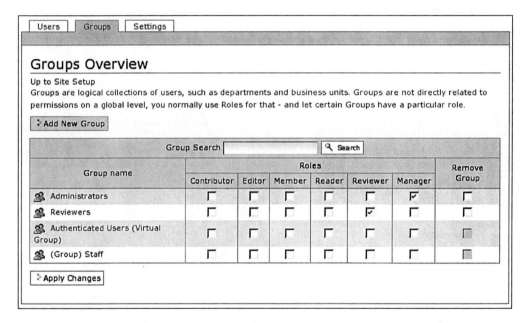

Here, you'll see a list of groups available on your Plone site, including some inherent Plone groups such as **Administrators**, **Reviewers**, and **Authenticated Users**. If your LDAP settings and connection are successful, you'll also see group entries prefixed with **(Group)**, which indicate group objects imported directly from your LDAP or Active Directory server.

You can add a new group via the **Add New Group** button, and assign Plone roles to groups or delete groups using this interface. You can also add users to or remove users from groups by clicking the group name, and editing the group's users on the **Group Members** screen.

If a group cannot be deleted via Plone, its **Remove Group** checkbox will be disabled in this interface.

As a final test to verify that your LDAP or Active Directory connection, log out of your Plone site as the **admin** user (you'll have to close and then reopen your browser to do so), and try logging in as one of your remote users by entering an LDAP or Active Directory user name and password. If such information is not available to you, have an actual user try to log in.

Advanced LDAP configuration

If you're not thoroughly satisfied with the options provided within the **LDAP Connections** configuration applet in **Site Setup**, or if you're simply curious and want to poke beneath the surface of the GUI to see what's really going on between Plone and your LDAP or Active Directory server, you can dig into the ZMI for your site and have a look at your **Access Control List (ACL)** settings.

In your Plone site's **Site Setup**, click on **Zope Management Interface**, and then click on **acl_users**.

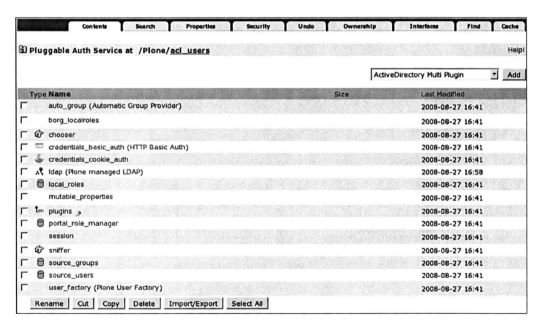

To examine your LDAP or Active Directory settings, click on **ldap (Plone managed LDAP)**.

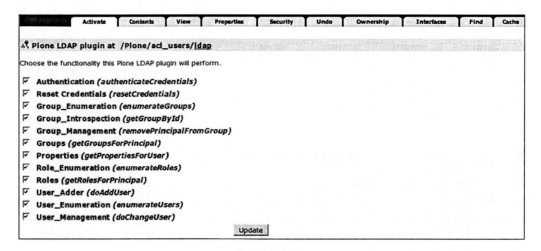

This screen displays a list of the functionalities enabled by Plone's plug-ins and the LDAP connections to your database. If you want to disable one or more of these functions, such as the ability to add new users via the **User_Added** tool, you could de-select those options on this screen, and click on **Update**. You can also examine the inner details of each functional plug-in listed here by clicking on the name of the plug-in.

For example, click on the **Authentication** plug-in to see a list of active plug-ins used by this module.

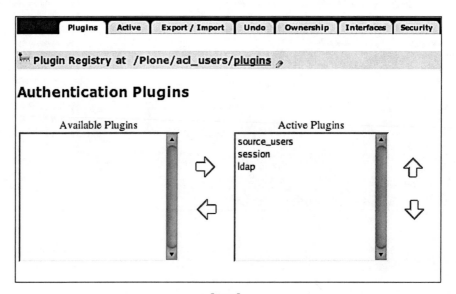

In this example, we see three active plug-ins: source_users, session, and the mandatory ldap. If we have a good reason to deactivate a plug-in (which we don't), we can select it in the **Active Plugins** list and click on the left-pointing arrow, to move it out of the **Active Plugins** list, and into the **Available Plugins** list.

The following example screen displays the default settings for **User_Enumeration**, which is similar to **Authentication**, also uses three plug-ins: **source_users**, **mutable_properties**, and the mandatory **ldap** plug-in.

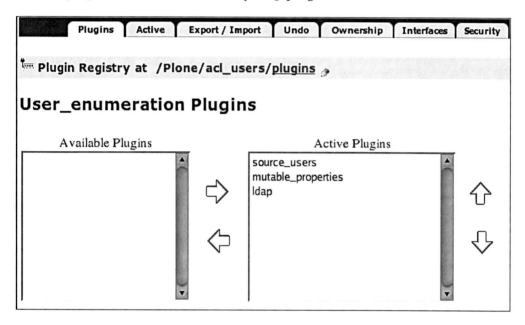

For more information on these plug-ins and their role in LDAP authentication in Plone, read about Zope's **Pluggable Authentication/Authorization Service (PAS)** framework at its package page on PyPI, which is available at the following location: http://pypi.python.org/pypi/Products.PluggableAuthService.

To see additional LDAP configuration information, go back to the **Activate** tab of the **ldap** folder, click on the **Contents** tab, and then click on **acl_users (Plone managed LDAP)**.

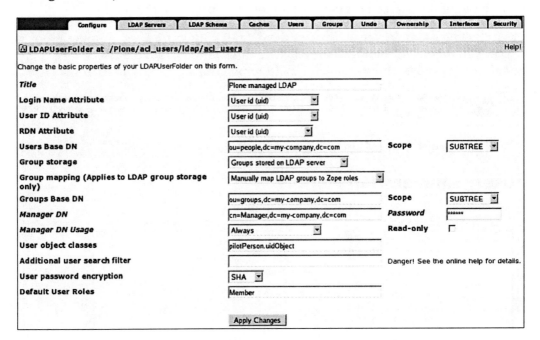

 This page can also be reached via the following path in your browser, from the site root:/ [your-site]/acl_users/ldap/acl_users/ manage_workspace

In the **Configure** tab, you'll see the fields and values that you established by completing the **Global Settings** section of the **LDAP Connection** configuration form. You can make changes in either of these two areas, with the exception of the parameters listed in the following table, which are found only in this section of the ZMI.

ZMI parameter	Description
Group storage	Specifies whether to store users' groups or role information in LDAP itself or within Zope's LDAP User Folder. The default setting is **Groups stored on LDAP server**.
Group mapping	Specifies whether a user's group memberships should be mapped automatically to the user's user object as a role. This option is effective only when the **Group storage** parameter is set to **Groups stored on LDAP server**. The default setting is **Manually map LDAP groups to Zope roles**.
Additional user search filter	As the descriptive on-screen text indicates, this option should be used with extreme caution and only for a deliberate purpose, as a misconfiguration here can block all users from gaining access to your site. When specified here, a custom LDAP filter expression is combined with the default search filter. This is disabled by default.
User password encryption	Specifies the encryption scheme to be applied to user password attributes. This must match an encryption scheme supported by your LDAP server. The default setting is **SHA**.
Default User Roles	Specifies the role or roles to be attributed automatically to all authenticated users; multiple values can be specified by separating the entries with commas; the default setting is **Member**.

For more information on these LDAP properties, click **Help!** in the upper-right corner of the page.

Similarly, click on the **LDAP Servers** tab to view the server settings that you created in the **LDAP Server** section of the **LDAP Connection** form.

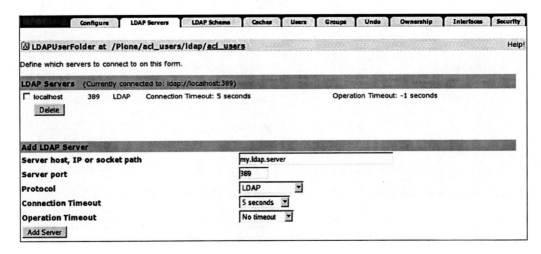

As with the previous tab, the displayed information and the changes that can be made are very much the same here as in the corresponding **LDAP Connection** section.

As you might expect, clicking on the **LDAP Schema** tab brings you to the ZMI counterpart of the **LDAP Schema** section of the **LDAP Connection** form.

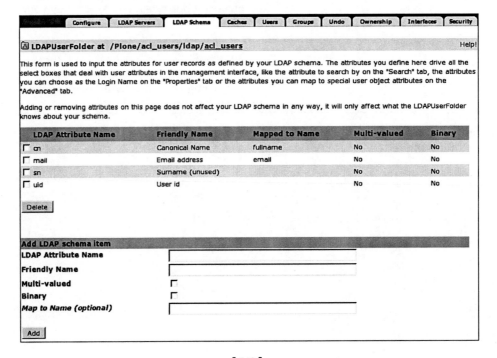

However, unlike the other two sections, the ZMI's **LDAP Schema** tool is not completely identical to its **LDAP Connections** counterpart. Although attributes can be added or removed here, changes to the mapping between existing attributes are not possible. You'll need to return to **LDAP Connections** in order to remap any attribute relationships between LDAP and Plone.

Click on the **Users** tab to search for users, or to add new user records.

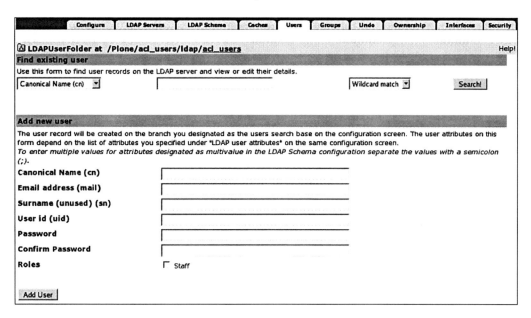

After performing a search, you can click on the **Distinguished Name** of a returned entry to view the user's attributes, change their group memberships, or set a new user password.

Click on the **Groups** tab to view, add, or delete LDAP groups, and to manage the mappings between LDAP groups and Zope roles, as shown in the following screenshot:

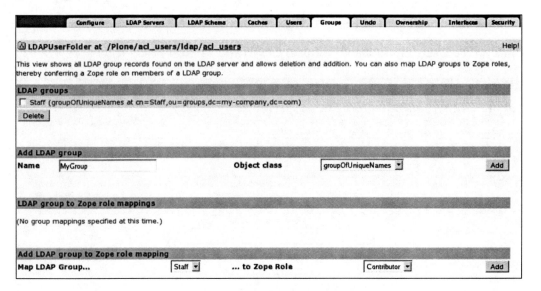

Summary

In this chapter, we have learned:

- About LDAP and Active Directory
- How to install Plone's prerequisite software for LDAP on multiple platforms
- How to install LDAP and Active Directory packages into a Plone site
- How to activate LDAP support on your site
- How to connect to your LDAP or Active Directory database server
- How to test the connection from your Plone site to your LDAP or Active Directory database
- How to perform advanced configuration via the ZMI

Using what you have learned in this chapter, you should be able to access your organization's LDAP or Active Directory database server via Plone, and use the information stored in this database to help authenticate, authorize, and categorize your Plone site's users and groups.

Index

creating 95
events folder 95
fields 95
iCal icon 100
vCal icon 99
extension profiles 385

F

favicon 419
feedback, Plone products
PloneFromGen, 281
Poi, 280
Trac, 280
files, Plone site
about 102
adding 103-105
filesystem
developing 393
filesystem product
about 341
writing 384
filesystem product, writing
GenericSetup 384
profile, exporting 388
profile, importing 389, 390
snapshots, taking 387, 388
folder actions category, CMF action
categories
about 348
contents 348
form
creating, PloneFormGen used 289
form, creating
form basic properties, configuring 290
form fields, adding 292-297
form fields, editing 293
form folder, adding 290
multi-select fields, adding 297-302
selection fields, adding 297, 299
formatting tools, Plone
bold and italics 59
default styles 63
definition list 61
indent text 62
left, center, and right align 60
numbered and bullet lists 60, 61

style menu 62
freshness headers
about 512
Cache-Control header 512
Expire header 512

G

GenericSetup, filesystem product
about 384
base profiles 384, 385
configuration profile 384
extension profiles 384, 385
plonetheme.ace example, extension profiles 385-387
Gentlewares Poseidon 315
Getpaid 282
global settings, LDAP connections
about 534
configuring 534
contents 536, 537
GNU tools
G++ 29
GCC 29

H

header sets, aggressively cached items
cache-in-browser-24-hours 521
cache-in-browser-forever 521
header sets, moderately-cached items
cache-in-proxy-1-hour 521
cache-in-proxy-24-hours 521
header sets, weakly-cached items
cache-in-memory 522
cache-with-etag 523
home page, Plone site
about 42
accessibility 44
change password section, personal dashboard 46
contact 44
logo 43
navigating 42
personal dashboard 45
personal dashboard, editing 46
profile, personal dashboard 45
search function 44

T

tabs, Plone site
  breadcrumbs 50
  colophon 51
  events tab 50
  home tab 48
  my folder 50
  news tab 49
  users tab 48
tagged values, UML 319
TALES 308
TAL portlet, adding
  conditionals 183
  HTML tag, filling in with a given value 184
  HTML tag attributes 184, 186
  random item, selecting 184
  variables, declaring 183
Template Attribute Language Expression
    Syntax. *See* **TALES**
terminology, content rules
  actions 201, 202
  conditions 201
  triggering events 201
theme, developing
  prerequisites 394
theme product
  installing on Plone site 399
theme product, installing
  about 399
  buildout, updating 399, 400
  Plone site, creating 400, 401
  product, installing 402, 403
  site, putting in debug mode 402
theme product example
  about 403
  Andreas09 theme 404
  boilerplate code, modifying 408
  buildout, downloading 404
  file structure 405, 406
  images, working with 413
  Plone installer, bootstrapping 404
  stylesheets, working with 422
  theme product, generating 406
  Zope instance, logging into 404
tools, content types
  Archetypes 313

ArchGenXML 320
Object-Oriented Programming 313
OOP 314
schema 313
UML 315
traditional product installation
  instance products directory, searching 273
  ownership, checking 274
  permissions, checking 274
  Zope, restarting 274
transitions 154

U

UML
  about 315
  ArchGenXML 315
  ArgoUML 315
  Gentleware's Poseidon 315
  programs, for diagrams 315
  stereotypes 318
  tagged values 318
UML symbols
  about 316
  aggregation 318
  class 316
  composition 317
  generalization 318
  package 316, 317
Unified Modeling Language. *See* **UML**
user category, CMF action categories
  about 353
  add to favorites link 354
  join link 354
  login link 353
  logout link 354
  member folder 353
  preferences link 353
  undo link 354

V

validation headers
  about 513
  ETag header 513
  Last-Modified header 513
Varnish, caching proxy 498

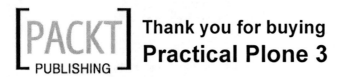

Packt Open Source Project Royalties

When we sell a book written on an Open Source project, we pay a royalty directly to that project. Therefore by purchasing Practical Plone 3, Packt will have given some of the money received to the Plone project.

In the long term, we see ourselves and you — customers and readers of our books — as part of the Open Source ecosystem, providing sustainable revenue for the projects we publish on. Our aim at Packt is to establish publishing royalties as an essential part of the service and support a business model that sustains Open Source.

If you're working with an Open Source project that you would like us to publish on, and subsequently pay royalties to, please get in touch with us.

Writing for Packt

We welcome all inquiries from people who are interested in authoring. Book proposals should be sent to author@packtpub.com. If your book idea is still at an early stage and you would like to discuss it first before writing a formal book proposal, contact us; one of our commissioning editors will get in touch with you.

We're not just looking for published authors; if you have strong technical skills but no writing experience, our experienced editors can help you develop a writing career, or simply get some additional reward for your expertise.

About Packt Publishing

Packt, pronounced 'packed', published its first book "Mastering phpMyAdmin for Effective MySQL Management" in April 2004 and subsequently continued to specialize in publishing highly focused books on specific technologies and solutions.

Our books and publications share the experiences of your fellow IT professionals in adapting and customizing today's systems, applications, and frameworks. Our solution-based books give you the knowledge and power to customize the software and technologies you're using to get the job done. Packt books are more specific and less general than the IT books you have seen in the past. Our unique business model allows us to bring you more focused information, giving you more of what you need to know, and less of what you don't.

Packt is a modern, yet unique publishing company, which focuses on producing quality, cutting-edge books for communities of developers, administrators, and newbies alike. For more information, please visit our website: www.PacktPub.com.

Building Websites with Plone

ISBN: 1-904811-02-7   Paperback: 398 pages

An in-depth and comprehensive guide to the Plone content management system

1. A comprehensive guide for Plone website administrators and developers

2. Design, build, and manage content rich websites using Plone

3. Extend Plone's skins and content types

4. Customize, secure, and optimize Plone websites

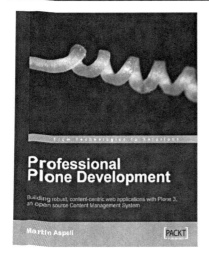

Professional Plone Development

ISBN: 978-1-847191-98-4   Paperback: 398 pages

Building robust, content-centric web applications with Plone 3, an open source Content Management System.

1. Plone development fundamentals

2. Customizing Plone

3. Developing new functionality

4. Real-world deployments

Please check **www.PacktPub.com** for information on our titles

Printed in the United States
141638LV00006B/2/P

9 781847 191786